File Formats for Popular PC Software

A Programmer's Reference

Jeff Walden

Wiley IBM PC Series
Laurence Press, Series Editor

A Wiley Press Book
John Wiley & Sons, Inc.
New York • Chichester • Brisbane • Toronto • Singapore

Publisher: Stephen Kippur
Editor: Theron Shreve
Managing Editor: Katherine Schowalter
Electronic Book Publishing Services: The Publisher's Network, Morrisville, PA

Copyright © 1986 by John Wiley & Sons, Inc.

All rights reserved. Published simultaneously in Canada.

Reproduction or translation of any part of this work beyond that permitted by Section 107 or 108 of the 1976 United States Copyright Act without the permission of the copyright owner is unlawful. Requests for permission or further information should be addressed to the Permissions Department, John Wiley & Sons, Inc.

Library of Congress Cataloging-in-Publication Data

Walden, Jeffrey B., 1951-
   File Formats for popular PC software
   1. File organization (Computer science)
2. Microcomputers—Programming   I. Title.
QA76.9.F5W34   1986   005.74   85-26430

ISBN 0-471-83671-0

Printed in the United States of America

    10 9

Wiley Press books can be used as premiums to promote products or services, for training, or in mail-order catalogs. For information on quantity discounts, please write to the Special Sales Department, John Wiley & Sons, Inc.

For my mother:
Who always likes things in order.

Ability is a trademark of Xanaro Technologies, Ltd.

1-2-3, Lotus, Symphony and VisiCalc are registered trademarks and DIF is a trademark of Lotus Development Corp.

dBase, dBase II, dBase III and Ashton-Tate are registered trademarks and MultiMate is a trademark of Ashton-Tate. Used by permission.

Microsoft and Multiplan are registered trademarks, and MS-DOS is a trademark of Microsoft, Inc.

IBM is a registered trademark and PC-DOS is a trademark of International Business Machines, Inc.

SuperCalc is a registered trademark and SuperData Interchange is a trademark of Computer Associates International, Inc.

WordStar is a registered trademark of MicroPro International Corporation.

Turbo Pascal is a trademark of Borland International.

This file format documentation is as complete as is practical; however, neither the author, publisher nor software manufacturers make any warranty, express or implied, as to its completeness or any fitness of use. The user of this reference guide assumes all risk. Manufacturers whose formats are documented reserve all rights to change these formats without notice and without liability.

Acknowledgments

Special thanks must be conveyed to several people (the order is not significant) who made this project infinitely more pleasant and complete: Dave Brown from Xanaro Technologies, who dug into code to find "the table"; tireless Dan Druid from MicroPro; Lee Barrett at MultiMate; and Martin Raffauf at IBM, who knows which side of the diskette holds the data. And special thanks to Lotus Development Corporation for the foresight and kindness to place the information about their file format in the public domain. To other folks at Ashton-Tate, Microsoft, and Lotus too numerous to mention—Thanks!

                                                                 Jeff Walden

Contents

Detailed Contents		viii
Preface		xv
Chapter 1	**Lotus 1-2-3** Version 1, 1A, 2.0 **and Symphony** Version 1, 1.1	1
Chapter 2	**Ability** Version 1.0	34
Chapter 3	**dBase II** Version 2.43 **and dBase III** Version 1.1	46
Chapter 4	**Data Interchange Format (DIF)**	53
Chapter 5	**MultiMate Professional Word Processor** Version 3.30	59
Chapter 6	**Microsoft MultiPlan and the SYLK File Format** Version 1.2	75
Chapter 7	**IBM Plans**+ Version 1.0	81
Chapter 8	**SuperCalc3** Release 2 **and the Super Data Interchange** Version 2.0	102
Chapter 9	**VisiCalc** Version 177Y2	108
Chapter 10	**WordStar** Versions 2.2x through 3.31	112
Chapter 11	**WordStar 2000** Version 1.01d	117
Appendixes Introduction		143
Appendix A Example File Contents		147
Appendix B Sample Files		151
	Sample Spreadsheet in Lotus 1-2-3 .WKS File 153	
	Gettysburg Address as a Symphony DOC File 156	
	Sample Spreadsheet as an Ability File 178	
	Gettysburg Address as an Ability File 193	
	Lincoln's Gettysburg Address as a MultiMate File 201	
	Sample File in SYLK Format as an ASCIII Dump 223	
	Sample Spreadsheet as an IBM Plans+ . ~ MD File 225	
	Sample Spreadsheet as an IBM Plans+ . ~ MF File 253	
	Gettysburg Address as a WordStar File 256	
	Gettyburg Address as a WordStar 2000 File 265	
Appendix C FilePrint Utility Source Code		279

Detailed Contents

Chapter 1   Lotus 1-2-3 and Symphony   1

.WKS and .WK1 File Formats   2
.WKS and .WK1 Record Opcodes
- 00h (00d) BOF   3
- 01h (01d) EOF   3
- 02h (02h) CalcMode   3
- 03h (03d) Calcorder   3
- 04h (04d) Split   3
- 05h (05d) Sync   4
- 06h (06d) Range   4
- 07h (07d) Window1   4
- 08h (08d) ColW1   5
- 09h (09d) WinTwo   5
- 0Ah (10d) ColW2   5
- 0Bh (11d) Name   5
- 0Ch (12d) Blank   5
- 0Dh (13d) Integer   6
- 0Eh (14d) Number   6
- 0Fh (15d) Label   6
- 10h (16d) Formula   7
- 18h (24d) Table   7
- 19h (25d) QRange   8
- 1Ah (26d) PRange   8
- 1Bh (27d) SRange   8
- 1Ch (28d) FRange   9
- 1Dh (29d) KRange   9
- 20h (32d) HRange   9
- 23h (35d) KRange2   9
- 24h (36d) Protec   10
- 25h (37d) Footer   10
- 26h (38d) Header   10
- 27h (39d) Setup   10
- 28h (40d) Margins   10
- 29h (41d) LabelFMT   10
- 2Ah (42d) Titles   11
- 2Dh (45d) Graph   11
- 2Eh (46d) NGraph   11
- 2Fh (47d) CalcCount   11
- 30h (48d) Unformatted   11
- 31h (49d) CursorW12   11
- 32h (50d) Window   12
- 33h (51d) String   12
- 37h (55d) Lock Password   12
- 38h (56d) Locked   12
- 3Ch (60d) Query   12
- 3Dh (61d) QueryName   12
- 3Eh (62d) Print   13
- 3Fh (63d) PrintName   13
- 40h (64d) Graph2   13
- 41h (65d) GraphName   13
- 42h (66d) Zoom   13
- 43h (67d) SymSplit   13
- 44h (68d) NSRows   14
- 45h (69d) NSCols   14
- 46h (70d) Ruler   14
- 47h (71d) NName   14
- 48h (72d) AComm   14
- 49h (73d) AMacro   15
- 4Ah (74d) Parse   15
- 4Bh (75d) WKSpword   15
- 64h (100d) Hidvec/Hidvec1   15
- 65h (101d) Hidvec2   16
- 66h (102d) ParseRanges   16
- 67h (103d) RRanges   16
- 69h (105d) MatrixRanges   17
- 96h (150d) CPI   17

Tables:
- 1.1 Cell Format Byte   18
- 1.2 Floating Point Format   19
- 1.3 Format Opcodes   19
- 1.4 Operation Codes   20
- 1.5 Multiple Argument Opcodes   21
- 1.6 Operator Precedence   23
- 1.7 Graph Record Structure   23
- 1.8 Named Graph Record Structure   25
- 1.9 Symphony Window Record   27
- 1.10 Symphony Query Record   29
- 1.11 Symphony Print Record   30
- 1.12 Symphony Graph Record   30
- 1.13 Data File Record Order   33

Chapter 2 Ability 34

Ability File Format 35
Ability File Structure 35
Header Line 36
Type-Dependent Information 36
Text Section of File 37
  In Spreadsheets 37
    Justification Control 38
  In Word Processing 38
    Linked Information 38
  In Graphs, Data-Base and
    Communications 39
Parameter Section of File 39
Field Description 40
  Links to Spreadsheets from Write 40
  Links to Graphs from Write 42
Field Display Formats 42

Tables:
2.1 Special Formatting Chars 44
2.2 RaC Parameter Values 44

Chapter 3 dBase II and dBase III 46

The dBase File Structure 47
dBase II Data 47
  Header 47
    Program ID 47
    Records in File 48
    Last Update 48
    Size of Record 48
    Field Descriptors 48
      Field Name 48
      Field Type 48
      Field Length 48
      Field Data Address 48
      Field Decimal Count 48
    End of Header 48
  Index File Structure 49
    Anchor Node 49
      Reserved Bytes 49
      Root Node Number 49
      Key Entry Length 49
      Key Entry Size 49
      Max Keys Per Node 49
      Numeric Key Flag 49
      Key Expression 49
      Unused Bytes 50
    Other Nodes 50
      Number of Keys 50
      Array of Key Entries 50
dBase III Data 50
  Header 50
    Version Number 50
    Last Update 50
    Records in File 51
    Length of Header 51
    Length of a Record 51
    Reserved Bytes 51
    Field Descriptors 51
      Field Name 51
      Field Type 51
      Field Data Address 51
      Field Length 51
      Field Decimal Count 51
      Reserved Bytes 51

Tables:
3.1 Program Limitations 52

Chapter 4 Data Interchange Format (DIF) 53

DIF File Structure 54
  Header 54
    Table 54
    Vectors(columns) 55
    Tuples(rows) 55
    Data 55
  Optional Header Items 55
    Label 55
    Comment 56
    Size 56
    Periodicity 56
    MajorStart 56
    MinorStart 57
    Truelength 57
    Units 57
    DisplayUnits 57
  Data Section 58
    Value Indicator 58

Chapter 5	**MultiMate Professional Word Processor**	**59**

MultiMate File Format 60
Document Header Section 60
  Relative Record 0 60
    Required Fields 60
      Bytes 0 - 511 60
        Document Name 62
        Author 62
        Addressee 62
        Operator 62
        Identification Keys 62
        Comments 62
        Creation Date 62
        Modification Date 63
        Reserved 63
        Left Margin 63
        Start Print Page 63
        Last Print Page 63
        Header/Footer First Page 63
        Printer Number 63
        Original Copies 63
        Page Length 64
        Print Flags 65
        Document Type 65
        Default Pitch 65
        Printer Action Table 66
        Lines Per Inch 66
        Top Margin 66
        Print Direction 66
        Sheetfeed Bins 66
        Sheetfeed Action Table 66
        Reserved Bytes 66
        Keystrokes Last Session 67
        Total Keystrokes Typed 67
        Decimal Tab Character 67
        Default Word 67
        Default Lines Per Page 68
        CWT Name 68
        Print Date Format 68
        Reserved Bytes 68
        MultiMate Version Number 68
        Total Number of Pages 68
        File Status 69
        File ID 69
        Library Documents 69
  Relative Record 1 69
    Page Start Map (byte 512-767) 69
    Record Allocation Table
      (byte 768-1023) 70
Data Section 70
  Link Section 71
    Next Relative Record 71
    Prior Relative Record 71
  Text Section 71
    Format Line 71
    Text Stream 72
    Text Formatting Codes 72
    Program Limitations 72

Tables:
5.1 MultiMate Formatting Codes 74

Diagrams:
5.1 MultiMate File Structure 61
5.2 MultiMate Admin Header 64
5.3 Print Flags Format 65
5.4 Default Word Bits 67
5.5 Relative Records 70

Chapter 6	**Microsoft MultiPlan and the SYLK File Format**	**75**

The SYLK File Format 76
  SYLK Overview 76
    RTDs and FTDs 76
  Record Type Descriptors (RTD) 76
    ID 77
    F (Formatting) 77
    B (Boundaries) 78
    C (Cell Properties) 78
    NN (Union of Named Areas) 79
    NE (Link to Another Sheet) 79
    NV (External Filename) 79
    W (Window Structure) 79
    E (End of File) 80
  SYLK File Organization 80

Chapter 7   IBM Plans+   81

Plans+ File Structure   82
  ~MD Model Definition File Layout   82
    Rec_Type   83
    Spd_ID   83
    Free_Chain   83
    Spd_Desc   83
    Last_Data   83
    Reserved Field   84
      Calc_Size   84
      No_Calcs   84
    Cell_Global   84
    Format_Global   85
    Reserved Field   85
    Col_Width   85
    Cur_Window   87
    Num_Windows   87
    Margin   87
    Data_Wds   87
    Scroll_Next   89
    Sync   89
    Printer Settings   89
      Head_Text   89
      Foot_Text   89
      PRange   90
      PName   90
      PNO   90
      LPI   90
      FLen   90
      LPP   90
      MLW (max line width)   91
      FMat   91
      LMG (left margin)   91
      PStyle   91
      SubDesc   91
      SubVal   92
    Graph Specifications   92
      Graph_Name   92
      Graph_Type   92
      First_Title   93
      Second_Title   93
      X_Axis_Name   93
      Y_Axis_Name   93
      Grid_Type   93
      Label_Type   93
      Start_Value   94
      End_Value   94
      Scale_Type   94
      Unused Byte   94
      Lower_Scale   94
      Upper_Scale   94
      Reference_Line   94
      Unused Byte   94
      Ref_Value   94
      Float_Bar   94
      Marked_Line   95
      Scatter_Gram   95
      Unused Byte   95
      No_Data_Sets   95
      Palette   95
      Save_File   95
      View_Print   95
      LPT   95
      PRCodes   95
      PRCodeP   96
      View_Display   96
      Point_Value   96
      Point_Label   96
      Data_Set_Name   96
      Data_Set_Points   96
      Data_Range   97
      PutGDat   97
    Sort Specifications   97
      SRange   97
    Calculation Record   97
      First   97
      Current   97
      Last   98
      HiCalc   98
    Saved Graph Information   98
      Graph_Info_Array   98
      Calculation Record Array   98
  .~MF Model Data File Layout   99
    Row Header Format   99
    Numeric Cell Format   99
    Text Cell Format   100
    NULL Cell Format   100

Tables:
  7.1 Format Flag Word Details   101

Diagrams:
  7.1 Organization of a .~MD File   86

Chapter 8   **SuperCalc3 and the Super Data Interchange Format**   **102**

SuperCalc3 and the SDI Format   103
SDI File Organization   103
  Format Strings   103
  SDI Header   104
    Table   104
    Vectors(columns)   104
    Tuples(rows)   104
    GDisp-Format   105
    Col-Format   105
    Row-Format   105
    Data   105

SDI Data Section   105
  Data Types   106
  Text Entry   106
  Numeric Entry   106
  Data Definition Entry   106
  Origin Specifier(Goto)   106
  Display Formatting Entry   107
  Formula Entry   107
  Repeat Count Entry   107

Chapter 9   **VisiCalc**   **108**

VisiCalc File Format   109
  VisiCalc Data Section   109
    Numeric Values   109
    Textual Values   109
    Formulas   109

VisiCalc Footer Section   110
  W - Window Command   110
  G - Global Command   110
  /X- Catch-All Command   111
File Organization   111

Chapter 10   **WordStar**   **112**

WordStar File Format   113
  The Text Stream   113
  High-Bit Characters   113
  WordStar Format Codes   114

Tables:
  10.1 Commands Used In Pairs   115
  10.2 Commands Used Alone   115
  10.3 Other Codes   116
  10.4 Dot Commands   116

Chapter 11   WordStar 2000   117

WordStar 2000 File Format   118
  File Contents   118
    Text Characters   118
    Control Characters   118
  Symmetrical Sequences   118
  Format Block   119
    File_ID (32d/20h)   119
    Font (28d/1Ch)   120
    Height (105d/69h)   120
    HeadOff (94d/5Eh)   120
    FootOff (95d/5Fh)   121
    Ruler (91d/5Bh)   121
    LPerPage (97d/61h)   122
    EvenPOff (92d/5Ch)   122
    OddPOff (93d/5Dh)   122
    TJustify (98d/62h)   122
    THyphen (101d/65h)   122
    TFormFeed (24d/18h)   122
    TUndGaps (102d/66h)   123
    TPageBreak (103d/67h)   123
    FootEven (67d/43h)   123
    FootOdd (68d/44h)   123
    FootBoth (69d/45h)   124
    Top (118d/76h)   124
  Text Block   125
    Appendix (111d/6Fh)   125
    AskV (79d/4Fh)   125
    BIndent (21d/15h)   125
    Bold (05d/05h)   126
    BUndent (23d/17h)   126
    Center (19d/13h)   126
    Cndshn (82d/52h)   126
    Color (29d/1Dh)   126
    Comment (70d/46h)   127
    Contents (112d/70h)   127
    DataF (76d/4Ch)   127
    Disp (80d/50h)   127
    Double (07d/07h)   127
    EndCnd (84d/54h)   127
    EvenPOff (92d/5Ch)   128
    Figure (113d/71h)   128
    File_ID (32d/20h)   128
    Font (28d/1Ch)   128
    FootBoth (69d/45d)   129
    FootEven (67d/43h)   129
    FootNote (26d/1Ah)   130
    FootOdd (68d/44h)   130
    FootOff (95d/5Fh)   130
    HardPage (71d/47h)   131

    HeadBoth (66d/42h)   131
    HeadEven (62d/40h)   131
    HeadOdd (65d/41h)   131
    HeadOff (94d/5Eh)   132
    Height (105d/69h)   132
    IHyphen (31d/1Fh)   132
    Index (18d/12h)   132
    InsertF (81d/51h)   133
    Lev1Num (116d/74h)   133
    Level1 (107d/6Bh)   133
    Level2 (108d/6Ch)   133
    Level3 (109d/6Dh)   133
    Level4 (110d/6Eh)   134
    LIndent (20d/14h)   134
    LPerPage (97d/61h)   134
    LUndent (22d/16h)   134
    MarkPage (11d/0Bh)   134
    Need (73d/49h)   134
    NonBreak (16d/10h)   135
    NxtCpy (85d/55h)   135
    OddPOff (93d/5Dh)   135
    Othrwis (83d/53h)   135
    OverPrint (17d/11h)   135
    PageNum (74d/4Ah)   135
    Pause (14d/0Eh)   135
    ReadV (75d/46h)   136
    Refer (12d/0Ch)   136
    Repeat (78d/4Eh)   136
    Ruler (91d/5Bh)   136
    SetV (77d/4Dh)   137
    SoftHyphen (30d/1Eh)   137
    SoftLine (03d/03h)   137
    SoftPage (72d/48h)   137
    SoftSpace (02d/02h)   138
    StrikeOut (10d/0Ah)   138
    Sub (08d/08h)   138
    Super (09d/09h)   138
    Table (114d/72h)   138
    TFormFeed (24d/18h)   38
    THyphen (101d/65h)   139
    TJustify (98d/62h)   139
    Top (118d/76h)   139
    TPageBreak (103d/67h)   139
    Tray (106d/6Ah)   139
    TSpell (99d/63h)   139
    TUndGaps (102d/66h)   140
    UnderLine (06d/06h)   140

Tables:
  11.1 WordStar 2000 Command Codes
  11.2 Program Limitations

Preface

"What goes in, must come out" is as true of computer systems as the pilot's "What goes up, must come down" is true of airplanes. Yet, without a roadmap to the information stored by a program on its data diskette, deciphering stored information is nearly impossible. How could you guess, for example, that a single byte (the value 185, say) really stored the formatting for an entire spreadsheet row?

The demand for this kind of data file format information is just getting started. Compatibility between programs is an acknowledged requirement in corporate America. It's important to be able to trade information between standalone programs on PCs.

And on the horizon is a whole new reason to comprehend the native file formats of the programs in which you've invested. It's the concept of creating *elsewhere* the spreadsheet templates, graphs, databases and other documents that you will use with application programs on the personal computer.

Already, mainframe programs extract data from corporate databases and create finished Lotus worksheets for downloading to PCs. Increased use of local area networks and PC communications will make this type of arrangement even more convenient in the future. Increased use of artificial intelligence techniques may make the creation of these downloaded templates more efficient.

File Formats for Popular PC Software is for corporate programmers, data-processing managers, software authors or anyone who needs to know how several popular personal computer programs or data interchange methods store formatted information on disk.

This book contains no source code for any of these programs, nor is it a tutorial in any way. It lists, byte by byte, offset by offset, and code by code, the digital information these programs place on diskette when they store a file.

Each format from byte 0 through the end of the file is documented. In general, the software manufacturers themselves graciously supplied the information about their formats. In almost every case, these formats have not been published before.

We try to provide both hex and decimal values (we know how irritating it is to be caught without a converting calculator), and organized tables of formatting codes. The format information we provide, however, is highly condensed. You should have some programming experience to help you understand how to apply this information. Tables referred to in the text will follow at the end of each chapter.

Each file format is introduced with company name and address, data on the files it produces and some points of interest about the product that produced the files. These "points of interest" are not software reviews, although some do carry the author's opinions.

Appendix B contains annotated sections of sample files produced by a number of the programs whose formats we've documented. As a control factor, word processing programs were fed the first two paragraphs of the Gettysburg Address, and spreadsheet programs were fed a 7 column by 15 row spreadsheet that included formatting, formulas and labels.

CHAPTER 1

LOTUS 1-2-3® and SYMPHONY®

Lotus 1-2-3, Version 1, 1A, 2.0
Symphony, Version 1, 1.1

**Lotus Development Corporation
161 First Street
Cambridge, MA 02142**

TYPE OF PRODUCT   Integrated software
1-2-3: Spreadsheet, Graphics, Data base
Symphony: Spreadsheet, Word Processing, Data base, Graphics, Communications

FILES PRODUCED   Binary; some ASCII text

POINTS OF INTEREST

1-2-3 and Symphony share one of the most complex file format approaches on the market. Information in a 1-2-3 or Symphony file is like a computer program. It is organized as an opcode, followed by a record length delimiter, followed by the data.

CONVERSION INFORMATION

Lotus provides facilities in 1-2-3 and Symphony to translate files between the following formats

From	To
VisiCalc	1-2-3
VisiCalc	Symphony
DIF	1-2-3
DIF	Symphony
1-2-3	DIF
Symphony	DIF
1-2-3	dBase II
Symphony	dBase II
dBase II	1-2-3
dBase	Symphony

Lotus .WKS File Format

Lotus 1-2-3 and Symphony are mutifunction, integrated software packages. They share many of the same file structures, which makes it practical to cover both products in the same chapter.

The Lotus .WKS file format uses special records, each one controlling some aspect of the file: ranges, cell formats, etc. The record format is

    <opcode> <record_length> <data>

where

    <**opcode**> represents a two-byte hexadecimal number (least significant byte first) indicating the meaning of, or the operation to perform on, the <**data**> section.

    <**record_length**> represents a two-byte hexadecimal number (LSB first) giving the length in bytes of the following data section. It serves in lieu of a carriage return or other end-of-record delimiter.

    <**data**> represents a series of 0 or more hexadecimal bytes. 1-2-3 and Symphony often supply data (particularly row and column locations) in pairs of bytes (LSB first). We will refer to the data bytes of any given record as data byte 0, data byte 1, etc.

This handbook lists the Lotus opcodes in numerical order. See Table 1.13 for a list of the order in which the opcodes appear in a file.

Rows and Columns

Traditionally, spreadsheet rows are numbered and spreadsheet columns are lettered. However, both 1-2-3 and Symphony refer to numbered rows and columns only. Internally, on-screen row #1 becomes 00h 00h (LSB first) and on-screen row #2 becomes 01h 00h (LSB first). On-screen column A becomes 00h 00h (LSB first) and on-screen column B becomes 01h 00h.

.WKS Records

Opcodes are listed in numeric order. *Length* is the length of the data segment. 1-2-3 uses some opcodes and Symphony uses others; most apply to both products.

Each opcode is a two-byte hexadecimal, LSB first. Each length is a two-byte hexadecimal, LSB first. Data is a series of 0 or more hexadecimal bytes, given for each record as byte 0, byte 1, etc.

00h (00d)   **BOF**
- Length   2 bytes
- Meaning   Beginning of file
- Program(s)   1-2-3 and Symphony
- Byte #   0-1   file format version number:
  - 1028 (0404h) is 1-2-3 file
  - 1029 (0405h) is Symphony file
  - 1030 (0406h) is 1-2-3/2 and Symphony 1.1

01h (01d)   **EOF**
- Length   0 bytes
- Meaning   End of file
- Program(s)   1-2-3 and Symphony
- Byte #   No data bytes.

02h (02d)   **CALCMODE**
- Length   1 byte
- Meaning   Calculation method
- Program(s)   1-2-3 and Symphony
- Byte #   0   00h is manual recalculation
  - FFh is automatic recalculation

03h (03d)   **CALCORDER**
- Length   1 byte
- Meaning   Order of calculation
- Program(s)   1-2-3 and Symphony
- Byte #   0   00h is natural recalculation order
  - 01h is recalculation by column
  - FFh is recalculation by row

04h (04d)   **SPLIT**
- Length   1 byte
- Meaning   Shows type of window split
- Program(s)   1-2-3 only
- Byte #   0   00h is not split
  - 01h is vertical split
  - FFh is horizontal split

05h (05d)   **SYNC**
- Length: 1 byte
- Meaning: Synchronizes windows to cursor movement
- Program(s): 1-2-3 only
- Byte #: 0   00h is windows not synchronized
  FFh is synchronized

06h (06d)   **RANGE**
- Length: 8 bytes
- Meaning: The range of cells to be written to a file.
- Program(s): 1-2-3 and Symphony
- Byte #:
  - 0-1   start column
  - 2-3   start row
  - 4-5   end column
  - 6-7   end row

Range describes the active area if a file was created with **File Save** command, and the extract range if created by **File Xtract**. In both cases, trailing blank rows and columns are removed. If there is no data in the range, the starting column value is set to −1. When creating a worksheet file externally, place this record as near to the BOF (Opcode 00h) record as possible.

07h (07d)   **WINDOW1**
- Length: 31 bytes
- Meaning: Describes window #1
- Program(s): 1-2-3 only
- Byte #:
  - 0-1   current cursor column
  - 2-3   current cursor row
  - 4   cell format byte (See Table 1.1)
  - 5   unused (must be 00h)
  - 6-7   column width
  - 8-9   number of columns on screen
  - 10-11   number of rows on screen
  - 12-13   leftmost column
  - 14-15   top row
  - 16-17   number of title columns
  - 18-19   number of title rows
  - 20-21   left title column
  - 22-23   top title row
  - 24-25   border width column
  - 26-27   border width row
  - 28-29   window width
  - 30   unused (must be 00h)

08h (08d)   **COLW1**
Length	3 bytes
Meaning	Defines column width
Program(s)	1-2-3 and Symphony
Byte #	0-1 hexadecimal number of a column
	2 width

In 1-2-3, COLW1 contains width of a column in window #1 specifically. In Symphony, it contains the width information for the widow record it follows.

09h (09d)   **WINTWO**
Length	31 bytes
Meaning	Window #2 record
Program(s)	1-2-3 only

Data is the same as WINDOW1.

0Ah (10d)   **COLW2**
Length	3 bytes
Meaning	Defines column width in window #2
Program(s)	1-2-3 only

Data is the same as COLW1.

0Bh (11d)   **NAME**
Length	24 bytes
Meaning	Describes name of range
Program(s)	1-2-3 only
Byte #	0-15 NULL terminated ASCII string
	16-17 start column
	18-19 start row
	20-21 end column
	22-23 end row

One record is present for each range name.

0Ch (12d)   **BLANK**
Length	5 bytes
Meaning	Defines blank cell
Program(s)	1-2-3 and Symphony
Byte #	0 format byte (See Table 1.1)
	1-2 column number
	3-4 row number

These records appear only for protected or formatted blank cells; otherwise empty cells are not saved.

0Dh (13d)   **INTEGER**
- Length: 7 bytes
- Meaning: Describes integer number cell
- Program(s): 1-2-3 and Symphony
- Byte #:
  - 0   format byte (See Table 1.1)
  - 1-2   column number
  - 3-4   row number
  - 5-6   integer value

A cell may hold an integer value in the range of −32767 to +32767 (decimal).

0Eh (14d)   **NUMBER**
- Length: 13 bytes
- Meaning: Defines floating point number
- Program(s): 1-2-3 and Symphony
- Byte #:
  - 0   format byte
  - 1-2   column number
  - 3-4   row number
  - 5-12   a 64-bit IEEE long real; uses 8087 double-precision floating point format

Lotus stores floating point numbers on disk in IEEE double-precision format. In memory, Lotus stores floating point numbers in its own unique format (See Table 1.2).

0Fh (15d)   **LABEL**
- Length: variable to 245 bytes
- Meaning: Defines a label cell
- Program(s): 1-2-3 and Symphony
- Byte #:
  - 0   format byte
  - 1-2   column number
  - 3-4   row number
  - 5-245(max) NULL (00h) terminated ASCII string; 240 bytes maximum

Byte 5 is always one of the following characters:

|	Printer command string parse line format line (1-2-3/2 only)
\\	repeating character
'	left alignment
"	right alignment
^	centered alignment

10h (16d)   **FORMULA**
Length   variable to 2064 bytes
Meaning   Defines a formula cell
Program(s)   1-2-3 and Symphony
Byte #

Byte	Description
0	format byte
1-2	column number
2-4	row number
5-12	formula numeric value (expressed as IEEE 64-bit long real)
13-14	formula size in bytes
15-2063 (max)	formula code; 2048 bytes maximum

Both 1-2-3 and Symphony compile formulas into "reverse Polish internal notation" (See Tables 1.3 through 1.6).

18h (24d)   **TABLE**
Length   25 bytes
Meaning   Describes a table range
Program(s)   1-2-3 and Symphony
Byte #

Byte	Description
0	0 is no table / 1 is table 1 / 2 is table 2
1-2	table range start column number
3-4	table range start row number
5-6	table range ending column number
7-8	table range ending row number
9-10	input cell 1 start column
11-12	input cell 1 start row
13-14	input cell 1 end column
16-17	input cell 1 end row
17-18	input cell 2 start column
19-20	input cell 2 start row
21-22	input cell 2 end column
23-24	input cell 2 end row

In 1-2-3, these are data tables 1 and 2. In Symphony, these are what-if tables 1 and 2.

19h (25d)   **QRANGE**
Length   25 bytes
Meaning   Describes query range
Program(s)   1-2-3 only
Byte #

Byte #	Description
0-1	input range start column
2-3	input range start row
4-5	input range ending column
6-7	input range ending row
8-9	output range start column
10-11	output range start row
12-13	output range end column
14-15	output range end row
16-17	criteria start column
18-19	criteria start row
20-21	criteria end column
22-23	criteria end row
24	Command 0 is no command
	1 is find
	2 is extract
	3 is delete
	4 is unique

1Ah (26d)   **PRANGE**
Length   8 bytes
Meaning   Defines print range
Program(s)   Symphony 1.1 and Lotus 1-2-3
Byte #

Byte #	Description
0-1	start column
2-3	start row
4-5	end column
6-7	end row

1Bh (27d)   **SRANGE**
Length   8 bytes
Meaning   Defines sort range
Program(s)   1-2-3 only
Byte #

Byte #	Description
0-1	start column
2-3	start row
4-5	end column
6-7	end row

1Ch (28d) **FRANGE**
Length 8 bytes
Meaning Defines fill range
Program(s) 1-2-3 and Symphony
Byte # 0-1 start column
2-3 start row
4-5 end column
6-7 end row

1Dh (29d) **KRANGE**
Length 9 bytes
Meaning Defines the primary sort key range
Program(s) 1-2-3 only
Byte # 0-1 start column
2-3 start row
4-5 end column
6-7 end row
8 order   00h is descending order
            FFh is ascending order

20h (32d) **HRANGE**
Length 16 bytes
Meaning Defines distribution range
Program(s) 1-2-3 and Symphony
Byte # 0-1 values range start column
2-3 values range start row
4-5 values range end column
6-7 values range end row
8-9 bin range start column
10-11 bin range start row
12-13 bin range end column
14-15 bin rage end row

23h (35d) **KRANGE2**
Length 9 bytes
Meaning Defines secondary sort key range
Program(s) 1-2-3 only
Byte # 0-1 start column
2-3 start row
4-5 end column
6-7 end row
8 order   00h is descending
            FFh is ascending

24h (36d)   PROTEC
Length	1 byte
Meaning	Toggles global protection
Program(s)	1-2-3 and Symphony
Byte #	0 00h means global protection off
	01h means global protection on

25h (37d)   FOOTER
Length	242 bytes
Meaning	Print footer
Program(s)	1-2-3 only
Byte #	0-241 NULL terminated ASCII string

26h (38d)   HEADER
Length	242 bytes
Meaning	Print header
Program(s)	1-2-3 only
Byte #	0-241 NULL terminated ASCII string

27h (39d)   SETUP
Length	40 bytes
Meaning	Describes print setup
Program(s)	1-2-3 only
Byte #	0-39 NULL terminated ASCII string

28h (40d)   MARGINS
Length	10 bytes
Meaning	Describes print margins mode
Program(s)	1-2-3 only
Byte #	0-1 left margin
	2-3 right margin
	4-6 page length
	6-7 top margin
	8-9 bottom margin

29h (41d)   LABELFMT
Length	1 byte
Meaning	Defines label alignment
Program(s)	1-2-3 and Symphony
Byte #	0 27h is left
	22h is right
	5Eh is center

2Ah (42d)   **TITLES**
Length	16 bytes	
Meaning	Print borders	
Program(s)	1-2-3 only	
Byte #	0-1	row border start column
	2-3	row border start row
	4-5	row border end column
	6-7	row border end row
	8-9	column border start column
	10-11	column border start row
	12-13	column border end column
	14-15	column border end row

2Dh (45d)   **GRAPH**
Length	437 bytes
Meaning	Describes current graph setting; 3 is unused
Program(s)	1-2-3 only
Byte #	See Table 1.7

2Eh (46d)   **NGRAPH**
Length	453 bytes
Meaning	Provided for named, current graph settings
Program(s)	1-2-3 only
Byte #	See Table 1.8

2Fh (47d)   **CALCCOUNT**
Length	1 byte	
Meaning	Contains iteration count	
Program(s)	1-2-3 and Symphony	
Byte #	0	iteration count

30h (48d)   **UNFORMATTED**
Length	1 byte	
Meaning	Toggles formatted/unformatted print	
Program(s)	1-2-3 only	
Byte #	0	00h is formatted
		01h is unformatted

31h (49d)   **CURSORW12**
Length	1 byte	
Meaning	Describes cursor location	
Program(s)	1-2-3 only	
Byte #	0	01h is cursor in window #1
		02h is cursor in window #2

32h (50d)   **WINDOW**
- Length   144 bytes
- Meaning   Describes window record
- Program(s)   Symphony only
- Byte #   See Table 1.9

33h (51d)   **STRING**
- Length   variable
- Meaning   Describes value of string function
- Program(s)   Symphony only
- Byte #
  - 0   format byte
  - 1-2   column number
  - 3-4   row number
  - 5 . . .   NULL terminated ASCII string

37h (55d)   **LOCK PASSWORD**
- Length   4 bytes
- Meaning   Restricts writing to a defined range
- Program(s)   Symphony only

Do not confuse this opcode with the Worksheet Password function, opcode 48h (75d). Further details were not available from Lotus.

38h (56d)   **LOCKED**
- Length   1 byte
- Meaning   Toggles lock flag
- Program(s)   Symphony only
- Byte #
  - 0   00h is off
  -        01h is on

3Ch (60d)   **QUERY**
- Length   127 bytes
- Meaning   Describes query settings
- Program(s)   Symphony only
- Byte #   See Table 1.10

3Dh (61d)   **QUERYNAME**
- Length   16 bytes
- Meaning   Describes current query name
- Program(s)   Symphony only
- Byte #   0-15   NULL terminated ASCII string

3Eh (62d)   **PRINT**
- Length: 679 bytes
- Meaning: Describes print record
- Program(s): Symphony only
- Byte #: See Table 1.11

3Fh (63d)   **PRINTNAME**
- Length: 16 bytes
- Meaning: Describes current print record name
- Program(s): Symphony only
- Byte #: 0-15   NULL terminated ASCII string

40h (64d)   **GRAPH2**
- Length: 499 bytes
- Meaning: Describes graph record
- Program(s): Symphony only
- Byte #: See Table 1.12

41h (65d)   **GRAPHNAME**
- Length: 16 bytes
- Meaning: Describes current graph record name
- Program(s): Symphony only
- Byte #: 0-15   NULL terminated ASCII string

42h (66d)   **ZOOM**
- Length: 9 bytes
- Meaning: Describes original coordinates of expanded window
- Program(s): Symphony only
- Byte #:
  - 0   Indicates window zoom
    - 00h is no
    - 01h is yes
  - 1-2   X coordinates
  - 3-4   Y coordinates
  - 5-6   column depth
  - 7-8   row depths

43h (67d)   **SYMSPLIT**
- Length: 2 bytes
- Meaning: Describes number of split windows
- Program(s): Symphony only
- Byte #: 0-1   number of split windows

44h (68d)   **NSROWS**
- Length: 2 bytes
- Meaning: Describes number of screen rows
- Program(s): Symphony only
- Byte #: 0-1   number of rows

45h (69d)   **NSCOLS**
- Length: 2 bytes
- Meaning: Describes number of screen columns
- Program(s): Symphony only
- Byte #: 0-1   number of columns

46h (70d)   **RULER**
- Length: 25 bytes
- Meaning: Describes named ruler range
- Program(s): Symphony only
- Byte #:
  - 0-15   name; NULL terminated ASCII string
  - 16-17   range start column
  - 18-19   range start row
  - 20-21   range end column
  - 22-23   range end row
  - 24   range type   00h is single cell
  -                                  01h is range

47h (71d)   **NNAME**
- Length: 25 bytes
- Meaning: Describes named sheet range
- Program(s): Symphony only
- Byte #:
  - 0-15   name; NULL terminated ASCII string
  - 16-17   range start column
  - 18-19   range start row
  - 20-21   range end column
  - 22-23   range end row
  - 24   range type   00h is single cell
  -                                  01h is range

48h (72d)   **ACOMM**
- Length: 65 bytes
- Meaning: Name of autoload communications file
- Program(s): Symphony only
- Byte #: 0-64   pathname; NULL terminated ASCII string

49h (73d)   **AMACRO**
                 Length   8 bytes
                 Meaning   Describes autoexecute macro address
                 Program(s)   Symphony only
                 Byte #   0-1   start column
                                         2-3   start row
                                         4-5   end column
                                         6-7   end row

4Ah (74d)   **PARSE**
                 Length   16 bytes
                 Meaning   Describes query parse information
                 Program(s)   Symphony only
                 Byte #   0-1   parse range start column
                                           2-3   parse range start row
                                           4-5   parse range end column
                                           6-7   parse range end row
                                           8-9   review range start column
                                           10-11   review range start row
                                           12-13   review range end column
                                           14-15   review range end row

4Bh (75d)   **WKSPWORD**
                 Length   4 bytes
                 Meaning   Worksheet password function
                 Program(s)   1-2-3/2, Symphony 1.1

This record encrypts the worksheet. Do not confuse it with opcode 37h (55d). Further details were not available from Lotus.

64h (100d)   **HIDVEC1 (1-2-3/2)**
                 HIVEC (Symphony 1.1)
                 Length   32 bytes
                 Meaning   Hidden columns record
                 Program(s)   1-2-3/2, Symphony

These 32 bytes correspond to an array of 256 bits. Each bit represents a worksheet column. A bit value of 1 represents a hidden column. The array is arranged LSB to MSB, byte 0 through byte 31. Byte 0, bit 0 represents column A. In 1-2-3/2, this record normally represents the entire worksheet. When the window is split, it represents the columns of Window 1.

65h (101d)   **HIDVEC2**
Length   32 bytes
Meaning   Hidden columns record
Program(s)   1-2-3/2

Operates in the same way as opcode 64h, but for Window #2 in 1-2-3/2.

66h (102d)   **PARSERANGES**
Length   16 bytes
Meaning   Parse ranges
Program(s)   1-2-3/2
Byte #
    0-1   Parse Input Range start column
    2-3   start row
    4-5   end column
    6-7   end row
    8-9   Parse Output Range start column
    10-11   start row
    12-13   end column
    14-15   end row

67h (103d)   **RRANGES**
Length   25 bytes
Meaning   Linear regression ranges
Program(s)   1-2-3/2
Byte #   Dependent variable range
    0-1   start column
    2-3   start row
    4-5   end column
    6-7   end row
    Indep. variable range
    8-9   start column
    10-11   start row
    12-13   end column
    14-15   end row
    Output range
    16-17   start column
    18-19   start row
    20-21   end column
    22-23   end row
    24   Zero intercept flag
               0 is not forced; zero intercept;
               −1 is forced intercept at origin

69h (105d)   **MATRIXRANGES**
Length	40 bytes	
Meaning	Matrix mathematics ranges	
Program(s)	1-2-3/2	
Byte #	0-1	Matrix inversion source start column
	2-3	start row
	4-5	end column
	6-7	end row
	8-9	Matrix inversion destination start column
	10-11	start row
	12-13	end column
	14-15	end row
	16-17	Matrix multiplicand range start column
	18-19	start row
	20-21	end column
	22-23	end row
	24-25	Matrix multiplier range start column
	26-27	start row
	28-29	end column
	30-31	end row
	32-33	Matrix product range start column
	34-35	start row
	36-37	end column
	38-39	end row

96h (150d)   **CPI**
Length	variable	
Meaning	Cell pointer index	
Program(s)	1-2-3/2, Symphony 1.1	

This record is a list of columns that contains one or more active cells.

Byte #	0-1	Column number, integer
	2-3	Lowest row number of active cell
	4-5	Highest row number of active cell

Table 1.1 Cell Format Byte

The following is a diagram of how 1-2-3 and Symphony organize the cell format byte.

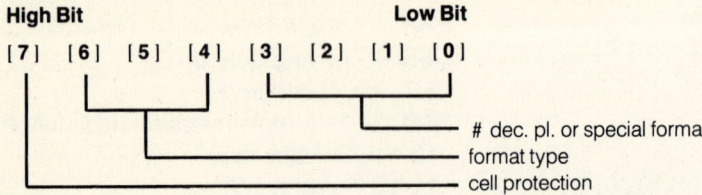

Bit	Description	Code	Binary	Meaning
7	protect	1	1	protected cell
		0	0	unprotected
6, 5, 4	format type	0	000	fixed
		1	001	scientific notation
		2	010	currency
		3	011	percent
		4	100	comma
		5	101	unused
		6	110	unused
		7	111	special
3, 2, 1, 0	If format type 0-6, these bits = # decimal places	0-15	000 to 1111	
	If format type is 7	0	0000	+/−
		1	0001	general format
		2	0010	day - month - year
		3	0011	day - month
		4	0100	month - year
		5	0101	text
	Symphony only	6	0110	hidden
	Symphony only	7	0111	date; hour - minute - second
	Symphony only	8	1000	date; hour - minute
	Symphony only	9	1001	date; international 1
	Symphony only	10	1010	date; international 2
	Symphony only	11	1011	time; international 1
	Symphony only	12	1100	time; international 2
		13	1101	unused
		14	1110	unused
		15	1111	default

LOTUS 1-2-3 and SYMPHONY

Table 1.2	Lotus Internal Floating Point Format

Lotus 1-2-3 and Symphony store floating point numbers in memory (but not on disk) in the following 11-byte format.

Byte	Value	SPECIAL CASES Byte	Value
0	0 is a positive number −1 is a negative number 2 is a range 3 is a string	ERR 0 1-2 2-10	0 2047 0
1-2	exponent, a signed integer	NA 0 1-2 3-10	−1 2047 0
3-10	64-bit unsigned fraction		

Table 1.3	Formula Opcodes: Format Opcodes

Dec	Hex	Operation	Notes
0	00	constant	followed by 64 bit IEE real
1	01	variable	followed by 4-byte row/column coordinate: byte 0-1 = column, byte 2-3 = row. LSB first.
2	02	range	followed by 8-byte range: byte 0-1 start column number byte 2-3 start row number byte 4-5 end column number byte 6-7 end row number
3	03	return	signifies end of formula
4	04	parentheses	indicates parentheses in original formula; ignored during recalculation
5	05	2-byte integer constant	followed by 2-byte signed integer
6	06	string constant	variable length, NULL terminated

Table 1.4 Formula Opcodes: Operation Codes

Dec	Hex	Operation	Notes
8	08	unary -	unary minus (negation)
9	09	+	addition
10	0A	-	subtraction
11	0B	*	multiplication
12	0C	/	division
13	0D	^	exponentiation
14	0E	=	equal to
15	0F	< >	not equal to
16	10	< =	less than or equal to
17	11	> =	greater than or equal to
18	12	<	less than
19	13	>	greater than
20	14	#AND#	logical AND
21	15	#OR#	logical OR
22	16	#NOT#	logical NOT
23	17	unary +	(ignored during recalculation)
31	1F	na	@na - not applicable
32	20	err	@err - error
33	21	abs	@abs - absolute value
34	22	int	@int - integer value
35	23	sqrt	@sqrt - square root
36	24	log	@log - log base 10
37	25	ln	@ln - log base e (natural log)
38	26	pi	@pi
39	27	sin	@sin - sine
40	28	cos	@cos - cosine
41	29	tan	@tan - tangent
42	2A	atan2	@atan2 - 4 quadrant arctangent
43	2B	atan	@atan - 2 quadrant arctangent
44	2C	asin	@asin - arcsine
45	2D	acos	@acos - arc cosine
46	2E	exp	@exp - exponential anti-log
47	2F	mod	@mod(x,y) - X mod Y
48	30	sel	@choose
49	31	isna	@isna(x) - x=NA then 1
50	32	iserr	@iserr(x) - x=ERR then 1
51	33	false	@false - return 0
52	34	true	@true - return 1
53	35	rand	@rand - generate random number between 0 and 1
54	36	date	@date - generate the number of days since 1/1/1900
55	37	today	@today - output serial date number
56	38	pmt	@pmt - payment
57	39	pv	@pv - present value
58	3A	fv	@fv - future value
59	3B	if	@if - boolean
60	3C	day	@day - output day of month
61	3D	month	@month - output month of year
62	3E	year	@year - output year

(continued)

Table 1.4   Continued

Dec	Hex	Operation	Notes
63	3F	round	@round - round number x to d decimal places
64	40	time	@time -
65	41	hour	@hour -
66	42	minute	@minute -
67	43	second	@second -
68	44		@ISNumber -
69	45		@ISString -
70	46	length	@length -
71	47	value	@value -
72	48		@fixed -
73	49		@mid -
74	4A		@chr -
75	4B		@ASCII -
76	4C		@find -
77	4D		@Datevalue -
78	4E		@Timevalue -
79	4F		@Cellpointer -

Table 1.5   Formula Opcodes: Multiple Argument Opcodes

NOTE: Commas generally separate arguments. The character "|" signifies the option to use more than one argument in a single expression.

Dec	Hex	Operation	Notes
80	50	sum	@sum (range | cell | constant)
81	51	avg	@avg (range | cell | constant)
82	52	cnt	@cnt (range | cell | constant)
83	53	min	@min (range | cell | constant)
84	54	max	@max (range | cell | constant)
85	55	vlookup	@vlookup (x,range,offset) x = cell address or constant range = table offset = row in table
86	56	npv	@npv (int,range) - net present no value int = interest range = cash flows
87	57	var	@var (range) - variance
88	58	std	@std (range) - standard deviation
89	59	irr	@irr (guess,range) - internal rate of return guess = % estimate range = cash flows
90	5A	hlookup	@hlookup(x,range,offset) x = cell address or constant range = table offset = row in table

(continued)

Table 1.5 Continued

Dec	Hex	Operation	Notes
91	5B	dsum	data base statistical function
92	5C	avg	data base statistical function
93	5D	dcnt	data base statistical function
94	5E	dmin	data base statistical function
95	5F	dmax	data base statistical function
96	60	dvar	data base statistical function
97	61	dstd	data base statistical function
98	62		@Index
99	63		@Cols
100	64		@Rows
101	65		@Repeat
102	66		@Upper
103	67		@Lower
104	68		@Left
105	69		@Right
106	6A		@Replace
107	6B		@Proper
108	6C		@Cell
109	6D		@Trim
110	6E		@Clean
111	6F		@S
112	70		@V
113	71		@Streq
114	72		@Call
115	73		@App (Symphony 1.0) @Indirect (Symphony 1.1)
116	74		@Rate
117	75		@Term
118	77		@CTerm
119	77		@SLN
120	78		@SOY
121	79		@DDB
156	9C		@@ @aafstart
206	CE		@aafunkown (1-2-3/2)
255	FF		@aafend (1-2-3/2) @aafmax (Symphony 1.1)

Table 1.6 Operator Precedence

Operator	Unary Precedence	Binary Precedence	Operator	Unary Precedence	Binary Precedence
+	6	4	<=	na	3
-	6	4	>=	na	3
*	na	5	<	na	3
/	na	5	>	na	3
^	na	7	#AND#	na	1
=	na	3	#OR#	na	1
<>	na	3	#NOT#	2	na

Table 1.7 Graph Record Structure

Byte #	Name	Meaning	Byte #	Name	Meaning
0- 1	X range	start column	68-69		end column
2- 3		start row	70-71		end row
4- 5		end column	72-73	C labels	start column
6- 7		end row	74-75		start row
8- 9	A range	start column	76-77		end column
10-11		start row	78-79		end row
12-13		end column	80-81	D labels	start column
14-15		end row	82-83		start row
16-17	B range	start column	84-85		end column
18-19		start row	86-87		end row
20-21		end column	88-89	E labels	start column
22-23		end row	90-91		start row
24-25	C range	start column	92-93		end column
26-27		start row	94-95		end row
28-29		end column	96- 97	F labels	start column
30-31		end row	98- 99		start row
32-33	D range	start column	100-101		end column
34-35		start row	102-103		end row
36-37		end column	104	Graph type:	00h = XY
38-39		end row			01h = bar
40-41	E range	start column			02h = pie
42-43		start row			04h = line
44-45		end column			05h = stacked bar
46-47		end row	105	Grid:	00h = none
48-49	F range	start column			01h = horizontal
50-51		start row			02h = vertical
52-53		end column			03h = both
54-55		end row	106	Color:	00h = black & white
56-57	A labels	start column			FFh = color
58-59		start row			
60-61		end column			
62-63		end row			
64-65	B labels	start column			
66-67		start row			

(continued)

Table 1.7 Continued

Byte #	Name	Meaning	Byte #	Name	Meaning
107	A range line format:	00h = none 01h = line 02h = symbol 03h = line-symbol	115	C range data label alignment	00h = center 01h = right 02h = below 03h = left 04h = above
108	B range line format:	00h = none 01h = line 02h = symbol 03h = line-symbol	116	D range data label alignment	00h = center 01h = right 02h = below 03h = left 04h = above
109	C range line format:	00h = none 01h = line 02h = symbol 03h = line-symbol	117	E range data label alignment	00h = center 01h = right 02h = below 03h = left 04h = above
110	D range line format:	00h = none 01h = line 02h = symbol 03h = line-symbol	118	F range data label alignment	00h = center 01h = right 02h = below 03h = left 04h = above
111	E range line format:	00h = none 01h = line 02h = symbol 03h = line-symbol	119	Scale	00h = auto FFh = manual
112	F range line format:	00h = none 01h = line 02h = symbol 03h = line-symbol	120-127	X lower limit	64-bit long real floating point format
			128-135	X upper limit	64-bit long real floating point format
113	A range data label alignment	00h = center 01h = right 02h = below 03h = left 04h = above	136	Y scale:	00h = auto FFh = manual
			137-144	Y lower limit	64-bit long real floating point format
			145-152	Y upper limit	64-bit long real floating point format
114	B range data label alignment	00h = center 01h = right 02h = below 03h = left 04h = above	153-192	First title	Text
			193-232	Second title	Text
			233-272	X title	Text
			273-312	Y title	Text

(continued)

Table 1.7	Continued				
Byte #	Name	Meaning	Byte #	Name	Meaning
313-332	A legend	Text	413-432	F legend	Text
333-352	B legend	Text	433	X format	Text
353-372	C legend	Text	434	Y format	Text
373-392	D legend	Text	435-436	Skip factor	
393-412	E legend	Text			

Table 1.8	NGraph Record Structure				
Byte #	Name	Meaning	Byte #	Name	Meaning
0-15	Name	NULL terminated ASCII string	80-81 82-83 84-85 86-87	B labels	start column start row end column end row
16-17 18-19 20-21 22-23	X range	start column start row end column end row	88-89 90-91 92-93 94-95	C labels	start column start row end column end row
24-25 26-27 28-29 30-31	A range	start column start row end column end row	96-97 98-99 100-101 102-103	D labels	start column start row end column end row
32-33 34-35 36-37 38-39	B range	start column start row end column end row	104-105 106-107 108-109 110-111	E labels	start column start row end column end row
40-41 42-43 44-45 46-47	C range	start column start row end column end row	112-113 114-115 116-117 118-119	F labels	start column start row end column end row
48-49 50-51 52-53 54-55	D range	start column start row end column end row	120	Graph type:	00h = XY 01h = bar 02h = pie 04h = line 05h = stacked bar 3 is unused
56-57 58-59 60-61 62-63	E range	start column start row end column end row	121	Grid:	00h = none 01h = horizontal 02h = vertical 03h = both
64-65 66-67 68-69 70-71	F range	start column start row end column end row	122	Color:	00h = black & white FFh = color
72-73 74-75 76-77 78-79	A labels	start column start row end column end row			

(continued)

Table 1.8 Continued

Byte #	Name	Meaning		Byte #	Name	Meaning	
123	A range line format:	00h = none 01h = line 02h = symbol 03h = line-symbol		132	D range data label alignment	00h = center 01h = right 02h = below 03h = left 04h = above	
124	B range line format:	00h = none 01h = line 02h = symbol 03h = line-symbol		133	E range data label alignment	00h = center 01h = right 02h = below 03h = left 04h = above	
125	C range line format:	00h = none 01h = line 02h = symbol 03h = line-symbol		134	F range data label alignment	00h = center 01h = right 02h = below 03h = left 04h = above	
126	D range line format:	00h = none 01h = line 02h = symbol 03h = line-symbol		135	Scale	00h = auto FFh = manual	
127	E range line format:	00h = none 01h = line 02h = symbol 03h = line-symbol		136-143	X lower limit	64-bit long real floating point format	
				144-151	X upper limit	64-bit long real floating point format	
128	F range line format:	00h = none 01h = line 02h = symbol 03h = line-symbol		152	Y scale:	00h = auto FFh = manual	
				153-160	Y lower limit	64-bit long real floating point format	
				161-168	Y upper limit	64-bit long real floating point format	
129	A range data label alignment	00h = center 01h = right 02h = below 03h = left 04h = above		209-224	First title	Text	
				225-248	Second title	Text	
				249-288	X title	Text	
				289-328	Y title	Text	
130	B range data label alignment	00h = center 01h = right 02h = below 03h = left 04h = above		329-348	A legend	Text	
				349-368	B legend	Text	
				369-388	C legend	Text	
				389-408	D legend	Text	
131	C range data label alignment	00h = center 01h = right 02h = below 03h = left 04h = above		409-428	E legend	Text	
				429-448	F legend	Text	
				449	X format	Text	
				450	Y format	Text	
				451-452	Skip factor		

Table 1.9		Symphony Window Record Structure	
Byte #	Name		Meaning
0- 15	window name		NULL terminate ASCII string
16- 17	cursor position		column
18- 19	cursor position		row
20	format byte		
21	unused		
22- 23	column width		
24- 25	total number of columns		
26- 27	total number of rows		
28- 29	non-title home position column		
30- 31	non-title home position row		
32- 33	number of title columns		
34- 35	number of title rows		
36- 37	left title column		
38- 39	top title row		
40- 41	home position column		
42- 43	home position row		
44- 45	number of screen columns		
46- 47	number of screen rows		
48	hidden status		00h = hidden FFh = not hidden
49	previous window		00h = SHEET 01h = DOC 02h = GRAPH 03h = COMM 04h = FORM 05h = APPLICATION
50	border display		00h = cell FFh = no cell
51	border display lines		00h = lines FFh = no lines
52- 53	window range		start column
54- 55			start row
56- 57			end column
58- 59			end row
60- 61	offset		
62	insert mode flag		00h = off non-zero = on
63- 78	graph name		

(continued)

Table 1.9 Continued

Byte #	Name	Meaning
79	window type	00h = SHEET 01h = DOC 02h = GRAPH 03h = COMM 04h = FORM 05h = APPLICATION
80	automatic display mode flag	"a" = automatic (61h) non- "a" = manual
81	forms filter	00h = filter non-00h = no filter
82- 97	associated form name	
98- 99	forms current record	
100	space display	00h = no spaces non-00h = spaces
101	line spacing	01h = 1 space 02h = 2 spaces 03h = 3 spaces
102	justify type	"l" = left (6Ch) "r" = right (72h) "c" = center (63h) "e" = even (65h)
103-104	right margin	00h-F0h = right margin FFh = no user-defined right margin; use default
105-106	left margin	00h-F0h = left margin
107-108	tab interval	
109	return display	00h = soft carriage ret. non 00h = hard return
110	autojustify	00h = no non-00h = yes
111-126	associated application name	
127-143	reserved	

Table 1.10 Symphony Query Record

Byte #	Name	Meaning	Byte #	Name	Meaning
0-15	name	NULL terminated ASCII string	88-89 90-91 92-93 94-95	input cell	start column start row end column end row
16-17 18-19 20-21 22-23	input range	start column start row end column end row	96-97 98-99 100-101 102-103	1st key range	start column start row end column end row
24-25 26-27 28-29 30-31	output range	start column start row end column end row	104-105 106-107 108-109 110-111	2nd key range	start column start row end column end row
32-33 34-35 36-37 38-39	criteria range	start column start row end column end row	112-113 114-115 116-117 118-119	3rd key range	start column start row end column end row
40-41 42-43 44-45 46-47	form entry	start column start row end column end row	120	last command	00h = no command 01h = find 02h = extract 03h = delete 04h = unique
48-49 50-51 52-53 54-55	form definition range	start column start row end column end row	121	1st key order	00h = descending order FFh = ascending order
56-67 58-59 60-61 62-63	report output	start column start row end column end row	122	2nd key order	00h = descending FFh = ascending
64-65 66-67 68-69 70-71	report header	start column start row end column end row	123 124	3rd key order report number of records	00h = descending FFh = ascending 00h = multiple FFh = single
72-73 74-75 76-77 78-79	report footer	start column start row end column end row	125	number of records	00h = multiple FFh = single
80-81 82-83 84-85 86-87	table range	start column start row end column end row	126	marks	00h = yes FFh = no

Table 1.11 Symphony Print Record

Byte #	Name	Meaning	Byte #	Name	Meaning
0-15	setting name	NULL terminated ASCII string	57-58	top	
			59-60	bottom of page	
16-17	source range	start column	61-101	setup string	NULL terminated ASCII string
18-19		start row			
20-21		end column			
22-23		end row	102-342	header	NULL terminated ASCII string
24-25	row border	start column			
26-27		start row	343-584	footer	NULL terminated ASCII string
28-29		end column			
30-31		end row	585-600	source data-base name	NULL terminated ASCII string
32-33	column border	start column			
34-35		start row			
36-37		end column	601	attribute	00h = no non-00h = yes
38-39		end row			
40-41	destination	start column	602	space compression	00h = no non-00h = yes
42-43		start row			
44-45		end column			
46-47		end row	603	print destination	00h = printer 01h = file 02h = range
48	print format	00h = as displayed non-00h = formulas			
49	page breaks	00h = yes non-00h = no	604-605	start page	
			606-607	end page	
50	line spacing		608-677	destination filename	NULL terminated ASCII string
51-52	left margin				
53-54	right margin				
55-56	page length		678	wait	00h = no non-00h = yes

Table 1.12 Symphony Graph Record

Byte #	Name	Meaning	Byte #	Name	Meaning
0-15	name	NULL terminated ASCII string	32-33	B range	start column
			34-35		start row
16-17	X range	start column	36-37		end column
18-19		start row	38-39		end row
20-21		end column	40-41	C range	start column
22-23		end row	42-43		start row
24-25	A range	start column	44-45		end column
26-27		start row	46-47		end row
28-29		end column	48-49	D range	start column
30-31		end row	50-51		start row
			52-53		end column
			54-55		end row

(continued)

Table 1.12 Continued

Byte #	Name	Meaning	Byte #	Name	Meaning
56-57	E range	start column	123	A range line format:	
58-59		start row			00h = none
60-61		end column			01h = line
62-63		end row			02h = symbol
					03h = line-symbol
64-65	F range	start column	124	B range line format:	
66-67		start row			00h = none
68-69		end column			01h = line
70-71		end row			02h = symbol
					03h = line-symbol
72-73	A labels	start column	125	C range line format:	
74-75		start row			00h = none
76-77		end column			01h = line
78-79		end row			02h = symbol
					03h = line-symbol
80-81	B labels	start column	126	D range line format:	
82-83		start row			00h = none
84-85		end column			01h = line
86-87		end row			02h = symbol
					03h = line-symbol
88-89	C labels	start column	127	E range line format:	
90-91		start row			00h = none
92-93		end column			01h = line
94-95		end row			02h = symbol
					03h = line-symbol
96-97	D labels	start column	128	F range line format:	
98-99		start row			00h = none
100-101		end column			01h = line
102-103		end row			02h = symbol
					03h = line-symbol
104-105	E labels	start column	129	A range data label alignment	00h = center
106-107		start row			01h = right
108-109		end column			02h = below
110-111		end row			03h = left
					04h = above
112-113	F labels	start column			
114-115		start row	130	B range data label alignment	00h = center
116-117		end column			01h = right
118-119		end row			02h = below
					03h = left
					04h = above
120	graph type	00h = XY			
		01h = bar			
		02h = pie	131	C range data label alignment	00h = center
		04h = line			01h = right
		05h = stacked bar			02h = below
					03h = left
121	grid	00h = none			04h = above
		01h = horizontal			
		02h = vertical	132	D range data label alignment	00h = center
		03h = both			01h = right
					02h = below
122	color	00h = black & white			03h = left
		FFh = color			04h = above

(continued)

Table 1.12 Continued

Byte #	Name	Meaning	Byte #	Name	Meaning
133	E range data label alignment	00h = center 01h = right 02h = below 03h = left 04h = above	451-452	Skip factor	
			453	X scale flag (x1K)	00h = on FFh = off
			454	Y scale flag (x1K)	00h = on FFh = off
134	F range data label alignment	00h = center 01h = right 02h = below 03h = left 04h = above	455	suppress	00h = no non-00h = yes
			456-463	bar origin (float)	
135	X Scale	00h = auto FFh = manual	464-471	X linear scale (float)	
136-143	X lower limit	64-bit long real floating point format	472-479	Y linear scale (float)	
144-151	X upper limit	64-bit long real floating point format	480	X log scale	
			481	Y log scale	
152	Y scale	00h = auto FFh = manual	482	graph region color	X hue
153-160	Y lower limit	64-bit long real floating point format	483	graph region color	A hue
161-168	Y upper limit	64-bit long real floating point format			
169-208	first title		484	graph region color	B hue
209-248	second title		485	graph region color	C hue
249-288	X title				
289-328	Y title		486	graph region color	D hue
329-348	A legend				
349-368	B legend		487	graph region color	E hue
369-388	C legend				
389-408	D legend		488	graph region color	F hue
409-428	E legend				
429-448	F legend		489-490	Y width	
449	X format		491-498	aspect (float)	
450	Y format				

Table 1.13   Record Order Within the Data File

1-2-3 Record Order	Symphony Record Order
BOF	BOF
WKSPASS	WKSPASS
RANGE	RANGE
CPI	CPI
CALCCOUNT	CALCCOUNT
CALCMODE	CALCMODE
CALCORDER	CALCORDER
SPLIT	NSPLIT
SYNC	NSROWS
WINDOW 1 DESCRIPTOR:	NSCOLS
WINDOW1	WINDOW DESCRIPTORS(S)—one group of these three records for each defined window.
COLW1	
HIDCOL1	WINDOW
WINDOW 2 DESCRIPTOR:	COLW
WINDOW2	HIDCOL
COLW2	PASSWORD
HIDCOL2	LOCKED
CURSORW12	AMACRO
AAF	ACOMM
RNAME	Range Names:
NGRAPH	NRANGE
TABLE	Query Names:
QRANGE	QUERY
PRANGE	Print Names:
FORMAT	PRINT
FRANGE	Graph Names:
SRANGE	SGRAPH
KRANGE1	Ruler Names:
KRANGE2	RULER
RRANGES	TABLE
MRANGES	QUERYNAME
HRANGE	PRINTNAME
PARSE	GRAPHNAME
PROTECT	FRANGE
FOOTER	HRANGE
HEADER	PROTECT
SETUP	LABELFMT
MARGINS	Cell List:
LABELFMT	BLANK
TITLES	OR INTEGER
GRAPH	OR NUMBER
Cell List:	OR LABEL
BLANK	OR FORMULA
OR INTEGER	OR FORMULA AND STRING
OR NUMBER	ZOOM
OR LABEL	SPLIT
OR FORMULA	PARSE
OR FORMULA AND STRING	EOF
EOF	

CHAPTER 2

ABILITY™
Version 1.0

Xanaro Technologies, Inc.
321 Bloor Street East, Suite 815
Toronto, Ontario
Canada, M4W 1G9

TYPE OF PRODUCT   Integrated software
Spreadsheet, Word Processing, Data Base, Business Graphics, Communications, Presentation Graphics

FILES PRODUCED   ASCII text

POINTS OF INTEREST

Ability™ is a program whose whole may be greater than the sum of its parts. Although each function is part of a single program, each of the major file-producing functions (spreadsheet, word processing, data base and graphics) creates a separate and distinct file.

Files may refer to each other. This most frequently takes place in word processing (for example, preparing a report) so that a document can include spreadsheet, graphics and tabular information.

In memory, this cross-reference information is changeable and active; an alteration to a spreadsheet in memory changes the table derived from it that has been included in a word-processing document.

File data is almost completely ASCII text. High bits are toggled on soft carriage returns in word-processing documents. This changes the 0Dh return character to 8Dh, and takes it out of the ASCII range.

According to Xanaro, the advantages of using ASCII text files include: smaller files, numbers may be stored with required precision (or lack of it), the files are machine-transparent, a text editor can correct simple file damage, and the human eye can read the files.

CONVERSION INFORMATION

Ability can read and write DIF format files and exchange data with other programs that read and write DIF. Ability's word-processing files are similar to (but not identical to) WordStar® files. Xanaro Technologies offers source code for Turbo Pascal access routines that allow external programs to read and write Ability format data-base files.

The Ability File Format

Ability is a multiple-function, integrated (all-in-one) software product. It performs the functions of spreadsheet, word processing, data base, business graphics, communications and presentation graphics.

Four of the six functions (spreadsheet, word processing, data base and business graphics) produce useful files of similar type. The business graphics function generally obtains its data series from spreadsheet files (although users may enter data directly).

Newline and EOF

Under PC-DOS, Ability uses as its newline character the carriage return/linefeed combination (0Dh, 0Ah). The high bit of the carriage return is sometimes set on, generating the code 8Dh and signifying a "soft" carriage return when used with the linefeed character. Ability's end of file (EOF) marker is PC-DOS' control-Z (1Ah).

Ability File Structures

The following sections make up each file:

- **a header line** which contains version number, document length, and document type-dependent information
- **the text section** which includes written text, spreadsheet constants and labels, data-base records, and graphic display
- **the parameters section** which contains tab stops, margins, and cursor position
- **field definitions** which define formulas, range and list specifications, and references to other files
- **field display formats** which include parentheses for negative numbers, decimal points and commas

Between text and parameters, Ability places a CTRL-L (0Ch, 12d) character as a division marker.

Not all sections need to be present. The header line and text section must be present. The parameters section will generally contain only information that has been changed from the default conditions. If there are no fields or references to other files (typical of word-processing documents that do not include spreadsheet or graphic data), then the last two sections will not be present.

As a rule, Ability saves only information that is in conflict with its defaults, rather than saving all file details. In word-processing documents for example, header lines and parameters are left out of the file if tabs, headers, footers, left and right margins, justification and page length settings have been left at default, if no fields have been defined and no graphs or spreadsheets have been included in the file.

Header Line

The header line tells Ability what type of file it has loaded. The header appears first in the file, starting at byte 0. It is a variable length string terminated by a newline (CR/LF) sequence in the format

>   --HDR<ver>--[S]<nlines>[S]<filetype>;<info>[newline]

>   *where*
>   [S] represents the ASCII space character (20h).
>   [newline] is the CR/LF sequence (0Dh, 0Ah).
>   <ver> is the version of the product (currently 1.0). Headers in Version 1.0 begin with --HDR1.0--.
>   <nlines> represents the number of lines expected in the text portion of the document.
>   <filetype> identifies the type of the file. It will be one of the following:
>   TX, text file (word processing); SS, spreadsheet; GR, graphics; DB, data base; or CO, communications.
>   <info> is type-dependent information.

Type-Dependent Information

For the different <filetypes> listed below, type-dependent information (<info>) contains the following items:

- **Spreadsheet** <info> holds a list of column widths that the user has changed from the default of 10 characters wide. These widths are listed as a series of space (20h) separated decimal numbers expressed as ASCII characters. The list represents values from column A rightwards until all remaining columns have the default widths. Ability uses a zero (30h) character to represent the default column width; it does not mean that the column has no width.
  A set of columns with the widths: A-12, B-10, C-15, would appear as: 12[S]0[S]15.
- **Write** has no type-dependent information for word-processing documents.
- **Graphics** has no type-dependent information for business graphics.
- **Data-base master form** is a form that can govern the entry and display of data. Type-dependent information consists of the string "PF". This indicates that the file is a data-base master form.

- **Data-base file** has type-dependent information that contains record size in bytes expressed as a decimal number; a space character (20h); the name of the master form for the data base; a space character; and the name of the parent data base (for sorted data bases).

Text Section

A newline character sequence separates the header section of a file from the text section. The text section is used somewhat differently in each file type.

The Text Section in Spreadsheets

Ability stores all labels (text strings within spreadsheet cells) and numeric constants that are not shared and do not have names in the text section.

Each newline-delimited line of text represents a row in the spreadsheet. Tab characters (09h) separate spreadsheet cells (fields). Each line also starts with a tab character.

Numeric constants appear as decimal numbers represented in ASCII characters with as much precision as required. Labels (text constants) appear as text strings. If a cell does not contain a label or constant, then nothing is written between the tab characters.

The following is an example of how Ability would store a spreadsheet row with the number 10 in Column A, a blank cell in Column B, the label "A Label" in Column C, and the number 3.14 in Column D.

[tab]10[tab][tab]'A[S]Label[tab]3.14[newline]

where

10 is the number placed in column A.

[tab][tab] shows that there is a blank cell in column B.

'A[S]Label indicates the label, "A Label", in column C.

3.14 is the number placed in column D.

[tab] signifies the tab character.

[S] signifies the space character.

[newline] signifies the newline sequence.

Justification Control for Labels

The four characters that may lead a label are:

1. **asterisk (*)**: This is a repeating label. The character or character string immediately following in the file will repeat to fill the width of the cell.
2. **single quote (')**: Text in the cell will be left justified within the cell limits.
3. **double quotes (")**: Text in the cell will be right justified within the cell limits.
4. **carat (^)**: Text in the cell will be centered within the cell limits.

The default is the single quote mark (').

The Text Section in Word Processing

The text section contains the body of Write documents. Each line of the text portion is a line of the document. A "soft carriage return"/linefeed (8Dh, 0Ah with the high bit set on the carriage return) combination ends each line within a paragraph. The newline sequence ends each blank line and each paragraph. Double- and triple-spaced paragraphs contain lines that consist only of the soft return/linefeed sequence. These indicate the position and number of blank lines between lines of the paragraph.

Ability embeds text formatting codes in the text stream similar to the way WordStar does. Table 2.1 gives a listing of the special characters that Ability embeds into text.

Linked Information in Documents

Text lines that contain fields (also called cells) use special control characters to indicate which character columns on the line the field uses.

There are two types of fields: fixed-width and variable-width. Fixed-width fields are fields for which the operator has specified a width or that are the result of bringing spreadsheet data into a word-processing document. A number of FIXCELL characters (05h) indicate a fixed-width field.

VARCELL characters (03h) indicate the variable-width field in much the same way that FIXCELL characters do. Ability will adjust the width of the variable-width fields enough to display the required information.

SEPCELL characters (01h) separate and define field positions. SEPCELL characters display as spaces, but the cursor will not rest on a SEPCELL character. The net effect of FIXCELL, VARCELL and SEPCELL is that they preserve the appearance of a table of numbers.

The Text Section in Graphs, Data-Base Forms and Communicate

The text section of these files appears essentially the same as that of a Write document. However, Ability uses the text section of these files differently. Typically, the user does not have access via the program to the text section of these files. The exception is data base, which has a CHANGE command to alter the appearance of the data-base form.

The top of a graphics file is actually a character representation of the graph and series display (less pixel graphics), built with the GREYBLOCK character. This section is followed by a data-base form containing series, color, graph type and labeling information.

Detailed information on the Graph text section, data-base forms, and Communicate was not available from Xanaro.

Data-Base File Information

Data-base files consist only of a header line and a text section. Each line in the file is one complete record. Ability pads fields with nulls (00h) if necessary to keep fields the same length. No characters separate data-base fields because the program obtains field width from the data-base master form.

Lines (records) terminate with a deletion-mark flag character followed by the newline sequence. If a record is marked for deletion, the flag character is "A" (41h, 65d), otherwise it is an "@" (40h, 64d).

The header line records the number of lines and the line length (not including the flag character, carriage return or linefeed characters at the end of the line).

Parameter Section

A CTRL-L (0Ch, 12d) separates the parameter section from the text section. The parameter section contains tab stops, margins, page length, cursor position, and other global file parameters. The format for each line in this section is

RaC <num> [tab] <name> = <description> [newline]

where

<num> represents the RaC parameter number (see Table 2.2). These are decimal integers that identify the parameter.

<name> is the RaC parameter name.

<description> is the value of the parameter. Some parameters are decimal numbers, some are strings written as labels with a prefix apostrophe.

Field Definitions

The field definitions section contains information on named fields or formula fields. The section also holds the links to other files.

Field Description

Only forms with names or formulas are listed in the file. The format for each field (spreadsheet cell) is

> R<row>C<col>[tab]<name>=<formula>[newline]

where

<dl>

<row> is a decimal number represented by ASCII characters giving the line of the cell or field. 0 is the first possible line.

<col> is a decimal number represented by ASCII characters giving the column of the cell or field. Note that 0 is the first possible column. Although spreadsheet columns are lettered on the screen in the Ability program, the program refers to columns by number in the file.
The first field may start at character column 17 in Write (word-processing) documents. The program locates the starting character by scanning the line for the control characters that specify where fields occur in the line.

<name> is present only if the field has been named.

<formula> is the text of the formula for the field. This text appears just as it appears in the editing box on the screen, with two minor exceptions.
Ability uses the character "!" to signify that a formula is the same as the formula for the field on the preceding line. "!" saves characters in the file.
The other exception is that the program changes references to named fields in other files from the "filename/fieldname" syntax to "filename.ext/fieldname" whenever the program can determine the extension of the file that the field "fieldname" comes from.

When Ability encounters the first formula, it scans the rest of the spreadsheet looking for derivative formulas. These are listed following the first. The program then continues to scan from left to right beginning where it paused to pick up the derivative formulas, looking for the next, different formula. (See Figure 2.1).

Links to Spreadsheets from Write Documents

Write documents may contain spreadsheet tables. Ability places the link in the field definition section.

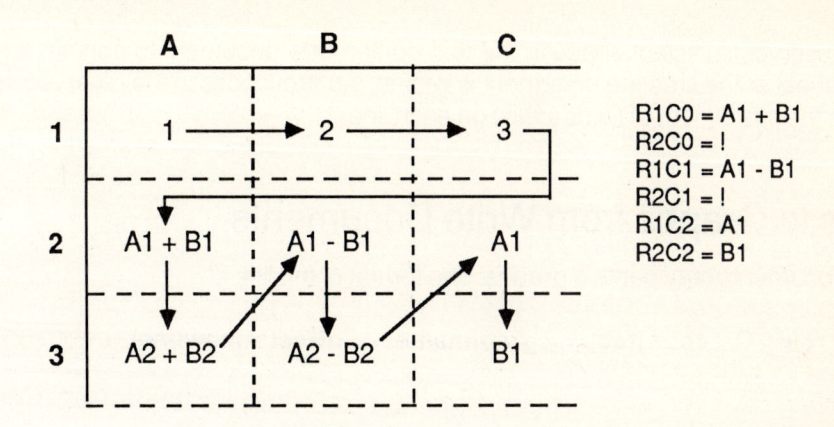

```
                A        B        C
                                              R1C0 = A1 + B1
        1    1 ──────▶ 2 ──────▶ 3            R2C0 = !
                                              R1C1 = A1 - B1
                                              R2C1 = !
        2    A1 + B1   A1 - B1    A1          R1C2 = A1
                                              R2C2 = B1
        3    A2 + B2   A2 - B2    B1
```

Figure 2.1 Ability uses this pattern to scan spreadsheet formulas for similarities before saving.

The format for the link is

R<row>C<col>[tab] = <ssname><range>[newline]

or

R<row>C<col>[tab] = <ssname><range>C[newline]

where

<row> is a decimal number represented by ASCII characters giving the line location of the upper left corner of the spreadsheet within the word-processing document. Zero (0) is the first possible line.

<col> is a decimal number represented by ASCII characters giving the character column of the upper left corner of the spreadsheet in the word-processing document. Note that 0 is the first possible column.

<ssname> is the name of the referenced spreadsheet. It takes the form **NAME.XSS ** where **NAME.XSS** is the PC-DOS name for the file.

<range> is the area of the spreadsheet included in the document. Range takes the form **R<rowUL>C<colUL>..R<rowLR>C<colLR>**. Row and col are decimal numbers in ASCII text. <rowUL> and <colUL> refer to the row and column of the upper left corner of the included spreadsheet; <rowLR> and <colLR> refer to the lower right corner.

C is a flag that indicates that the document includes the entire spreadsheet. Ability will adjust the space set aside in the text section at read-time if the size of the spreadsheet file has changed.

Ability reserves sufficient space in the text portion of a document to contain a given spreadsheet at the time the document is written. Control codes in the reserved space indicate the placement of fields (cells) on each line.

Links to Graphs from Write Documents

Write documents may contain graphs. The format of the link is

R<row>C<col>[tab] = <graphname> <offset> [newline]

where

<row> and <col> define the position in the write document of the referenced graph.

<graphname> is the name of the referenced graph. It takes the form **NAME.XGR ** where NAME.XGR is the PC-DOS name for the graph file.

<offset> is a decimal number indicating the offset of the graph in character columns from the left margin of the document.

Ability reserves sufficient space in the text portion of the document to contain the graph. The text lines in this reserved space may contain any text or fields that the operator has typed into the graph.

Field Display Formats

The field display formats section contains the display formats of all the fields in the file. A CTRL-L separates this section from the field definitions section.

As is true elsewhere of Ability, only changes from the default display format are written. Formats "carry." If R3C7 has a specified format, and R6C3 has another, all fields between those two fields have the same format as R3C7.

The format for each line in this section is

R<row>C<col>[tab] <format> [newline]

where

<row> and <col> are decimal numbers in ASCII indicating the formatted field.

<format> is a string containing the display format for the field.

The format parameter is a string. In the following definition, items in square brackets ([ ]) are optional, and or-bars (|) indicate a single choice from a set of options. <format> may be:

[#] [$] [(] [,] [%]
[L] [C]
[0 | 1 | 2 | 3 | 4 | 5 | 6 | 7 | 8 | 9 | 10 | 11 | 12 | ? | E | .]

The characters and their meanings are as follows:

Character	Meaning
#	Locked field
$	Display leading currency symbol
(	Display negative numbers in parentheses
,	Commas separate thousands
%	Display numbers as percentages
L	Left justify a number
C	Center a number
0-12	Number of digits after the decimal point
?	Reserved
E	Scientific notation
.	Variable precision (as many digits as necessary)

Table 2.1 Special Ability Formatting Characters

Hex	Dec	ASCII	Meaning
01	01	CRTL-A	SEPCELL
03	03	CTRL-C	VARCELL
05	05	CRTL-E	FIXCELL
1F	31	CTRL-_	GREYBLOCK—Default DB field value
02	02	CRTL-B	Boldface toggle
13	19	CTRL-S	Continuous underline toggle
15	21	CTRL-U	Word underline toggle
17	23	CTRL-W	Italics toggle
0E	14	CRTL-N	Indentation marker
8D	141		Phantom end of line (Soft CR)
14	20	CTRL-T	Reserved for superscript toggle
1A	26	CTRL-Z	End of file
16	22	CTRL-V	Reserved for superscript toggle

Table 2.2 RaC Parameter Values

RaC #	Text	Default	Meaning
0	typeid=		
1	stattext=		
2	border=	0, 1 or 2	0 - no borders, titles
			1 - SS row/col titles
			2 - page borders
3	pgwidth=	65 or 30000	Right Marg - Left Marg + 1
			30000 for spreadsheets
4	pgdepth=	54 or 9998	# lines per printed page
			9998 for spreadsheets
5	fixtop=	0	# fixed SS title lines
6	fixleft=	0	# fixed SS title columns
7	page=	0, −1	cursor page; −1 for spreadsheet
8	curline=	0	cursor line
9	curpos=	0	cursor column
10	windline=	0	virtual row of the first line in the window (after adjusting for page borders)
11	windcol=	0	virtual column of the first column in the window (after adjusting for page borders)
12	tabs=	every 8 cols	tab settings
13	pghead0=	none	left side header line 1
14	pghead1=	none	center of header line 1
15	pghead2=	none	right side header line 1
16	pghead3=	none	left side footer

(continued)

ABILITY 45

Table 2.2 Continued

RaC #	Text	Default	Meaning
17	pghead4 =	none	center footer
18	pghead5 =	none	right side footer
19	justflag =	0 (off)	Right justify toggle
20	spacing =		
21	limittop =	0	top row limit of cursor movement
22	limitbot =	9998	bottom row limit of cursor movement
23	limitleft =	0	left column limit of cursor movement
24	limitright =	pgwidth − 1	right column limit of cursor movement
25	pgoffset =	10	left margin
26	firsthead =	1 (on)	show headers on page 1:
			0 - no headers on page 1
			1 - headers all pages
			2 - headers on p1 only
27	firstfoot =	1 (on)	show footers on page 1: (same as firsthead)
28	pghead6 =	none	left side header line 2
29	pghead7 =	none	center header line 2
30	pghead8 =	none	right side header line 2
31	pghead9 =	none	left side header line 3
32	pghead10 =	none	center header line 3
33	pghead11 =	none	right side header line 3
34	dformat =	'.	display format for created fields
35	dtabs =	none	decimal tab settings

According to Xanaro, if a parameter is left out of a file, Ability will assume the default value. In this case the user may need to reformat or change a setting from within the program. The lack of any parameter is not fatal.

CHAPTER 3

dBASE II® and dBASE III®

dBase II - Version 2.43
dBase III - Version 1.1

Ashton-Tate
20101 Hamilton Avenue
Torrance, CA 90502

TYPE OF PRODUCT   Data base managers

FILES PRODUCED   ASCII text, some binary

POINTS OF INTEREST
Ashton-Tate's venerable dBase II probably has the largest installed base of any microcomputer data base manager. Its file structure is simple and direct. It is, however, not the data structure, but the dBase application programs that give these products their power. The application programs are ASCII text files that dBase interprets and uses to act on the stored data. Programming in dBase II or III is beyond the scope of this reference guide.

CONVERSION INFORMATION
dBase III can read comma-delimited files and files where the field length of the information in the input file is known.

	Field A	Field B	Field C
Record 1			
Record 2			
Record 3			

Figure 3.1 Envision data in dBase II or III as a row-and-column table.

The dBase File Structure

dBase II and dBase III are data-base management programs. They act on commands entered at the keyboard or from an input file (the dBase program).

Envision data in dBase II or III as displayed in an array of rows and columns, much like a spreadsheet. An example of how this might look is illustrated in Figure 3.1.

Data in any one field (or column) is of the same type (ASCII, numeric, logical, etc.). Each field name is unique and each record has a unique number. See Table 3.1 for information on the total numbers of these records and fields, and other program file size limitations.

dBase II Data

Data records begin where the file header ends. One byte precedes each record. The value of this byte is an ASCII space (20h) if the record is not deleted, and an asterisk (2Ah) if the record is deleted. There are no separators, delimiters or terminators used in the data records. All the fields are packed.

dBase II Header

dBase II files consist of a file header and a set of data records. The header provides information about the structure of the data records.

Byte 0   **Program ID**
Must contain 02h to denote a dBase II file.

Byte 1-2   **2-byte integer**
Number of records in data file (up to FFFFh—a maximum of 65,535 in dBase II).

Byte 3-5   **Last update**
Shows the date that the last update was performed on the file. The order of the three bytes are: MM, DD, and YY.

Byte 6-7   **2-byte integer indicating size of record**
A dBase II file may hold up to 1000 bytes in each record.

Byte 8-519   **Field descriptors**
This is a 32-field array, one field for each of the possible data fields (columns) in a dBase II file. The final array field containing data terminates with a carriage return (0Dh). If all 32 fields are not defined, NULLs (00h) pad out the array through byte 519.

Each of the 32 fields consists of 16 bytes. These bytes are organized in the following manner:

Byte 0-10   field name in ASCII
(11 bytes)

If all the bytes are not defined, it will be padded by NULLs (00h).

Byte 11   field type in ASCII
(1 byte)
Field types:

C (character)	ASCII characters
N (numeric)	. 0 1 2 3 4 5 6 7 8 9
L (logical)	Y y N n T t F f
	(or 20h if not initialized)

Byte 12   field length
(1 byte)
This byte can hold a value of 00h to maximum FFh.

Byte 13-14   field data address
(2 byte integer)
dBase II sets the contents of this field in memory.

Byte 15   field decimal count
(1 byte)

Byte 520   **End of header**
This single byte will be a carriage return (0Dh) if all 32 data fields are defined. If not, it will be a NULL (00h).

dBase II Index File Structure

The index structure used by dBase II permits both index and sequential searches. Each node of the tree structure is fixed at 512 bytes. The first node is called the anchor node. It contains information on the key expression, root node, next available node and maximum number of keys per node. Other nodes are made up of key values and pointers to lower nodes.

Index files are organized in the following manner:

Anchor Node

Byte 0-1 **RESERVED**

Byte 2-3 **16-bit number**
This is the node number of the root node.

Byte 4-5 **16-bit number**
This is the node number of the next available node.

Byte 6 **8-bit number**
This is the length of a key entry (Key__Length).
Key__Length is defined as the number of bytes in the record number (always 2) plus the number of bytes in the key expression.

Byte 7 **8-bit number**
This is the size of a key entry (Key__Entry).
Key__Entry is defined as the number of bytes in the pointer to the lower level (always 2), plus the number of bytes in the record number (always 2), plus the number of bytes in the key expression.

Byte 8 **8-bit number**
This is the maximum number of keys per node.

Byte 9 **Numeric key flag**
The contents are 00h if this is a character key, non-00h if it is a numeric key.

Byte 10-109 **Key expression**
This is a NULL-terminated ASCII string, 100 bytes maximum. These are padded to the end of the field by Nulls (00h).

Byte 110-511   **UNUSED**

All other nodes are organized in the following manner:

Byte 0   **8-bit number**
                    This is the number of keys in this node.

Byte 1-511   **Array of key entries**

A key entry is organized in the following manner:

Byte 0-1   **Pointer to lower level**

Byte 2-3   **Record number**

Byte 4-n   **Key expression value in ASCII**

dBase III Data

Data records begin where the file header ends. One byte precedes each record. The value of this byte is an ASCII space (20h) if the record is not deleted, or an asterisk (2Ah) if the record is deleted. No separators, delimiters or terminators are used in the data records. All fields are packed.

dBase III Header

dBase III files consist of a file header and a set of data records. The header provides information about the structure of the data records.

Byte 0   **Version number**
                    This byte holds:
                        03h, no .DBT (memo) file is present
                        83h, a .DBT file is present

Byte 1-3   **Last update**
                    These three bytes hold the date of the last update of the file. The order of these bytes are: YY, MM, DD.

Byte 4-7   **Number of records in data file**
             This is a 32-bit number.

Byte 8-9   **2-byte integer**
             These bytes indicate the length of the header structure.

Byte 10-11   **2-byte integer**
             These bytes indicate the length of a record.

Byte 12-31   **RESERVED**

Byte 32-n   **Field descriptors**
             This is an array of 32-byte descriptors, one for each field in the record. A dBase III record may have up to 128 fields. Each field descriptor is organized in the following manner:

   Byte 0-10   field name in ASCII characters
   If the byte is not filled, it will be padded by NULLs (00h).

   Byte 11   field type in ASCII
   Field types:

C (character)	ASCII characters
N (numeric)	- . 0 1 2 3 4 5 6 7 8 9
L (logical)	Y y N n T t F f (contains ? when not initialized)
M (memo)	10 digits representing a .DBT block number
D (date)	8 digits in YYYY MM DD format

   Byte 12-15   field data address
   This is a 32-bit number set by dBase III in memory.

   Byte 16   field length
   This byte can hold a value of 00h to maximum FFh.

   Byte 17   field decimal count

   Byte 18-21   RESERVED

Byte n+1   **Carriage return (0Dh)**
             This is used as a field terminator.

Table 3.1 — Program Limitations

File Limits (max.)	dBase II	dBase III
Number of records in file	65,535	1 billion
Record size (bytes)	1000	4000 (.DBF file)
Number of fields in record	32	128

Field Limits	dBaseII	dBaseIII
Character fields (bytes)	254	254
Logical fields (bytes)	1	1
Numeric fields (bytes)	254 (to v2.41) 63 (v.2.42)	19
Date fields (bytes)	n/a	8
Memo fields (bytes)	n/a	10 (in .DBF) (.DBT file size limit by Hardware, Operating System and word processor)

CHAPTER 4

DATA INTERCHANGE FORMAT™ (DIF)

**Lotus Development Corporation
161 First Street
Cambridge, MA 02142**

TYPE OF PRODUCT Interchange format; not a product.

FILES PRODUCED ASCII text

POINTS OF INTEREST

DIF is a proposed "standard" method of exchanging data between non-compatible programs. Numerous software companies support DIF input and output for their programs. By its nature, DIF cannot support program-specific information, such as cell formats.

For extensions and alterations to the DIF "standard" which *do* support formatting and spreadsheet formulas (at least for input to one specific program), see SuperCalc3® and the Super Data Interchange.

The DIF File Structure

DIF (Data Interchange Format) is a program-independent method of storing data. DIF files are ASCII text files. The format uses a brief line length to make the files as universally compatible as possible with application software, languages, operating systems and computer hardware.

A DIF file is oriented towards row-and-column data, such as a spreadsheet or database manager might produce. Because individual programs may "rotate" the rows and columns, DIF uses the terms *vector* and *tuple*. You may generally interpret vector as column and tuple as row.

DIF files contain two sections: a file header and a data section.

The DIF Header

There are four required entries in the DIF header, and a number of optional entries. The format of all header entries is

<topic>
<vector #>,<numerical value>
"<string value>"

where

<topic> is a "token," generally 32 characters or fewer.

<vector #> is 0 if specifying the entire file.

<numerical value> is 0 unless a value is specified.

<string value> is "" (double quotations with no space between) if it is not used.

The first required item in a DIF file is the title. For a typical spreadsheet, this would look like:

TABLE
0,<version #>
"<title>"

where

<version #> is 1.

<title> is the title of the table.

The next required item is the vector count. This specifies the number of vectors (columns). Its format is

VECTORS
0,<count>
" "

where

    <count> is the number of vectors. This entry may appear anywhere in the header, but must appear before any entries that specify vector numbers.

The third required item is the tuple count. This specifies the length of the vectors (the number of rows). Its format is

TUPLES
0,<count>
" "

where

    <count> is the number of tuples.

The final required header item is DATA, which specifies the division of the header information from the data proper. DATA must be the last header item. Its format is:

DATA
0,0
" "

Optional Header Items

Other header entries are optional. DIF Clearinghouse has included optional entries. Some are "standard" as a result of their being used in particular software products. The optional header entry items are: label, comment, field size, time series, significant values, and measure.

- *Labels a specific vector:*

    LABEL
    <vector # >,<line # >
    "<label>"

    where

        <vector # > is the labeled vector.

        <line # > allows for labeling more than one line.

        <label> is the label string.

- **Permits enhanced description of a vector:**

    COMMENT
    <vector # >, <line # >
    "<comment>"

    where

    <vector # > is the commented vector.
    <line # > may refer to more than one line.
    <comment> is the comment string.

- **Allocates fixed field sizes for each vector:**

    SIZE
    <vector # >, <# bytes>
    " "

    where

    <vector # > is the vector being sized.
    <# bytes> is the size.

- **Specifies the period in a time series:**

    PERIODICITY
    <vector # >, <period>
    " "

    where

    <vector # > is the specified vector.
    <period> is the time period.

- **Indicates first year of a time series:**

    MAJORSTART
    <vector # >, <start>
    " "

    where

    <vector # > is the specified vector.
    <start> is the start of the time series.

- **Indicates first period of a time series:**

    MINORSTART
    <vector #>,<start>
    " "

    where
    <vector #> is the specified vector.
    <start> is the start of the time series.

- **Indicates the portion of a vector that contains significant values:**

    TRUELENGTH
    <vector #>,<length>
    " "

    where
    <vector #> is the specified vector.
    <length> is the length of that vector that contains significant values.

- **Units of measure for a given vector:**

    UNITS
    <vector #>,0
    "<name>"

    where
    <vector #> is the specified vector.
    <name> is the name string of the units to be applied.

- **Units in which a given vector should be displayed:**

    DISPLAYUNITS
    <vector #>,0
    "<name>"

    where
    <vector #> is the specified vector.
    <name> is the name string of the units used to display the vector. (This may be different from the units used to measure the vector.)

DIF Data Section

The data section is organized in a series of tuples. Data within each tuple is organized in vector sequence. Essentially, using a spreadsheet as a data model, this means one data entry to a cell, in ascending column position, then by ascending row position.

There are two "special data values," BOT (Beginning of Tuple) and EOD (End of Data). BOT marks the start of each tuple. EOD terminates the DIF file.

Each data entry is organized in the following manner

<type indicator> , <numerical value>
<string value>

where

<type indicator> is one of three different indicators:

- **−1**   **special data value**
  <numeric value> is 0
  <string value> is BOT, EOD
- **0**   **numeric data (signed decimal number)**
  <numeric value> is numeric data
  <string value> is one of the Value Indicators (see below)
- **1**   **string data**
  <numeric value> is 0
  <string value> is string data

Value Indicator

There are five value indicators to use as the <string value> when the <type indicator> = 0:

V	value
NA	not available <numeric value> must be 0
ERROR	error condition <numeric value> must be 0
TRUE	<numeric value> is 1
FALSE	<numeric value> is 0

CHAPTER 5

MULTIMATE™ PROFESSIONAL WORD PROCESSOR
Version 3.30

MultiMate
Div. of Ashton-Tate, Inc.
52 Oakland Avenue North
East Hartford, CT 06108

TYPE OF PRODUCT   Word processor

FILES PRODUCED   Binary/ASCII text

POINTS OF INTEREST
Emulates the operation of Wang word processing. The program produces document text in ASCII characters with embedded formatting codes which may have the high bit set. MultiMate files begin with a header that contains historical document information such as the name of the author and computer operator, and the creation date of the document. Users may search their files based on this information.

CONVERSION INFORMATION
MultiMate supplies software that converts between the following formats:
- MultiMate document format
- ASCII (most formatting functions are lost)
- COMM, a 7-bit ASCII format useful for telecommunications. When converting from MultiMate to COMM and back to MultiMate, format and function characters from the original file are maintained.
- DCA, the format commonly used on IBM's Displaywriter system. A common filename extension is .RF.
- DIF, a format commonly used for spreadsheet data. MultiMate converts from DIF to MultiMate document format. The usual filename extension is .DIF.
- VCDIF, DIF format used by the VisiCalc™ spreadsheet.

DCA and VCDIF format conversions are available from MultiMate on written request.

The MultiMate File Format

MultiMate Professional Word Processing is a page-oriented word processor. Documents may hold up to 254 pages.

MultiMate files consist of a series of 512-byte records, referred to as relative record 0, relative record 1, relative record 2, and so on. Figure 5.1 illustrates the relative record structure and the organization of a MultiMate file.

The first two relative records are reserved to the document header. This consists of document description data, printer configuration parameters, the page start map and the record allocation map. The data section, beginning at relative record 2, is variable in length but contains a maximum of 254 records containing 512-bytes. Text data that does not reach the end of its 512-byte section is padded with NULLs.

MultiMate produces three types of documents: normal documents, merge documents and library documents. Normal and merge documents share identical header structures. Library documents differ and are described on page 69.

Document Header Section

Relative Record 0 (Byte 0-511)

This record is called the MultiMate Administrative Header and contains the document description data found on the document summary screen, document default screen, and the print parameter screen from inside MultiMate. Some values are optional and some are required. The following nine fields must contain data:

1. File name
2. Creation date
3. Modification date
4. Decimal tab character
5. Default word
6. Default lines per page
7. Print date format
8. Total number of pages
9. File status

Optional fields must be NULL-filled if there is no data for them (See Figure 5.2).

MultiMate File Structure

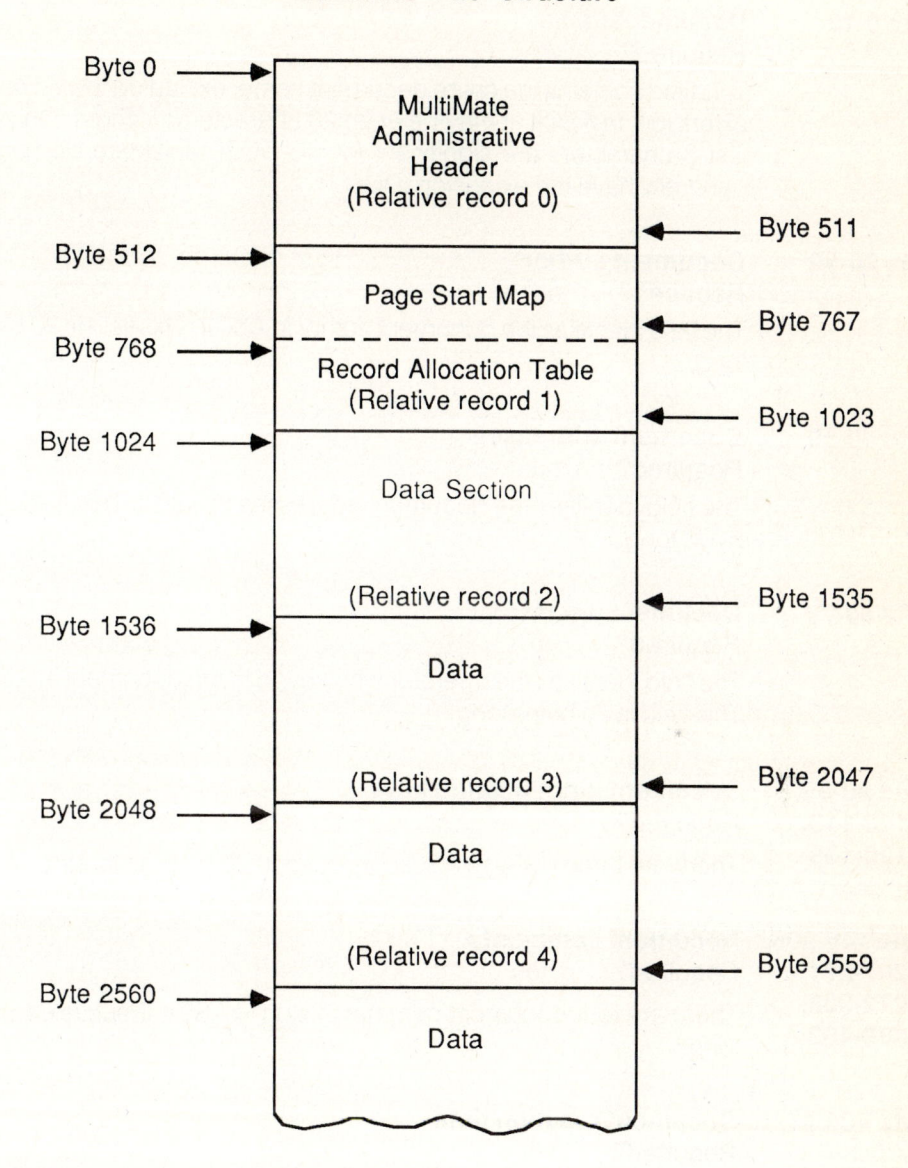

```
Byte 0    ──▶ ┌─────────────────────────┐
              │      MultiMate          │
              │    Administrative       │
              │        Header           │
              │   (Relative record 0)   │
              │                         │◀── Byte 511
Byte 512  ──▶ ├─────────────────────────┤
              │     Page Start Map      │
              │                         │◀── Byte 767
Byte 768  ──▶ ├ ─ ─ ─ ─ ─ ─ ─ ─ ─ ─ ─ ─┤
              │  Record Allocation Table│
              │   (Relative record 1)   │
              │                         │◀── Byte 1023
Byte 1024 ──▶ ├─────────────────────────┤
              │      Data Section       │
              │                         │
              │                         │
              │   (Relative record 2)   │◀── Byte 1535
Byte 1536 ──▶ ├─────────────────────────┤
              │          Data           │
              │                         │
              │   (Relative record 3)   │◀── Byte 2047
Byte 2048 ──▶ ├─────────────────────────┤
              │          Data           │
              │                         │
              │   (Relative record 4)   │◀── Byte 2559
Byte 2560 ──▶ ├─────────────────────────┤
              │          Data           │
              │                         │
              └──────────∿∿∿────────────┘
```

Figure 5.1 Organization of a MultiMate File

The following listing of items are all contained within bytes 0-511:

Byte 0-19   **Document name**
Required?   yes
This field contains the entire document name, excluding the file name extension, in ASCII. It may be up to 20 characters in length. Only the first 8 characters are significant for PC-DOS. MultiMate file names generally have the extension .DOC.

Byte 20-39   **Document author**
Required?   no
The field identifies the document author in ASCII. This field is 20 bytes long.

Byte 40-59   **Document addressee**
Required?   no
The field identifies the document addressee in ASCII. This field is 20 bytes long.

Byte 60-79   **Document operator**
Required?   no
The field identifies the operator who keyed in the document in ASCII. This field is 20 bytes long.

Byte 80-99, 100-119, 120-139   **Document identification keys**
Required?   no
There are three of these ASCII fields, each 20 bytes in length.

Byte 140-206, 207-271, 272-338, 339-403   **Document comments**
Required?   no
There are four document comment fields in ASCII. Each is 64 bytes long.

Byte 404-411   **Document creation date**
Required?   yes
This field is an 8-byte ASCII string formatted as mm/dd/yy (including slashes) where mm denotes the month, dd the day and yy the year.

Byte 412-419 **Document modification date**
Required?   yes

This is the same format as *creation date*. It stores the date that the document was last modified.

Byte 420-421 **RESERVED**
Required?   no

This field is unused and *must be NULL-filled*.

Byte 422-423 **Left margin**
Required?   no

This field contains the number of spaces from the left side of the page, where printing will begin. This is a 2-byte binary field; least significant byte (LSB) first.

Byte 424-425 **Start print page**
Required?   no

This field contains the page number within the document where printing will start. This is a 2-byte binary field; LSB first.

Byte 426-427 **Last print page**
Required?   no

This field contains the page number within the document where printing will stop. This is a 2-byte binary field; LSB first.

Byte 428-29 **Header/Footer first page number**
Required?   no

If auto page numbering is used in either the headers or the footers, numbering will begin with this value. This is a 2-byte binary field; LSB first.

Byte 430-431 **Printer number**
Required?   no

This field contains a number that represents the device number of the printer. Range: 1, 2 or 3. This is a 2-byte binary field; LSB first.

Byte 432-433 **Number of original copies**
Required?   no

This field contains the number of times the document will print. This is a 2-byte binary field; LSB first.

64 File Formats for Popular PC Software

MultiMate Administrative Header Document Description Record Layout

0 / 0	20 / 14H	40 / 28H	60 / 3CH	80 / 50H	100 / 64H
File Name	Author	Addressee	Operator	I.D. Key Field 1	I.D. Key Field 2

120 / 78H	140 / 8CH	206 / CEH	272 / 110H	338 / 152H	404 / 194H
I.D. Key Field 3	Comment Field 1	Comment Field 2	Comment Field 3	Comment Field 4	Creation Date

412 / 19CH	420 / 1A4H	422 / 1A6H	424 / 1A8H	426 / 1AAH	428 / 1ACH
Modification Date	Reserved Area	Left Margin	Start Print Page	Last Print Page	Hdr/Ftr 1st Page

430 / 1AEH	432 / 1B0H	434 / 1B2H	436 / 1B4H	438 / 1B6H	440 / 1B8H
Printer Number	# of Orig. Copies	Page Length	Print Flags	Document Type	Default Pitch

442 / 1BAH	450 / 1C2H	451 / 1C3H	453 / 1C5H	454 / 1C6H	455 / 1C7H
Pat Name	Lines Per Inch	Top Margin	Print Direction	Sheet Feeder Bin 1	Sheet Feeder Bin 2

456 / 1C8H	457 / 1C9H	465 / 1D1H	472 / 1D8H	476 / 1DCH	480 / 1E0H
Sheet Feeder Bin 3	SAT Name	Reserved Area	# Keys Typed, Last	# Keys Typed, Tot.	Dec Tab Character

481 / 1E1H	483 / 1E3H	484 / 1E4H	492 / 1ECH	493 / 1EDH	507 / 1FBH
Default Word	Default Lines/Page	CWT Name	Print Data Format	Reserved Area	Version Number

508 / 1FCH	510 / 1FEH	511 / 1FFH
Total # of Pages	File Status	File I.D.

Figure 5.2 MultiMate Administrative Header Document Description Record Layout

Byte 434-435   Page length
Required?   no

This field contains the total number of lines which will fit on the paper being printed on (not the number of lines you may wish to print on the paper). Range: 1 to 195. A usual value is 66. This is a 2-byte binary field; LSB first.

Print Flags (Stored LSB First)

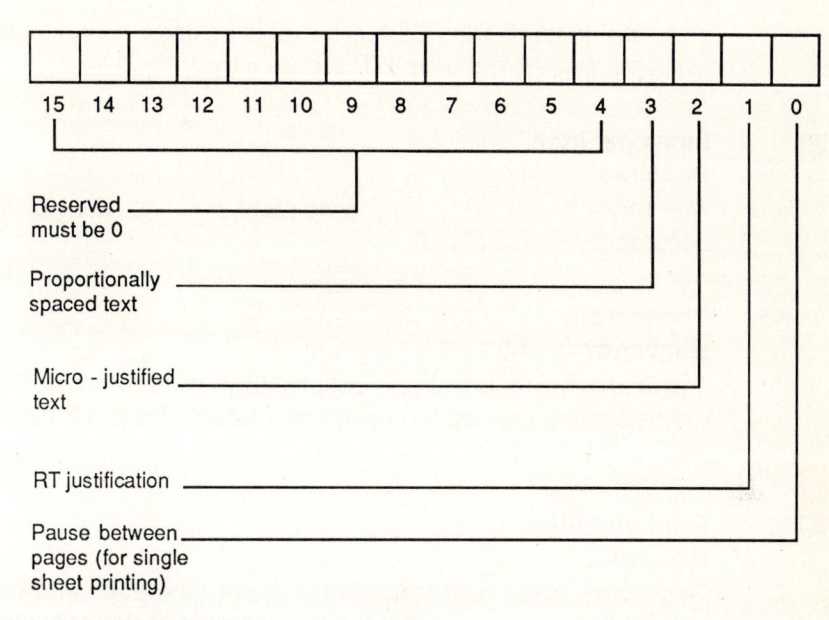

```
| 15 | 14 | 13 | 12 | 11 | 10 | 9 | 8 | 7 | 6 | 5 | 4 | 3 | 2 | 1 | 0 |
```

- Reserved must be 0 (bits 15–4)
- Proportionally spaced text (bit 3)
- Micro - justified text (bit 2)
- RT justification (bit 1)
- Pause between pages (for single sheet printing) (bit 0)

Figure 5.3 Print Flags Format. A 1 value signifies on.

Byte 436-437 **Print flags**
Required?   no
This field is a 2-byte binary field; LSB first. A 1 stored in each bit position signifies ON; a 0 signifies OFF (See Figure 5.3).

Byte 438-439 **Document type**
Required?   no
This field determines whether printout is draft or non-draft mode. This is a binary field; LSB first. If the first byte (byte 438) is 00, the document is being printed in draft mode. If the first byte (byte 438) is 01, the document is being printed in non-draft mode.

Byte 440-441 **Default pitch**
Required?   no
This field contains the character pitch at which the document will print. It must be a 2-byte binary value between 1 and 9 (LSB first). The values are mapped against the range of pitches available to the specified printer, with 1 being the largest and 9 being the smallest pitch.

Byte 442-449   **Printer action table**
Required?   no
This field contains the ASCII name of the printer action table used when printing the document. This is an 8-byte ASCII field.

Byte 450   **Lines per inch**
Required?   no
This 1-byte binary field contains the number of lines per inch that the document will print (6 or 8).

Byte 451-452   **Top margin**
Required?   no
This field contains the number of lines down from the top of the paper where printing will begin on each new page. This is a 2-byte binary field; LSB first.

Byte 453   **Print direction**
Required?   no
This 1-byte ASCII field tells the computer where to send the print stream. It may contain one of the following ASCII characters:

P	(50h)	Print to parallel port
S	(53h)	Print to serial port
A	(41h)	Print to DOS auxiliary device
L	(4Ch)	Print to DOS LIST device
F	(46h)	Print to disk file

Byte 454, 455, 456   **Sheetfeed bins 1, 2, 3**
Required?   no
This field contains the bin number from which the first, second and third sheets will be taken when printing. These are each 1-byte binary fields.

Byte 457-464   **Sheet feed action table**
Required?   no
This 8-byte ASCII field contains the name of the sheet feed action table (similar to printer action table).

Byte 465-471   **RESERVED**
Required?   no
This field is unused and must be NULL-filled.

Byte 472-475　Keystrokes typed last session
Required?　no

This 4-byte binary field contains the 'keystrokes last session' number that appears on the document summary screen.

Byte 476-479　Total keystrokes typed
Required?　no

This 4-byte binary field contains the count of total keystrokes typed since the document was created. This information also appears on the document summary screen.

Byte 480　Decimal tab character
Required?　no

This 1-byte ASCII field contains either a period (2Eh) or comma (2Ch).

Byte 481-482　Default word
Required?　no

These two binary bytes (LSB first) are used to hold various default conditions as bit flags (see Figure 5.4).

Default Word Bits

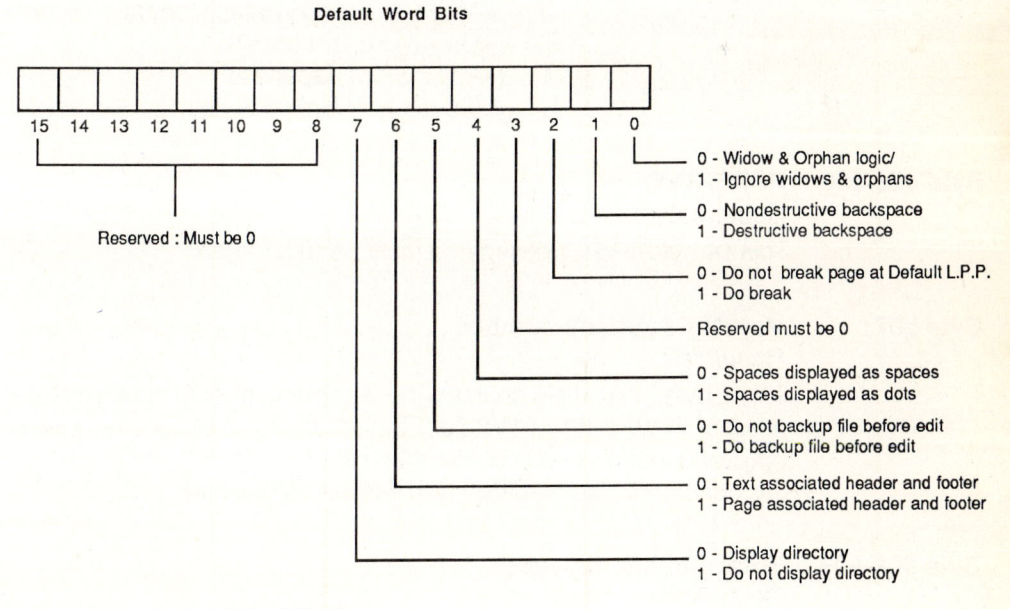

| 15 | 14 | 13 | 12 | 11 | 10 | 9 | 8 | 7 | 6 | 5 | 4 | 3 | 2 | 1 | 0 |

Bits 15-8: Reserved : Must be 0

- Bit 0: 0 - Widow & Orphan logic / 1 - Ignore widows & orphans
- Bit 1: 0 - Nondestructive backspace / 1 - Destructive backspace
- Bit 2: 0 - Do not break page at Default L.P.P. / 1 - Do break
- Bit 3: Reserved must be 0
- Bit 4: 0 - Spaces displayed as spaces / 1 - Spaces displayed as dots
- Bit 5: 0 - Do not backup file before edit / 1 - Do backup file before edit
- Bit 6: 0 - Text associated header and footer / 1 - Page associated header and footer
- Bit 7: 0 - Display directory / 1 - Do not display directory

Figure 5.4　Default Word Bit Flags

Byte 483　　　**Default lines per page**
　　　　　　　　Required?　no
　　　　　　　　This 1-byte binary field contains the default number of lines which will print out per document page. (Do not confuse this with the total number of lines per page). The default lines per page determine the point at which an auto page break will occur during the edit mode (1 to 195).

Byte 484-491　**CWT name**
　　　　　　　　Required?　no
　　　　　　　　This 8-byte ASCII field contains the name of the character width table to be used with this document. The CWT defines the character widths for each character that the printer can print (primarily for dot matrix printers). It is used with printers that support more than one character size as an alternate to the CWT table contained in the PAT for the specific printer.

Byte 492　　　**Print date format**
　　　　　　　　Required?　no
　　　　　　　　This 1-byte ASCII field contains the character indicating which format is used to print the date. The field must contain one of the following values:

D	(44h)	DOS default format
E	(45h)	European
J	(4Ah)	Japanese
U	(55h)	United States

Byte 493-506　**RESERVED**
　　　　　　　　Required?　no
　　　　　　　　This 14-byte field is unused and must be NULL-filled.

Byte 507　　　**MultiMate version number**
　　　　　　　　Required?　no
　　　　　　　　This 1-byte binary field contains the version number of the MultiMate release. A zero (0) in this field indicates that the document was prepared with a version earlier than version 3.20; a 1 indicates that this document was prepared with version 3.20 or later.

Byte 508-509　**Total number of pages**
　　　　　　　　Required?　yes
　　　　　　　　This 2-byte binary field (LSB first) contains the total number of pages in this document.

Byte 510 **File status**
Required?   yes
This 2-byte binary field should always contain a 1. It will be used in the future to validate a MultiMate document.

Byte 511 **File I.D.**
Required?   no
This field is currently not used, and must be NULL-filled. It will eventually hold a 0 to denote a MultiMate document or a 1 to denote a library document.

A Note About Library Documents

The header for a MultiMate library document differs substantially from that of a normal document. The bytes from byte 20 to byte 420 consist of 101 4-byte fields. Each field contains three ASCII characters followed by a NULL. A field holding the ASCII literal 000<nul> denotes an entry that exists; and ASCII literal of 001<nul> denotes an entry that does not exist. Further information was unavailable from MultiMate.

Relative Record 1

Relative record 1 (byte 512-1024) holds the document file description data. These are essentially pointers to the beginnings of each of the 254 permissible MultiMate pages and where that information is found in the following sequence of 512-byte relative records.

Relative record 1 is divided into equal 256-byte parts: the *page start map* and the *record allocation table*.

Byte 512-767 **Page start map**
Each byte of the PSM represents a page in a MultiMate document. The final two bytes of the PSM are unused and must be null (a MultiMate document may only hold 254 pages, not 256). The value stored in each byte is the number of the 512-byte relative record (counting from record 0 in the header) that holds the start of the text intended for the page that the byte represents. Each stored value also serves as an index into the record allocation table.

Relationship Between PSM, RAC, and Relative Records

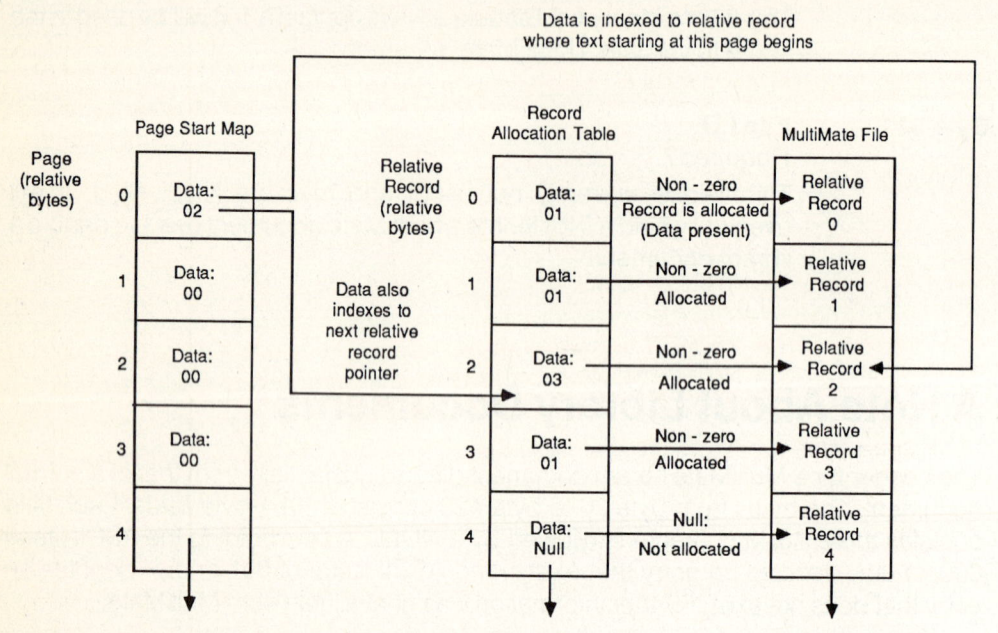

Figure 5.5 Relationship between PSM, RAC, and Relative Records (based on sample file).

Byte 768-1023 Record allocation table

This field is where each byte of the page start map represented a page of output. Each byte of the record allocation table represents a 512-byte relative record. The record allocation table determines which 512-byte relative records have been used to store information. Any unallocated record must contain a NULL. The first two entries in the record allocation table must be binary 1's. This reflects the fact that relative record numbers 0 and 1 are allocated and used in the header (see Figure 5.5).

Data Section

The MultiMate data section consists of a series of 512-byte records addressed relative to record 0. Relative record 0 is the document description data; relative record 1 is the page start map and record allocation table; relative record 2 begins the text data. Each data record consists of a 2-byte link section and a 510-byte stream of attributes, text formatting codes and ASCII printable characters.

Link Section

The first two bytes of each record are pointers to the next relative record and to the previous relative record containing *text*. The first link byte (in the sample file, byte 1024) is the forward pointer to the next record. The following byte (byte 1025 in the sample) contains the record number of the previous relative data record.

Byte offset 0 from start of record
This field contains the relative record number of the next record in this page. If there is no next record, this field contains the binary value 1.

Byte offset 1 from start of record
This field contains the relative record number of the previous record in this page. If there is no previous record, this field contains the binary value 0.

Text Section

The remaining 510 bytes of each 512-byte relative record contain a stream of attributes, text-formatting characters and ASCII printable characters.

After the link bytes (offset bytes 2 and 3 in the sample), each new page (but not new record) begins with MultiMate's 1-byte internal format-change character (FFh), followed by one attribute byte. The first two bytes of the text section, in the first record of any page, must be an attribute change (even if this change confirms the preceding attribute). The attribute byte value may be one of the following:

03h	Normal character
01h	Underscore character
83h	Normal placemark
81h	Underline placemark

The attribute may be changed anywhere in a file. In all cases, the change consists of the format-change character followed by one of the attribute byte values.

Other text changes—bold print, header text, etc.—are signaled by a single formatting value. Formatting values do not always have their high bit set (see Text Formatting Codes on page 74).

Format Line

Every page of a MultiMate document must begin with a format line. The program displays this line at the top of the screen during editing. The maximum line length is 156 characters.

The format line follows the link bytes and format change bytes. It's signaled by the one-byte format character (B3h), followed by a one-byte ASCII character giving the line spacing of the document. The line itself is made up of ASCII period characters (2Eh) to the length of the line. The line is closed with a MultiMate return character (AEh). There may be tab characters (AFh) within the line. Each one occupies a space and acts as the tab setting.

Text Stream

Sequential document text begins following the format line and its terminating return (AEh). If the text does not reach a 512-byte relative record border, the remaining bytes are padded with NULLs.

Text Formatting Codes

MultiMate text formatting codes are 1-byte binary codes embedded in the sequential text stream. Many work as toggles: B2h turns on bold print, but also turns it off when text is to revert to normal.

Note that some characters are changed from their traditional ASCII values. For example, while carriage return continues as 0Dh, the return character that Multimate stores in the file is actually AEh. Any document previously made with Version 2 Multimate or before will automatically be updated to the Version 3 formatting codes when loaded into 3.2 Multimate.

The following is a list of the MultiMate program limitations:

Max. number of text pages
254 (limited by page maps) pages

Max. document size
131,072 characters (256 x 512) including administrative header

Max. characters in document
130,048 (254 x 512) characters

Merge document
Maximum number of variable entries is 254 or one set per page. For libraries, the maximum number of entries is 101 as limited by the area in the administrative header.

Format line
Every MultiMate page begins with a format line. Maximum line length is 156 characters. Text formatting characters are included in this number.

Max. lines per page
195 lines including format lines

Max. characters per page
6144 characters

Max. document records per page
12 records

Table 5.1 Formatting Codes

Hex Value	Decimal	Description
00	000	End of Data
08	008	Backspace key code
09	009	Tab character
0D	013	Carriage return
13	019	Expanded text char (pre-3.20)
18	024	Superscript char
19	025	Subscript char
1A	026	Indent char
1B	027	Escape key code
1D	029	Center char
7F	127	Stop print char
9E	158	Pitch char
9F	159	Footer char
AE	174	Return char
AF	175	Tab char
B2	178	Bold print char
B3	179	Format character
BA	186	Format character
C1	193	Req'd page break char
C3	195	Merge character
C5	197	Strikeout char
C7	199	Shadow print char
D7	215	Header char
E0	224	Compressed print ch (pre-3.20)
E6	230	Print control code
EB	235	Draft print character
ED	237	Hard space character
EF	239	Enhanced print char
F7	247	Soft hyphen char
FE	254	Decimal tab char
FF	255	Internal attribute change char

CHAPTER 6

MICROSOFT MULTIPLAN™ and the SYLK FILE FORMAT
Version 1.2

Microsoft Corporation
10700 Northup Way
Bellevue, WA 98009

TYPE OF PRODUCT MultiPlan is Microsofts' spreadsheet product. SYLK is an *external* file specification written and read by MultiPlan and other Microsoft products.

FILES PRODUCED ASCII text

POINTS OF INTEREST

SYLK (Symbolic Link) format is designed to permit complete representation of a worksheet or other program session in a format external to the host program.

With SYLK, you may develop entire working spreadsheet templates, including cell formats, formulas, window splits and all the other elements resulting from a session with MultiPlan. The details are preserved in a file format that is not the native format of the program, but which the program can read and write and convert into its working internal format.

Like DIF or SDI, SYLK is an interchange format, but extends to areas of data representation that the other interchange formats do not.

Microsoft is the final arbiter of the SYLK file format, and may choose to extend it. They have made a number of extensions to SYLK specific to the Microsoft Chart™ product which are not covered here.

CONVERSION INFORMATION

MultiPlan may read and write its own binary format, read and write SYLK format, and read (only) VisiCalc™ format.

The SYLK File Format

SYLK format is an ASCII text file designed to completely represent a template in a format external to the native file format of any given product.

It has a strong orientation towards MultiPlan in that the formatting commands, formula representations and row-and-column references used are MultiPlan-derived. It is, however, a program-independent interchange format, much like DIF or SDI.

Because Microsoft may extend SYLK further, programs using the format should be written to ignore records and fields they aren't prepared to handle.

SYLK Overview

SYLK files are divided into records by carriage return/linefeed characters. Empty records are ignored. Non-empty records take the format

<RTD> <FTD> <Fields>

where

<RTD> is a record type descriptor

<FTD> is an optional field type descriptor

<Fields> is an optional and variable number of data items

The interpretation of the FTD depends on which RTD is used; the interpretation of the Fields often depends on which FTD is used. FTDs within a particular RTD may or may not be mutually exclusive, depending on use.

An RTD may be up to two letters long. By convention, all RTDs are capitalized. The FTD takes the form of a semicolon followed by a single letter: **;<letter>**. The FTDs ;U, ;V, ;W, ;X, ;Y and ;Z are the same for all records. Others vary. Fields may not contain carriage return or linefeed characters. Any field containing the reserved semicolon character must have two of them, as is the practice in some programming languages.

In entries labeled as (diff), the last prior field values will be substituted if the field value of the current entry is empty. For example, if formatting commands are given for different cells in a given row, only the column number needs to be supplied. The row number will be assumed to be the last prior given field value.

The FTDs ;X and ;Y determine the column and row coordinates, respectively. The spreadsheet origin is 1,1.

SYLK Record Type Descriptors (RTD)

In the descriptions that follow, items enclosed in angle brackets (< >) signify fields; the character [S] signifies an ASCII space character (20h).

MICROSOFT MULTIPLAN and the SYLK FILE FORMAT

RTD ID
First record in SYLK file
FTD   ;P<name>
<name> is the name of the program that produced the file.

RTD F
Formatting of entire template or cell
There are seven possible FTDs to consider:

(1) ;X ;Y
(diff) cell coordinates

(2) ;F<c1>[S]<n>[S]<c2>
(diff) cell formatting properties

<c1> is one of the following 1-character formatting codes:
- D default
- C continuous cross-cell display
- E scientific exponentiation
- F fixed decimal point
- G general format
- $ leading $ and 2 decimal points
- * bar graph, one asterisk per unit (5 would be *****)

<n> is the number of digits.
<c2> is one of the following 1-character alignment codes:
- D default
- C center
- G general (text left, numbers right)
- L left justify
- R right justify

(3) ;R ;C
;F properties applied to an entire row or column

(4) ;D<c1>[S]<n>[S]<c2>[S]<n3>
default format defined as in ;F. ;D codes cannot be used.
<n3> is the default column width

(5) ;K
if present, commas are set

(6) ;E
if present, the formula format option is set

(7) ;W <n1> [S] <n2> [S] <n3>
defines the widths of a group of columns:
        <n1> is the first column
        <n2> is the last column
        <n3> is the width of columns in number of characters

RTD B   **Defines the boundaries of the rows and columns. Appears near the beginning of a SYLK file.**
        FTD   ;Y ;X
                        row and column numbers

RTD C   **Supplies the numerical or text value of a cell, the formula it contains, whether it is protected, and other properties.**
There are eight possible FTDs to consider:

    FTD

(1) ;X ;Y
(diff) cell coordinates

(2) ;K
Value of the cell, either numerical or textual, follows. Text values must be in double quotes. Logical values "TRUE" and "FALSE" must also be quoted. An ERROR value is preceded by #.

(3) ;P
if present, cell is locked (protected)

(4) ;E <expr>
MultiPlan formula (expression) follows

(5) ;R ;C
(diff) see ;S, below

(6) ;S
expression for this cell is given by another coordinate, where X = C and Y = R. The field contents are decimal coordinates. ;E cannot appear in the same set of FTDs with ;S. The cell at ;R ;C must be marked with either a ;D or a ;G.

(7) ;D
;E expression is shared with another cell

(8) ;G
;K value is shared with another cell. ;E does not appear.

RTD NN	**Defines a MultiPlan name as a union of rectangular spreadsheet areas, expressed as absolute references.**

There are two possible FTDs to consider:

    FTD   **(1) ;N < name >**
                  name of the area

                  (2) ;E < expr >
                  expression describing the area

RTD NE	**Defines a link to another (inactive) spreadsheet**

There are three possible FTDs to consider:

    FTD   **(1) ;F < name >**
                  filename of the source sheet

                  (2) ;S
                  description of the source area (name of the cell group)

                  (3) ;E
                  expression describing the area

RTD NV	**External filename substitution**

There are two possible FTDs to consider:

    FTD   **(1) ;L**
                  filename

                  (2) ;F
                  filename to be used instead

RTD W	**MultiPlan window structure**

Before trying to set up a window structure from scratch, Microsoft recommends dumping an available window structure to see how it is organized.

    FTD   **(1) ;N**
                  window number

                  (2) ;A y x
                  coordinates of current cell as shown in upper left corner of window cited in ;N

                  (3) ;B
                  bordered flag

(4) ;ST cy cx
split window with title. cx is cursor position in new window. cy is number of screen lines in new window.

(5) ;SH 1cy
split window horizontal. cx is cursor position in new window. cy is number of screen lines in new window. 1 = L if windows are linked or scrolling.

(6) ;SV 1cx
split window vertical. cx is cursor position in new window. cy is number of screen lines in new window. 1 = L if windows are linked or scrolling.

RTD E   **End of SYLK file.**

Organization of a SYLK File

1. ID must be the first record.
2. The B RTD should be used for MultiPlan input, although it is not required.
3. For MultiPlan C records: ;D or ;G must appear before another C record that refers to it (with ;S, ;R, ;C)
4. Name definition should precede name use for efficiency, although not required.
5. Window splits and window properties must be in strict logical order.
6. NU records must precede NE records.
7. E must be the last record.

CHAPTER 7

IBM PLANS+™
Personal Decision Series
IBM Plans+ Version 1.0 and Version 1.0 Updates 1 and 2

IBM Corporation
Information Services
472 Wheelers Farms Road
Milford, CT 06460

TYPE OF PRODUCT   Spreadsheet with graphics

FILES PRODUCED   Binary/ASCII text

POINTS OF INTEREST
IBM's *Personal Decision* series of software is unique in that it requires a central data manager called the *PDS Data Edition*. Users must install the Data Edition to run spreadsheet, graphics, word processing and other PDS applications.

This approach to software integration means that users may trade data between and extract subsets of data from PDS software and a variety of other packages. This is true only if those other packages put out and accept DIF or ASCII files, and if you know the layout of those files. This benefit is not without its organizational overhead; designing such a system requires forethought.

Plans+ more closely resembles its mainframe-based planning cousins than it does the "traditional" PC spreadsheet. There are three "windows" on the screen: the spreadsheet matrix, a rules window, and a command window (for immediate mode calculation and data entry, rules may be input here, but are not saved). The program produces separate files for spreadsheet data and calculation rules (each is saved differently). Users can mix and match rule sets and data sets.

CONVERSION INFORMATION
Users can import and export data to and from ASCII text files and DIF files via PDS Data Edition.

> **AUTHOR'S NOTE**
> IBM was most cooperative with this file format project—up to a point. IBM did supply the file layout information, but drew the line at answering certain questions about legal values for the offset locations, or the bit arrangement in some flag words. Consequently, some range and organizational information in the file layout may be missing. The data was supplied by the author where it could be deduced.
>
> The file byte offset figures received from IBM appeared to be 256 (100h) off when we examined files actually produced by Plans+. The locations below reflect the offset locations achieved through experiment. You may obtain the locations as supplied by IBM by adding 100h to the hex offset figures listed below.
>
> Updates 1 and 2 add two new integer fields (CALC__SIZE and NO__CALCS) and change the size of COL__WIDTH from an array of 99 integers to an array of 255 to accommodate an increase in the number of spreadsheet columns.

IBM PLANS+ (Version 1) File Structure

Plans+ is a spreadsheet/financial planning tool with business graphics capability. Plans+ creates two files for every spreadsheet, a model definition file with the extension .~MD, and a data file with the extension .~MF. The program stores both files in the directory (or on the floppy disk) named LIB1. You must have both files for running a Model.

.~MD (Model Definition) File Layout

We can map the first 2532 bytes of the model definition file; the offset location of the final bytes of the file depends on variably sized graphics definitions.

The following is the order in which the fields appear in a .~MD file:

Byte 0-1   REC__TYPE
                      Offset   00h
                      Data Type 2-byte string
                      Description Record type is stored here.

                      This field contains the ASCII literal "10" (31h 30h).

Byte 2-11   **SPD_ID**
             Offset   02h
             Data Type   10-byte string
             Description   This field contains the ASCII literal
                            "<<SPDDEF>>".

Byte 12-13 **FREE__CHAIN**
             Offset   0Ch
             Data Type   integer
             Description   "Free Chain record number" is stored here.

             In the experimental sample file, the program set this field to two NULLs (00h).

Byte 14-55 **SPD__DESC**
             Offset   0Eh
             Data Type   40-byte string
             Description   This field contains the spreadsheet description.

             This field is a NULL-terminated ASCII string. The first byte (#14) is a size-indicator of the length of the non-NULL string. The program uses space characters (20h) to pad to the end of the field (indicated by a NULL-byte) if it's unfilled by ASCII text.

Byte 56-97 **LAST__DATA**
             Offset   38h
             Data Type   40-byte string
             Description   DOS file identification is contained in these bytes.

             This field is a NULL-terminated ASCII string. The first byte is a size-indicator to the length of the significant characters in the entered string.

             Author's Note: The last data field does hold the DOS file identification but if the full 40 bytes are not used, spurious data may fill the remainder of the field.

Byte 98-255
RESERVED FIELD
    Offset   62h
    Description   In Version 1, this field is officially reserved and unused. Most of this field is NULL-filled. Entries in quotation marks below are literal. In our sample file, data occurred at the following locations:

Byte	Data
100-103	"ATA3"
128	08h, length of succeeding text
129-136	"PDSS.EXE"
150	20h, space character
162	05h, length of succeeding text
163-167	"DATA1"
192	08h, length of succeeding text
193-200	"PDSX.EXE"
214	20h, space character
226	05h, length of succeeding text
227-231	"DATA1"

The remainder of the bytes in this field were NULL-filled.

Author's Note: In the updated version of Plans+, the following two fields appear at bytes 98 and 100. These fields appear in an otherwise reserved area, and do not affect offset locations of the following fields (See Figure 7.1):

Byte 98-99   CALC_SIZE
    Offset   62h
    Data Type   integer
    Description   This stores the calculations length.

Byte 100-101   NO_CALCS
    Offset   64h
    Data Type   integer
    Description   This contains the total number of calculations defined.

Byte 256-257   CELL_GLOBAL
    Offset   100h
    Data Type   word
    Description   Default flags stored here with each cell when a row is created.

Author's Note: IBM has declined to make the bit map of this word available. In our sample file (where no global format changes had been made), the values of these bytes were 18h and 28h, respectively. Assuming LSB first, these values produce the following bit map of the word:

```
15         byte 257                 byte 256         0
[0] [0] [1] [0] [1] [0] [0] [0]/[0] [0] [0] [1] [1] [0] [0] [0]
```

Byte 258-259   **FORMAT__GLOBAL**
Offset   102h
Data Type   word
Description   This contains the global formatting default.

Byte 259 is NULL. The range of legal values for byte 258 was unavailable. In the sample file (where no global format changes had been made) this location contained 14h.

Byte 260-261   **RESERVED FIELD**
Offset   104h
Description   This field is officially reserved and unused.

The sample file contained a value of 06h in byte 260. This field does not exist in the updated version (see Figure 7.1).

Byte 262-459   **COL__WIDTH**
Offset   106h
Data Type   integer array
Description   These bytes contain a 99-member array of 2-byte (LSB first) integers.

Each member of the array represents the width of one of the Plans+'s 99 spreadsheet columns. In the updated version of Plans+, this field begins at byte 260 (offset 104h), and consists of a 255-member array of 2-byte integers. Expanding this field in the updated version affects the offset locations of all following fields, but not their order, size or contents.

You may obtain the offset figure for the following fields by adding 312 to their decimal offset or 138h to their hexadecimal offset (See Figure 7.1).

86 File Formats for Popular PC Software

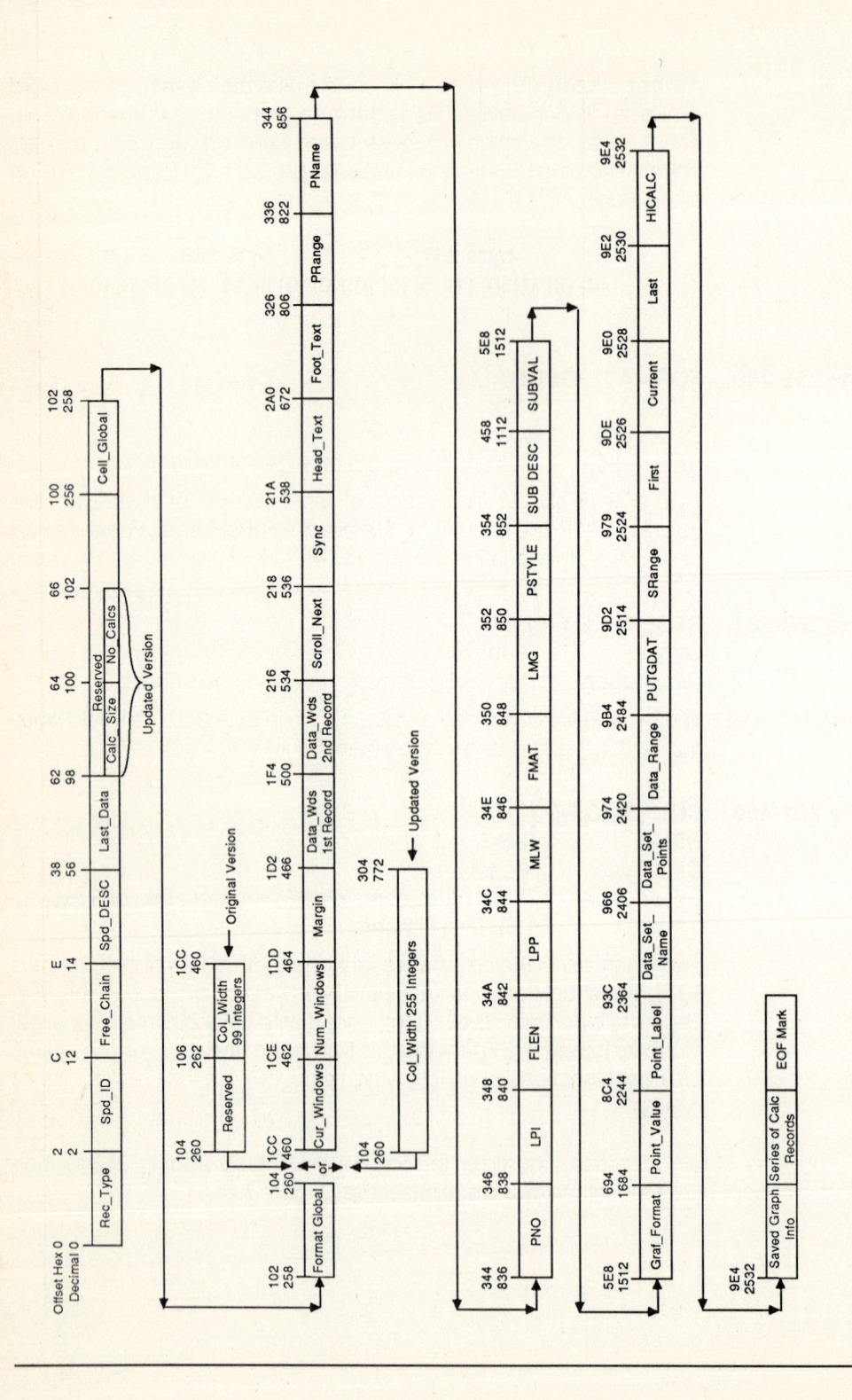

Figure 7.1 IBM Plans + File Layout

Byte 460-461 **CUR_WINDOW**
  Offset   1CCh
  Data Type   integer
  Description   The integer (LSB first) containing the number of the current data window is stored here.

  Plans+ can have two data windows.

Byte 462-463 **NUM_WINDOWS**
  Offset   1CEh
  Data Type   integer
  Description   Stores the integer (LSB first) containing the number of windows in the data area (the spreadsheet display).

  Plans+ can have two data windows.

Byte 464-465 **MARGIN**
  Offset   1D0h
  Data Type   integer
  Description   Stores the integer (LSB first) containing the right column margin for using the enter key advance.

Byte 466-499 **DATA_WDS**
  Offset   1D2h

and

Byte 500-533 **DATA_WDS**
  Offset   1F4h
  Description   These are two 33-byte records made up of 2-byte integer fields. Each record contains scrolling information for one of the two spreadsheet windows. Plans+ organizes the records as follows:

  DATA-WDS (466-499)
466	TITLE	0 is none, 1 is vert, 2 is horizontal, and 3 is both
468	WIDTH	# of characters across in window
470	T_FIRST_INST	first TITLE row
472	T_OCCURR	# of TITLE instances
474	T_FIRST_COL	# of first TITLE column displayed

476	T_LAST_COL	# of last TITLE column displayed
478	S_FIRST_INST	instance of first scrollable row
480	S_OCCURR	# of scrollable instances
482	S_FIRST_COL	# of first scrollable column display
484	S_LAST_COL	# of last scrollable column display
486	CUR_ROW	current row
488	CUR_COL	current column for current cell
490	CUR_INST	cursor pointer instance
492	CUR_POS	cursor pointer character position
494	CUR_WIDTH	current cell cursor width
496	LEFT_BORDER	left character edge of DATA window
498	TOP_BORDER	top line edge of DATA window

DATA_WDS (500-533)

500	TITLE	0 is none, 1 is vert, 2 is horizontal, and 3 is both
502	WIDTH	# of characters across in window
504	T_FIRST_INST	first TITLE row
506	T_OCCURR	# of TITLE instances
508	T_FIRST_COL	# of first TITLE column displayed
510	T_LAST_COL	# of last TITLE column displayed
512	S_FIRST_INST	instance of first scrollable row
514	S_OCCURR	# of scrollable instances
516	S_FIRST_COL	# of first scrollable column display
518	S_LAST_COL	# of last scrollable column display
520	CUR_ROW	current row
522	CUR_COL	current column for current cell
524	CUR_INST	cursor pointer instance
526	CUR_POS	cursor pointer character position
528	CUR_WIDTH	current cell cursor width
530	LEFT_BORDER	left character edge of DATA window
532	TOP_BORDER	top line edge of DATA window

Byte 534-535   **SCROLL__NEXT**
                   Offset   216h
                   Data Type   word
                   Description   These bytes contain the data window scroll direction flag. Plans+ saves (and displays) the most recent direction that it has moved the pointer cursor in the data window. If the user enters a carriage return, that directional move is repeated. We believe that byte 534 may hold one of four values, depending on which way the cursor direction indicator was facing when the file was saved:
                                       00h   up
                                       40h   right
                                       80h   down
                                       C0h   left

Byte 536-537   **SYNC**
                   Offset   218h
                   Data Type   word
                   Description   These bytes determine whether the split data windows scroll in a synchronized manner.

Printer Setting Information

Byte 538-671   **HEAD__TEXT**
                   Offset   21Ah
                   Data Type   string
                   Description   These bytes contain text for printed heading.

                   Byte 538 may be a size-indicator byte as in SPD__DESC.

Byte 672-805   **FOOT__TEXT**
                   Offset   2A0h
                   Data Type   string
                   Description   These bytes contain text for printed footer.

                   Byte 672 may be a size-indicator byte as in SPD__DESC.

Byte 806-821   **PRANGE**
      Offset   326h
      Data Type   array
      Description   These bytes store the range of cells to print.

Organized as an array of two, each member of the array contains four 2-byte integers.

Byte 822-835   **PNAME**
      Offset   336h
      Data Type   string
      Description   This is a 14-byte field believed to be the destination port or device for the print function, expressed as a legal PC-DOS name in a NULL-terminated ASCII string. Byte 822 is a size-indicator byte. In the sample file, bytes 823-827 held the value "LPT1:"; the remainder of the field was NULL-filled.

Byte 836-837   **PNO**
      Offset   344h
      Data Type   integer
      Description   This field stores page numbering.

Byte 838-839   **LPI**
      Offset   346h
      Data Type   integer
      Description   These bytes store lines per inch.

The default is 6. A 2-byte integer (LSB first).

Byte 840-841   **FLEN**
      Offset   348h
      Data Type   integer
      Description   These bytes contain the form length.

The default is 66. A 2-byte integer (LSB first).

Byte 842-843   **LPP**
      Offset   34Ah
      Data Type   integer
      Description   These bytes contain the number of lines to print per page.

The default is 58. A 2-byte integer (LSB first).

Byte 844-845   **MLW**
                    Offset   34Ch
                    Data Type   integer
                    Description   These bytes holds the maximum line width (in characters).

The default is 80. A 2-byte integer (LSB first).

Byte 846-847   **FMAT**
                    Offset   34Eh
                    Data Type   integer
                    Description   This is a 2-byte integer (LSB first) which signifies formatted or unformatted output.

You may print a Plans+ spreadsheet with page breaks and assorted other formatting options. How these options map into the formatting integer was not available from IBM. In the sample file, the default value for byte 846 was 04h, byte 847 was NULL.

Byte 848-849   **LMG**
                    Offset   350h
                    Data Type   2-byte integer
                    Description   These bytes determine the left margin.

The default is 00.

Byte 850-851   **PSTYLE**
                    Offset   352h
                    Data Type   string
                    Description   Print style may be normal or compressed.

The default value for byte 850 is 4Eh. This is the ASCII code for "N". The code for compressed print is ASCII "C".

Byte 852-1111   **SUBDESC**
                    Offset   354h
                    Data Type   string
                    Description   An array of ten substitute descriptions, each is a 25-byte field. Each substitute description is a NULL-terminated ASCII string. The first byte of each description may be a size-indicator.

Byte 1112-1511 SUBVAL
        Offset   458h
        Data Type   string
        Description An array of ten substitute value fields, each is a 40-byte field.

In the sample file, the first byte of each field contained the value 3Fh (ASCII "?"). The next byte contained the hex value of the ASCII character from "1" - "9" ("1", "0" in two bytes in the case of the tenth field).

Graph Specifications

Byte 1512-2483 GRAF_FORMAT
        Offset   5E8h
        Data Type   record
        Description A record comprised of the following offset locations and information:

Byte 1512-1521 GRAPH_NAME
        Offset   5E8h
        Data Type   string

This is a 10-byte field.

Byte 1512 is a size-indicator byte, followed by a NULL-terminated ASCII string of up to eight characters (excluding the NULL). When no graph has been named, Plans+ stores the following data:

        Byte 1512   01h
        Byte 1513   2Ah(ASCII "*")
        Byte 1514-1521   NULLs

Byte 1522-1523 GRAPH_TYPE
        Offset   5F2h
        Data Type   integer

A 2-byte integer field (LSB first),this field holds a number from 1-9 signifying graph type. There are eight types of graph; 9 may signify no graph. Our sample file, which had no graph defined, contained a 09h at this location.

Byte 1524-1563 FIRST__TITLE
        Offset   5F4h
        Data Type   string

Contains the top line title of the displayed or printed graph.

Byte 1524 is a size-indicator byte. In the case of a titleless graph, Plans+ saves the value 01h in the indicator byte, followed in the next byte by 20h (ASCII space). The remainder of the string is NULL.

Byte 1564-1603 SECOND__TITLE
        Offset   61Ch
        Data Type   string

Contains the second line title of the displayed or printed graph. This is the same construction as FIRST__TITLE.

Byte 1604-1623 X__AXIS__NAME
        Offset   644h
        Data Type   string

Stores the name given to x-axis of graph.

The first byte is a size-indicator, followed by ASCII space if there is no name.

Byte 1624-1643 Y__AXIS__NAME
        Offset   658h
        Data Type   string

Name given to y-axis of graph. This is the same construction as X__AXIS__NAME.

Byte 1644   GRID__TYPE
        Offset   66Ch
        Data Type   byte

This byte determines whether Plans+ draws grid lines on the graph. This field holds either the ASCII value "y" (70h) or "n" (6Eh).

Byte 1645   LABEL__TYPE
        Offset   66Dh
        Data Type   byte

This byte determines whether the graph labels become days, months, a range, or values. The default is "n". The byte may hold one of the following ASCII values:

"d"	(64h)	days
"i"	(69h)	include a range
"m"	(6Dh)	months
"n"	(6Eh)	none

Byte 1646-1647 START_VALUE
                Offset   66Eh
                Data Type   integer

These bytes contain the start location for the range of labels.

Byte 1648-1649 END_VALUE
                Offset   670h
                Data Type   integer

These bytes contain the ending location for the range of labels.

Byte 1650   SCALE_TYPE
                Offset   672h
                Data Type   byte

This byte determines whether scaling is automatic or manual. This field holds either an ASCII "y" for automatic, or an ASCII "n" for manual.

Byte 1651   UNUSED   This byte contains a NULL.

Byte 1652-1655 LOWER_SCALE
                Offset   674h
                Data Type   long real

A 64-bit, 8087-format long real number is stored here.

Byte 1656-1659 UPPER_SCALE
                Offset   678h
                Data Type   long real

A 64-bit, 8087-format long real number is stored in these bytes.

Byte 1660   REFERENCE_LINE
                Offset   67Ch
                Data Type   byte

Is a reference line used on the graph? This byte holds the ASCII value "y" or "n".

Byte 1661   UNUSED   This byte must be NULL.

Byte 1662-1665 REF_VALUE
                Offset   67Eh
                Data Type   long real

A 64-bit, 8087-format long real number is stored here. This field determines where to place the reference line along an axis.

Byte 1666   FLOAT_BAR
                Offset   682h
                Data Type   byte

"No input required," according to IBM. The sample file held the ASCII value "n".

Byte 1667   **MARKED_LINE**
              Offset   683h
              Data Type   byte

"No input required," according to IBM. The sample file held the ASCII value "y".

Byte 1668   **SCATTER_GRAM**
              Offset   684h
              Data Type   byte

This byte may hold the ASCII value "y" or "n".

Byte 1669   **UNUSED**

This byte is unused and must be NULL.

Byte 1670-1671 NO_DATA_SETS
              Offset   686h
              Data Type   2-byte integer

This integer may hold the values 00h to 07h.

Byte 1672-1673 PALETTE
              Offset   688h
              Data Type   2-byte word

This field holds the values 0 or 1. 0 signifies a graph using the colors cyan, magenta and white; 1 signifies green, yellow and red.

Byte 1674   **SAVE_FILE**
              Offset   68Ah
              Data Type   byte

This byte may hold the ASCII values "n" or "y".

Byte 1675   **VIEW_PRINT**
              Offset   68Bh
              Data Type   byte

This byte may hold the ASCII values "n" or "y".

Byte 1676-1677 LPT
              Offset   68Ch
              Data Type   2-byte integer

May hold the values 01h to 03h.

Seems to signify the printer destination for the graph, as in "LPT1:", "LPT2:", etc.

Byte 1678-1679 PRCODES
              Offset   68Eh
              Data Type   integer

These bytes store the background color.

The default for this field is 03h.

Byte 1680-1681 PRCODEP
    Offset   690h
    Data Type integer

This byte contains the printer type.

The default for this field is 01h.

Byte 1682 VIEW__DISPLAY
    Offset   692h
    Data Type byte

This byte may hold the ASCII values "y" or "n".

The default for this field is "n".

Byte 1684-2243 POINT__VALUE
    Offset   694h
    Data Type array of reals

This byte contains the current graph points.

This is an array of 20 fields; each field is made up of seven 4-byte (32-bit) long reals.

Byte 2244-2363 POINT__LABEL
    Offset   8C4h
    Data Type array of strings

This byte holds the current graph labels.

This is an array of 20 fields. Each field is six bytes long: a size-indicator byte followed by up to 4 ASCII characters and terminated with a NULL. The default condition is an indicator byte of value 01h, followed by an ASCII space character (20h), followed by four NULLS.

Byte 2364-2405 DATA__SET__NAME
    Offset   93Ch
    Data Type array

The current data set names are stored here.

This is an array of seven fields. Each field is six bytes long: a size indicator byte followed by up to 4 ASCII characters and terminated with a NULL. The default condition is an indicator byte of value 01h, followed by an ASCII space character, followed by four NULLS.

Byte 2406-2419 DATA__SET__POINTS
    Offset   966h
    Data Type array

This is an array of seven fields. Each field is a 2-byte integer (LSB first) containing the number of points in each data set. The default values are NULL.

Byte 2420-2483 DATA__RANGE
        Offset   974h
        Data Type   array
        Description This is an array of eight fields which stores the ranges to be graphed. Each field consists of four 2-byte integers. The default values are NULL.

Byte 2484-2513 PUTGDAT
        Offset   9B4h
        Data Type   array
        Description This field is officially reserved and unused.

These bytes are defined by IBM as an array of 29 fields, each one a character. PUTGDAT appears to be a 30-byte, NULL-terminated ASCII string. The first byte may be a size-indicator byte. The default contents for PUTGDAT are ASCII space characters. Byte 2513 is NULL.

Sort Specifications

Byte 2514-2523 SRANGE
        Offset   9D2h
        Data Type   array
        Description This is an array of five 2-byte integers.

Calculation Record Information

Note: Plans+ numbers calculations in order of entry, starting from 1.

Byte 2524-2525 FIRST
        Offset   979h
        Data Type   2-byte integer
        Description Stores the number of the first calculation on the screen.

Byte 2526-2527 CURRENT
        Offset   9DEh
        Data Type   2-byte integer
        Description Stores the number of the current calculation.

Byte 2528-2529 LAST
    Offset   9E0h
    Data Type   2-byte integer
    Description   Contains the number of the last calculation appearing on the screen.

Byte 2530-2531 HICALC
    Offset   9E2h
    Data Type   2-byte integer
    Description   Stores the highest calculation defined.

Saved Graph Information

Byte 2532 - variable GRAPH__INFO__ARRAY
    Offset   9E4h
    Data Type   This array contains 10 records for user-defined graph specifications.
    Description   For each user-named set of graph specifications, there will be a variable sized record that contains the following information:

- A GRAF__FORMAT record for each named graph.

- A DATA__SET__NAME, a DATA__SET__POINTS, and a DATA__RANGE array for each named graph.

According to IBM, the program represents all of the array information in rowwise fashion just as though it were a text cell in the .~MF file (explained below). Each value of the three arrays is stored as a 2-byte integer, rather than as two characters.

Calculation Records

The Calculation Array follows the GRAF__INFO__ARRAY. If the GRAF__INFO__ARRAY is not present, the Calculation Array immediately follows the last byte of HICALC. Each member of the array represents one calculation rule. Each member has the following format:

    LENGTH   2-byte integer   length of row
    ROW__NUMBER 2-byte integer   row number
    NUMB__CELLS 1-byte   # of cells (always 1)
    CELL   string   length of text in the calculation

Byte   **EOF__MARK**
                  Data Type   integer
                  Description   A 2-byte end-of-file marker.
                  This field always contains the value FFFFh.

.~MF Model Data File Layout

The .~MF file is composed of a number of variable length records. Each record represents a row in the spreadsheet matrix. Plans+ organizes the records by ascending row number, and within each record, the cells appear from left to right (ascending column number). The file ends with the last row that contains non-NULL cells. The EOF__MARK (FFFFh) closes the file.

Each row begins with a 5-byte header, followed by information that varies depending on whether the particular cell is numeric, text or NULL (empty, no entry). A NULL row (no cells containing data values, but not the final row of a model) has only a header. NULL cells occur in rows where data cells follow the NULL cell.

Header Format (5 bytes long)

LENGTH   Length   2-byte integer
                  Description   This field contains the length of the row record, including header, in bytes.

ROWNUMB   Length   2-byte integer
                  Description   This field contains the row number.

COLUMN   Length   1 byte
                  Description   This field contains the number of spreadsheet columns in this row. COLUMN is 0 for a NULL row.

Numeric Cell Format (10 bytes long)

FLAG   Length   2-byte word
                  Description   This field contains information flags (See Table 7.1).

NUMBER   Length   8-byte real
                  Description   This field contains the number value of the cell.

Text Cell Format (3 bytes plus text)

FLAG Length   2-byte word
          Description This field contains information flags (See Table 7.1).

LEN   Length   1 byte
          Description This field contains the size-indicator byte.

TEXT Length   Variable
          Description This field contains the NULL-terminated ASCII string.

NULL Cell Format (2-bytes long)

FLAG Length   2-byte word
          Description This field contains hex 8400h or C400h.

Table 7.1 — Flag Word Details

```
        high byte            low byte
    ┌─┬─┬─┬─┬─┬─┬─┬─┬─┬─┬─┬─┬─┬─┬─┬─┐
    │7│6│5│4│3│2│1│0│7│6│5│4│3│2│1│0│
    └─┴─┴─┴─┴─┴─┴─┴─┴─┴─┴─┴─┴─┴─┴─┴─┘
```

Byte	Bit #	Meaning
Low Byte	0, 1	Justify left (00), right (01), center (10)
	2	on if cell is null
	3	on to break on assignment
	4	on to protect against change by calculation
	5	on if cell holds a calculation-assigned value
	6	on to protect against manual change
	7	on if text cell, off if numeric
Hi Byte	0, 1, 2	number of decimal places (to 7)
	3, 4, 5	display format (unknown)
	6	date
	7	reserved

CHAPTER 8

SUPERCALC 3®
Release 2
and SUPER DATA INTERCHANGE™ FORMAT
Version 2.0

**Computer Associates International, Inc.
2195 Fortune Drive
San Jose, CA 95131**

TYPE OF PRODUCT   Spreadsheet with graphics

FILES PRODUCED   SuperCalc3 produces binary and special format; Super Data Interchange produces ASCII text.

POINTS OF INTEREST

No information is available on the native data file format produced by SupeCalc3. Sorcim suggests that all input to SuperCalc, other than via the keyboard, be done through the Super Data Interchange (SDI) format. SDI can handle the input of most cell formatting and formulas. However, SuperCalc is not designed to output formulas or cell formatting information via SDI.

Obtaining formula and data output from SuperCalc becomes a matter of producing an ASCII text file of the formulas (which the program does allow), and combining it with the data available from the SDI output. Cell formatting information is lost.

CONVERSION INFORMATION

Super Data Interchange handles all conversion between SuperCalc3 and other programs. Specifically, SDI can convert the following ASCII text file formats into SuperCalc3:

- **Comma separated value**   A comma separates each field of a CSV file. Each field becomes the contents of a cell. No formula or formatting information is converted. SuperCalc3 can read and write CSV files.

- **Super Data Interchange format** SuperCalc3 reads and writes SDI; reads it with formulas and formatting, and writes it without.
- **VisiCalc® file** SDI conversion programs can read a VisiCalc file, formulas and formats.
- **Lotus 1-2-3® .WKS file** SDI can read a 1-2-3 file and convert formulas and formats.

SuperCalc3 and the SDI Format

SuperCalc3 Release 2 is a spreadsheet with business graphics. Besides its native file format, which only SuperCalc can read or write, the program accepts text and numeric data, formula and formatting input via a Super Data Interchange (SDI) file. The SDI function in SuperCalc3 will also output files. These, however, contain text and numeric data only.

SDI is based on the Data Interchange Format (DIF) created by Software Arts, Inc. (now part of Lotus Development Corporation). The SDI format is primarily intended to handle row-and-column information. It shares some vocabulary with DIF. A *vector* is a column. A *tuple* is a row.

Because SDI files are ASCII text files, there is an assumed <**carriage return**> <**linefeed**> at the end of each line of text. Rows are numbered from 1 to 9999 in SuperCalc3 (1 to 245 in earlier releases). While columns are lettered on screen, in SDI files they are numbered from 1 to 128 in SuperCalc3 (1-63 in earlier releases). SDI makes no provision for graphic data.

SDI File Organization

SDI files are divided into a file header and a data section. Both sections are of variable length.

Formatting Strings

Both the header and data sections use unquoted strings of ASCII characters to control the formatting of rows, columns, data and cells. Multiple characters can make up these formatting strings. Legal values and their meanings are:

L	left justify numerical values
R	right justify numerical values
TL	left justify text values
TR	right justify text values
$	format numerical values with 2 decimal places and trailing zeros if necessary

*	display numerical values as asterisks, one asterisk for each unit (5 is *****). A 0 is a blank cell.
I	displays a truncated integer of the numerical value
G	general format, best fit for cell width
D	remove any format and replace with default
E	exponential format

As an example, the unquoted string R$ signifies right justified numbers with two decimal places. Please note that not all formatting controls are available. For instance, you cannot input an instruction for three decimal places.

SDI Header

There are two required and five optional entries in the SDI header. The two required entries are TABLE and DATA.

The first entry must be of the form:

TABLE
0,1
" "

There is no space between the double quotation marks.
The next entry contains the number of columns (vectors) in the spreadsheet.

VECTORS
0, <count>
" "

where

<count> is the number of columns.

The following entry lists the number of rows (tuples) in the spreadsheet.

TUPLES
0, <count>
" "

where

<count> is the number of rows.

The fourth entry controls the global formatting of the spreadsheet.

GDISP-FORMAT
< width >,0
< format string >

where

   < width > is the global column width.

   < format string > is an unquoted text string made up of the legal characters in the Format String section (see page 103).

An SDI file header may have multiple instances of the next two entries. They control the formatting of individual columns and rows, respectively.

COL-FORMAT
< col # >,< width >
< format string >

and

ROW-FORMAT
< row # >,0
< format string >

where

   < col # > or **< row # >** is the number of the column or row being formatted.

   < width > is the column width of the column being formatted.

   < format string > is an unquoted text string made up of the legal characters in the Format String section (see page 103).

The final entry in the SDI header section determines the end of the header section and the beginning of the data section. It must take the form:

DATA
0,0
" "

SDI Data Section

The basic organization of an SDI data section is an entry for each cell of the spreadsheet beginning at location A1 and continuing in ascending columnar order and then in ascending row order. Each row is a tuple; a BOT (Beginning of Tuple) entry acts much as a carriage return or other delimiter.

An "origin specifier" (essentially a GOTO) makes it unnecessary to create entries for large blocks of unfilled cells.

Each data entry must take the form:

<data type>,<numerical value>
<string value>

There are seven data types, each corresponding to a signed integer:

1	text
0	numeric value
-1	data definition
-2	origin specifier (GOTO)
-3	entry level display formatting
-4	formula
-5	repeat count

For the following types of entries, the <data type>, <numeric values> and <string values> fields of the SDI data section contain the information below:

Text Entry

<data type>	1
<numeric value>	0 is regular text entry
	1 is repeating text entry
<string value>	text; if blanks, must be enclosed in double quotes

Numeric Entry

<data type>	0
<numeric value>	number
<string value>	V is valid numeric entry
	NA is not available, <numeric value> = 0
	NULL is unoccupied cell, <numeric value> = 0
	ERROR is an error condition, <numeric value> = 0

Data Definition Entry

<data type>	-1
<numeric value>	always 0
<string value>	BOT (Beginning of Tuple) separates rows
	EOD (End of Data)

Origin Specifier (GOTO)

<data type>	-2
<numeric value>	always 0
<string value>	cell address in the form: column:row
	1 – 127 : 1 – 9999 SuperCalc 3
	1 – 63 : 1 – 254 earlier versions

Entry Level Display Formatting Entry
            <data type>   −3
   <numeric value>   always 0
    <string value>   formatting string for the previous cell. If no previous cell, SDI generates an input error.

Formula Entry
            <data type>   −4
   <numeric value>   always 0
    <string value>   formula (must be a valid SuperCalc 3 formula.)

Repeat Count Entry
            <data type>   −5
   <numeric value>   # times to repeat
    <string value>   always and only **R**. Previous data item repeated across the cells of a given row for a <**numeric value**> number of cells.

CHAPTER 9

VISICALC®
Version 177Y2

**Lotus Development Corp.
161 First Street
Cambridge, MA 02142**

TYPE OF PRODUCT   Spreadsheet

FILES PRODUCED   ASCII text

POINTS OF INTEREST

VisiCalc was the first electronic spreadsheet program, available in 1978. It almost single-handedly forged the managerial market for personal computers and "productivity software." At the height of its popularity, the program was said to have had a million users. Many people still use and are satisfied with VisiCalc.

Being first may have had its price. VisiCalc has been surpassed in power and in the market by Lotus 1-2-3 and other programs. In the summer of 1985, it was taken off the market. The company that created it, Software Arts, was merged into Lotus.

CONVERSION INFORMATION

VisiCalc reads and writes DIF. Many packages offer conversion programs that transfer VisiCalc models to their own format.

The VisiCalc File Format

VisiCalc is the original spreadsheet program. It stores its data in record-oriented, carriage return/linefeed delimited, ASCII text files.

The files are divided into two sections: a data section and a footer. The data section contains the contents of each non-empty cell location, including formatting information. The footer section contains window and global formatting information, and the position of the cursor.

The VisiCalc Data Section

Each cell record in the data section takes the form

>   \><cell>:<format><cell contents>

where

>   \> is a right brace (3Eh).

>   <**cell**> is the cell reference coordinates expressed as column-row (A4, B26).

>   <**format**> is a number of optional format parameters for the individual cell only.

>   <**cell contents**> is a numerical or textual value, or VisiCalc formula. There are no spaces anywhere in a record, except inside of strings.

Numeric values may be signed or unsigned, with or without decimals, or in scientific notation.

Textual values are led with a single instance of a double quote ("A Label). The exception to this is a repeating label, which uses the format: /<characters>. A repeating dash in A5, for example, would be written as: >A5:/-

Formulas begin with numbers (0 to 9) or, if cell coordinates or a function begins a formula, start with one of the following symbols: + − (. # or @.

The forward slash character (/) signals the formatting command. For individual cells (the only type of formatting allowed in the data section) the command is: /-F<options>.

The <options> are:

D	default—resets to global format
G	general—uses maximum precision
I	integer
L	left justified
R	right justified
$	2 decimal places (VisiCalc displays no $ character)
*****	graph—one asterisk per unit (5 is *****)

When VisiCalc saves a file, it does so from the lowermost, non-empty, right-hand corner of the spreadsheet, working leftwards across each row, then upwards to the rightmost limit of the previous row. The process skips empty cells. When cell A1 is saved (or the non-empty cell closest to the upper left hand corner of the sheet is reached), the program begins to save the footer.

The VisiCalc Footer Section

The footer contains global format information, order of recalculation, a flag to signify automatic or manual recalc, current cursor position and any set title rows or columns.

The format for almost all footer records is

/<command> <command options>

where

<command> is either a **W** (window) command or a **G** (global) command.

<command options> depends on <command>. The exception to this format is /X (see page 111).

W	Description	Window command
	Options	**1** one window
		S synchronized windows
		U unsynchronized windows

Usually, /W1 is the format that appears in the file (even when windows are split). Splitting the window is handled under the /X command.

G	Description	Global command
	Options	**C** sets all column widths to a specified number
		F sets global display format (see /F on page 109)
		O sets order of recalculation
		C down columns
		R across rows
		R recalculation
		A automatic whenever an entry is made
		M manual, whenever ! is entered

All options act globally on the spreadsheet.

/X—The Catch-All Command

This command serves many masters. Generally, its format is

>/X> <upper left>:> <current cursor>:<options>

where

> <**upper left**> are the coordinates of the cell in the upper left corner of the window.
>
> <**current cursor**> is the cell where the cursor is currently positioned or where an activity is to take place (such as locking titles).
>
> <**options**> include window, titles or global formatting for one of the two possible windows. (see /W, /G, /F above.) However, /X may also split the window. The command /XH10 splits the screen horizontally at row 10. Title options are:
>
> | | | |
> |---|---|---|
> | **H** | lock titles horizontally at <current cursor> | |
> | **V** | lock titles vertically at <current cursor> | |
> | **B** | lock titles both vertically and horizontally at <current cursor> | |

File Organization

The data section is saved from the lowermost, non-empty, right-hand corner of the spreadsheet, leftward across each row in decreasing row numbers. Because each entry retains its cell coordinates, no empty cells are saved.

  The footer begins where the data section leaves off. Its format is generally:

> /W1
> /Global <order of recalculation>
> /Global <recalculation auto or manual>
> /X <window split if any>
> /Global <formatting>
> /Global <column width window 1>
> /X <window 1 - titles set if any>
> /X <window 1 - current cursor, formatting>
> /Global <column width window 2>
> /X <window 2 - titles set if any>
> /X <window 2 - current cursor, window synch>

CHAPTER 10

WORDSTAR®
Versions 2.2x through 3.31

MicroPro International Corporation
33 San Pablo Avenue
San Rafael, CA 94903

TYPE OF PRODUCT   Word processor

FILES PRODUCED   Binary/ASCII text

POINTS OF INTEREST

WordStar files potentially contain a host of embedded commands. Many of these are multi-byte, ASCII, print-time layout formatting strings made up of multiple ASCII characters. They begin with a period character and are called DOT COMMANDS. Others are single-byte control codes.

Aside from Dot Commands and control codes, most of WordStar is controlled from the user interface or the original installation procedure—including selecting the printer driver, setting margins, setting tabs and electing right/left justification. WordStar stores the results of these settings as they have affected the file; it does not store the settings themselves. Users must realize they may have to manually reformat documents which were stored under a different line length.

CONVERSION INFORMATION

MicroPro supplies no software with the WordStar package specifically for converting between WordStar and other programs. However, WordStar can read ASCII text files with each line either delimited by the carriage return/linefeed combination, or in "long line" format with a single paragraph delimited by CR/LF. For line-delimited files, the user must perform a global search-and-replace on all the CR/LFs *except* the final one for *each paragraph*. The user then issues a ^B reformat command for each paragraph. Files can then be saved in WordStar's Document format.

The WordStar File Format

WordStar is a file-oriented word processor. Only available disk storage limits the size of documents; but the manufacturer warns in the program documentation against creating extremely large files because program efficiency suffers.

There are no file headers or footers. Files are organized in 128-byte sections. The unused balance of the final 128-byte section in each file (if any) is padded with PC DOS end-of-file marks (^ Z or 1Ah).

Embedded Dot Commands and format commands can be interspersed among printable ASCII text characters in a WordStar file (See Format Codes). In Document Mode, detailed here, the high bit of the final character of each word in a word-wrapped line is set on. Table 10.1 lists the Dot Commands and a description of each.

The Text Stream

Unless told otherwise via an embedded formatting character, WordStar assumes that text is to be printed "normally"—without underlining, boldfacing, etc. To boldface an area of text, for example, you embed the boldface character (02h) in the text stream prior to the text to be altered. You again embed it after that text to turn the function off. The program filters out these characters at print time; but a justified line may appear unjustified on screen because such control codes become visible during editing.

Normally, the first character of a WordStar document is the first character appearing in the file —Dot Command, ASCII character, or formatting control code. When a character moves away from that first position (because of centering, for example), the preceding positions are padded with space characters (20h).

WordStar represents commands such as center, justify right or line length, by multiple "hard" spaces (20h), by "phantom spaces" (A0h) inserted by the program to even off a justified line or by the "soft" carriage return/line feed combination of 8Dh 0Ah, instead of the "hard" return 0Dh 0Ah. The soft CR/LF appears at a position in the line corresponding to the number of character positions in the line length set at the page ruler.

High-Bit Characters

The high-order bit of the final character of each word is set on when it occurs in a line ending with a "soft" or word-wrapped, carriage return/line feed combination. These characters are offset by 128 (80h). Any program written to read WordStar files should generally strip the high bits from these characters prior to interpreting them. WordStar considers a punctuation mark (comma, period, quotation, etc.) to be the final character of the preceding word. Often, the final words of a paragraph occur in a line *without* a word-wrapped CR/LF. These words will not have the high bits of their final characters set on.

Spaces entered by the WordStar program in order to justify lines also have their high-order bit set on (A0h). These "phantom spaces" may change or disappear as the file is reformatted.

The carriage-return character (0Dh) of the CR/LF combination may have the high bit set on (8Dh) if it is a CR/LF created by automatic word-wrap. This two-byte combination character occurs at or before the end of the line length under which the file was saved. A CR/LF combination entered by the user is represented conventionally (0Dh 0Ah). A WordStar file loaded into an empty document will maintain its saved line length *even if the current line length is set differently*. The user must reformat each paragraph (by using ^B) to change the positions of the soft CR/LFs.

The line-feed character of a page break marker (normally 0Ah) has its high bit set on (becomes 8Ah). The CR/LF combination for a page-break marker becomes 0Dh 8Ah.

WordStar Format Codes

Format codes may appear once or twice in the file. If they appear twice, the first occurrence turns the function on, and the second turns it off.

Table 10.1 Commands Used in Pairs

Hex	WS Command	Function
02	^PB	Bold Print
04	^PD	Double strike
09	^PI (or Tab)	Hard tab, used mostly in non-document mode
0A	^PJ	LF prt of line terminator, not used by itself, but user may enter
0B	^PK	Odd/even page offset for headers and footers
0C	^PL	Alternate method for creating page break, creates 0Ch in file
01		NOT USED
13	^PS	Underline
14	^PT	Superscript
16	^PV	Subscript
18	^PX	Strikeout
1A		End of file marker
1B		Escape—NOT USED*
1C		NOT USED*
1D		NOT USED*
1E	^p~	Soft hyphen
1F		NOT USED*

*In European versions of WordStar, Versions 3.4x, 1Bh is a prefix for a character for which the high bit should not be stripped before interpreting. 1Ch is used as a suffix for such a character.

Table 10.2 Commands Used Alone

Hex	WS Command	Function
01	^PA	Alternate pitch
03	^PC	Print pause
05	^PE	User printer command
06	^PF	Phantom space
07	^PG	Phantom rubout
08	^PH	Strikeover character
0D	^P<CR> or ^PM	Strikeover line and part of line terminator. 0D appears alone for strikeover
0E	^PN	Standard pitch
0F	^PO	Non-break space
11	^PQ	User printer command
12	^PW	User printer command
17	^PW	User printer command
19	^PY	Ribbon Color change

Table 10.3 Other Codes Used by WordStar

0Dh	8Ah	Page break
0Dh	0Ah	Line terminator on non-word-wrapped lines, last line of paragraph ("hard carriage return")
8Dh	0Ah	Line terminator on word-wrapped lines ("soft carriage return")

Table 10.4 Dot Commands

Command	Description	Command	Description
.BP	Bidirectional printing	.LH	Line height
.UJ	Micro-justification	.MT	Top margin
.PO	Page offset, left margin	.MB	Bottom margin
.CW	Character width	.PA	New page (page break)
.IG or ..	Comment (not printed)	.OP	Omit page number
.CP	Conditional page	.PN	Page number
.FO	Footer	.PC	Page number column
.HE	Header	.SR	Subscript/superscript roll
.HM	Header margin	.PL	Paper length
.FM	Footer margin		

WordStar places dot commands in a file exactly as though they were written words of a document.

CHAPTER 11
WORDSTAR® 2000™
Version 1.01d

MicroPro International Corporation
33 San Pablo Avenue
San Rafael, CA 94903

TYPE OF PRODUCT   Word processor

FILES PRODUCED   Binary/ASCII text

POINTS OF INTEREST

MicroPro states categorically that WordStar 2000 is not a successor to the original WordStar program. But the similarities are there; and though WS2000 may be compiled from totally different source code, it may best be comprehended as a modernization of the original WordStar.

WordStar 2000 has a much simpler user interface than the original WordStar program. English language prompts reflect formatting codes enterable from a menu as well as via control codes.

The ASCII text stream produced by the program still has embedded codes in it, however, and the codes are now a good bit more complex. A file header carries additional information: program version, printer driver name, page ruler, font, heading and footing information, and more as covered below.

CONVERSION INFORMATION

Software supplied by MicroPro with this package allows conversion both ways between WordStar and WordStar 2000 files. Like the original version of the program, WordStar 2000 may read and write CR/LF-delimited ASCII text files not containing formatting information.

The WordStar 2000 File Format

WordStar 2000 is a file-based word processor that can use floppy or hard disk as a virtual memory extension of the document in memory. A WordStar 2000-formatted document consists of a format block of variable length (some information is optional), a "top of editable portion" marker, the document body with embedded codes, and an end-of-file marker.

File Contents

The characters that make up a WordStar 2000 file fall into three types: text characters, control characters, and symmetrical sequences.

Text Characters

Text characters are printable and displayable ASCII characters.

Control Characters

WordStar 2000 uses a restricted set of control characters. Control characters are used in text formatting in a fashion similar to their standard ASCII interpretation. These characters appear singly in the file.

Name	Dec	Hex	Meaning
Overstrike	16	10	overprint one character
Tab	09	09	space to next tab
Hardline	10	0A	end of paragraph
Carriage ret.	14	0E	unformatted file line delimiter
Attention char.	127	7F	lead-in character for symmetrical sequence

Symmetrical Sequences

WordStar 2000 stores most of the formatting information in its files in sequences of bytes bracketed by the attention (or lead-in) character and a one-byte code that carries the formatting command itself. The symmetrical sequence looks like this:

[attn][command][parameters][command][attn]

Symmetrical sequences come in two types: compound, which carry parameters; and simple, which do not.

Some symmetrical sequences occur in pairs and bracket intervening text — for example, the sequence that triggers an even page header brackets the header text itself. Other sequences are "standalone." A Hardline character (10d/0Ah) or another standalone sequence must precede a standalone sequence.

The WordStar 2000 program internally scans its files backwards and forwards. Hence, the symmetrical sequences assure that the program can read formatting information conveniently either way.

Format Block

The format block precedes the text block. It begins at offset byte 0 and continues until the top-of-text sequence ([7Fh][76h][7Fh]). A number of the fields in the format block are optional, making it difficult to provide absolute byte number offsets from the 0 byte. A few of the commands used in the format block are also used in the text block. For the sake of clarity and completeness, the format block command characters are listed below in the order that they appear. They are also included with the alphabetic listing of command sequences. Table 11.1 lists all command codes in numerical order in both format and text blocks.

Parameters are ASCII characters (rather than binary) except where noted. Thus the number 1, when included as a parameter, is the ASCII character "1" (31h) instead of the binary 01h. In all cases, the attention character (7Fh) is assumed to precede and follow each sequence. [S] signifies the space character (20h). WS2000 uses space characters between command code parameters.

File__ID   **32d/20h**
                Description   formatted file identification
                Format   [20h][Str1][S][Str2][S][Byt1][20h]

[Str1] is the version number. This string is a 15-byte field with all hardspaces converted to FFh. The valid string for this version is "WS2000[S]1.00[S][S][S][S]".

[Str2] is the printer identifier. This string is a 15-byte field with hardspaces converted to FFh. The default is "*NONE*[S][S][S][S][S][S][S][S][S]". WS2000 rewrites this field on closing and the value doesn't matter on opening.

[Byt1] is the formatted line count. This string is a 6-byte field. This is a pointer to the last formatted line of the document. WS2000 fills in this parameter. A file prepared for use with WS2000 should contain 5 space characters (20h) and ASCII zero (30h).

File__ID must be the first sequence in the file. A space character ([S] - 20h) separates each of the three parameters from the other.

Font   **28d/1Ch**
　　　　　　　Description　select font
　　　　　　　Format　　　[1Ch][Byt1][S][Byt2][1Ch]

[Byt1] is the previous font. This is a 2-byte number in ASCII characters used as index into font information.

[Byt2] is the subsequent font. This is a 2-byte number in ASCII characters.

The correspondence of number to actual fonts selected depends on the printer identifier selected for the file. As a rule, Font 0 is "almost always" a 10 point non-proportional font, and Font 1 is "almost always" a 12 point font. Selecting Font 0 will usually result in a "reasonable" effect, according to MicroPro. This sequence must be preceded by a hardline (0Ah) character.

Height   **105d/69h**
　　　　　　　Description　select line height - standalone
　　　　　　　Format　　　[69h][Byt1][S][Byt2][69h]

[Byt1] is the previous line height. This is a 2-byte field used as an index into an array of line heights.

[Byt2] is the subsequent line height. This is a 2-byte field.

WS2000 uses "printer points" to place text graphically on the page.

Author's Note: A discussion of printer points is beyond the scope of this handbook. Documents prepared for use with WS2000 can safely replace both of these 2-byte parameters with the bytes: [20h][30h] (space and zero). WordStar 2000 will alter the parameters internally.

Headoff   **94d/5Eh**
　　　　　　　Description　header offset - standalone
　　　　　　　Format　　　[5Eh][Byt1][5Eh]

[Byt1] is the header offset in number of lines. This is a 3-byte field, expressed as ASCII.

For a 6-line offset, the three bytes will hold two ASCII space characters (20h) and an ASCII "6" (36h). This sequence indicates the number of lines from the top of page to the first line of printed text.

Footoff   **95d/5Fh**
             Description   footer offset - standalone
             Format   [5Fh][Byt1][5Fh]

             [Byt1] is the footer offset in number of lines. This is a 3-byte field, expressed in ASCII.

This field indicates the number of lines from the bottom of the page up to the last line of printed text.

Ruler   **91d/5Bh**
             Description   new ruler line - standalone
             Format   [5Bh][Byt1] . . . [Byt128][5Bh]

             [Byt1] is the old left margin position in column units.
             [Byt2] is the old right margin position in column units.
             [Byt3] is the old first tab type (1 is normal, 2 is decimal).
             [Byt4] is the old first tab position in column units.
             [Byt5] is the old second tab type (1 is normal, 2 is decimal).
             [Byt6] is the old second tab position in column units.
                .
                .
                .
             [Byt63] is the old 31st tab type (must be FFh).
             [Byt64] is the old 31st tab position (must be FFh).
             [Byt65] is the new left margin position in column units.
             [Byt66] is the new right margin position in column units.
             [Byt67] is the new first tab type (1 is normal, 2 is decimal).
             [Byt68] is the new first tab position in column units.
             [Byt69] is the new second tab type.
             [Byt70] is the new second tab position in column units.
                .
                .
                .
             [Byt127] is the new 31st tab type (must be FFh).
             [Byt128] is the new 31st tab position (must be FFh).

Up to 30 tabstops may be set. Unused tabstops are set to FFh. Ruler sequences are 128 bytes long.

LPerPage **97d/61h**
Description lines per page - standalone
Format [61h][Byt1][61h]

[Byt1] is the number of lines per page. This is a 2-byte field.

A usual value for this field is 66, handled as two bytes, each containing the value 36h (ASCII character "6").

EvenPOff **92d/5Ch**
Description even page offset - standalone
Format [5Ch][Byt1][5Ch]

[Byt1] is the left-right offset of the even page in column units. This is a 2-byte field.

OddPOff **93d/5Dh**
Description odd page offset - standalone
Format [5Dh][Byt1][5Dh]

[Byt1] is the left-right offset of the odd-numbered pages in column units. This is a 2-byte field.

TJustify **98d/62h**
Description set justification - standalone
Format [62h][Byt1][Byt2][62h]

[Byt1] is the previous justification selected. This is a 1-byte field.

[Byt2] is the subsequent justification selected. This is a 1-byte field. 1 is justification on; 0 is justification off.

THyphen **101d/65h**
Description toggle hyphen - format block only
Format [65h][Byt1][65h]

[Byt1] sets automatic hyphenation mode. This is a 1-byte field, found only in the format block. 1 is hyphenation on; 0 is hyphenation off.

TFormFeed **24d/18h**
Description form feed toggle - format block only
Format [18h]

This field indicates that the form feeds are not to be used during printing.

TUndGaps   **102d/66h**
   Description   set underline - format block only
   Format   [66h][Byt1][66h]

   [Byt1] sets the underline word gaps flag. This is a 1-byte field. 1 is set; 0 is not set.

TPageBreak   **103d/67h**
   Description   page break display - format block only
   Format   [67h][Byt1][67h]

   [Byt1] sets the status of the page break display. This is a 1-byte field, found only in format block. 1 is display page breaks; 0 is no display.

FootEven   **67d/43h**
   Description   even page footer - standalone
   Format   [43h][Byt1][S][Byt2][S][Byt3][S][Byt4][S][Byt5][43h]

   [Byt1] represents the previous header or footer vertical dots ("Most of the time," according to MicroPro). This is a 3-byte field, expressed as ASCII.

   [Byt2] is the previous header or footer in vertical dots. This is a 3-byte field.

   [Byt3] is the number of lines in the footer just crossed, plus one. This is a 3-byte field.

   [Byt4] is the number of vertical dots in the footer just crossed. This is a 4-byte field.

   [Byt5] is the number of vertical dots on the page so far (including the footer just crossed). This is a 4-byte field.

The FootEven field only appears in conjunction with the FootOdd field. It indicates the text to be printed within the bottom margin on even numbered pages.

FootOdd   **68d/44h**
   Description   odd page footer - standalone
   Format   [44h][Byt1][S][Byt2][S][Byt3][S][Byt4][S][Byt5][44h]

   [Byt1] represents the previous header or footer vertical dots ("Most of the time," according to MicroPro). This is a 3-byte field, expressed as ASCII.

   [Byt2] is the previous header or footer in vertical dots. This is a 3-byte field.

[Byt3] is the number of lines in the footer just crossed, plus one. This is a 3-byte field.

[Byt4] is the number of vertical dots in the footer just crossed. This is a 4-byte field.

[Byt5] is the number of vertical dots on the page so far (including the footer just crossed). This is a 4-byte field.

The FootOdd field indicates text to be printed within the bottom margin on odd numbered pages.

FootEven and FootOdd must be used together on alternating numbered pages. They must be the last two sequences before TOP if they exist.

FootBoth   **69d/45h**
Description   both-page footer - standalone
Format   [45h][Byt1][S][Byt2][S][Byt3][S][Byt4][S][Byt5][45h]

[Byt1] represents the previous header or footer vertical dots ("Most of the time," according to MicroPro). This is a 3-byte field, expressed in ASCII.

[Byt2] previous header or footer in vertical dots.
This is a 3-byte field.

[Byt3] is the number of lines in the footer just crossed, plus one. This is a 3-byte field.

[Byt4] is the number of vertical dots in the footer just crossed. This is a 4-byte field.

[Byt5] is the number of vertical dots on the page so far (including the footer just crossed). This is a 4-byte field.

FootBoth indicates the text to be printed within the bottom margin on both even and odd numbered pages. It must be the last sequence before TOP if it exists.

If the Footer information is present, the paired sequence will contain a ruler line and one text line with at least "%PAGE%" on the line.

Top   **118d/76h**
Description   top of editable portion marker
Format   [76h]

TOP marks the end of the format block and the beginning of the text.

Text Block

The text block is made up of printable ASCII text characters and formatting sequences. The following listing provides all legal sequences up to and including Version 1.01d in alphabetical order by field name. A listing of command codes in numerical order is provided in Table 11.1.

Appendix **111d/6Fh**
                Description   appendix heading - paired and standalone
                Format   [6Fh][Byt1][S][Byt2] . . . [Byt5][6Fh]

[Byt1], [Byt2], and [Byt3] are each 3-byte fields of ASCII characters.

[Byt4] and [Byt5] are each 4-byte fields of ASCII characters.

Appendix is a special form of a Level-1 heading. The first occurrence of an Appendix heading results in a Level-1 letter of "A" and the second results in "B" when processed by the Index program.

    [Byt1] to [Byt5] are similar in content to those described in FootBoth. MicroPro recommends that each of these fields be set to space-led ASCII zeros. The WS2000 program will update them.

AskV **79d/4Fh**
                Description   ask for value - standalone
                Format   [4Fh][STR1][S][STR2][S][Byt1][4Fh]

[STR1] is the name of the variable wanted. It has a maximum length of 31 characters and must begin with a letter.

[STR2] is the text of the on-screen prompt which will ask for the value. It has a maximum of 54 characters.

[Byt1] is the maximum user-determined length of allowable input. The maximum program-allowable input is 40 characters. This is a 1-byte field.

AskV permits print-time keyboard entry of values into a document.

BIndent **21d/15h**
                Description   indent both sides
                Format   [15h]

This field indents both left and right sides to the next tab position.

Bold 05d/05h
Description boldface toggle
Format [05h]

This field toggles boldface printing on and off.

BUndent 23d/17h
Description un-indent both sides
Format [17h][Byt1][S][Byt2][17h]

[Byt1] is a field showing the number of active left indents. This is a 2-byte field.

[Byt2] is a field showing the number of active right indents. This is a 2-byte field.

BUndent turns off all active indents. MicroPro advises that Byt1 and Byt2 may be set to zero, and that the program will produce the correct values.

Center 19d/13h
Description center current line
Format [13h]

Cndshn 82d/52h
Description conditional statement (mailmerge)
Format [52h][STR1][52h]

[STR1] is a string of text from 1 to 64 chracters long. Space characters (20h) are converted to FFh within the string.

Color 29d/1Dh
Description printer ribbon color select
Format [1Dh][Byt1][S][Byt2][1Dh]

[Byt1] is the previous color select. This is a 2-byte field.

[Byt2] is the subsequent color select. This is a 2-byte field.

Each field (Byt1 and Byt2) is an index into a list of available colors from 0 to 7 dependent on the selected printer. A given printer may or may not have a color mapped against all eight color choices. Color 0 is "defined as something reasonable" for all supported printers, according to MicroPro.

Comment **70d/46h**
Description   unprinted comment-paired, standalone
Format   [46h][Byt1][S][Byt2]...[Byt5][46h]

[Byt1], [Byt2], and [Byt3] are 3-byte fields.

[Byt3] and [Byt5] are 4-byte fields.

[Byt1] through [Byt5] may be set to space-led ASCII zero (30h). The program will fill in appropriate values.

Contents **112d/70h**
Description   contents summary-paired, standalone
Format   [70h][Byt1][S][Byt2]...[Byt5][70h]

[Byt1], [Byt2], and [Byt3] are 3-byte fields.

[Byt4] and [Byt5] are 4-byte fields.

Allows for a table of contents entry to contain a summary of the contents of one section of a document. [Byt1] through [Byt5] may be set to space-led ASCII zero (30h). The program will fill in appropriate values.

DataF **76d/4Ch**
Description   select data file (mailmerge) - standalone
Format   [4Ch][STR1][4Ch]

[STR1] is a field of 1 to 64 characters. DataF supplies the data file pathname for use in a mailmerge document.

Disp **80d/50h**
Description   display message (mailmerge) - standalone
Format   [50h][STR1][50h]

[STR1] is a message displayed at print time and may contain from 1 to 79 characters.

Double **07d/07h**
Description   doublestrike toggle
Format   [07h]

This field toggles doublestrike printing on and off.

EndCnd **84d/54h**
Description   end merge condition
Format   [54h]

This field indicates the end of a conditionally-printed section of a document.

EvenPOff   **92d/5Ch**
                  Description   even page offset - standalone
                  Format   [5Ch][Byt1][5Ch]

[Byt1] is a left-right offset of the even page in column units. This is a 2-byte field.

Figure   **113d/71h**
                  Description   figure heading - paired, standalone
                  Format   [71h][Byt1][S][Byt2] . . . [Byt5][71h]

[Byt1], [Byt2], [Byt3] are 3-byte fields.

[Byt4] and [Byt5] are 4-byte fields.

This field permits applying a label to a figure within a document. [Byt1] through [Byt5] may be set to space-led ASCII zero (30h). The program will fill in appropriate values.

File__ID   **32d/20h**
                  Description   formatted file identification
                  Format   [20h][STR1][S][STR2][S][Byt1][20h]

[STR1] is the version number. This is a 15-byte field with all hard-spaces converted to FFh. The valid string for this version is "WS2000[S]1.00[S][S][S][S]".

[STR2] is the printer identifier. This is a 15-byte field with all hard-spaces converted to FFh. The default is "*NONE*[S][S][S][S][S][S][S][S]". WS2000 rewrites this field on closing and the value doesn't matter on opening.

[Byt1] is the formatted line count. This is a pointer to the last formatted line of the document. This field is a 6-byte field. WS2000 fills in this parameter. A file prepared for use with WS2000 should contain 5 space characters (20h) and an ASCII zero (30h).

File__ID must be the first sequence in the file.

Font   **28d/1Ch**
                  Description   select font
                  Format   [1Ch][Byt1][S][Byt2][1Ch]

[Byt1] is the previous font number. This is a 2-byte number in ASCII characters used as index into font information.

[Byt2] is the subsequent font number. This is a 2-byte number in ASCII characters.

This field must be preceded by a hard line character (0Ah). The correspondence of numbers to actual fonts selected depends on the printer identifier selected for the file. As a rule, Font 0 is "almost always" a 10 point, non-proportional font, and Font 1 is "almost always" a 12 point font. Selecting Font 0 will usually result in a "reasonable" effect, according to MicroPro.

FootBoth **69d/45h**
Description both-page footer - standalone
Format [45h][Byt1][S][Byt2][S][Byt3][S][Byt4][S][Byt5][45h]

[Byt1] represents the previous header or footer vertical dots ("Most of the time," according to MicroPro). This is a 3-byte field, expressed as ASCII.

[Byt2] is the previous header or footer in vertical dots. This is a 3-byte field.

[Byt3] is the number of lines in the footer just crossed, plus one. This is a 3-byte field.

[Byt4] is the number of vertical dots in the footer just crossed. This is a 4-byte field.

[Byt5] is the number of vertical dots on the page so far (including the footer just crossed). This is a 4-byte field.

The FootBoth field indicates text to be printed within the bottom margin on both even- and odd-numbered pages. It must be the last sequence before TOP if it exists.

As already stated, a discussion of printer points and the vertical dot structure of a document is beyond the scope of this reference book. MicroPro advises that these fields may be safely set to space character-led zeros, and that the WS2000 program will update them correctly after the file has been loaded. If the Footer information is present, the paired sequence will contain a ruler line and one text line with a least "%PAGE%" on the line.

FootEven **67d/43h**
Description even page footer - standalone
Format [43h][Byt1][S][Byt2][S][Byt3][S][Byt4][S][Byt5][43h]

[Byt1] represents the previous header or footer vertical dots ("Most of the time," according to MicroPro). This is a 3-byte field, expressed as ASCII.

[Byt2] is the previous header or footer in vertical dots. This is a 3-byte field.

[Byt3] is the number of lines in the footer just crossed, plus one. This is a 3-byte field.

[Byt4] is the number of vertical dots in the footer just crossed. This is a 4-byte field.

[Byt5] is the number of vertical dots on the page so far (including the footer just crossed). This is a 4-byte field.

The FootEven field only appears in conjunction with the FootOdd field. It indicates the text to be printed within the bottom margin on even numbered pages.

FootNote **26d/1Ah**
Description end note - paired
Format [1Ah][Byt1][S][Byt2] . . . [Byt5][1Ah]

[Byt1], [Byt2], and [Byt3] are 3-byte fields.

[Byt4] and [Byt5] are 4-byte fields.

FootNote indicates text to be printed at the end of the document. WS2000 automatically numbers footnotes. MicroPro advises that WS2000 automatically fills the five fields in FootNote. In documents prepared for use with WS2000, these fields should be set to space-led ASCII zeros.

FootOdd **68d/44h**
Description odd page footer - standalone
Format [44h][Byt1][S][Byt2][S][Byt3][S][Byt4][S][Byt5][44h]

[Byt1] represents the previous header or footer vertical dots ("Most of the time," according to MicroPro). This is a 3-byte field, expressed in ASCII.

[Byt2] is the previous header or footer in vertical dots. This is a 3-byte field.

[Byt3] is the number of lines in the footer just crossed, plus one. This is a 3-byte field.

[Byt4] is the number of vertical dots in the footer just crossed. This is a 4-byte field.

[Byt5] is the number of vertical dots on the page so far (including the footer just crossed). This is a 4-byte field.

The FootOdd field indicates text to be printed within the bottom margin on odd numbered pages.

FootEven and FootOdd must be used together on alternating numbered pages. They must be the last two sequences before TOP if they exist.

Footoff **95d/5Fh**
Description footer offset - standalone
Format [5Fh][Byt1][5Fh]

[Byt1] is the footer offset in number of lines. This is a 3-byte field, expressed in ASCII. This field indicates the number of lines from the bottom of the page up to the last line of printed text.

HardPage   **71d/47h**
                      Description   hard (forced) page break
                      Format   [47h][Byt1][S][Byt2]...[Byt4][47h]

[Byt1] is the number of print lines on the previous page. This is a 3-byte field.

[Byt2] is the number of dots consumed on the page. This is a 4-byte field.

[Byt3] is the number of dots available on the page. This is a 4-byte field.

[Byt4] is used as a flag set if printed characters have been crossed. This is a 1-byte field.

WS2000 will set these fields itself when a file is loaded.

HeadBoth   **66d/42h**
                      Description   both page header - paired, standalone
                      Format   [42h][Byt1][S][Byt2] . . . [Byt5][42h]

[Byt1], [Byt2], and [Byt3] are 3-byte fields.

[Byt4] and [Byt5] are 4-byte fields.

HeadBoth indicates text to be printed within the top margin on both even and odd numbered pages. WS2000 should set these fields to the correct values when the file is loaded.

HeadEven   **62d/40h**
                      Description   even page header - paired, standalone
                      Format   [40h][Byt1][S][Byt2] . . . [Byt5][40h]

[Byt1], [Byt2], and [Byt3] are 3-byte fields.

[Byt4] and [Byt5] are 4-byte fields.

HeadEven indicates text to be printed within the top margin on even numbered pages. WS2000 should set these fields to the correct values when the file is loaded.

HeadOdd   **65d/41h**
                      Description   odd page header - paired, standalone
                      Format   [41h][Byt1][S][Byt2] . . . [Byt5][41h]

[Byt1], [Byt2], and [Byt3] are 3-byte fields.

[Byt4] and [Byt5] are 4-byte fields.

HeadOdd indicates text to be printed within the top margin on odd-numbered pages. WS2000 should set these fields to the correct values when the file is loaded.

Headoff   **94d/5Eh**
                    Description   header offset - standalone
                    Format   [5Eh][Byt1][5Eh]

[Byt1] is the header offset in number of lines. This is a 3-byte field, expressed in ASCII.

For a 6-line offset, the three bytes will hold two ASCII space characters (20h) and an ASCII "6" (36h). This sequence indicates the number of lines from the top of page to the first line of printed text.

Height   **105d/69h**
                    Description   select line height - standalone
                    Format   [69h][Byt1][S][Byt2][69h]

[Byt1] is the previous line height. This is a 2-byte field used as an index into an array of line heights.

[Byt2] is the subsequent line height. This is a 2-byte field.

WS2000 uses "printer points" to place text graphically on the page. A discussion of printer points is beyond the scope of this handbook. Documents prepared for use with WS2000 can safely replace both these 2-byte parameters with the bytes: [20h][30h] (space and zero). WordStar 2000 will alter the parameters internally.

IHyphen   **31d/1Fh**
                    Description   invisible soft hyphen
                    Format   [1Fh]

A soft hyphen is inserted by the program during formatting. It may be removed automatically if the format changes.

Index   **18d/12h**
                    Description   index entry
                    Format   [12h][STR1][S][STR2][S][STR3][12h]

[STR1] is the index entry text.

[STR2] is the index sub-entry text.

[STR3] is the boldface flag.

Index permits an entry and subentry to be entered into the index.

InsertF **81d/51h**
Description   insert file (mailmerge) - standalone
Format   [51h][STR1][51h]

[STR1] is the pathname of the file to insert. The maximum length is from 1 to 64 characters. InsertF selects the name of this file for insertion at print time.

Lev1Num **116d/74h**
Description   level-1 starting number (index) - standalone
Format   [74h][Byt1][74h]

[Byt1] determines the starting number for the first level-1 entry. This is a 1-byte ASCII character. Allowable values are from 0 to 9.

Level1 **107d/6Bh**
Description   level-1 heading - paired, standalone
Format   [6Bh][Byt1][S][Byt2] . . . [Byt5][6Bh]

[Byt1], [Byt2], and [Byt3] are 3-byte fields.

[Byt4] and [Byt5] are 4-byte fields.

Level1 brackets the description of the first level of section headings.

Level2 **108d/6Ch**
Description   level-2 heading - paired, standalone
Format   [6Ch][Byt1][S][Byt2] . . . [Byt5][6Ch]

[Byt1], [Byt2], and [Byt3] are 3-byte fields.

[Byt4] and [Byt5] are 4-byte fields.

Level2 brackets the description of the second level of section headings.

Level3 **109d/6Dh**
Description   level-3 heading - paired, standalone
Format   [6Dh][Byt1][S][Byt2] . . . [Byt5][6Dh]

[Byt1], [Byt2], and [Byt3] are 3-byte fields.

[Byt4] and [Byt5] are 4-byte fields.

Level3 brackets the description of the third level of section headings.

Level4 **110d/6Eh**
          Description   level-4 heading - paired, standalone
          Format   [6Eh][Byt1][S][Byt2] . . . [Byt5][6Eh]

[Byt1], [Byt2], and [Byt3] are 3-byte fields.

[Byt4] and [Byt5] are 4-byte fields.

Level4 brackets the description of the fourth level of section headings.

LIndent **20d/14h**
          Description   indent left side
          Format   [14h]

This field indents the left side to the next higher tabstop.

LPerPage **97d/61h**
          Description   lines per page - standalone
          Format   [61h][Byt1][61h]

[Byt1] is the number of lines per page. This is a 2-byte field.

A usual value for this field is 66, handled as two bytes each containing the value 36h (ASCII character "6").

LUndent **22d/16h**
          Description   un-indent left side
          Format   [16h]

This field deactivates one currently active left indent.

MarkPage **11d/0Bh**
          Description   mark page reference
          Format   [0Bh][STR1][0Bh]

[STR1] is the name of the page for reference.

MarkPage labels a page so that it may be referenced by name rather than by absolute page number.

Need **73d/49h**
          Description   group lines
          Format   [49h][Byt1][49h]

[Byt1] contains the number of lines to be kept together and not interrupted by a page break. This is a 1-byte field.

NonBreak **16d/10h**
             Description   non-break space
             Format   [10h]

   NonBreak prevents ending a line on this space and prevents automatically hyphenating words connected by the non-break spaces.

NxtCpy   **85d/55h**
             Description   next copy (mailmerge)
             Format   [55h]

   NxtCpy indicates end of a Repeat loop. It must be preceded by a Repeat command.

OddPOff **93d/5Dh**
             Description   odd page offset - standalone
             Format   [5Dh][Byt1][5Dh]

   [Byt1] is the left-right offset of the odd numbered pages in the column units. This is a 2-byte field.

Othrwis **83d/53h**
             Description   otherwise clause
             Format   [53h]

   This field specifies the start of text to be printed if the associated Cndshn command is FALSE.

Overprint **17d/11h**
             Description   overprint line
             Format   [11h]

   This field causes the current line to overprint the previous line.

PageNum **74d/4Ah**
             Description   set page number
             Format   [4Ah][Byt1][4Ah]

   [Byt1] sets the current page number to the specified value. This is a 1-byte field.

Pause   **14d/0Eh**
             Description   pause printing
             Format   [0Eh]

   This field makes the printer pause during printing.

ReadV **75d/46h**
Description   read value from data file (mailmerge)
Format   [46h][STR1][46h]

[STR1] is the name of the variable to load from the data file declared in the previous DataF sequence.

Refer **12d/0Ch**
Description   refer to page marker
Format   [0Ch][STR1][0Ch]

[STR1] is the name of the referenced page. This field inserts the correct page number for the referenced page, as marked by a MarkPage sequence.

Repeat **78d/4Eh**
Description   repeat printing (mailmerge) - standalone
Format   [4Eh][STR1][4Eh]

[STR1] contains a count of the number of times to repeat, or the string "$", which causes a repeat to the end of the current data file.

Ruler **91d/5Bh**
Description   new ruler line - standalone
Format   [5Bh][Byt1] . . . [Byt128][5Bh]

[Byt1] is the old left margin position in column units.
[Byt2] is the old right margin position in column units.
[Byt3] is the old first tab type (1 is normal, 2 is decimal).
[Byt4] is the old first tab position in column units.
[Byt5] is the old second tab type (1 is normal, 2 is decimal).
[Byt6] is the old second tab position in column units.
.
.
.

[Byt63] is the old 31st tab type (must be FFh).
[Byt64] is the old 31st tab position (must be FFh).
[Byt65] is the new left margin position in column units.
[Byt66] is the new right margin position in column units.
[Byt67] is the new first tab type (1 is normal, 2 is decimal).
[Byt68] is the new first tab position in column units.
[Byt69] is the new second tab type.
[Byt70] is the new second tab position in column units.
.
.
.

[Byt127] is the new 31st tab type (must be FFh).
[Byt128] is the new 31st tab position (must be FFh).

Up to 30 tabstops may be set. Unused tabstops are set to FFh. Ruler sequences are 128 bytes long.

SetV **77d/4Dh**
Description   set variable (mailmerge) - standalone
Format   [4Dh][STR1][S][STR2][4Dh]

[STR1] is the name of the variable.

[STR2] is the value to which the variable is set.

SoftHyphen **30d/1Eh**
Description   soft hyphen
Format   [1Eh]

This field indicates a soft hyphen entered by the user. It may become active or inactive if the format changes. The soft hyphen is not removed during reformatting.

Softline **03d/03h**
Description   soft line end
Format   [03h]

Indicates the end of a line of text, but not the end of a paragraph. The softline is inserted and deleted during reformatting.

SoftPage **72d/48h**
Description   soft page break - standalone
Format   [48h][Byt1][S][Byt2]...[Byt4][48h]

[Byt1] is the number of print lines on the previous page. This is a 3-byte field.

[Byt2] is the number of dots consumed on the page. This is a 4-byte field.

[Byt3] is the number of dots available on the page. This is a 4-byte field.

[Byt4] is used as a flag. It is set if printed characters have been crossed. This is a 1-byte field.

This field indicates a page break has been inserted by the program to show page accounting. The reformatting process may insert or delete the softpage break.

SoftSpace 02d/02h
      Description   soft space
      Format   [02h][Byt1][Byt2][02h]
      [Byt1] is a 1-byte field.
      [Byt2] is a 1-byte field.

A softspace is a space inserted by the program (usually for right-left justification) during reformatting. In files prepared for use with WS2000, the contents of the two bytes should be binary NULLs (00h). The program will insert soft spaces as needed.

StrikeOut 10d/0Ah
      Description   strikeout toggle
      Format   [0Ah]
      This field toggles printing of strikeout characters ("-") over current text.

Sub 08d/08h
      Description   subscript toggle
      Format   [08h]
      This field toggles printing of subscript text.

Super 09d/09h
      Description   superscript toggle
      Format   [09h]
      This field toggles printing of superscript text.

Table 114d/72h
      Description   table of contents title - paired and standalone
      Format   [72h][Byt1][S][Byt2] . . . [Byt5][72h]
      [Byt1], [Byt2], and [Byt3] are each 3-byte fields of ASCII characters.
      [Byt4] and [Byt5] are each 4-byte fields of ASCII characters.

Table specifies text used to label the table of contents. The five fields are set by the program after the file is loaded.

TFormFeed 24d/18h
      Description   form-feed toggle - format block only
      Format   [18h]
      This field indicates that form feeds are not to be used during printing.

THyphen   **101d/65h**
                 Description   toggle hyphen - format block only
                 Format   [65h][Byt1][65h]

                 [Byt1] sets automatic hyphenation mode. This is a 1-byte field, found only in the format block. 1 is hyphenation on; 0 is hyphenation off.

TJustify   **98d/62h**
                 Description   set justification - standalone
                 Format   [62h][Byt1][Byt2][62h]

                 [Byt1] is the previous justification selected. This is a 1-byte field.

                 [Byt2] is the subsequent justification selected. This is a 1-byte field. 1 is justification on; 0 is justification off.

TOP   **118d/76h**
                 Description   top of editable portion marker
                 Format   [76h]

                 TOP marks the end of the format block and the beginning of the text.

TPageBreak   **103d/67h**
                 Description   page break display
                 Format   [67h][Byt1][67h]

                 [Byt1] sets the status of the page break display. This is a 1-byte field found only in the format block. 1 is display page breaks; 0 is no display.

Tray   **106d/6Ah**
                 Description   select sheet feeder tray
                 Format   [6Ah][Byt1][S][Byt2][6Ah]

                 [Byt1] is the forward sheet feeder tray select. This is a 2-byte field.

                 [Byt2] is the reverse sheet feeder tray select. This is a 2-byte field.

This field selects the paper tray for the sheet feeder. Not implemented in Version 1.00 or 1.01d.

TSpell   **99d/63h**
                 Description   toggle spelling corrector - standalone
                 Format   [63h][Byt1][S][Byt2][63h]

                 [Byt1] is the forward spelling toggle. This is a 1-byte field.

                 [Byt2] is the reverse spelling toggle. This is a 1-byte field.

This field causes the spelling corrector to skip a portion of the document.

TUndGaps   **102d/66h**
                  Description   set underline - format block only
                  Format   [66h][Byt1][66h]

[Byt1] is the field that sets the flag that makes the program underline word gaps. This is a 1-byte field. 1 is set; 0 is not set.

Underline   **06d/06h**
                  Description   toggles underlining
                  Format   [06h]

This field turns underlining on and off.

Table 11.1 WordStar 2000 Command Codes

Dec	Hex	Command	Dec	Hex	Command
01	01	Unused	65	41	HeadOdd (Odd number page header)
02	02	Softspace			
03	03	Softline feed	66	42	HeadBoth (header on both pages)
04	04	Unused			
05	05	Boldface toggle	67	43	FootEven
06	06	Underline toggle	68	44	FootOdd
07	07	Doublestrike toggle	69	45	FootBoth
08	08	Subscript toggle	70	46	Comment
09	09	Superscript toggle	71	47	HardPage (forced page break)
10	0A	Strikeout toggle	72	48	SoftPage
11	0B	Markpage	73	49	Need (Mailmerge)
12	0C	Refer	74	4A	PageNum
13	0D	Unused	75	4B	ReadV (Mailmerge)
14	0E	Pause	76	4C	DataF (datafile—mailmerge)
15	0F	Unused			
16	10	Overstrike	77	4D	SetV (Mailmerge)
17	11	Overprint	78	4E	Repeat (Mailmerge)
18	12	Index	79	4F	AskV (Mailmerge)
19	13	Center text	80	50	Disp (Mailmerge)
20	14	Left indent (Lindent)	81	51	InsertF (Mailmerge)
21	15	Both sides indent (Bindent)	82	52	Cndshn (Mailmerge)
22	16	Left Unindent (Lundent)	83	53	Othrwis (Mailmerge)
23	17	Both Unindent (Bundent)	84	54	EndCnd (Mailmerge)
24	18	TFormfeed—format block	85	55	NxtCpy
25	19	Unused	. . .		Codes between these numbers are unused in this version
26	1A	Footnote			
27	1B	Unused	91	5B	Ruler—format block and text
28	1C	Font			
29	1D	Color (ribbon)	92	5C	EvenPOff (even page offset)—format block
30	1E	Soft hyphen			
31	1F	IHyphen	93	5D	OddPOff—format block
32	20	File_ID—format block	94	5E	HeadOff (header offset)—format block
33	21	Unused . . .			
.		codes between these numbers are unused in this version	95	5F	FootOff—format block
.			96	60	Unused
			97	61	LPerPage (lines per page)—format block
64	40	HeadEven (even number page header)			

(continued)

Table 11.1 Continued

Dec	Hex	Command	Dec	Hex	Command
98	62	TJustify (justify)—format block and text	110	6E	Level4
			111	6F	Appendix
99	63	TSpell	112	70	Contents
100	64	Unused	113	71	Figure
101	65	THyphen—format block	114	72	Table
102	66	TUndGaps—format block	115	73	Unused
103	67	TPageBreak—format block	116	74	LevlNum
104	68	Unused	117	75	Unused
105	69	Height	118	76	Top—format block
106	6A	Tray	.		Codes between these numbers are unused in this version
107	6B	Level1	.		
108	6C	Level2			
109	6D	Level3	127	7F	Attention Character (lead-in char.)

Table 11.2 Program Limitations and Specifications

Disk storage	Minimum two 360kb floppy disks
Maximum file size	8,192,000 bytes
Maximum length of line in formatted file	240 columns (24 inches)
Range of top or bottom margin in format	0 to 500 lines
Right margin range	10 to 240 columns
Left margin range	1 to 70 columns
Number of lines per page	3 to 500
Even or odd page offset	0 to 132 columns
Number of lines that can be kept together	2 to 100 lines
Minimum page width	10 columns
Maximum number of colors, line heights or fonts	8

APPENDIXES

Introduction

A number of the programs covered in this Reference Guide have particularly complex file formats. While the byte offset documentation may be enough for most programmers, it can help to look at selected printouts from time to time.

As a spreadsheet sample, a fairly simple principal and interest calculation is used (see Sample 1). As a word-processing sample, most of the first two paragraphs of the Gettysburg Address was used (see Sample 2). As a control procedure, each sample was formatted the same way.

Only format printout for files that were complex, particularly interesting, or that required illustration for easier understanding are reproduced here. (The printout for the sample Lotus 1-2-3 file went on for 72 pages!) The original printouts were created by *Mr. Peepers*, a file reader/editor. The source code for creating the printouts is included in Appendix C. A more complete version is included with the software package that can be ordered with the business reply card in this book.

144 File Formats for Popular PC Software

```
              1           2           3           4              5           6           7           8
   1
   2                                            PAYMENT ANALYSIS WORKSHEET
                                                ==========================
   3  LOAN AMT  $4,800.00
   4  INTEREST     18.50%
   5  MO PMT     $174.73
   6  PERIODS         36
   7
   8  ------------------------------------------------------------------------------
   9  PMT NO    INT PD    PRC PD    REMAIN BAL  INT TO DATE  PRC TO DATE  PAID TO DATE
  10  ------------------------------------------------------------------------------
  11     1     $74.00   $100.73    $4,699.27       $74.00      $100.73      $174.73
  12     2     $72.45   $102.28    $4,596.99      $146.45      $203.01      $349.46
  13     3     $70.87   $103.86    $4,493.13      $217.32      $306.87      $524.19
```

Sample 1 Simple principal and interest calculation used as a control for spreadsheet programs.

The Gettysburg Address

Fourscore and seven years ago our fathers brought forth on this continent, a new nation, conceived in <u>Liberty</u>, and dedicated to the proposition that all men are created equal.

Now we are engaged in a great civil war, testing whether that nation or any nation so conceived and so dedicated can long endure. We are met on a great battlefield of that war. We have come to dedicate a portion of that field, as a final resting place for those who here gave their lives that that nation might live. It is altogether fitting and proper that we do this.

Sample 2 A portion of the Gettysburg address used as a control for word-processing programs.

APPENDIX A

Converting Data Files from One Format to Another

All the native file formats documented in this book have one thing in common: each is the most appropriate format for its particular program. Each is unique. The Lotus programs have their opcodes, Multimate has its header and page map, Plans+ divides a model into two files.

Because each file format is unique, converting one native file into another involves more than transferring row and column spreadsheet numbers into a table in a word processing program. You must create any required headers or footers, translate any formulas, and translate and carry over any formatting commands. You may need to ignore or create other information, depending on the two programs involved.

The file format specifications in this book should help you find those "points of congruency" where the information of one program can be translated directly into the information of another. As a simplistic example, Symphony, Ability, Multimate, WordStar and Wordstar 2000 all have a command to create boldface type.

These file specifications should also help you determine where information must be created or ignored. For example, not all the information in a Symphony window record will translate directly into Multiplan, even though both programs permit multiple windows.

Two Methods of Conversion

There are two basic methods to use when converting a source file format to a target file format. For convenience, we'll call these the *parsing method* and the *filter method* (although both involve parsing and filtering).

Parsing

The parsing method takes advantage of large personal computer memory to read an entire source file into memory. Once the source file is in memory, the conversion program reads through it (parses it) and writes it out to disk in the target format.

While it does require a large amount of memory, this method has the advantage that differences in file organization from source to target don't matter. The parser "knows" it's looking for the source-equivalent of the first item it must write to the target file, finds that item somewhere in the source, writes it to disk, and goes on to the next item to be looked for. Other advantages to the parsing method are speed and a minimum of disk accessing.

The disadvantage is that the source file *must* fit in memory. This is not too much of a disadvantage, considering the current size of PC memory. Despite the fact that spreadsheet templates have a tendency to butt up against memory limitations, on any individual machine, *if there's room enough for a spreadsheet program and its file, there should be room enough for a conversion program and the same file.*

Filter Method

The filter method is best when source and target are already very much alike, or when memory limitations are especially stringent. When source and target are alike, the filter conversion program reads the source and translates "on the fly" into the target. Conversion between WordStar and Ability can work this way; the files are nearly identical, and use most of the same formatting codes in the same ways.

It's obvious, though, that this type of conversion between an involved Multiplan model and Symphony would not be easy. The differences in file organization between the two programs require a temporary file either in memory or on disk to hold a stack. If memory is limited, a temporary file must be set up on disk.

The advantage of the filter method is its ability to work in limited memory; but it becomes more complicated the more dissimilar the source and target files are.

In both cases, we can sum up the technique this way:

- Find the congruencies (cell coordinates, formulas, formatting codes).
- Find what must be ignored (headers, untranslatable formats, complex window records, sub-application names, etc.).
- Find what must be created as required information in the target file and then create it (headers with key names, rulers, global formatting commands).
- Write the target file as completely as possible.

Conversion Made Easier

Wiley Professional Software produces a companion package to this book called *File Formats*. The package contains programs that handle the spreadsheet-to-spreadsheet and word processor-to-word processor file conversions for programs that are documented in this book. It also contains a program, called *Mr. Peepers*, which is used for reading and editing files, and was used to produce the sample file outputs in this appendix.

APPENDIX B

Sample Spreadsheet Files

Sample Spreadsheet in Lotus 1-2-3 .WKS File
Gettysburg Address as a Symphony DOC File
Sample Spreadsheet as an Ability File
Gettysburg Address as an Ability File
Lincoln's Gettysburg Address as a MultiMate File
Sample File in SYLK Format as an ASCII Dump
Sample Spreadsheet as an IBM Plans+ .~MD File
Sample Spreadsheet as an IBM Plans+ .~MF File
Gettysburg Address as a WordStar File
Gettyburg Address as a WordStar 2000 File

Sample Spreadsheet in Lotus 1-2-3.WKS File

BYTE	0	1	2	3	4	5	6	7	8	9	10	11	12	13	14	15
HEX	00	00	02	00	04	04	06	00	08	00	00	00	00	00	06	00
DEC	0	0	2	0	4	4	6	0	8	0	0	0	0	0	6	0
ASC	^@	^@	^B	^@	^D	^D	^F	^@	^H	^@	^@	^@	^@	^@	^F	^@
ALT SYM	NUL	NUL	STX	NUL	EOT	EOT	ACK	NUL	BS	NUL	NUL	NUL	NUL	NUL	ACK	NUL

| | BOF | Lenght=2 Bytes | 1028 (1-2-3 File) | Range | Length-8 Bytes | Starting Col=A | Starting Row=1 | Ending Col=F |

BYTE	16	17	18	19	20	21	22	23	24	25	26	27	28	29	30	31
HEX	C7	00	2F	00	01	00	01	02	00	01	00	FF	03	00	01	00
DEC	199	0	47	0	1	0	1	2	0	1	0	255	3	0	1	0
ASC	199	^@		^@	^A	^@	^A	^B	^@	^A	^@	255	^C	^@	^A	^@
ALT SYM	199	NUL	/	NUL	SOH	NUL	SOH	STX	NUL	SOH	NUL	255	ETX	NUL	SOH	NUL

| Ending Row=200 | Calc Count | 1 Byte long | Iteration | Calc mode | 1 Byte long | Auto mode | Calc order | 1 Byte long |

BYTE	32	33	34	35	36	37	38	39	40	41	42	43	44	45	46	47
HEX	00	04	00	01	00	00	05	00	01	00	FF	07	00	1F	00	00
DEC	0	4	0	1	0	0	5	0	1	0	255	7	0	31	0	0
ASC	^@	^D	^@	^A	^@	^@	^E	^@	^A	^@	255	^G	^@	^_	^@	^@
ALT SYM	NUL	EOT	NUL	SOH	NUL	NUL	ENQ	NUL	SOH	NUL	255	BEL	NUL	US	NUL	NUL

| Nat. Calc. Order | Window Split | 1 Byte long | Not Split | Split Window Synch | 1 Byte long | Synch | Window 1 | 31 Bytes Long | Cursor |

BYTE	48	49	50	51	52	53	54	55	56	57	58	59	60	61	62	63
HEX	00	00	00	02	00	0C	00	06	00	14	00	00	00	00	00	00
DEC	0	0	0	2	0	12	0	6	0	20	0	0	0	0	0	0
ASC	^@	^@	^@	^B	^@	^L	^@	^F	^@	^T	^@	^@	^@	^@	^@	^@
ALT SYM	NUL	NUL	NUL	STX	NUL	FF	NUL	ACK	NUL	DC4	NUL	NUL	NUL	NUL	NUL	NUL

| At A | Cursor at Row 1 | FMT 2 Dec. Place | Unused | Column Width | No. Cols. on Screen | No. Rows on Screen | Left Col. A | Top Row 1 | No. Title Cols. |

BYTE	64	65	66	67	68	69	70	71	72	73	74	75	76	77	78	79
HEX	00	00	00	00	00	05	00	04	00	04	00	48	00	09	08	00
DEC	0	0	0	0	0	5	0	4	0	4	0	72	0	9	8	0
ASC	^@	^@	^@	^@	^@	^E	^@	^D	^@	^D	^@		^@	^I	^H	^@
ALT SYM	NUL	NUL	NUL	NUL	NUL	ENQ	NUL	EOT	NUL	EOT	NUL	H	NUL	HT	BS	NUL

| No. Title Cols. | No. Title Rows | Left Title Column | Top Title Row | Border Width Col. | Border Width Row | Window Width | Unused | Col. Width |

LOTUS 1-2-3   **153**

BYTE	80	81	82	83	84	85	86	87	88	89	90	91	92	93	94	95
HEX	03	00	00	00	09	08	00	03	00	01	00	0A	08	00	03	00
DEC	3	0	0	0	9	8	0	3	0	1	0	10	8	0	3	0
ASC	^C	^@	^@	^@	^I	^H	^@	^C	^@	^A	^@	^J	^H	^@	^C	^@
ALT SYM	ETX	NUL	NUL	NUL	HT	BS	NUL	ETX	NUL	SOH	NUL	LF	BS	NUL	ETX	NUL

|← 3 Bytes Long →|← Column A →|← Width →|← Column Width →|← 3 Bytes Long →|← Column B →|← Width →|← Column Width →|← 3 Bytes Long →|

BYTE	96	97	98	99	100	101	102	103	104	105	106	107	108	109	110	111
HEX	02	00	0A	08	00	03	00	04	00	0D	08	00	03	00	05	00
DEC	2	0	10	8	0	3	0	4	0	13	8	0	3	0	5	0
ASC	^B	^@	^J	^H	^@	^C	^@	^D	^@	^M	^H	^@	^C	^@	^E	^@
ALT SYM	STX	NUL	LF	BS	NUL	ETX	NUL	EOT	NUL	CR	BS	NUL	ETX	NUL	ENQ	NUL

|← Column C →|← Width →|← Column Width →|← 3 Bytes Long →|← Column E →|← Width →|← Column Width →|← 3 Bytes Long →|← Column F →|

BYTE	112	113	114	115	116	117	118	119	120	121	122	123	124	125	126	127
HEX	0E	08	00	03	00	06	00	0E	18	00	19	00	00	FF	FF	00
DEC	14	8	0	3	0	6	0	14	24	0	25	0	0	255	255	0
ASC	^N	^H	^@	^C	^@	^F	^@	^N	^X	^@	^Y	^@	^@	255	255	^@
ALT SYM	SO	BS	NUL	ETX	NUL	ACK	NUL	SO	CAN	NUL	EM	NUL	NUL	255	255	NUL

|← Width →|← Column Width →|← 3 Bytes long →|← Column G →|← Width →| Table Range | 25 Bytes long | No Table | Starting Col. | Starting Row |

BYTE	128	129	130	131	132	133	134	135	136	137	138	139	140	141	142	143
HEX	00	FF	FF	00	00	FF	FF	00	00	FF	FF	00	00	FF	FF	00
DEC	0	255	255	0	0	255	255	0	0	255	255	0	0	255	255	0
ASC	^@	255	255	^@	^@	255	255	^@	^@	255	255	^@	^@	255	255	^@
ALT SYM	NUL	255	255	NUL	NUL	255	255	NUL	NUL	255	255	NUL	NUL	255	255	NUL

| Starting Row | Ending Col. | Ending Row | Input Cell 1 Starting Col. | Input Cell 1 Starting Row | Input Cell 1 Ending Col. | Input Cell 1 Ending Row | Input Cell 2 Starting Col. | Input Cell 2 → |

BYTE	144	145	146	147	148	149	150	151	152	153	154	155	156	157	158	159
HEX	00	FF	FF	00	00	19	00	19	00	FF	FF	00	00	FF	FF	00
DEC	0	255	255	0	0	25	0	25	0	255	255	0	0	255	255	0
ASC	^@	255	255	^@	^@	^Y	^@	^Y	^@	255	255	^@	^@	255	255	^@
ALT SYM	NUL	255	255	NUL	NUL	EM	NUL	EM	NUL	255	255	NUL	NUL	255	255	NUL

| Start Row | Input Cell 2 End Col. | Input Cell 2 End Row | Query Range | 25 Bytes long | Input Range Start Col. | Input Range Start Row | Input Range End Col. | Input Range → |

BYTE	160	161	162	163	164	165	166	167	168	169	170	171	172	173	174	175
HEX	00	FF	FF	00	00	FF	FF	00	00	FF	FF	00	00	FF	FF	00
DEC	0	255	255	0	0	255	255	0	0	255	255	0	0	255	255	0
ASC	^@	255	255	^@	^@	255	255	^@	^@	255	255	^@	^@	255	255	^@
ALT SYM	NUL	255	255	NUL	NUL	255	255	NUL	NUL	255	255	NUL	NUL	255	255	NUL

| End Row | Output Range Start Col. | Output Range Start Row | Output Range End Col. | Output range End Row | Criteria Start Col. | Criteria Start Row | Criteria End Col. | Criteria End Row |

154 LOTUS 1-2-3

BYTE	176	177	178	179	180	181	182	183	184	185	186	187	188	189	190	191
HEX	00	00	1A	00	08	00	FF	FF	00	00	FF	FF	00	00	30	00
DEC	0	0	26	0	8	0	255	255	0	0	255	255	0	0	48	0
ASC	^@	^@	^Z	^@	^H	^@	255	255	^@	^@	255	255	^@	^@		^@
ALT	NUL	NUL	SUB	NUL	BS	NUL	255	255	NUL	NUL	255	255	NUL	NUL		NUL
SYM															0	

| Criteria End Row | Command | Print Range | 8 Bytes long | Start Col. | Start Row | End Col. | End Row | Unformatted Print |

.WKS File continues ... (not shown)

LOTUS 1-2-3   **155**

Gettysburg Address as a Symphony File

BYTE	0	1	2	3	4	5	6	7	8	9	10	11	12	13	14	15
HEX	00	00	02	00	05	04	06	00	08	00	00	00	00	00	00	00
DEC	0	0	2	0	5	4	6	0	8	0	0	0	0	0	0	0
ASC	^@	^@	^B	^@	^E	^D	^F	^@	^H	^@	^@	^@	^@	^@	^@	^@
ALT	NUL	NUL	STX	NUL	ENQ	EOT	ACK	NUL	BS	NUL	NUL	NUL	NUL	NUL	NUL	NUL
SYM																

| Beginning of File | 2 Bytes long | 1029=Symphony | Range | 8 Bytes long | Start Col. | Start Row | End Col. |

BYTE	16	17	18	19	20	21	22	23	24	25	26	27	28	29	30	31
HEX	0C	00	2F	00	01	00	01	02	00	01	00	FF	03	00	01	00
DEC	12	0	47	0	1	0	1	2	0	1	0	255	3	0	1	0
ASC	^L	^@		^@	^A	^@	^A	^B	^@	^A	^@	255	^C	^@	^A	^@
ALT	FF	NUL		NUL	SOH	NUL	SOH	STX	NUL	SOH	NUL	255	ETX	NUL	SOH	NUL
SYM			/													

| End Row | Calc Count | Count 1 Byte | Count | Calc Mode | 1 Byte long | Automatic | Calc Order | 1 Byte long |

BYTE	32	33	34	35	36	37	38	39	40	41	42	43	44	45	46	47
HEX	00	44	00	02	00	19	00	45	00	02	00	50	00	32	00	90
DEC	0	68	0	2	0	25	0	69	0	2	0	80	0	50	0	144
ASC	^@		^@	^B	^@	^Y	^@		^@	^B	^@		^@		^@	144
ALT	NUL		NUL	STX	NUL	EM	NUL		NUL	STX	NUL		NUL		NUL	144
SYM		D						E				P		2		

| Natural | No. Screen Rows | 2 Bytes long | 19 Rows | No. Screen Cols. | 2 Bytes long | 50 Cols. | Window Record | 144 Bytes |

BYTE	48	49	50	51	52	53	54	55	56	57	58	59	60	61	62	63
HEX	00	4C	4F	47	41	00	00	00	00	00	00	00	00	00	00	00
DEC	0	76	79	71	65	0	0	0	0	0	0	0	0	0	0	0
ASC	^@					^@	^@	^@	^@	^@	^@	^@	^@	^@	^@	^@
ALT	NUL					NUL	NUL	NUL	NUL	NUL	NUL	NUL	NUL	NUL	NUL	NUL
SYM		L	O	G	A											

←─────────────────── Window Name ───────────────────→

BYTE	64	65	66	67	68	69	70	71	72	73	74	75	76	77	78	79
HEX	00	02	00	00	00	71	00	09	00	08	00	14	00	00	00	00
DEC	0	2	0	0	0	113	0	9	0	8	0	20	0	0	0	0
ASC	^@	^B	^@	^@	^@		^@	^I	^@	^H	^@	^T	^@	^@	^@	^@
ALT	NUL	STX	NUL	NUL	NUL		NUL	HT	NUL	BS	NUL	DC4	NUL	NUL	NUL	NUL
SYM						q										

| Cursor Col. | Cursor Row | Format Cell | Unused | Col. Width | Total No. Cols. | Total No. Rows | Non-Title Col. | Non-Title Row |

156 SYMPHONY

BYTE	80	81	82	83	84	85	86	87	88	89	90	91	92	93	94	95
HEX	00	00	00	00	00	00	00	00	00	00	00	02	00	50	00	16
DEC	0	0	0	0	0	0	0	0	0	0	0	2	0	80	0	22
ASC	^@	^@	^@	^@	^@	^@	^@	^@	^@	^@	^@	^B	^@		^@	^V
ALT	NUL	NUL	NUL	NUL	NUL	NUL	NUL	NUL	NUL	NUL	NUL	STX	NUL		NUL	SYN
SYM														P		

	No. Title Cols.	No. Title Rows	Left Title Col.	Top Title Row	Home Position Col.	Home Position Row	No. Screen Cols.	No. Screen Rows

BYTE	96	97	98	99	100	101	102	103	104	105	106	107	108	109	110	111
HEX	00	FF	01	FF	FF	00	00	00	00	08	00	FF	1F	07	00	FF
DEC	0	255	1	255	255	0	0	0	0	8	0	255	31	7	0	255
ASC	^@	255	^A	255	255	^@	^@	^@	^@	^H	^@	255	^_	^G	^@	255
ALT	NUL	255	SOH	255	255	NUL	NUL	NUL	NUL	BS	NUL	255	US	BEL	NUL	255
SYM																

	Not Hidden	Prev. Wind.	No Cell Border	No Line Border	Window Range Start Col.	Window Range Start Row	Window Range End Col.	Window Range End Row	Offset	Inset On

BYTE	112	113	114	115	116	117	118	119	120	121	122	123	124	125	126	127
HEX	4D	41	49	4E	00	00	00	00	00	00	00	00	00	00	00	00
DEC	77	65	73	78	0	0	0	0	0	0	0	0	0	0	0	0
ASC					^@	^@	^@	^@	^@	^@	^@	^@	^@	^@	^@	^@
ALT					NUL	NUL	NUL	NUL	NUL	NUL	NUL	NUL	NUL	NUL	NUL	NUL
SYM	M	A	I	N												

|←————————————————— Graph Name —————————————————→|

BYTE	128	129	130	131	132	133	134	135	136	137	138	139	140	141	142	143
HEX	01	61	FF	4D	41	49	4E	00	00	00	00	00	00	00	00	00
DEC	1	97	255	77	65	73	78	0	0	0	0	0	0	0	0	0
ASC	^A		255					^@	^@	^@	^@	^@	^@	^@	^@	^@
ALT	SOH		255					NUL	NUL	NUL	NUL	NUL	NUL	NUL	NUL	NUL
SYM		a		M	A	I	N									

| Window Type | Auto Display Mode | Forms Filter |←————————— Associated Form Name —————————→|

BYTE	144	145	146	147	148	149	150	151	152	153	154	155	156	157	158	159
HEX	00	00	00	00	00	00	31	65	40	00	00	00	05	00	01	01
DEC	0	0	0	0	0	0	49	101	64	0	0	0	5	0	1	1
ASC	^@	^@	^@	^@	^@	^@				^@	^@	^@	^E	^@	^A	^A
ALT	NUL	NUL	NUL	NUL	NUL	NUL				NUL	NUL	NUL	ENQ	NUL	SOH	SOH
SYM							1	e	@							

	Forms Current Rec.	Space Displ.	Line Space	Justify Type	Right Margin	Left Margin	Tab Interval	CR Displ.	Auto Just.

BYTE	160	161	162	163	164	165	166	167	168	169	170	171	172	173	174	175
HEX	00	00	00	00	00	00	00	00	00	00	00	00	00	00	00	00
DEC	0	0	0	0	0	0	0	0	0	0	0	0	0	0	0	0
ASC	^@	^@	^@	^@	^@	^@	^@	^@	^@	^@	^@	^@	^@	^@	^@	^@
ALT	NUL	NUL	NUL	NUL	NUL	NUL	NUL	NUL	NUL	NUL	NUL	NUL	NUL	NUL	NUL	NUL
SYM																

|←————————————————— Associated Application Name —————————————————→|

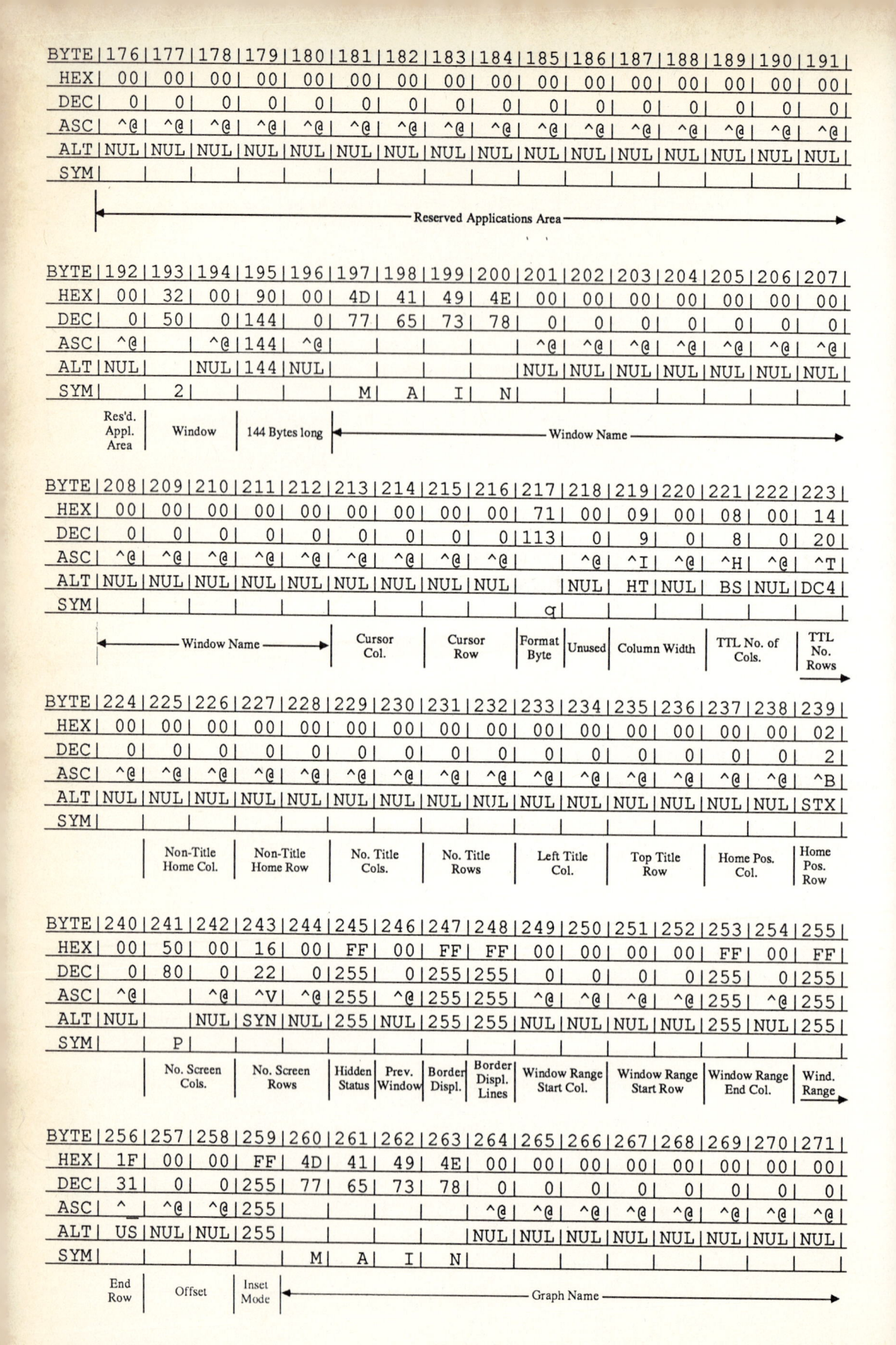

BYTE	176	177	178	179	180	181	182	183	184	185	186	187	188	189	190	191
HEX	00	00	00	00	00	00	00	00	00	00	00	00	00	00	00	00
DEC	0	0	0	0	0	0	0	0	0	0	0	0	0	0	0	0
ASC	^@	^@	^@	^@	^@	^@	^@	^@	^@	^@	^@	^@	^@	^@	^@	^@
ALT	NUL	NUL	NUL	NUL	NUL	NUL	NUL	NUL	NUL	NUL	NUL	NUL	NUL	NUL	NUL	NUL
SYM																

← ─────────────── Reserved Applications Area ─────────────── →

BYTE	192	193	194	195	196	197	198	199	200	201	202	203	204	205	206	207
HEX	00	32	00	90	00	4D	41	49	4E	00	00	00	00	00	00	00
DEC	0	50	0	144	0	77	65	73	78	0	0	0	0	0	0	0
ASC	^@		^@	144	^@					^@	^@	^@	^@	^@	^@	^@
ALT	NUL		NUL	144	NUL					NUL	NUL	NUL	NUL	NUL	NUL	NUL
SYM		2				M	A	I	N							

Res'd. Appl. Area | Window | 144 Bytes long | ← ──── Window Name ──── →

BYTE	208	209	210	211	212	213	214	215	216	217	218	219	220	221	222	223
HEX	00	00	00	00	00	00	00	00	00	71	00	09	00	08	00	14
DEC	0	0	0	0	0	0	0	0	0	113	0	9	0	8	0	20
ASC	^@	^@	^@	^@	^@	^@	^@	^@	^@		^@	^I	^@	^H	^@	^T
ALT	NUL	NUL	NUL	NUL	NUL	NUL	NUL	NUL	NUL		NUL	HT	NUL	BS	NUL	DC4
SYM										q						

← ─── Window Name ─── → | Cursor Col. | Cursor Row | Format Byte | Unused | Column Width | TTL No. of Cols. | TTL No. Rows

BYTE	224	225	226	227	228	229	230	231	232	233	234	235	236	237	238	239
HEX	00	00	00	00	00	00	00	00	00	00	00	00	00	00	00	02
DEC	0	0	0	0	0	0	0	0	0	0	0	0	0	0	0	2
ASC	^@	^@	^@	^@	^@	^@	^@	^@	^@	^@	^@	^@	^@	^@	^@	^B
ALT	NUL	NUL	NUL	NUL	NUL	NUL	NUL	NUL	NUL	NUL	NUL	NUL	NUL	NUL	NUL	STX
SYM																

Non-Title Home Col. | Non-Title Home Row | No. Title Cols. | No. Title Rows | Left Title Col. | Top Title Row | Home Pos. Col. | Home Pos. Row

BYTE	240	241	242	243	244	245	246	247	248	249	250	251	252	253	254	255
HEX	00	50	00	16	00	FF	00	FF	FF	00	00	00	00	FF	00	FF
DEC	0	80	0	22	0	255	0	255	255	0	0	0	0	255	0	255
ASC	^@		^@	^V	^@	255	^@	255	255	^@	^@	^@	^@	255	^@	255
ALT	NUL		NUL	SYN	NUL	255	NUL	255	255	NUL	NUL	NUL	NUL	255	NUL	255
SYM		P														

No. Screen Cols. | No. Screen Rows | Hidden Status | Prev. Window | Border Displ. | Border Displ. Lines | Window Range Start Col. | Window Range Start Row | Window Range End Col. | Wind. Range →

BYTE	256	257	258	259	260	261	262	263	264	265	266	267	268	269	270	271
HEX	1F	00	00	FF	4D	41	49	4E	00	00	00	00	00	00	00	00
DEC	31	0	0	255	77	65	73	78	0	0	0	0	0	0	0	0
ASC	^_	^@	^@	255					^@	^@	^@	^@	^@	^@	^@	^@
ALT	US	NUL	NUL	255					NUL	NUL	NUL	NUL	NUL	NUL	NUL	NUL
SYM					M	A	I	N								

End Row | Offset | Inset Mode | ← ──────── Graph Name ──────── →

158 SYMPHONY

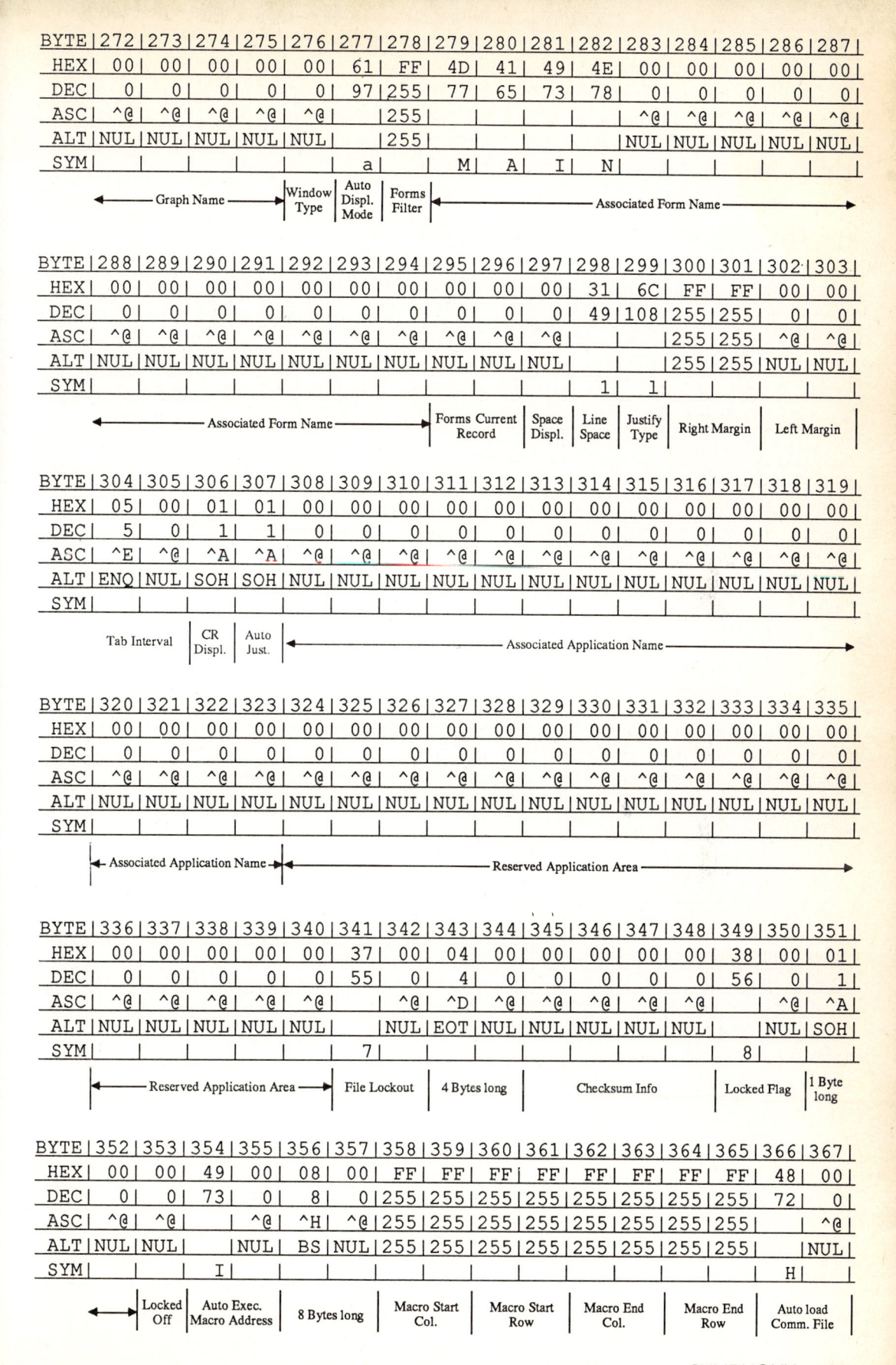

BYTE	272	273	274	275	276	277	278	279	280	281	282	283	284	285	286	287
HEX	00	00	00	00	00	61	FF	4D	41	49	4E	00	00	00	00	00
DEC	0	0	0	0	0	97	255	77	65	73	78	0	0	0	0	0
ASC	^@	^@	^@	^@	^@		255					^@	^@	^@	^@	^@
ALT	NUL	NUL	NUL	NUL	NUL		255					NUL	NUL	NUL	NUL	NUL
SYM						a		M	A	I	N					

←———— Graph Name ————→ | Window Type | Auto Displ. Mode | Forms Filter | ←———— Associated Form Name ————→

BYTE	288	289	290	291	292	293	294	295	296	297	298	299	300	301	302	303
HEX	00	00	00	00	00	00	00	00	00	00	31	6C	FF	FF	00	00
DEC	0	0	0	0	0	0	0	0	0	0	49	108	255	255	0	0
ASC	^@	^@	^@	^@	^@	^@	^@	^@	^@	^@			255	255	^@	^@
ALT	NUL	NUL	NUL	NUL	NUL	NUL	NUL	NUL	NUL	NUL			255	255	NUL	NUL
SYM											1	l				

←——— Associated Form Name ———→ | Forms Current Record | Space Displ. | Line Space | Justify Type | Right Margin | Left Margin

BYTE	304	305	306	307	308	309	310	311	312	313	314	315	316	317	318	319
HEX	05	00	01	01	00	00	00	00	00	00	00	00	00	00	00	00
DEC	5	0	1	1	0	0	0	0	0	0	0	0	0	0	0	0
ASC	^E	^@	^A	^A	^@	^@	^@	^@	^@	^@	^@	^@	^@	^@	^@	^@
ALT	ENQ	NUL	SOH	SOH	NUL	NUL	NUL	NUL	NUL	NUL	NUL	NUL	NUL	NUL	NUL	NUL
SYM																

Tab Interval | CR Displ. | Auto Just. | ←————— Associated Application Name —————→

BYTE	320	321	322	323	324	325	326	327	328	329	330	331	332	333	334	335
HEX	00	00	00	00	00	00	00	00	00	00	00	00	00	00	00	00
DEC	0	0	0	0	0	0	0	0	0	0	0	0	0	0	0	0
ASC	^@	^@	^@	^@	^@	^@	^@	^@	^@	^@	^@	^@	^@	^@	^@	^@
ALT	NUL	NUL	NUL	NUL	NUL	NUL	NUL	NUL	NUL	NUL	NUL	NUL	NUL	NUL	NUL	NUL
SYM																

←— Associated Application Name —→ | ←————— Reserved Application Area —————→

BYTE	336	337	338	339	340	341	342	343	344	345	346	347	348	349	350	351
HEX	00	00	00	00	00	37	00	04	00	00	00	00	00	38	00	01
DEC	0	0	0	0	0	55	0	4	0	0	0	0	0	56	0	1
ASC	^@	^@	^@	^@	^@		^D	^@	^@	^@	^@	^@		^@	^A
ALT	NUL	NUL	NUL	NUL	NUL		NUL	EOT	NUL	NUL	NUL	NUL	NUL		NUL	SOH
SYM						7								8		

←—— Reserved Application Area ——→ | File Lockout | 4 Bytes long | Checksum Info | Locked Flag | 1 Byte long

BYTE	352	353	354	355	356	357	358	359	360	361	362	363	364	365	366	367
HEX	00	00	49	00	08	00	FF	FF	FF	FF	FF	FF	FF	FF	48	00
DEC	0	0	73	0	8	0	255	255	255	255	255	255	255	255	72	0
ASC	^@	^@		^@	^H	^@	255	255	255	255	255	255	255	255		^@
ALT	NUL	NUL		NUL	BS	NUL	255	255	255	255	255	255	255	255		NUL
SYM			I												H	

←— | Locked Off | Auto Exec. Macro Address | 8 Bytes long | Macro Start Col. | Macro Start Row | Macro End Col. | Macro End Row | Auto load Comm. File

SYMPHONY 159

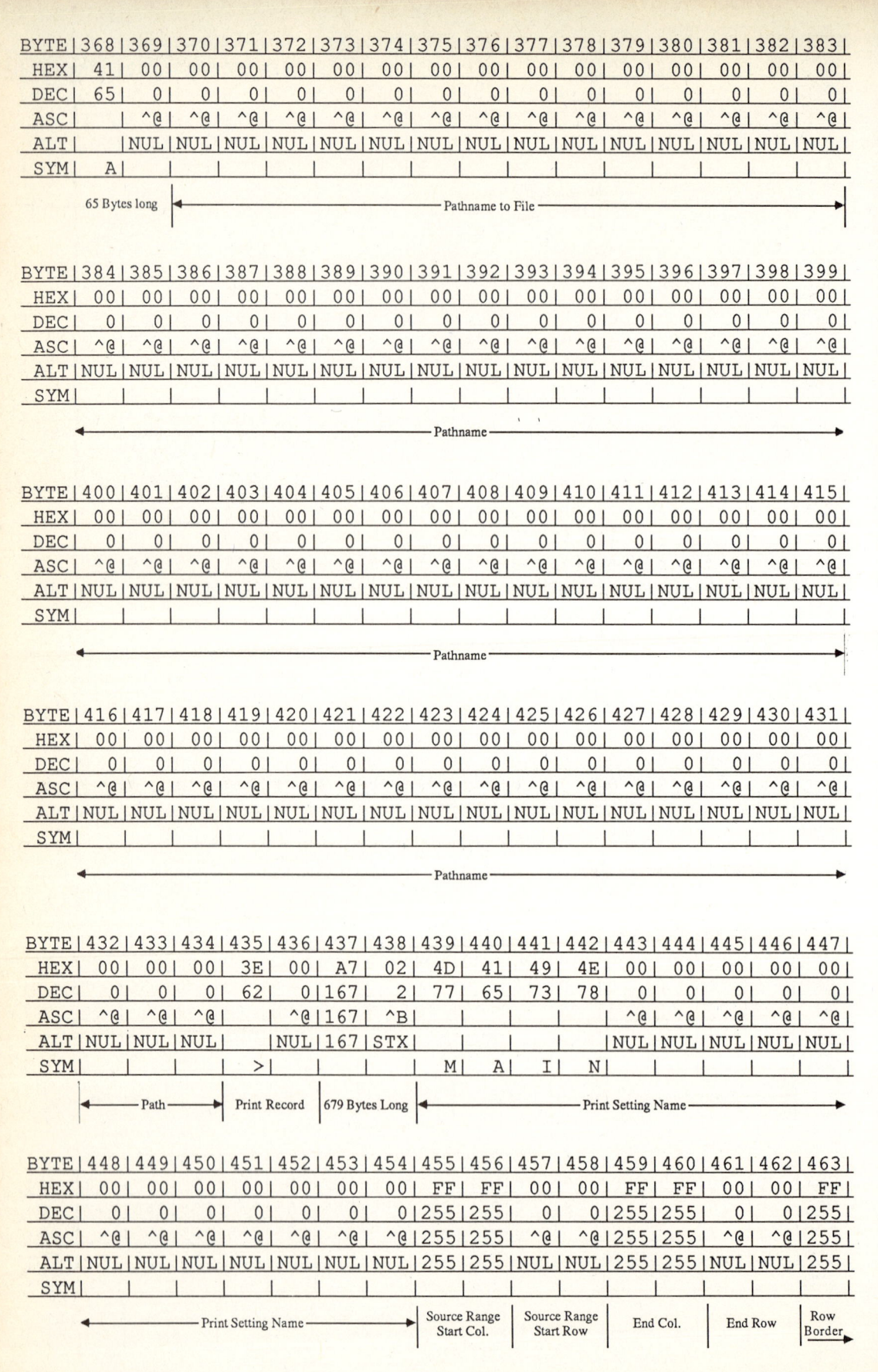

BYTE	368	369	370	371	372	373	374	375	376	377	378	379	380	381	382	383
HEX	41	00	00	00	00	00	00	00	00	00	00	00	00	00	00	00
DEC	65	0	0	0	0	0	0	0	0	0	0	0	0	0	0	0
ASC		^@	^@	^@	^@	^@	^@	^@	^@	^@	^@	^@	^@	^@	^@	^@
ALT		NUL	NUL	NUL	NUL	NUL	NUL	NUL	NUL	NUL	NUL	NUL	NUL	NUL	NUL	NUL
SYM	A															

|← 65 Bytes long →|←─────────────── Pathname to File ───────────────→|

BYTE	384	385	386	387	388	389	390	391	392	393	394	395	396	397	398	399
HEX	00	00	00	00	00	00	00	00	00	00	00	00	00	00	00	00
DEC	0	0	0	0	0	0	0	0	0	0	0	0	0	0	0	0
ASC	^@	^@	^@	^@	^@	^@	^@	^@	^@	^@	^@	^@	^@	^@	^@	^@
ALT	NUL	NUL	NUL	NUL	NUL	NUL	NUL	NUL	NUL	NUL	NUL	NUL	NUL	NUL	NUL	NUL
SYM																

←──────────────────── Pathname ────────────────────→

BYTE	400	401	402	403	404	405	406	407	408	409	410	411	412	413	414	415
HEX	00	00	00	00	00	00	00	00	00	00	00	00	00	00	00	00
DEC	0	0	0	0	0	0	0	0	0	0	0	0	0	0	0	0
ASC	^@	^@	^@	^@	^@	^@	^@	^@	^@	^@	^@	^@	^@	^@	^@	^@
ALT	NUL	NUL	NUL	NUL	NUL	NUL	NUL	NUL	NUL	NUL	NUL	NUL	NUL	NUL	NUL	NUL
SYM																

←──────────────────── Pathname ────────────────────→

BYTE	416	417	418	419	420	421	422	423	424	425	426	427	428	429	430	431
HEX	00	00	00	00	00	00	00	00	00	00	00	00	00	00	00	00
DEC	0	0	0	0	0	0	0	0	0	0	0	0	0	0	0	0
ASC	^@	^@	^@	^@	^@	^@	^@	^@	^@	^@	^@	^@	^@	^@	^@	^@
ALT	NUL	NUL	NUL	NUL	NUL	NUL	NUL	NUL	NUL	NUL	NUL	NUL	NUL	NUL	NUL	NUL
SYM																

←──────────────────── Pathname ────────────────────→

BYTE	432	433	434	435	436	437	438	439	440	441	442	443	444	445	446	447
HEX	00	00	00	3E	00	A7	02	4D	41	49	4E	00	00	00	00	00
DEC	0	0	0	62	0	167	2	77	65	73	78	0	0	0	0	0
ASC	^@	^@	^@		^@	167	^B					^@	^@	^@	^@	^@
ALT	NUL	NUL	NUL		NUL	167	STX					NUL	NUL	NUL	NUL	NUL
SYM				>				M	A	I	N					

|←─ Path ─→|Print Record|679 Bytes Long|←──── Print Setting Name ────→|

BYTE	448	449	450	451	452	453	454	455	456	457	458	459	460	461	462	463
HEX	00	00	00	00	00	00	00	FF	FF	00	00	FF	FF	00	00	FF
DEC	0	0	0	0	0	0	0	255	255	0	0	255	255	0	0	255
ASC	^@	^@	^@	^@	^@	^@	^@	255	255	^@	^@	255	255	^@	^@	255
ALT	NUL	NUL	NUL	NUL	NUL	NUL	NUL	255	255	NUL	NUL	255	255	NUL	NUL	255
SYM																

|←── Print Setting Name ──→|Source Range Start Col.|Source Range Start Row|End Col.|End Row|Row Border|

160 SYMPHONY

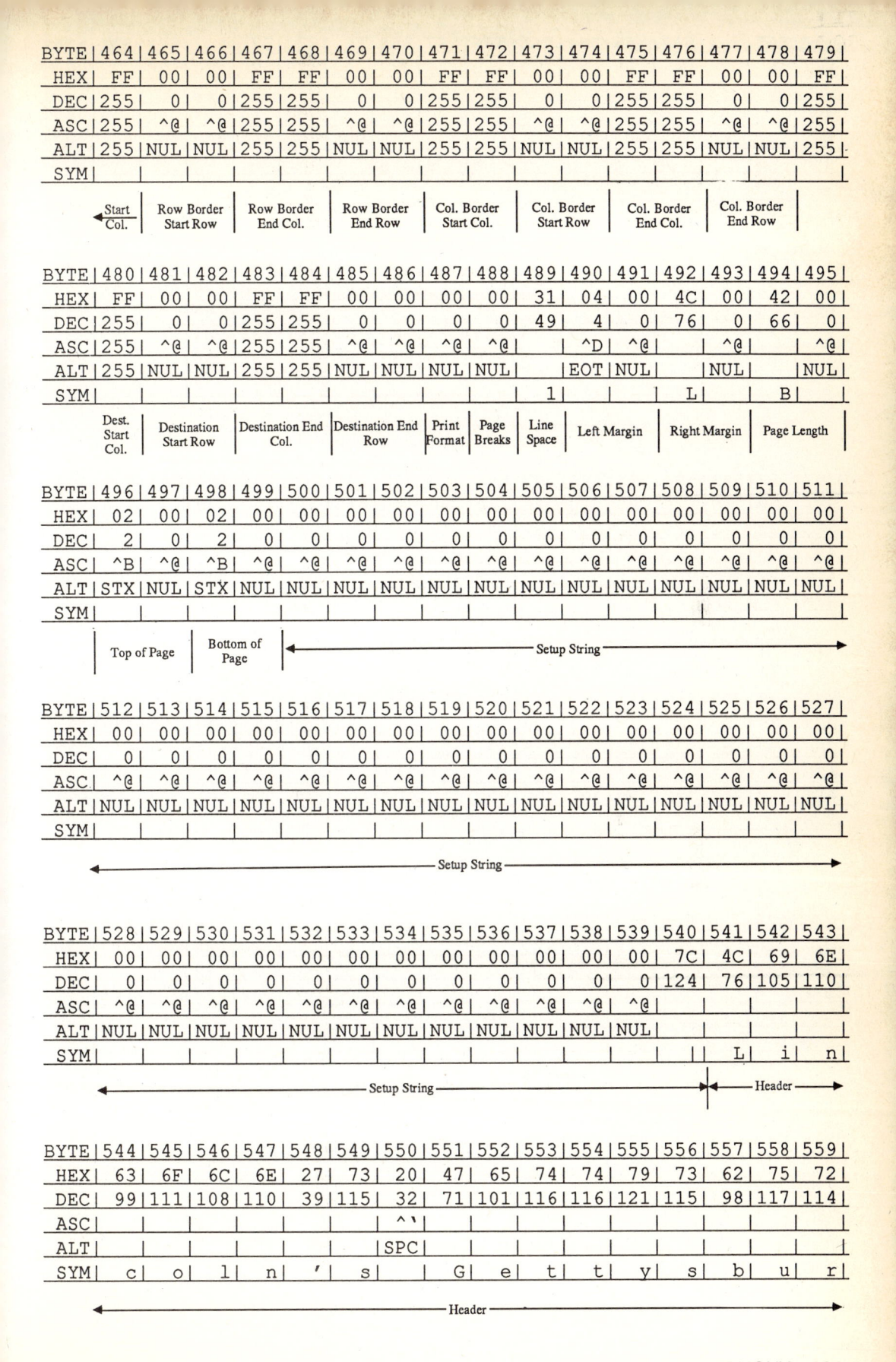

BYTE	464	465	466	467	468	469	470	471	472	473	474	475	476	477	478	479
HEX	FF	00	00	FF	FF	00	00	FF	FF	00	00	FF	FF	00	00	FF
DEC	255	0	0	255	255	0	0	255	255	0	0	255	255	0	0	255
ASC	255	^@	^@	255	255	^@	^@	255	255	^@	^@	255	255	^@	^@	255
ALT	255	NUL	NUL	255	255	NUL	NUL	255	255	NUL	NUL	255	255	NUL	NUL	255
SYM																

	Start Col.	Row Border Start Row	Row Border End Col.	Row Border End Row	Col. Border Start Col.	Col. Border Start Row	Col. Border End Col.	Col. Border End Row

BYTE	480	481	482	483	484	485	486	487	488	489	490	491	492	493	494	495
HEX	FF	00	00	FF	FF	00	00	00	00	31	04	00	4C	00	42	00
DEC	255	0	0	255	255	0	0	0	0	49	4	0	76	0	66	0
ASC	255	^@	^@	255	255	^@	^@	^@	^@	^D	^@		^@		^@	
ALT	255	NUL	NUL	255	255	NUL	NUL	NUL	NUL	EOT	NUL		NUL		NUL	
SYM										1			L		B	

	Dest. Start Col.	Destination Start Row	Destination End Col.	Destination End Row	Print Format	Page Breaks	Line Space	Left Margin	Right Margin	Page Length

BYTE	496	497	498	499	500	501	502	503	504	505	506	507	508	509	510	511
HEX	02	00	02	00	00	00	00	00	00	00	00	00	00	00	00	00
DEC	2	0	2	0	0	0	0	0	0	0	0	0	0	0	0	0
ASC	^B	^@	^B	^@	^@	^@	^@	^@	^@	^@	^@	^@	^@	^@	^@	^@
ALT	STX	NUL	STX	NUL	NUL	NUL	NUL	NUL	NUL	NUL	NUL	NUL	NUL	NUL	NUL	NUL
SYM																

	Top of Page	Bottom of Page	← Setup String →

BYTE	512	513	514	515	516	517	518	519	520	521	522	523	524	525	526	527
HEX	00	00	00	00	00	00	00	00	00	00	00	00	00	00	00	00
DEC	0	0	0	0	0	0	0	0	0	0	0	0	0	0	0	0
ASC	^@	^@	^@	^@	^@	^@	^@	^@	^@	^@	^@	^@	^@	^@	^@	^@
ALT	NUL	NUL	NUL	NUL	NUL	NUL	NUL	NUL	NUL	NUL	NUL	NUL	NUL	NUL	NUL	NUL
SYM																

← Setup String →

BYTE	528	529	530	531	532	533	534	535	536	537	538	539	540	541	542	543
HEX	00	00	00	00	00	00	00	00	00	00	00	00	00	7C	4C	69	6E
DEC	0	0	0	0	0	0	0	0	0	0	0	0	0	124	76	105	110
ASC	^@	^@	^@	^@	^@	^@	^@	^@	^@	^@	^@	^@	^@				
ALT	NUL	NUL	NUL	NUL	NUL	NUL	NUL	NUL	NUL	NUL	NUL	NUL	NUL				
SYM															L	i	n

← Setup String →|← Header →

BYTE	544	545	546	547	548	549	550	551	552	553	554	555	556	557	558	559
HEX	63	6F	6C	6E	27	73	20	47	65	74	74	79	73	62	75	72
DEC	99	111	108	110	39	115	32	71	101	116	116	121	115	98	117	114
ASC					^'											
ALT					SPC											
SYM	c	o	l	n	'	s		G	e	t	t	y	s	b	u	r

← Header →

SYMPHONY 161

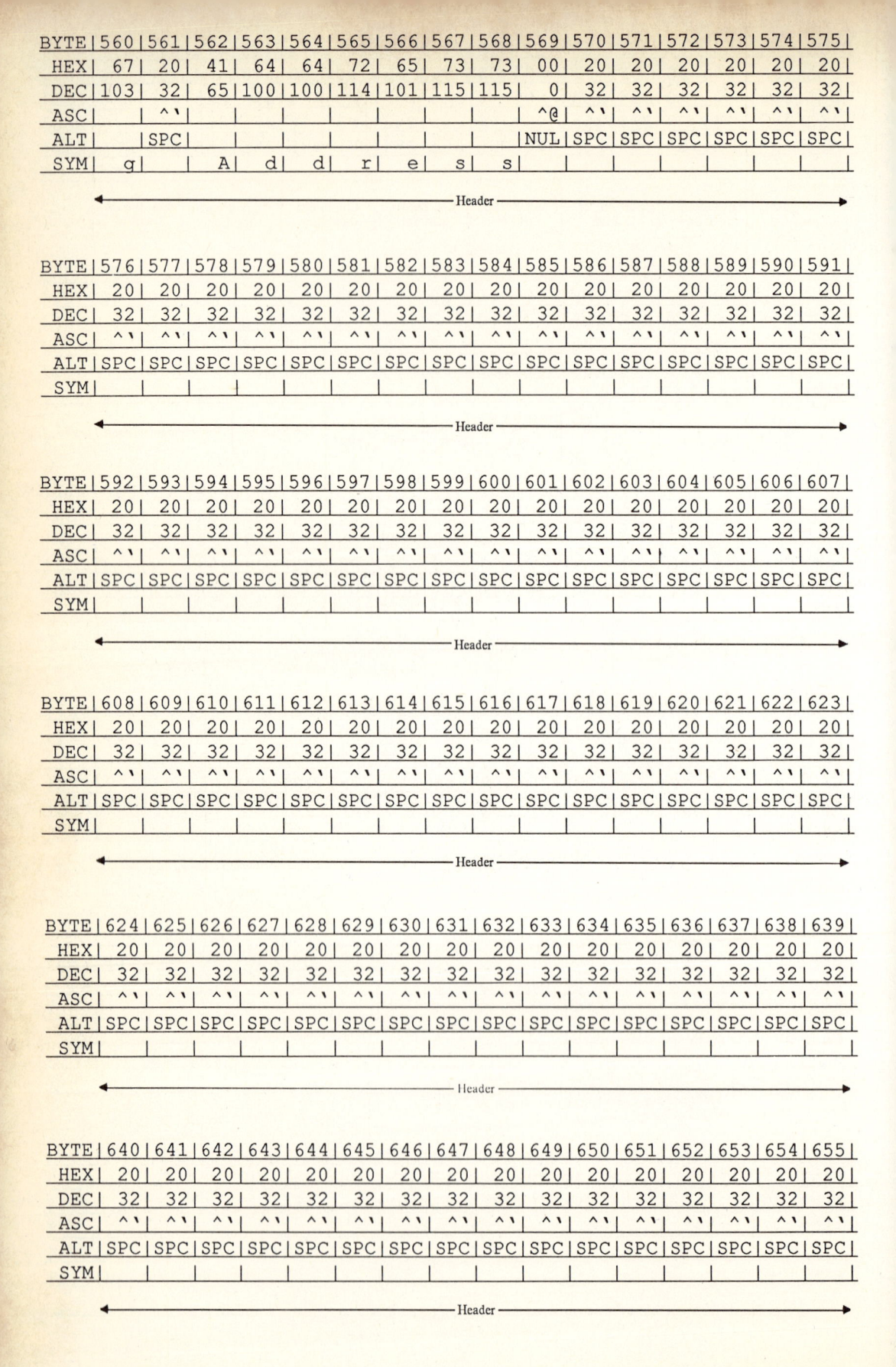

BYTE	560	561	562	563	564	565	566	567	568	569	570	571	572	573	574	575
HEX	67	20	41	64	64	72	65	73	73	00	20	20	20	20	20	20
DEC	103	32	65	100	100	114	101	115	115	0	32	32	32	32	32	32
ASC		^`								^@	^`	^`	^`	^`	^`	^`
ALT		SPC								NUL	SPC	SPC	SPC	SPC	SPC	SPC
SYM	g		A	d	d	r	e	s	s							

◄──────────────── Header ────────────────►

BYTE	576	577	578	579	580	581	582	583	584	585	586	587	588	589	590	591
HEX	20	20	20	20	20	20	20	20	20	20	20	20	20	20	20	20
DEC	32	32	32	32	32	32	32	32	32	32	32	32	32	32	32	32
ASC	^`	^`	^`	^`	^`	^`	^`	^`	^`	^`	^`	^`	^`	^`	^`	^`
ALT	SPC	SPC	SPC	SPC	SPC	SPC	SPC	SPC	SPC	SPC	SPC	SPC	SPC	SPC	SPC	SPC
SYM																

◄──────────────── Header ────────────────►

BYTE	592	593	594	595	596	597	598	599	600	601	602	603	604	605	606	607
HEX	20	20	20	20	20	20	20	20	20	20	20	20	20	20	20	20
DEC	32	32	32	32	32	32	32	32	32	32	32	32	32	32	32	32
ASC	^`	^`	^`	^`	^`	^`	^`	^`	^`	^`	^`	^`	^`	^`	^`	^`
ALT	SPC	SPC	SPC	SPC	SPC	SPC	SPC	SPC	SPC	SPC	SPC	SPC	SPC	SPC	SPC	SPC
SYM																

◄──────────────── Header ────────────────►

BYTE	608	609	610	611	612	613	614	615	616	617	618	619	620	621	622	623
HEX	20	20	20	20	20	20	20	20	20	20	20	20	20	20	20	20
DEC	32	32	32	32	32	32	32	32	32	32	32	32	32	32	32	32
ASC	^`	^`	^`	^`	^`	^`	^`	^`	^`	^`	^`	^`	^`	^`	^`	^`
ALT	SPC	SPC	SPC	SPC	SPC	SPC	SPC	SPC	SPC	SPC	SPC	SPC	SPC	SPC	SPC	SPC
SYM																

◄──────────────── Header ────────────────►

BYTE	624	625	626	627	628	629	630	631	632	633	634	635	636	637	638	639
HEX	20	20	20	20	20	20	20	20	20	20	20	20	20	20	20	20
DEC	32	32	32	32	32	32	32	32	32	32	32	32	32	32	32	32
ASC	^`	^`	^`	^`	^`	^`	^`	^`	^`	^`	^`	^`	^`	^`	^`	^`
ALT	SPC	SPC	SPC	SPC	SPC	SPC	SPC	SPC	SPC	SPC	SPC	SPC	SPC	SPC	SPC	SPC
SYM																

◄──────────────── Header ────────────────►

BYTE	640	641	642	643	644	645	646	647	648	649	650	651	652	653	654	655
HEX	20	20	20	20	20	20	20	20	20	20	20	20	20	20	20	20
DEC	32	32	32	32	32	32	32	32	32	32	32	32	32	32	32	32
ASC	^`	^`	^`	^`	^`	^`	^`	^`	^`	^`	^`	^`	^`	^`	^`	^`
ALT	SPC	SPC	SPC	SPC	SPC	SPC	SPC	SPC	SPC	SPC	SPC	SPC	SPC	SPC	SPC	SPC
SYM																

◄──────────────── Header ────────────────►

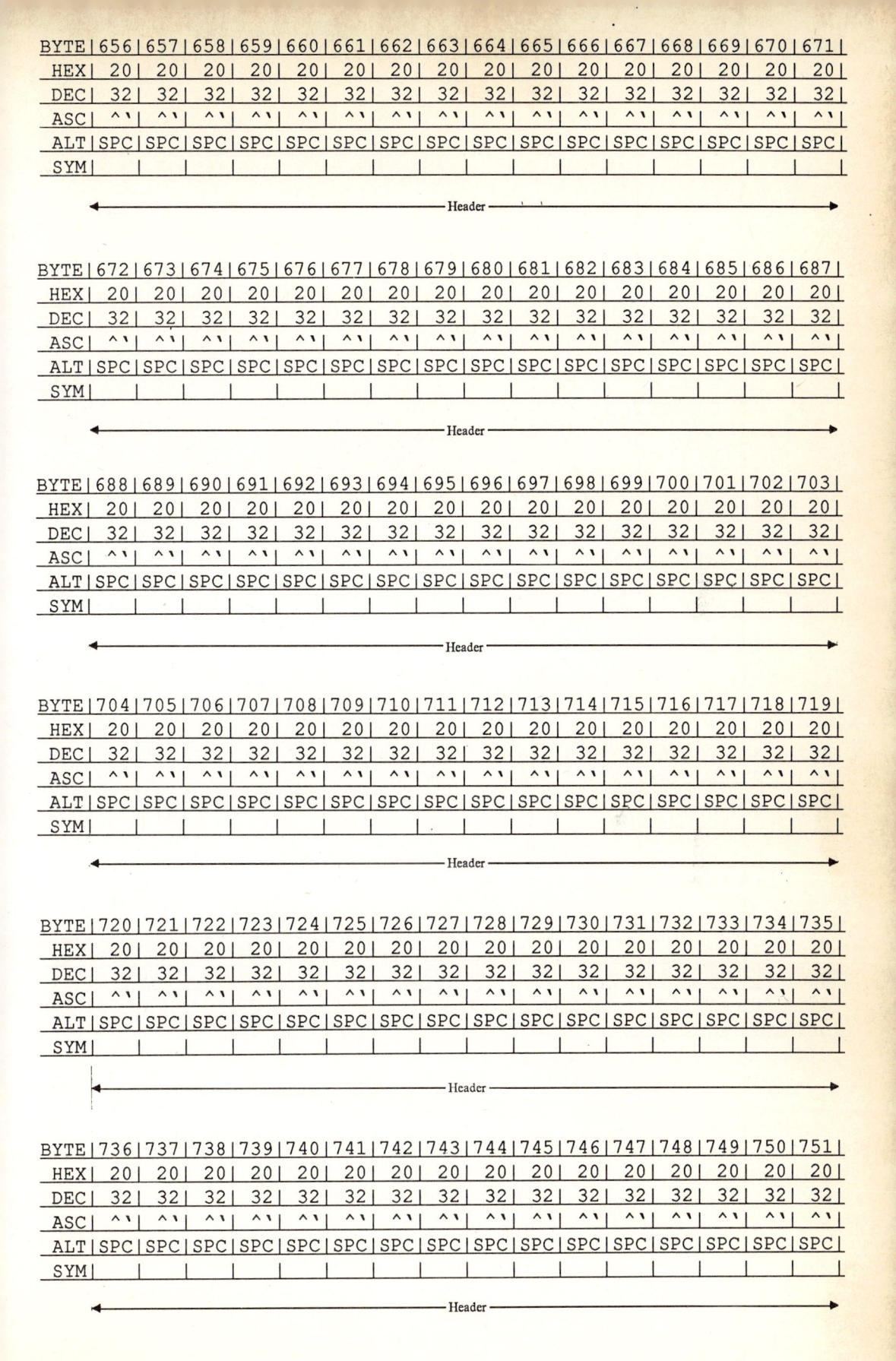

BYTE	656	657	658	659	660	661	662	663	664	665	666	667	668	669	670	671
HEX	20	20	20	20	20	20	20	20	20	20	20	20	20	20	20	20
DEC	32	32	32	32	32	32	32	32	32	32	32	32	32	32	32	32
ASC	^`	^`	^`	^`	^`	^`	^`	^`	^`	^`	^`	^`	^`	^`	^`	^`
ALT	SPC	SPC	SPC	SPC	SPC	SPC	SPC	SPC	SPC	SPC	SPC	SPC	SPC	SPC	SPC	SPC
SYM																

◄──────────────── Header ────────────────►

BYTE	672	673	674	675	676	677	678	679	680	681	682	683	684	685	686	687
HEX	20	20	20	20	20	20	20	20	20	20	20	20	20	20	20	20
DEC	32	32	32	32	32	32	32	32	32	32	32	32	32	32	32	32
ASC	^`	^`	^`	^`	^`	^`	^`	^`	^`	^`	^`	^`	^`	^`	^`	^`
ALT	SPC	SPC	SPC	SPC	SPC	SPC	SPC	SPC	SPC	SPC	SPC	SPC	SPC	SPC	SPC	SPC
SYM																

◄──────────────── Header ────────────────►

BYTE	688	689	690	691	692	693	694	695	696	697	698	699	700	701	702	703
HEX	20	20	20	20	20	20	20	20	20	20	20	20	20	20	20	20
DEC	32	32	32	32	32	32	32	32	32	32	32	32	32	32	32	32
ASC	^`	^`	^`	^`	^`	^`	^`	^`	^`	^`	^`	^`	^`	^`	^`	^`
ALT	SPC	SPC	SPC	SPC	SPC	SPC	SPC	SPC	SPC	SPC	SPC	SPC	SPC	SPC	SPC	SPC
SYM																

◄──────────────── Header ────────────────►

BYTE	704	705	706	707	708	709	710	711	712	713	714	715	716	717	718	719
HEX	20	20	20	20	20	20	20	20	20	20	20	20	20	20	20	20
DEC	32	32	32	32	32	32	32	32	32	32	32	32	32	32	32	32
ASC	^`	^`	^`	^`	^`	^`	^`	^`	^`	^`	^`	^`	^`	^`	^`	^`
ALT	SPC	SPC	SPC	SPC	SPC	SPC	SPC	SPC	SPC	SPC	SPC	SPC	SPC	SPC	SPC	SPC
SYM																

◄──────────────── Header ────────────────►

BYTE	720	721	722	723	724	725	726	727	728	729	730	731	732	733	734	735
HEX	20	20	20	20	20	20	20	20	20	20	20	20	20	20	20	20
DEC	32	32	32	32	32	32	32	32	32	32	32	32	32	32	32	32
ASC	^`	^`	^`	^`	^`	^`	^`	^`	^`	^`	^`	^`	^`	^`	^`	^`
ALT	SPC	SPC	SPC	SPC	SPC	SPC	SPC	SPC	SPC	SPC	SPC	SPC	SPC	SPC	SPC	SPC
SYM																

◄──────────────── Header ────────────────►

BYTE	736	737	738	739	740	741	742	743	744	745	746	747	748	749	750	751
HEX	20	20	20	20	20	20	20	20	20	20	20	20	20	20	20	20
DEC	32	32	32	32	32	32	32	32	32	32	32	32	32	32	32	32
ASC	^`	^`	^`	^`	^`	^`	^`	^`	^`	^`	^`	^`	^`	^`	^`	^`
ALT	SPC	SPC	SPC	SPC	SPC	SPC	SPC	SPC	SPC	SPC	SPC	SPC	SPC	SPC	SPC	SPC
SYM																

◄──────────────── Header ────────────────►

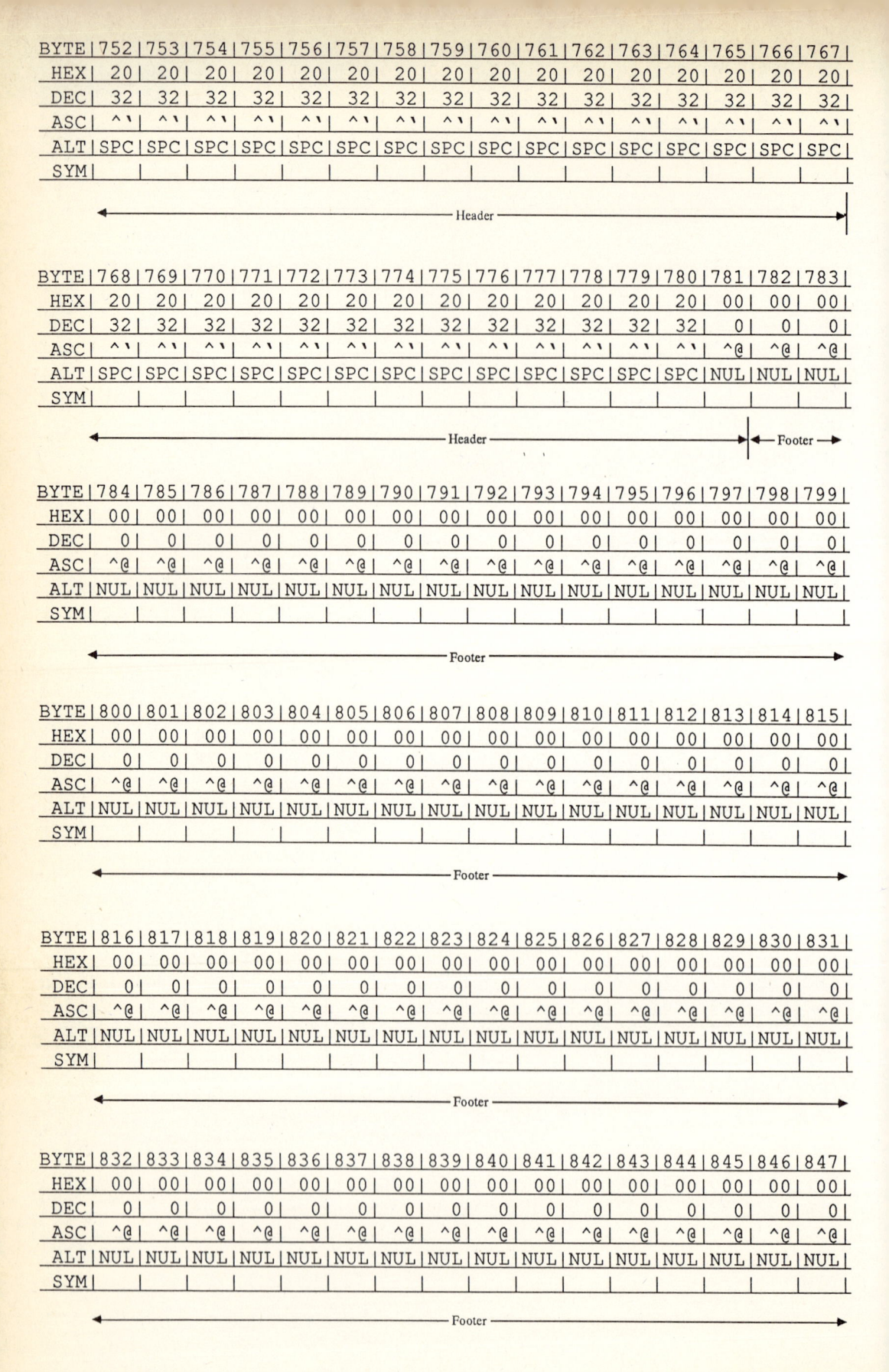

BYTE	752	753	754	755	756	757	758	759	760	761	762	763	764	765	766	767
HEX	20	20	20	20	20	20	20	20	20	20	20	20	20	20	20	20
DEC	32	32	32	32	32	32	32	32	32	32	32	32	32	32	32	32
ASC	^\`	^\`	^\`	^\`	^\`	^\`	^\`	^\`	^\`	^\`	^\`	^\`	^\`	^\`	^\`	^\`
ALT	SPC	SPC	SPC	SPC	SPC	SPC	SPC	SPC	SPC	SPC	SPC	SPC	SPC	SPC	SPC	SPC
SYM																

◄─────────────────────────────── Header ───────────────────────────────►

BYTE	768	769	770	771	772	773	774	775	776	777	778	779	780	781	782	783
HEX	20	20	20	20	20	20	20	20	20	20	20	20	20	00	00	00
DEC	32	32	32	32	32	32	32	32	32	32	32	32	32	0	0	0
ASC	^\`	^\`	^\`	^\`	^\`	^\`	^\`	^\`	^\`	^\`	^\`	^\`	^\`	^@	^@	^@
ALT	SPC	SPC	SPC	SPC	SPC	SPC	SPC	SPC	SPC	SPC	SPC	SPC	SPC	NUL	NUL	NUL
SYM																

◄────────────────────────── Header ──────────────────────────►◄── Footer ──►

BYTE	784	785	786	787	788	789	790	791	792	793	794	795	796	797	798	799
HEX	00	00	00	00	00	00	00	00	00	00	00	00	00	00	00	00
DEC	0	0	0	0	0	0	0	0	0	0	0	0	0	0	0	0
ASC	^@	^@	^@	^@	^@	^@	^@	^@	^@	^@	^@	^@	^@	^@	^@	^@
ALT	NUL	NUL	NUL	NUL	NUL	NUL	NUL	NUL	NUL	NUL	NUL	NUL	NUL	NUL	NUL	NUL
SYM																

◄─────────────────────────────── Footer ───────────────────────────────►

BYTE	800	801	802	803	804	805	806	807	808	809	810	811	812	813	814	815
HEX	00	00	00	00	00	00	00	00	00	00	00	00	00	00	00	00
DEC	0	0	0	0	0	0	0	0	0	0	0	0	0	0	0	0
ASC	^@	^@	^@	^@	^@	^@	^@	^@	^@	^@	^@	^@	^@	^@	^@	^@
ALT	NUL	NUL	NUL	NUL	NUL	NUL	NUL	NUL	NUL	NUL	NUL	NUL	NUL	NUL	NUL	NUL
SYM																

◄─────────────────────────────── Footer ───────────────────────────────►

BYTE	816	817	818	819	820	821	822	823	824	825	826	827	828	829	830	831
HEX	00	00	00	00	00	00	00	00	00	00	00	00	00	00	00	00
DEC	0	0	0	0	0	0	0	0	0	0	0	0	0	0	0	0
ASC	^@	^@	^@	^@	^@	^@	^@	^@	^@	^@	^@	^@	^@	^@	^@	^@
ALT	NUL	NUL	NUL	NUL	NUL	NUL	NUL	NUL	NUL	NUL	NUL	NUL	NUL	NUL	NUL	NUL
SYM																

◄─────────────────────────────── Footer ───────────────────────────────►

BYTE	832	833	834	835	836	837	838	839	840	841	842	843	844	845	846	847
HEX	00	00	00	00	00	00	00	00	00	00	00	00	00	00	00	00
DEC	0	0	0	0	0	0	0	0	0	0	0	0	0	0	0	0
ASC	^@	^@	^@	^@	^@	^@	^@	^@	^@	^@	^@	^@	^@	^@	^@	^@
ALT	NUL	NUL	NUL	NUL	NUL	NUL	NUL	NUL	NUL	NUL	NUL	NUL	NUL	NUL	NUL	NUL
SYM																

◄─────────────────────────────── Footer ───────────────────────────────►

BYTE	848	849	850	851	852	853	854	855	856	857	858	859	860	861	862	863
HEX	00	00	00	00	00	00	00	00	00	00	00	00	00	00	00	00
DEC	0	0	0	0	0	0	0	0	0	0	0	0	0	0	0	0
ASC	^@	^@	^@	^@	^@	^@	^@	^@	^@	^@	^@	^@	^@	^@	^@	^@
ALT	NUL	NUL	NUL	NUL	NUL	NUL	NUL	NUL	NUL	NUL	NUL	NUL	NUL	NUL	NUL	NUL
SYM																

◄──────── Footer ────────►

BYTE	864	865	866	867	868	869	870	871	872	873	874	875	876	877	878	879
HEX	00	00	00	00	00	00	00	00	00	00	00	00	00	00	00	00
DEC	0	0	0	0	0	0	0	0	0	0	0	0	0	0	0	0
ASC	^@	^@	^@	^@	^@	^@	^@	^@	^@	^@	^@	^@	^@	^@	^@	^@
ALT	NUL	NUL	NUL	NUL	NUL	NUL	NUL	NUL	NUL	NUL	NUL	NUL	NUL	NUL	NUL	NUL
SYM																

◄──────── Footer ────────►

BYTE	880	881	882	883	884	885	886	887	888	889	890	891	892	893	894	895
HEX	00	00	00	00	00	00	00	00	00	00	00	00	00	00	00	00
DEC	0	0	0	0	0	0	0	0	0	0	0	0	0	0	0	0
ASC	^@	^@	^@	^@	^@	^@	^@	^@	^@	^@	^@	^@	^@	^@	^@	^@
ALT	NUL	NUL	NUL	NUL	NUL	NUL	NUL	NUL	NUL	NUL	NUL	NUL	NUL	NUL	NUL	NUL
SYM																

◄──────── Footer ────────►

BYTE	896	897	898	899	900	901	902	903	904	905	906	907	908	909	910	911
HEX	00	00	00	00	00	00	00	00	00	00	00	00	00	00	00	00
DEC	0	0	0	0	0	0	0	0	0	0	0	0	0	0	0	0
ASC	^@	^@	^@	^@	^@	^@	^@	^@	^@	^@	^@	^@	^@	^@	^@	^@
ALT	NUL	NUL	NUL	NUL	NUL	NUL	NUL	NUL	NUL	NUL	NUL	NUL	NUL	NUL	NUL	NUL
SYM																

◄──────── Footer ────────►

BYTE	912	913	914	915	916	917	918	919	920	921	922	923	924	925	926	927
HEX	00	00	00	00	00	00	00	00	00	00	00	00	00	00	00	00
DEC	0	0	0	0	0	0	0	0	0	0	0	0	0	0	0	0
ASC	^@	^@	^@	^@	^@	^@	^@	^@	^@	^@	^@	^@	^@	^@	^@	^@
ALT	NUL	NUL	NUL	NUL	NUL	NUL	NUL	NUL	NUL	NUL	NUL	NUL	NUL	NUL	NUL	NUL
SYM																

◄──────── Footer ────────►

BYTE	928	929	930	931	932	933	934	935	936	937	938	939	940	941	942	943
HEX	00	00	00	00	00	00	00	00	00	00	00	00	00	00	00	00
DEC	0	0	0	0	0	0	0	0	0	0	0	0	0	0	0	0
ASC	^@	^@	^@	^@	^@	^@	^@	^@	^@	^@	^@	^@	^@	^@	^@	^@
ALT	NUL	NUL	NUL	NUL	NUL	NUL	NUL	NUL	NUL	NUL	NUL	NUL	NUL	NUL	NUL	NUL
SYM																

◄──────── Footer ────────►

BYTE	944	945	946	947	948	949	950	951	952	953	954	955	956	957	958	959
HEX	00	00	00	00	00	00	00	00	00	00	00	00	00	00	00	00
DEC	0	0	0	0	0	0	0	0	0	0	0	0	0	0	0	0
ASC	^@	^@	^@	^@	^@	^@	^@	^@	^@	^@	^@	^@	^@	^@	^@	^@
ALT SYM	NUL	NUL	NUL	NUL	NUL	NUL	NUL	NUL	NUL	NUL	NUL	NUL	NUL	NUL	NUL	NUL

◄──────────────── Footer ────────────────►

BYTE	960	961	962	963	964	965	966	967	968	969	970	971	972	973	974	975
HEX	00	00	00	00	00	00	00	00	00	00	00	00	00	00	00	00
DEC	0	0	0	0	0	0	0	0	0	0	0	0	0	0	0	0
ASC	^@	^@	^@	^@	^@	^@	^@	^@	^@	^@	^@	^@	^@	^@	^@	^@
ALT SYM	NUL	NUL	NUL	NUL	NUL	NUL	NUL	NUL	NUL	NUL	NUL	NUL	NUL	NUL	NUL	NUL

◄──────────────── Footer ────────────────►

BYTE	976	977	978	979	980	981	982	983	984	985	986	987	988	989	990	991
HEX	00	00	00	00	00	00	00	00	00	00	00	00	00	00	00	00
DEC	0	0	0	0	0	0	0	0	0	0	0	0	0	0	0	0
ASC	^@	^@	^@	^@	^@	^@	^@	^@	^@	^@	^@	^@	^@	^@	^@	^@
ALT SYM	NUL	NUL	NUL	NUL	NUL	NUL	NUL	NUL	NUL	NUL	NUL	NUL	NUL	NUL	NUL	NUL

◄──────────────── Footer ────────────────►

BYTE	992	993	994	995	996	997	998	999	0	1	2	3	4	5	6	7
HEX	00	00	00	00	00	00	00	00	00	00	00	00	00	00	00	00
DEC	0	0	0	0	0	0	0	0	0	0	0	0	0	0	0	0
ASC	^@	^@	^@	^@	^@	^@	^@	^@	^@	^@	^@	^@	^@	^@	^@	^@
ALT SYM	NUL	NUL	NUL	NUL	NUL	NUL	NUL	NUL	NUL	NUL	NUL	NUL	NUL	NUL	NUL	NUL

◄──────────────── Footer ────────────────►

BYTE	8	9	10	11	12	13	14	15	16	17	18	19	20	21	22	23
HEX	00	00	00	00	00	00	00	00	00	00	00	00	00	00	00	00
DEC	0	0	0	0	0	0	0	0	0	0	0	0	0	0	0	0
ASC	^@	^@	^@	^@	^@	^@	^@	^@	^@	^@	^@	^@	^@	^@	^@	^@
ALT SYM	NUL	NUL	NUL	NUL	NUL	NUL	NUL	NUL	NUL	NUL	NUL	NUL	NUL	NUL	NUL	NUL

◄──────────────── Footer ────────────────►

BYTE	24	25	26	27	28	29	30	31	32	33	34	35	36	37	38	39
HEX	00	00	00	00	00	00	00	00	00	00	00	00	00	00	00	00
DEC	0	0	0	0	0	0	0	0	0	0	0	0	0	0	0	0
ASC	^@	^@	^@	^@	^@	^@	^@	^@	^@	^@	^@	^@	^@	^@	^@	^@
ALT SYM	NUL	NUL	NUL	NUL	NUL	NUL	NUL	NUL	NUL	NUL	NUL	NUL	NUL	NUL	NUL	NUL

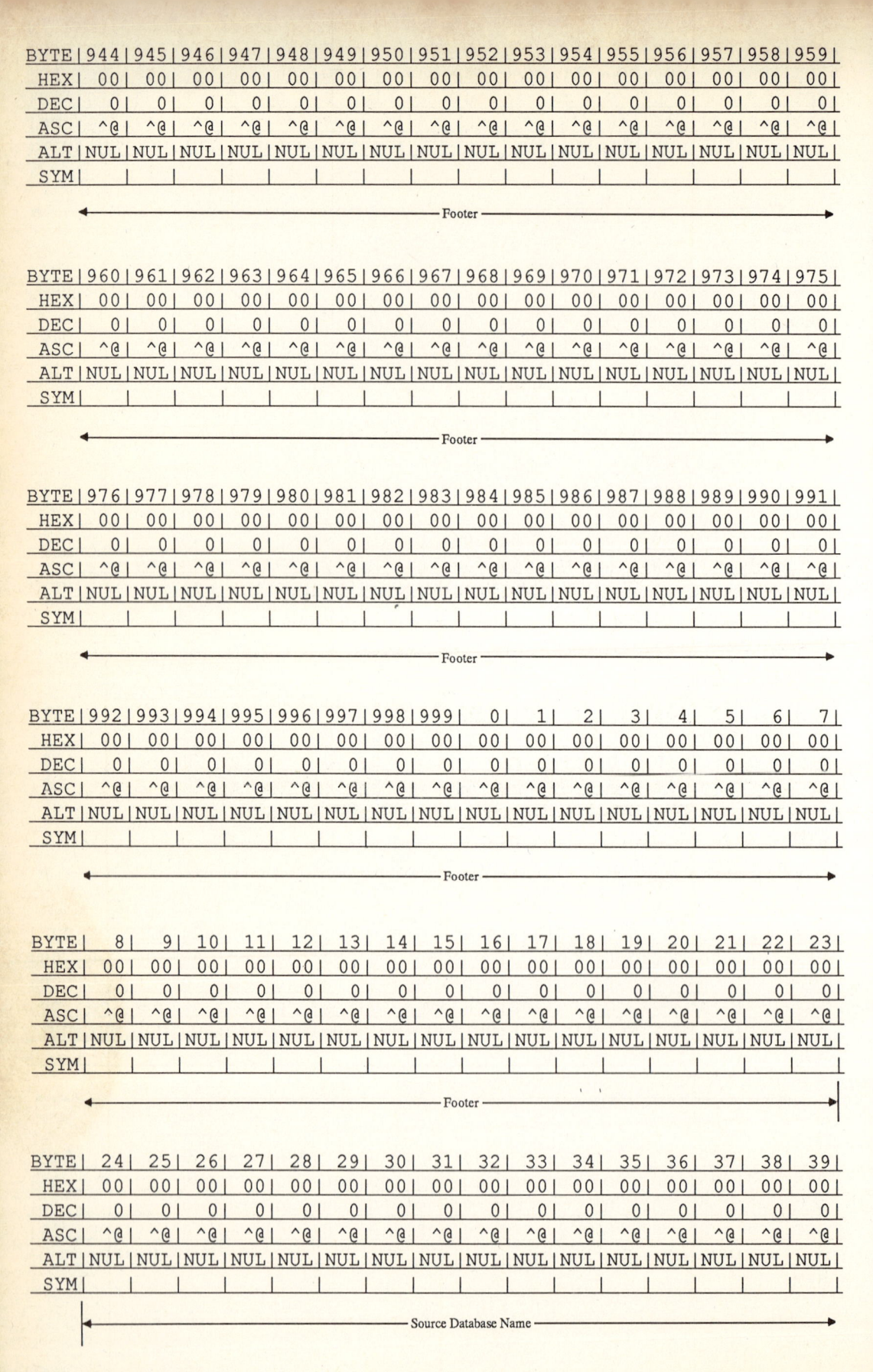

◄──────────── Source Database Name ────────────►

BYTE	40	41	42	43	44	45	46	47	48	49	50	51	52	53	54	55
HEX	FF	00	00	01	00	E7	03	00	00	00	00	00	00	00	00	00
DEC	255	0	0	1	0	231	3	0	0	0	0	0	0	0	0	0
ASC	255	^@	^@	^A	^@	231	^C	^@	^@	^@	^@	^@	^@	^@	^@	^@
ALT SYM	255	NUL	NUL	SOH	NUL	231	ETX	NUL	NUL	NUL	NUL	NUL	NUL	NUL	NUL	NUL

	Attribute	Space Compressn.	Print Dest.	Starting Page	Ending Page	◄─────── Destination Filename ───────►

BYTE	56	57	58	59	60	61	62	63	64	65	66	67	68	69	70	71
HEX	00	00	00	00	00	00	00	00	00	00	00	00	00	00	00	00
DEC	0	0	0	0	0	0	0	0	0	0	0	0	0	0	0	0
ASC	^@	^@	^@	^@	^@	^@	^@	^@	^@	^@	^@	^@	^@	^@	^@	^@
ALT SYM	NUL	NUL	NUL	NUL	NUL	NUL	NUL	NUL	NUL	NUL	NUL	NUL	NUL	NUL	NUL	NUL

◄─────── Destination Filename ───────►

BYTE	72	73	74	75	76	77	78	79	80	81	82	83	84	85	86	87
HEX	00	00	00	00	00	00	00	00	00	00	00	00	00	00	00	00
DEC	0	0	0	0	0	0	0	0	0	0	0	0	0	0	0	0
ASC	^@	^@	^@	^@	^@	^@	^@	^@	^@	^@	^@	^@	^@	^@	^@	^@
ALT SYM	NUL	NUL	NUL	NUL	NUL	NUL	NUL	NUL	NUL	NUL	NUL	NUL	NUL	NUL	NUL	NUL

◄─────── Destination Filename ───────►

BYTE	88	89	90	91	92	93	94	95	96	97	98	99	100	101	102	103
HEX	00	00	00	00	00	00	00	00	00	00	00	00	00	00	00	00
DEC	0	0	0	0	0	0	0	0	0	0	0	0	0	0	0	0
ASC	^@	^@	^@	^@	^@	^@	^@	^@	^@	^@	^@	^@	^@	^@	^@	^@
ALT SYM	NUL	NUL	NUL	NUL	NUL	NUL	NUL	NUL	NUL	NUL	NUL	NUL	NUL	NUL	NUL	NUL

◄─────── Destination Filename ───────►

BYTE	104	105	106	107	108	109	110	111	112	113	114	115	116	117	118	119
HEX	00	00	00	00	00	00	00	00	00	00	00	00	00	00	18	00
DEC	0	0	0	0	0	0	0	0	0	0	0	0	0	0	24	0
ASC	^@	^@	^@	^@	^@	^@	^@	^@	^@	^@	^@	^@	^@	^@	^X	^@
ALT SYM	NUL	NUL	NUL	NUL	NUL	NUL	NUL	NUL	NUL	NUL	NUL	NUL	NUL	NUL	CAN	NUL

◄─────── Destination Filename ───────► | Wait | Table Range |

BYTE	120	121	122	123	124	125	126	127	128	129	130	131	132	133	134	135
HEX	19	00	00	FF	FF	00	00	FF	FF	00	00	FF	FF	00	00	FF
DEC	25	0	0	255	255	0	0	255	255	0	0	255	255	0	0	255
ASC	^Y	^@	^@	255	255	^@	^@	255	255	^@	^@	255	255	^@	^@	255
ALT SYM	EM	NUL	NUL	255	255	NUL	NUL	255	255	NUL	NUL	255	255	NUL	NUL	255

25 Bytes long	No Table	Table Range Start Col.	Table Range Start Row	Table Range End Col.	Table Range End Row	Input Cell 1 Start Col.	Input Cell 1 Start Row	Input Cell 1

SYMPHONY 167

BYTE	136	137	138	139	140	141	142	143	144	145	146	147	148	149	150	151
HEX	FF	00	00	FF	FF	00	00	FF	FF	00	00	3D	00	10	00	00
DEC	255	0	0	255	255	0	0	255	255	0	0	61	0	16	0	0
ASC	255	^@	^@	255	255	^@	^@	255	255	^@	^@		^@	^P	^@	^@
ALT	255	NUL	NUL	255	255	NUL	NUL	255	255	NUL	NUL		NUL	DLE	NUL	NUL
SYM												=				

| End Col. | Input Cell 2 End Row | Input Cell 2 Start Col. | Input Cell 2 Start Row | Input Cell 2 End Col. | Input Cell 2 End Row | Query Name | 16 Bytes long |

BYTE	152	153	154	155	156	157	158	159	160	161	162	163	164	165	166	167
HEX	00	00	00	00	00	00	00	00	00	00	00	00	00	00	00	3F
DEC	0	0	0	0	0	0	0	0	0	0	0	0	0	0	0	63
ASC	^@	^@	^@	^@	^@	^@	^@	^@	^@	^@	^@	^@	^@	^@	^@	
ALT	NUL	NUL	NUL	NUL	NUL	NUL	NUL	NUL	NUL	NUL	NUL	NUL	NUL	NUL	NUL	
SYM																?

◄──────────────── Query Name String ────────────────► Print Name

BYTE	168	169	170	171	172	173	174	175	176	177	178	179	180	181	182	183
HEX	00	10	00	4D	41	49	4E	00	00	00	00	00	00	00	00	00
DEC	0	16	0	77	65	73	78	0	0	0	0	0	0	0	0	0
ASC	^@	^P	^@					^@	^@	^@	^@	^@	^@	^@	^@	^@
ALT	NUL	DLE	NUL					NUL	NUL	NUL	NUL	NUL	NUL	NUL	NUL	NUL
SYM				M	A	I	N									

| Print Name | 16 Bytes long | ◄──────────── Print Name ────────────► |

BYTE	184	185	186	187	188	189	190	191	192	193	194	195	196	197	198	199
HEX	00	00	00	41	00	10	00	00	00	00	00	00	00	00	00	00
DEC	0	0	0	65	0	16	0	0	0	0	0	0	0	0	0	0
ASC	^@	^@	^@		^@	^P	^@	^@	^@	^@	^@	^@	^@	^@	^@	^@
ALT	NUL	NUL	NUL		NUL	DLE	NUL	NUL	NUL	NUL	NUL	NUL	NUL	NUL	NUL	NUL
SYM				A												

◄── Print Name ──► | Graph Name | 16 Bytes long | ◄──────── Graph Name ────────►

BYTE	200	201	202	203	204	205	206	207	208	209	210	211	212	213	214	215
HEX	00	00	00	00	00	00	00	1C	00	08	00	FF	FF	00	00	FF
DEC	0	0	0	0	0	0	0	28	0	8	0	255	255	0	0	255
ASC	^@	^@	^@	^@	^@	^@	^@	^\	^@	^H	^@	255	255	^@	^@	255
ALT	NUL	NUL	NUL	NUL	NUL	NUL	NUL	FS	NUL	BS	NUL	255	255	NUL	NUL	255
SYM																

◄─────── Graph Name ───────► | F Range | 8 Bytes long | Start Col. | Start Row | End Col.

BYTE	216	217	218	219	220	221	222	223	224	225	226	227	228	229	230	231
HEX	FF	00	00	20	00	10	00	FF	FF	00	00	FF	FF	00	00	FF
DEC	255	0	0	32	0	16	0	255	255	0	0	255	255	0	0	255
ASC	255	^@	^@	^`	^@	^P	^@	255	255	^@	^@	255	255	^@	^@	255
ALT	255	NUL	NUL	SPC	NUL	DLE	NUL	255	255	NUL	NUL	255	255	NUL	NUL	255
SYM																

| End Col. | End Row | H Range | 16 Bytes long | VAL Start Col. | VAL Start Row | VAL End Col. | VAL End Row | BIN Start Col. |

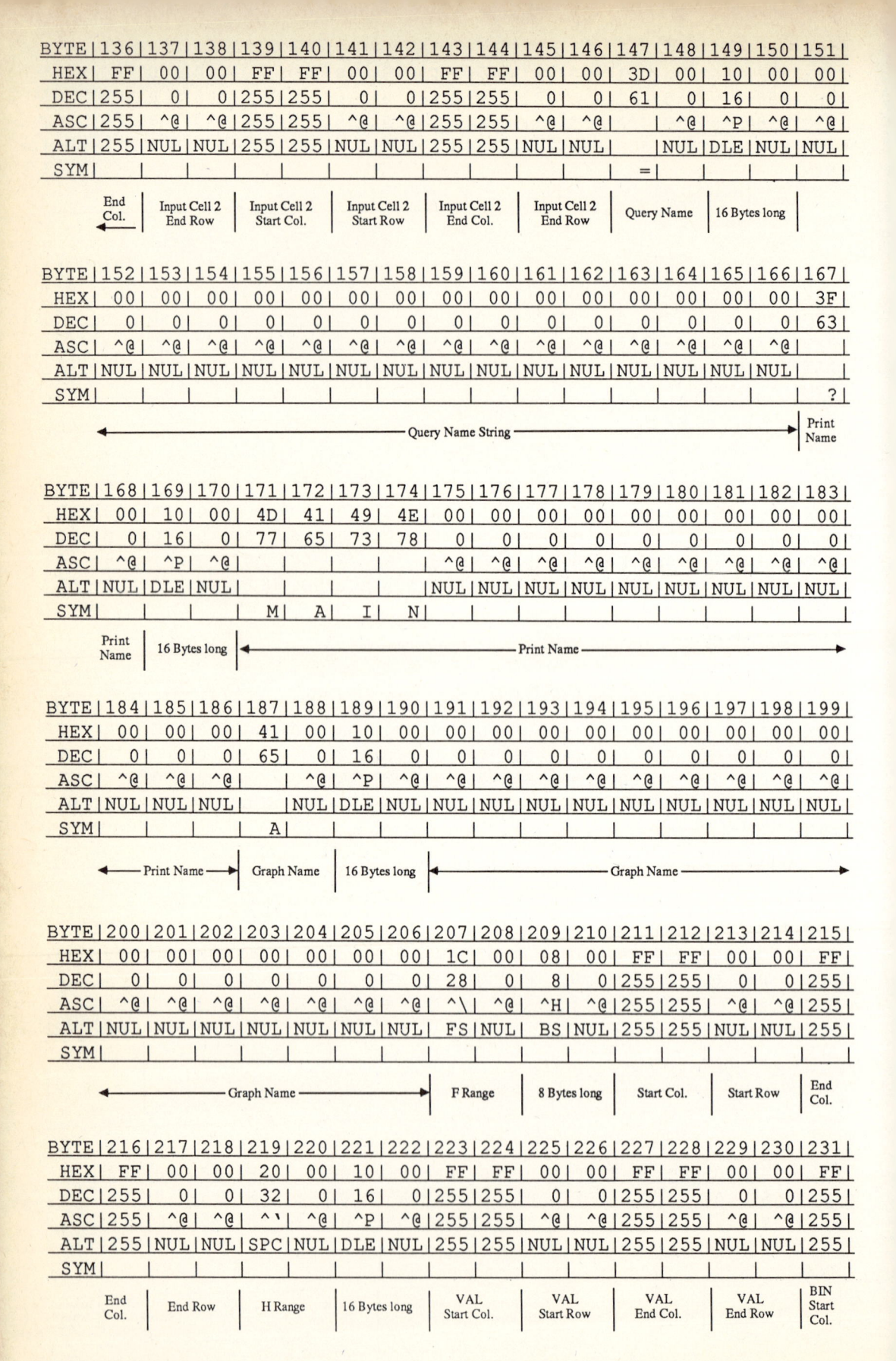

168 SYMPHONY

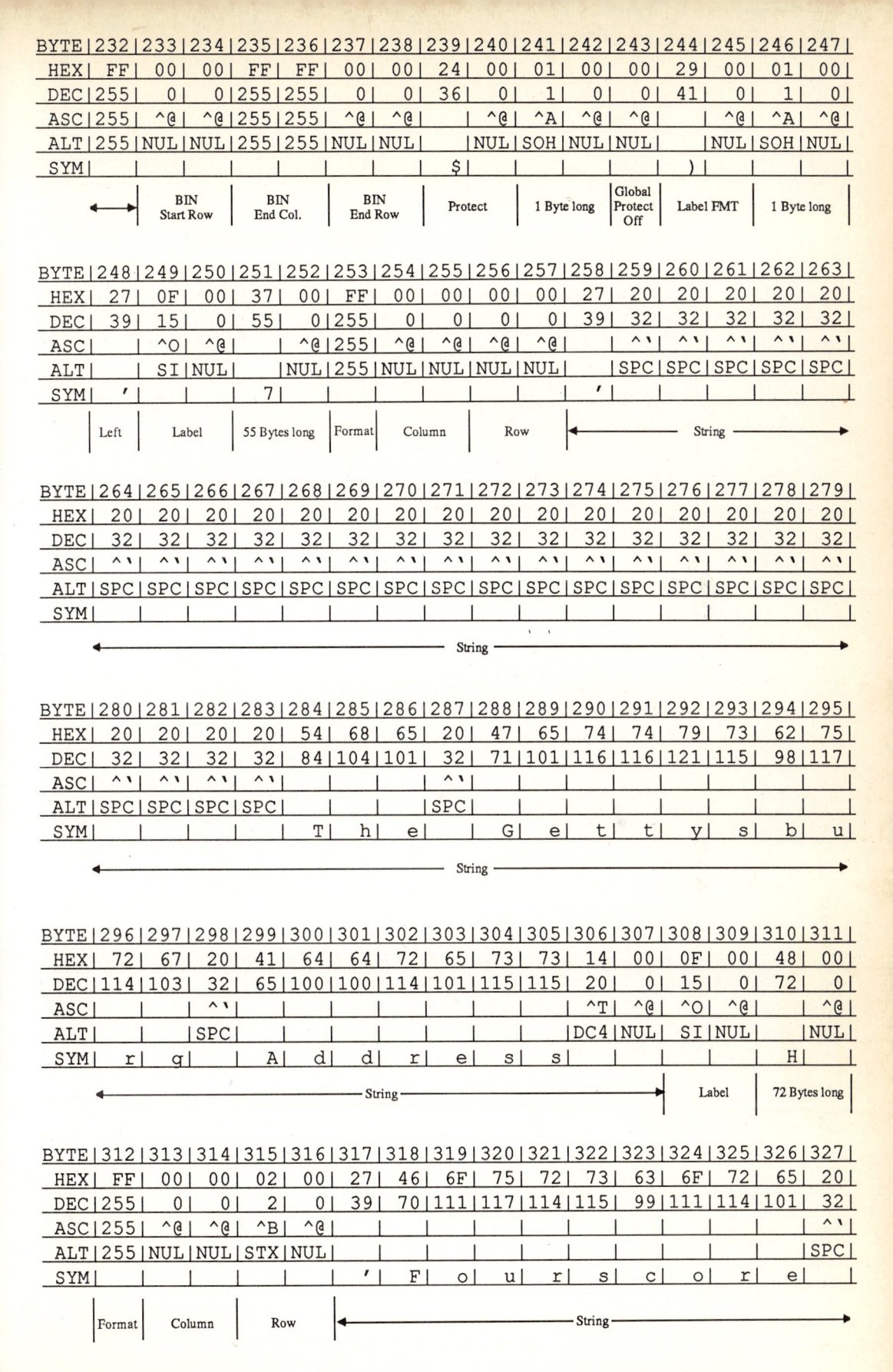

BYTE	232	233	234	235	236	237	238	239	240	241	242	243	244	245	246	247
HEX	FF	00	00	FF	FF	00	00	24	00	01	00	00	29	00	01	00
DEC	255	0	0	255	255	0	0	36	0	1	0	0	41	0	1	0
ASC	255	^@	^@	255	255	^@	^@		^@	^A	^@	^@		^@	^A	^@
ALT	255	NUL	NUL	255	255	NUL	NUL		NUL	SOH	NUL	NUL		NUL	SOH	NUL
SYM								$					)			

| ← → | BIN Start Row | BIN End Col. | BIN End Row | Protect | 1 Byte long | Global Protect Off | Label FMT | 1 Byte long |

BYTE	248	249	250	251	252	253	254	255	256	257	258	259	260	261	262	263
HEX	27	0F	00	37	00	FF	00	00	00	00	27	20	20	20	20	20
DEC	39	15	0	55	0	255	0	0	0	0	39	32	32	32	32	32
ASC		^O	^@		^@	255	^@	^@	^@	^@		^ '	^ '	^ '	^ '	^ '
ALT		SI	NUL		NUL	255	NUL	NUL	NUL	NUL		SPC	SPC	SPC	SPC	SPC
SYM	'			7							'					

| Left | Label | 55 Bytes long | Format | Column | Row | ← String → |

BYTE	264	265	266	267	268	269	270	271	272	273	274	275	276	277	278	279
HEX	20	20	20	20	20	20	20	20	20	20	20	20	20	20	20	20
DEC	32	32	32	32	32	32	32	32	32	32	32	32	32	32	32	32
ASC	^ '	^ '	^ '	^ '	^ '	^ '	^ '	^ '	^ '	^ '	^ '	^ '	^ '	^ '	^ '	^ '
ALT	SPC	SPC	SPC	SPC	SPC	SPC	SPC	SPC	SPC	SPC	SPC	SPC	SPC	SPC	SPC	SPC
SYM																

← String →

BYTE	280	281	282	283	284	285	286	287	288	289	290	291	292	293	294	295
HEX	20	20	20	20	54	68	65	20	47	65	74	74	79	73	62	75
DEC	32	32	32	32	84	104	101	32	71	101	116	116	121	115	98	117
ASC	^ '	^ '	^ '	^ '				^ '								
ALT	SPC	SPC	SPC	SPC				SPC								
SYM					T	h	e		G	e	t	t	y	s	b	u

← String →

BYTE	296	297	298	299	300	301	302	303	304	305	306	307	308	309	310	311
HEX	72	67	20	41	64	64	72	65	73	73	14	00	0F	00	48	00
DEC	114	103	32	65	100	100	114	101	115	115	20	0	15	0	72	0
ASC			^ '								^T	^@	^O	^@		^@
ALT			SPC								DC4	NUL	SI	NUL		NUL
SYM	r	g		A	d	d	r	e	s	s					H	

| ← String → | Label | 72 Bytes long |

BYTE	312	313	314	315	316	317	318	319	320	321	322	323	324	325	326	327
HEX	FF	00	00	02	00	27	46	6F	75	72	73	63	6F	72	65	20
DEC	255	0	0	2	0	39	70	111	117	114	115	99	111	114	101	32
ASC	255	^@	^@	^B	^@											^ '
ALT	255	NUL	NUL	STX	NUL											SPC
SYM						'	F	o	u	r	s	c	o	r	e	

| Format | Column | Row | ← String → |

SYMPHONY **169**

BYTE	328	329	330	331	332	333	334	335	336	337	338	339	340	341	342	343
HEX	61	6E	64	20	73	65	76	65	6E	20	20	79	65	61	72	73
DEC	97	110	100	32	115	101	118	101	110	32	32	121	101	97	114	115
ASC				^`						^`	^`					
ALT				SPC						SPC	SPC					
SYM	a	n	d		s	e	v	e	n			y	e	a	r	s

←——————————————— String ———————————————→

BYTE	344	345	346	347	348	349	350	351	352	353	354	355	356	357	358	359
HEX	20	61	67	6F	20	6F	75	72	20	66	61	74	68	65	72	73
DEC	32	97	103	111	32	111	117	114	32	102	97	116	104	101	114	115
ASC	^`				^`				^`							
ALT	SPC				SPC				SPC							
SYM		a	g	o		o	u	r		f	a	t	h	e	r	s

←——————————————— String ———————————————→

BYTE	360	361	362	363	364	365	366	367	368	369	370	371	372	373	374	375
HEX	20	62	72	6F	75	67	68	74	20	20	66	6F	72	74	68	20
DEC	32	98	114	111	117	103	104	116	32	32	102	111	114	116	104	32
ASC	^`								^`	^`						^`
ALT	SPC								SPC	SPC						SPC
SYM		b	r	o	u	g	h	t			f	o	r	t	h	

←——————————————— String ———————————————→

BYTE	376	377	378	379	380	381	382	383	384	385	386	387	388	389	390	391
HEX	6F	6E	20	74	68	69	73	00	0F	00	48	00	FF	00	00	03
DEC	111	110	32	116	104	105	115	0	15	0	72	0	255	0	0	3
ASC			^`					^@	^O	^@		^@	255	^@	^@	^C
ALT			SPC					NUL	SI	NUL		NUL	255	NUL	NUL	ETX
SYM	o	n		t	h	i	s				H					

←———————— String ————————→ |Label|72 Bytes long|Format|Column|Row|

BYTE	392	393	394	395	396	397	398	399	400	401	402	403	404	405	406	407
HEX	00	27	63	6F	6E	74	69	6E	65	6E	74	2C	20	61	20	6E
DEC	0	39	99	111	110	116	105	110	101	110	116	44	32	97	32	110
ASC	^@												^`		^`	
ALT	NUL												SPC		SPC	
SYM		'	c	o	n	t	i	n	e	n	t	,		a		n

Row|←——————————————— String ———————————————→

BYTE	408	409	410	411	412	413	414	415	416	417	418	419	420	421	422	423
HEX	65	77	20	20	6E	61	74	69	6F	6E	2C	20	63	6F	6E	63
DEC	101	119	32	32	110	97	116	105	111	110	44	32	99	111	110	99
ASC			^`	^`								^`				
ALT			SPC	SPC								SPC				
SYM	e	w			n	a	t	i	o	n	,		c	o	n	c

←——————————————— String ———————————————→

BYTE	424	425	426	427	428	429	430	431	432	433	434	435	436	437	438	439
HEX	65	69	76	65	64	20	69	6E	20	4C	69	62	65	72	74	79
DEC	101	105	118	101	100	32	105	110	32	76	105	98	101	114	116	121
ASC						^`		^`								
ALT						SPC		SPC								
SYM	e	i	v	e	d		i	n		L	i	b	e	r	t	y

◄──────────────────── String ────────────────────►

BYTE	440	441	442	443	444	445	446	447	448	449	450	451	452	453	454	455
HEX	2C	20	20	61	6E	64	20	64	65	64	69	63	61	74	65	64
DEC	44	32	32	97	110	100	32	100	101	100	105	99	97	116	101	100
ASC		^`	^`				^`									
ALT		SPC	SPC				SPC									
SYM	,			a	n	d		d	e	d	i	c	a	t	e	d

◄──────────────────── String ────────────────────►

BYTE	456	457	458	459	460	461	462	463	464	465	466	467	468	469	470	471
HEX	20	74	6F	00	0F	00	37	00	FF	00	00	04	00	27	74	68
DEC	32	116	111	0	15	0	55	0	255	0	0	4	0	39	116	104
ASC	^`			^@	^O	^@		^@	255	^@	^@	^D	^@			
ALT	SPC			NUL	SI	NUL		NUL	255	NUL	NUL	EOT	NUL			
SYM		t	o				7							'	t	h

◄─── String ───►│ Label │ 55 Bytes Long │ Format │ Column │ Row │◄─── String ───►

BYTE	472	473	474	475	476	477	478	479	480	481	482	483	484	485	486	487
HEX	65	20	70	72	6F	70	6F	73	69	74	69	6F	6E	20	74	68
DEC	101	32	112	114	111	112	111	115	105	116	105	111	110	32	116	104
ASC		^`												^`		
ALT		SPC												SPC		
SYM	e		p	r	o	p	o	s	i	t	i	o	n		t	h

◄──────────────────── String ────────────────────►

BYTE	488	489	490	491	492	493	494	495	496	497	498	499	500	501	502	503
HEX	61	74	20	61	6C	6C	20	6D	65	6E	20	61	72	65	20	63
DEC	97	116	32	97	108	108	32	109	101	110	32	97	114	101	32	99
ASC			^`				^`				^`				^`	
ALT			SPC				SPC				SPC				SPC	
SYM	a	t		a	l	l		m	e	n		a	r	e		c

◄──────────────────── String ────────────────────►

BYTE	504	505	506	507	508	509	510	511	512	513	514	515	516	517	518	519
HEX	72	65	61	74	65	64	20	65	71	75	61	6C	2E	14	00	0F
DEC	114	101	97	116	101	100	32	101	113	117	97	108	46	20	0	15
ASC							^`							^T	^@	^O
ALT							SPC							DC4	NUL	SI
SYM	r	e	a	t	e	d		e	q	u	a	l	.			

◄──────────────── String ────────────────►│ Label

SYMPHONY **171**

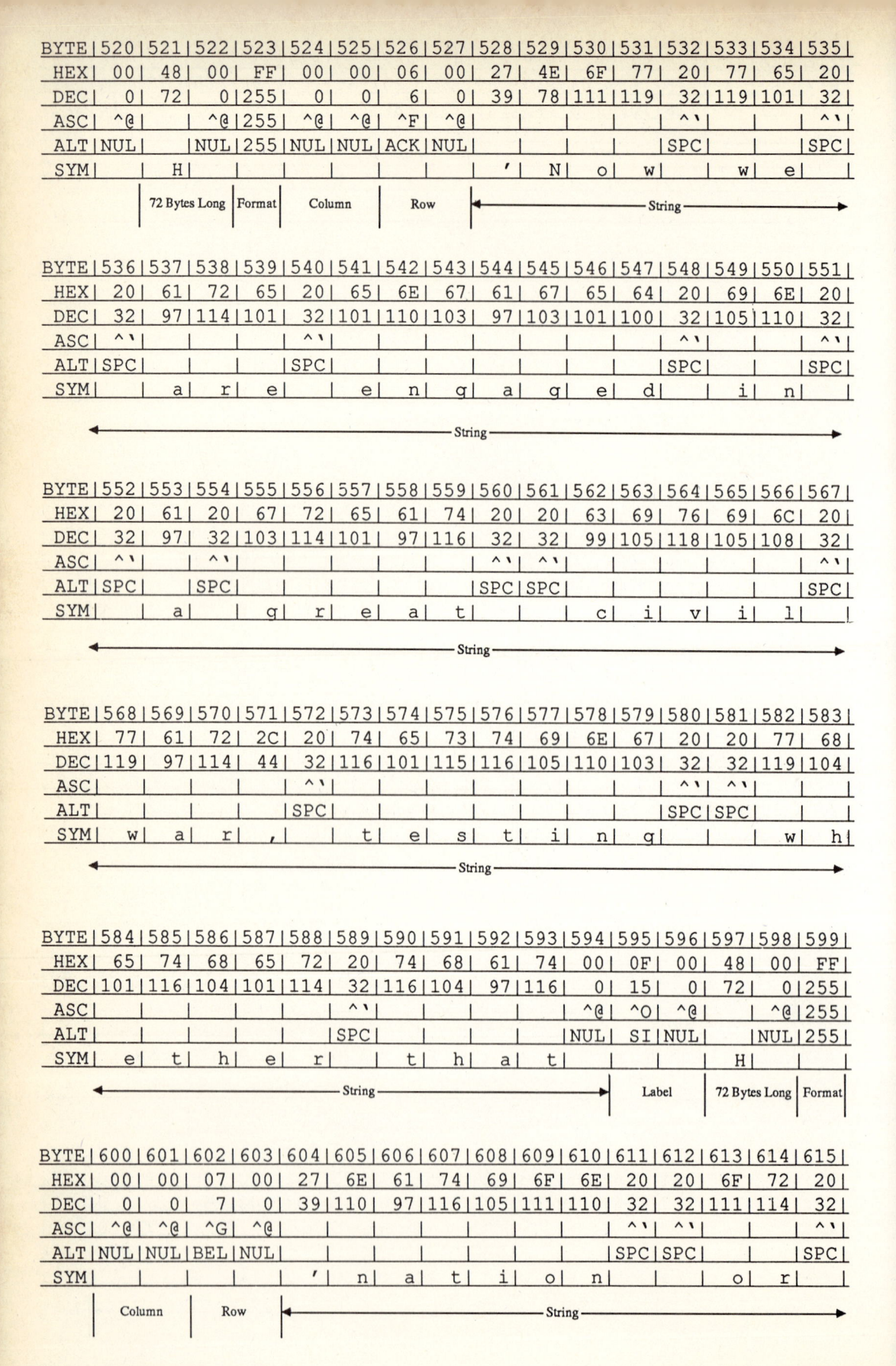

BYTE	520	521	522	523	524	525	526	527	528	529	530	531	532	533	534	535
HEX	00	48	00	FF	00	00	06	00	27	4E	6F	77	20	77	65	20
DEC	0	72	0	255	0	0	6	0	39	78	111	119	32	119	101	32
ASC	^@		^@	255	^@	^@	^F	^@					^`			^`
ALT	NUL		NUL	255	NUL	NUL	ACK	NUL					SPC			SPC
SYM		H							'	N	o	w		w	e	

|72 Bytes Long | Format | Column | Row | ←———— String ————→ |

BYTE	536	537	538	539	540	541	542	543	544	545	546	547	548	549	550	551
HEX	20	61	72	65	20	65	6E	67	61	67	65	64	20	69	6E	20
DEC	32	97	114	101	32	101	110	103	97	103	101	100	32	105	110	32
ASC	^`				^`								^`			^`
ALT	SPC				SPC								SPC			SPC
SYM		a	r	e		e	n	g	a	g	e	d		i	n	

←———————————— String ————————————→

BYTE	552	553	554	555	556	557	558	559	560	561	562	563	564	565	566	567
HEX	20	61	20	67	72	65	61	74	20	20	63	69	76	69	6C	20
DEC	32	97	32	103	114	101	97	116	32	32	99	105	118	105	108	32
ASC	^`		^`						^`	^`						^`
ALT	SPC		SPC						SPC	SPC						SPC
SYM		a		g	r	e	a	t			c	i	v	i	l	

←———————————— String ————————————→

BYTE	568	569	570	571	572	573	574	575	576	577	578	579	580	581	582	583
HEX	77	61	72	2C	20	74	65	73	74	69	6E	67	20	20	77	68
DEC	119	97	114	44	32	116	101	115	116	105	110	103	32	32	119	104
ASC					^`								^`	^`		
ALT					SPC								SPC	SPC		
SYM	w	a	r	,		t	e	s	t	i	n	g			w	h

←———————————— String ————————————→

BYTE	584	585	586	587	588	589	590	591	592	593	594	595	596	597	598	599
HEX	65	74	68	65	72	20	74	68	61	74	00	0F	00	48	00	FF
DEC	101	116	104	101	114	32	116	104	97	116	0	15	0	72	0	255
ASC						^`					^@	^O	^@		^@	255
ALT						SPC					NUL	SI	NUL		NUL	255
SYM	e	t	h	e	r		t	h	a	t				H		

←———— String ————→ | Label | 72 Bytes Long | Format |

BYTE	600	601	602	603	604	605	606	607	608	609	610	611	612	613	614	615
HEX	00	00	07	00	27	6E	61	74	69	6F	6E	20	20	6F	72	20
DEC	0	0	7	0	39	110	97	116	105	111	110	32	32	111	114	32
ASC	^@	^@	^G	^@								^`	^`			^`
ALT	NUL	NUL	BEL	NUL								SPC	SPC			SPC
SYM					'	n	a	t	i	o	n			o	r	

| Column | Row | ←———— String ————→ |

172 SYMPHONY

BYTE	616	617	618	619	620	621	622	623	624	625	626	627	628	629	630	631
HEX	61	6E	79	20	20	6E	61	74	69	6F	6E	20	73	6F	20	20
DEC	97	110	121	32	32	110	97	116	105	111	110	32	115	111	32	32
ASC				^`	^`							^`			^`	^`
ALT				SPC	SPC							SPC			SPC	SPC
SYM	a	n	y			n	a	t	i	o	n		s	o		

◄──────────────────── String ────────────────────►

BYTE	632	633	634	635	636	637	638	639	640	641	642	643	644	645	646	647
HEX	63	6F	6E	63	65	69	76	65	64	20	20	61	6E	64	20	73
DEC	99	111	110	99	101	105	118	101	100	32	32	97	110	100	32	115
ASC										^`	^`				^`	
ALT										SPC	SPC				SPC	
SYM	c	o	n	c	e	i	v	e	d			a	n	d		s

◄──────────────────── String ────────────────────►

BYTE	648	649	650	651	652	653	654	655	656	657	658	659	660	661	662	663
HEX	6F	20	20	64	65	64	69	63	61	74	65	64	20	63	61	6E
DEC	111	32	32	100	101	100	105	99	97	116	101	100	32	99	97	110
ASC		^`	^`										^`			
ALT		SPC	SPC										SPC			
SYM	o			d	e	d	i	c	a	t	e	d		c	a	n

◄──────────────────── String ────────────────────►

BYTE	664	665	666	667	668	669	670	671	672	673	674	675	676	677	678	679
HEX	20	20	6C	6F	6E	67	00	0F	00	48	00	FF	00	00	08	00
DEC	32	32	108	111	110	103	0	15	0	72	0	255	0	0	8	0
ASC	^`	^`					^@	^O	^@		^@	255	^@	^@	^H	^@
ALT	SPC	SPC					NUL	SI	NUL		NUL	255	NUL	NUL	BS	NUL
SYM			l	o	n	g				H						

◄─── String ───► | Label | 72 Bytes Long | Format | Column | Row |

BYTE	680	681	682	683	684	685	686	687	688	689	690	691	692	693	694	695
HEX	27	65	6E	64	75	72	65	2E	20	20	57	65	20	61	72	65
DEC	39	101	110	100	117	114	101	46	32	32	87	101	32	97	114	101
ASC									^`	^`			^`			
ALT									SPC	SPC			SPC			
SYM	'	e	n	d	u	r	e	.			W	e		a	r	e

◄──────────────────── String ────────────────────►

BYTE	696	697	698	699	700	701	702	703	704	705	706	707	708	709	710	711
HEX	20	6D	65	74	20	6F	6E	20	61	20	20	67	72	65	61	74
DEC	32	109	101	116	32	111	110	32	97	32	32	103	114	101	97	116
ASC	^`				^`			^`		^`	^`					
ALT	SPC				SPC			SPC		SPC	SPC					
SYM		m	e	t		o	n		a			g	r	e	a	t

◄──────────────────── String ────────────────────►

SYMPHONY **173**

BYTE	712	713	714	715	716	717	718	719	720	721	722	723	724	725	726	727
HEX	20	62	61	74	74	6C	65	66	69	65	6C	64	20	6F	66	20
DEC	32	98	97	116	116	108	101	102	105	101	108	100	32	111	102	32
ASC	^`												^`			^`
ALT	SPC												SPC			SPC
SYM		b	a	t	t	l	e	f	i	e	l	d		o	f	

←——————————————— String ———————————————→

BYTE	728	729	730	731	732	733	734	735	736	737	738	739	740	741	742	743
HEX	74	68	61	74	20	77	61	72	2E	20	20	57	65	20	68	61
DEC	116	104	97	116	32	119	97	114	46	32	32	87	101	32	104	97
ASC					^`					^`	^`			^`		
ALT					SPC					SPC	SPC			SPC		
SYM	t	h	a	t		w	a	r	.			W	e		h	a

←——————————————— String ———————————————→

BYTE	744	745	746	747	748	749	750	751	752	753	754	755	756	757	758	759
HEX	76	65	00	0F	00	48	00	FF	00	00	09	00	27	63	6F	6D
DEC	118	101	0	15	0	72	0	255	0	0	9	0	39	99	111	109
ASC			^@	^O	^@		^@	255	^@	^@	^I	^@				
ALT			NUL	SI	NUL		NUL	255	NUL	NUL	HT	NUL				
SYM	v	e				H							'	c	o	m

←— String —→ Label 72 Bytes Long Format Column Row ←— String —→

BYTE	760	761	762	763	764	765	766	767	768	769	770	771	772	773	774	775
HEX	65	20	74	6F	20	20	64	65	64	69	63	61	74	65	20	61
DEC	101	32	116	111	32	32	100	101	100	105	99	97	116	101	32	97
ASC		^`			^`	^`									^`	
ALT		SPC			SPC	SPC									SPC	
SYM	e		t	o			d	e	d	i	c	a	t	e		a

←——————————————— String ———————————————→

BYTE	776	777	778	779	780	781	782	783	784	785	786	787	788	789	790	791
HEX	20	20	70	6F	72	74	69	6F	6E	20	6F	66	20	20	74	68
DEC	32	32	112	111	114	116	105	111	110	32	111	102	32	32	116	104
ASC	^`	^`								^`			^`	^`		
ALT	SPC	SPC								SPC			SPC	SPC		
SYM			p	o	r	t	i	o	n		o	f			t	h

←——————————————— String ———————————————→

BYTE	792	793	794	795	796	797	798	799	800	801	802	803	804	805	806	807
HEX	61	74	20	66	69	65	6C	64	2C	20	20	61	73	20	61	20
DEC	97	116	32	102	105	101	108	100	44	32	32	97	115	32	97	32
ASC			^`							^`	^`			^`		^`
ALT			SPC							SPC	SPC			SPC		SPC
SYM	a	t		f	i	e	l	d	,			a	s		a	

←——————————————— String ———————————————→

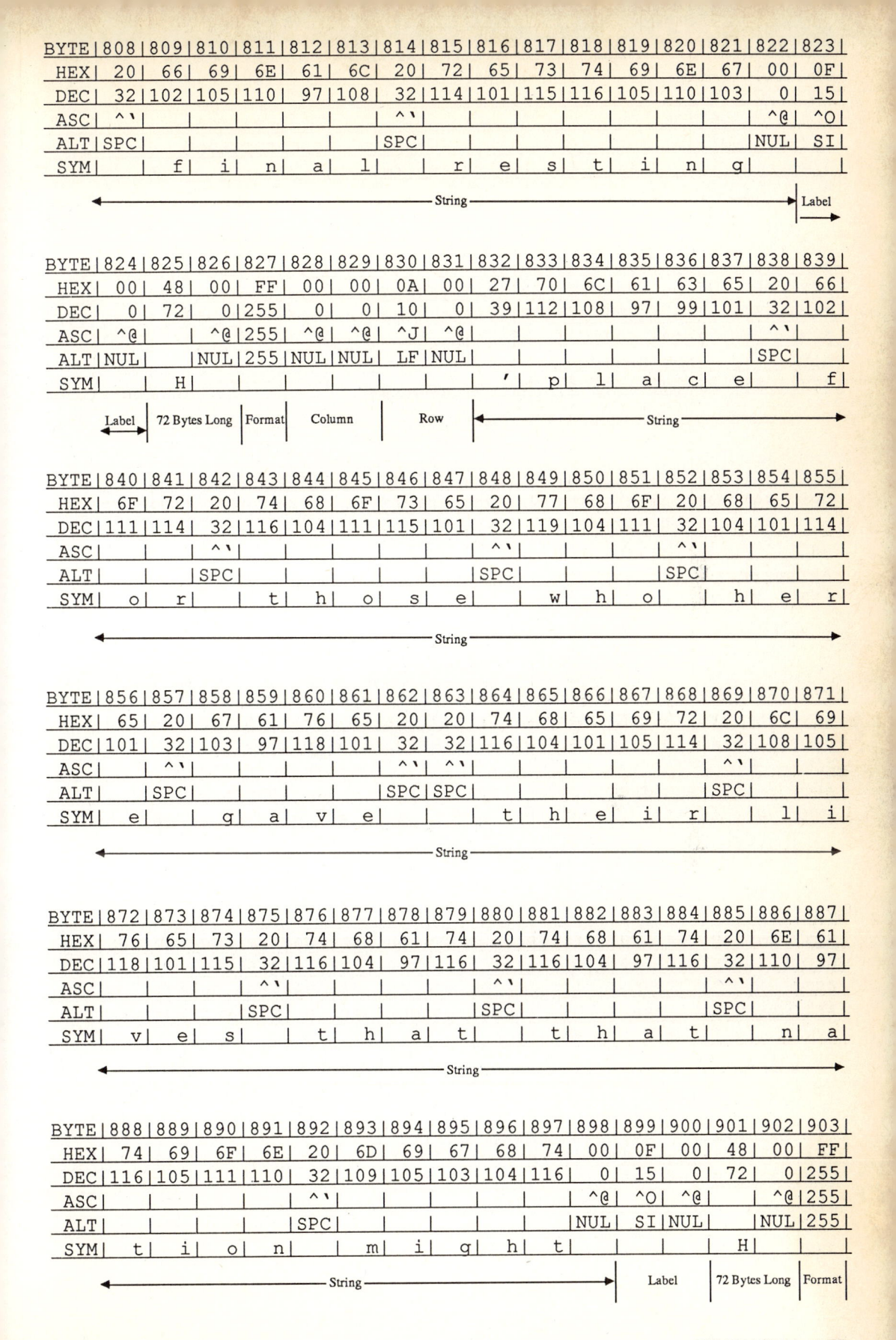

BYTE	808	809	810	811	812	813	814	815	816	817	818	819	820	821	822	823
HEX	20	66	69	6E	61	6C	20	72	65	73	74	69	6E	67	00	0F
DEC	32	102	105	110	97	108	32	114	101	115	116	105	110	103	0	15
ASC	^`						^`								^@	^O
ALT	SPC						SPC								NUL	SI
SYM		f	i	n	a	l		r	e	s	t	i	n	g		

◀──────────────────── String ────────────────────▶ Label ▶

BYTE	824	825	826	827	828	829	830	831	832	833	834	835	836	837	838	839
HEX	00	48	00	FF	00	00	0A	00	27	70	6C	61	63	65	20	66
DEC	0	72	0	255	0	0	10	0	39	112	108	97	99	101	32	102
ASC	^@		^@	255	^@	^@	^J	^@							^`	
ALT	NUL		NUL	255	NUL	NUL	LF	NUL							SPC	
SYM		H							'	p	l	a	c	e		f

Label | 72 Bytes Long | Format | Column | Row | ◀──────── String ────────▶

BYTE	840	841	842	843	844	845	846	847	848	849	850	851	852	853	854	855
HEX	6F	72	20	74	68	6F	73	65	20	77	68	6F	20	68	65	72
DEC	111	114	32	116	104	111	115	101	32	119	104	111	32	104	101	114
ASC			^`						^`				^`			
ALT			SPC						SPC				SPC			
SYM	o	r		t	h	o	s	e		w	h	o		h	e	r

◀──────────────────── String ────────────────────▶

BYTE	856	857	858	859	860	861	862	863	864	865	866	867	868	869	870	871
HEX	65	20	67	61	76	65	20	20	74	68	65	69	72	20	6C	69
DEC	101	32	103	97	118	101	32	32	116	104	101	105	114	32	108	105
ASC		^`					^`	^`						^`		
ALT		SPC					SPC	SPC						SPC		
SYM	e		g	a	v	e			t	h	e	i	r		l	i

◀──────────────────── String ────────────────────▶

BYTE	872	873	874	875	876	877	878	879	880	881	882	883	884	885	886	887
HEX	76	65	73	20	74	68	61	74	20	74	68	61	74	20	6E	61
DEC	118	101	115	32	116	104	97	116	32	116	104	97	116	32	110	97
ASC				^`					^`					^`		
ALT				SPC					SPC					SPC		
SYM	v	e	s		t	h	a	t		t	h	a	t		n	a

◀──────────────────── String ────────────────────▶

BYTE	888	889	890	891	892	893	894	895	896	897	898	899	900	901	902	903
HEX	74	69	6F	6E	20	6D	69	67	68	74	00	0F	00	48	00	FF
DEC	116	105	111	110	32	109	105	103	104	116	0	15	0	72	0	255
ASC					^`						^@	^O	^@		^@	255
ALT					SPC						NUL	SI	NUL		NUL	255
SYM	t	i	o	n		m	i	g	h	t				H		

◀──────────── String ────────────▶ Label | 72 Bytes Long | Format

SYMPHONY 175

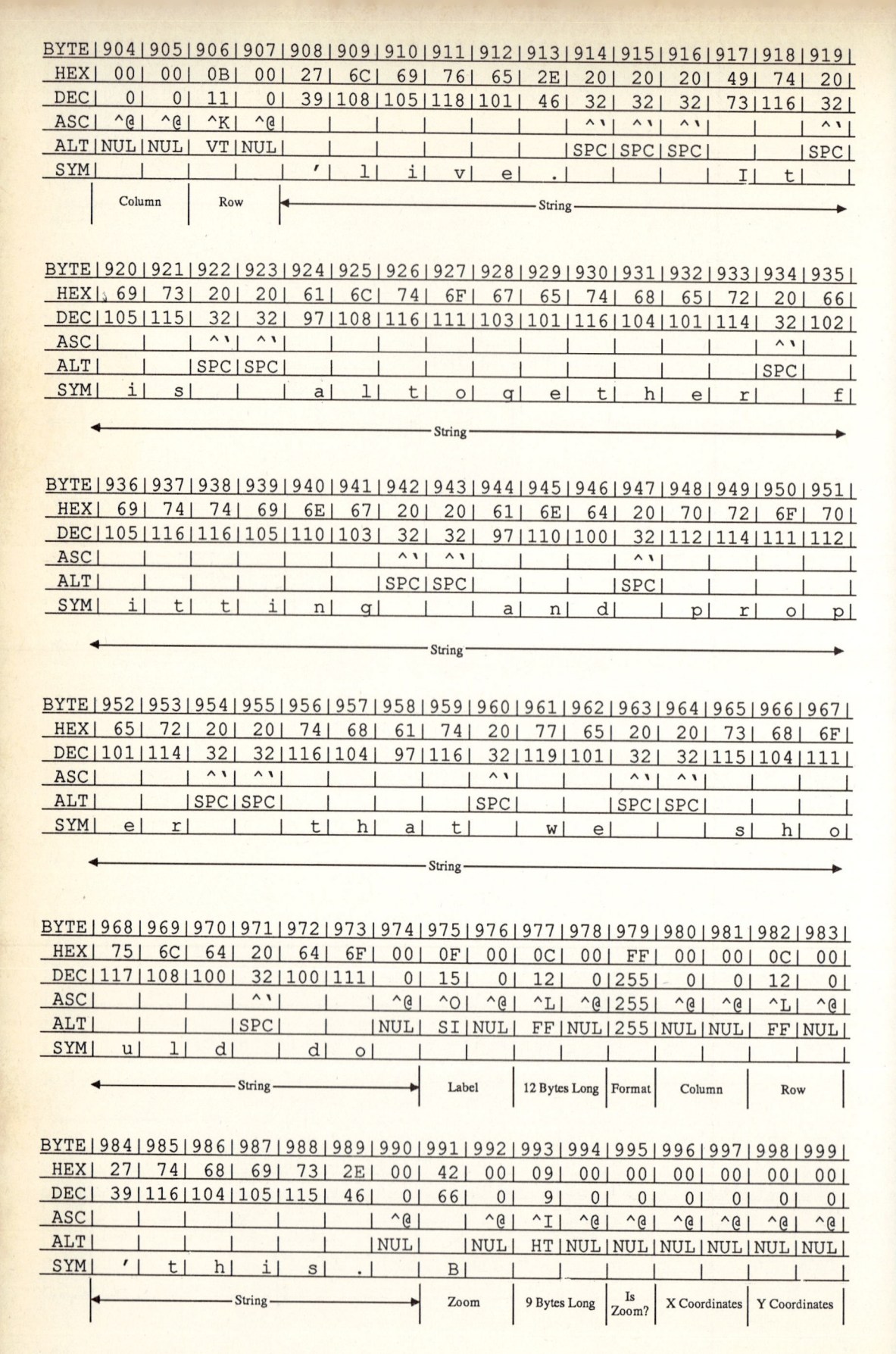

BYTE	904	905	906	907	908	909	910	911	912	913	914	915	916	917	918	919
HEX	00	00	0B	00	27	6C	69	76	65	2E	20	20	20	49	74	20
DEC	0	0	11	0	39	108	105	118	101	46	32	32	32	73	116	32
ASC	^@	^@	^K	^@							^\	^\	^\			^\
ALT	NUL	NUL	VT	NUL							SPC	SPC	SPC			SPC
SYM					'	l	i	v	e	.				I	t	

Column | Row | String

BYTE	920	921	922	923	924	925	926	927	928	929	930	931	932	933	934	935
HEX	69	73	20	20	61	6C	74	6F	67	65	74	68	65	72	20	66
DEC	105	115	32	32	97	108	116	111	103	101	116	104	101	114	32	102
ASC			^\	^\											^\	
ALT			SPC	SPC											SPC	
SYM	i	s			a	l	t	o	g	e	t	h	e	r		f

String

BYTE	936	937	938	939	940	941	942	943	944	945	946	947	948	949	950	951
HEX	69	74	74	69	6E	67	20	20	61	6E	64	20	70	72	6F	70
DEC	105	116	116	105	110	103	32	32	97	110	100	32	112	114	111	112
ASC							^\	^\				^\				
ALT							SPC	SPC				SPC				
SYM	i	t	t	i	n	g			a	n	d		p	r	o	p

String

BYTE	952	953	954	955	956	957	958	959	960	961	962	963	964	965	966	967
HEX	65	72	20	20	74	68	61	74	20	77	65	20	20	73	68	6F
DEC	101	114	32	32	116	104	97	116	32	119	101	32	32	115	104	111
ASC			^\	^\					^\			^\	^\			
ALT			SPC	SPC					SPC			SPC	SPC			
SYM	e	r			t	h	a	t		w	e			s	h	o

String

BYTE	968	969	970	971	972	973	974	975	976	977	978	979	980	981	982	983
HEX	75	6C	64	20	64	6F	00	0F	00	0C	00	FF	00	00	0C	00
DEC	117	108	100	32	100	111	0	15	0	12	0	255	0	0	12	0
ASC				^\			^@	^O	^@	^L	^@	255	^@	^@	^L	^@
ALT				SPC			NUL	SI	NUL	FF	NUL	255	NUL	NUL	FF	NUL
SYM	u	l	d		d	o										

String | Label | 12 Bytes Long | Format | Column | Row

BYTE	984	985	986	987	988	989	990	991	992	993	994	995	996	997	998	999
HEX	27	74	68	69	73	2E	00	42	00	09	00	00	00	00	00	00
DEC	39	116	104	105	115	46	0	66	0	9	0	0	0	0	0	0
ASC							^@		^@	^I	^@	^@	^@	^@	^@	^@
ALT							NUL		NUL	HT	NUL	NUL	NUL	NUL	NUL	NUL
SYM	'	t	h	i	s	.		B								

String | Zoom | 9 Bytes Long | Is Zoom? | X Coordinates | Y Coordinates

176 SYMPHONY

BYTE	0	1	2	3	4	5	6	7	8	9	10	11	12	13	14	15
HEX	00	00	00	00	43	00	02	00	00	00	4A	00	10	00	FF	FF
DEC	0	0	0	0	67	0	2	0	0	0	74	0	16	0	255	255
ASC	^@	^@	^@	^@		^@	^B	^@	^@	^@		^@	^P	^@	255	255
ALT	NUL	NUL	NUL	NUL		NUL	STX	NUL	NUL	NUL		NUL	DLE	NUL	255	255
SYM					C						J					

| Column Depth | Row Depth | Symsplit | 2 Bytes Long | Number of Split Windows | Parse | 16 Bytes Long | Parse Range Start Column |

BYTE	16	17	18	19	20	21	22	23	24	25	26	27	28	29	30	31
HEX	00	00	FF	FF	00	00	FF	FF	00	00	FF	FF	00	00	01	00
DEC	0	0	255	255	0	0	255	255	0	0	255	255	0	0	1	0
ASC	^@	^@	255	255	^@	^@	255	255	^@	^@	255	255	^@	^@	^A	^@
ALT	NUL	NUL	255	255	NUL	NUL	255	255	NUL	NUL	255	255	NUL	NUL	SOH	NUL
SYM																

| Parse Range Start Row | Parse Range End Column | Parse Range End Row | Review Start Column | Review Start Row | Review End Column | Review End Row | End of File |

BYTE	32	33	0	0	0	0	0	0	0	0	0	0	0	0	0	0
HEX	00	00	XX	XX	XX	XX	XX	XX	XX	XX	XX	XX	XX	XX	XX	XX
DEC	0	0	0	0	0	0	0	0	0	0	0	0	0	0	0	0
ASC	^@	^@	XXX	XXX	XXX	XXX	XXX	XXX	XXX	XXX	XXX	XXX	XXX	XXX	XXX	XXX
ALT	NUL	NUL	XXX	XXX	XXX	XXX	XXX	XXX	XXX	XXX	XXX	XXX	XXX	XXX	XXX	XXX
SYM																

End of Symphony File

Sample Spreadsheet as an Ability File

BYTE	0	1	2	3	4	5	6	7	8	9	10	11	12	13	14	15
HEX	2D	2D	48	44	52	31	2E	30	2D	2D	20	32	33	20	53	53
DEC	45	45	72	68	82	49	46	48	45	45	32	50	51	32	83	83
ASC									^'				^'			
ALT									SPC				SPC			
SYM	-	-	H	D	R	1	.	0	-	-		2	3		S	S

- Bytes 0–9: Header String and Version Number
- Bytes 10–12: Lines in Document
- Bytes 13–15: Document Type

BYTE	16	17	18	19	20	21	22	23	24	25	26	27	28	29	30	31
HEX	3B	30	20	30	20	30	20	31	32	20	31	33	20	31	33	20
DEC	59	48	32	48	32	48	32	49	50	32	49	51	32	49	51	32
ASC			^'		^'		^'			^'			^'			^'
ALT			SPC		SPC		SPC			SPC			SPC			SPC
SYM	;	0		0		0		1	2		1	3		1	3	

- Byte 16–17: Col. A Change FM Default
- Column B
- Column C
- Column D Width in Characters
- Column E Width in Characters
- Column F Width in Characters

BYTE	32	33	34	35	36	37	38	39	40	41	42	43	44	45	46	47
HEX	0D	0A	09	09	09	09	27	50	61	79	6D	65	6E	74	20	41
DEC	13	10	9	9	9	9	39	80	97	121	109	101	110	116	32	65
ASC	^M	^J	^I	^I	^I	^I									^'	
ALT	CR	LF	HT	HT	HT	HT									SPC	
SYM							'	P	a	y	m	e	n	t		A

- Newline, Tab (Start of Text), Tab, Tab, Tab (Nothing in Column), L Just — Contents Column D

BYTE	48	49	50	51	52	53	54	55	56	57	58	59	60	61	62	63
HEX	6E	61	6C	79	73	69	73	20	57	6F	72	6B	73	68	65	65
DEC	110	97	108	121	115	105	115	32	87	111	114	107	115	104	101	101
ASC								^'								
ALT								SPC								
SYM	n	a	l	y	s	i	s		W	o	r	k	s	h	e	e

- Contents Column D

BYTE	64	65	66	67	68	69	70	71	72	73	74	75	76	77	78	79
HEX	74	0D	0A	09	09	09	09	2A	3D	09	2A	3D	09	2A	3D	0D
DEC	116	13	10	9	9	9	9	42	61	9	42	61	9	42	61	13
ASC		^M	^J	^I	^I	^I	^I			^I			^I			^M
ALT		CR	LF	HT	HT	HT	HT			HT			HT			CR
SYM	t							*	=		*	=		*	=	

- Newline, Tab, Tab, Tab, Tab, D2-Repeating Character, Column Divider Tab, E2, Tab, F2, Newline

178 ABILITY SPREADSHEET

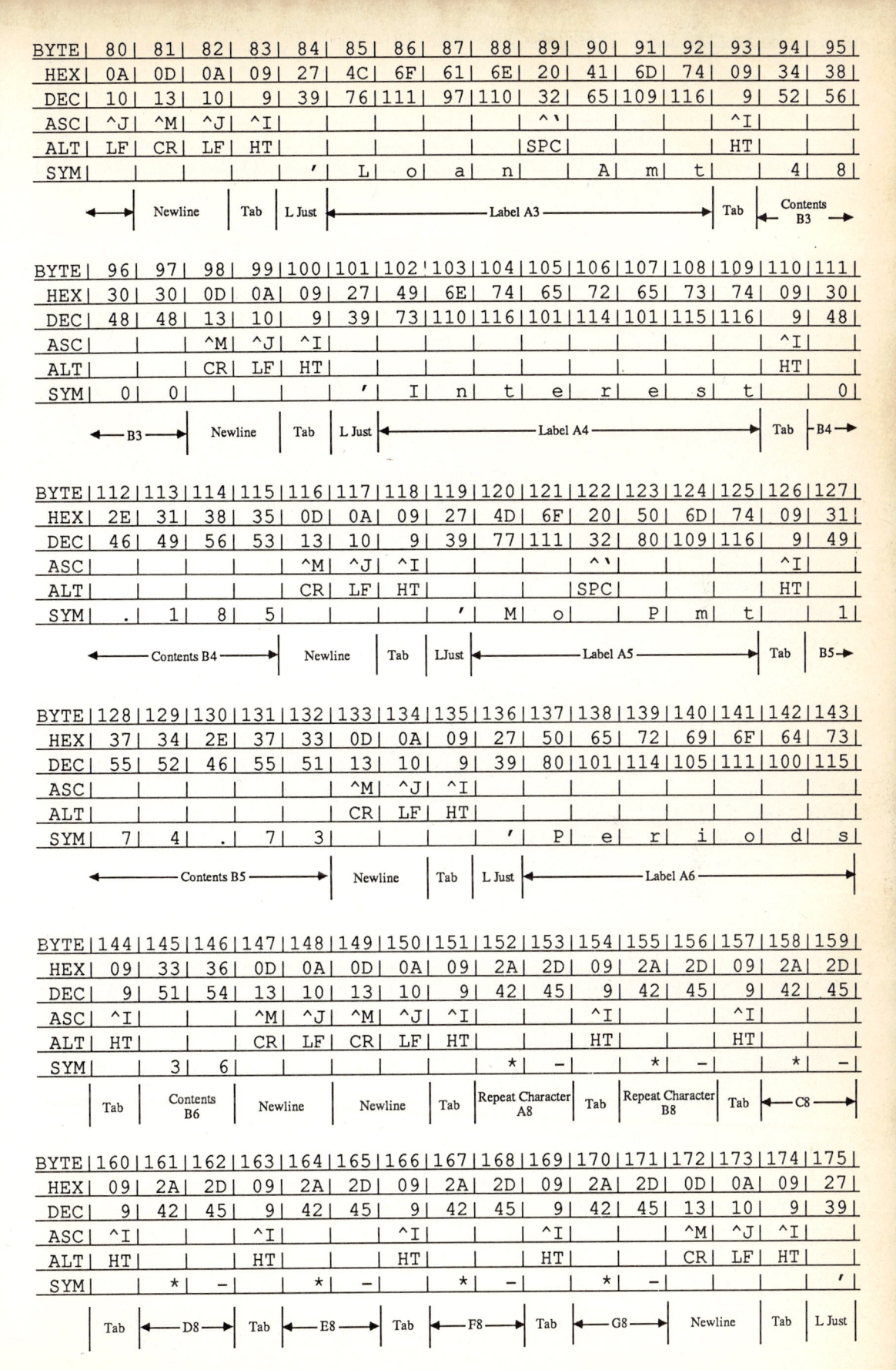

BYTE	80	81	82	83	84	85	86	87	88	89	90	91	92	93	94	95
HEX	0A	0D	0A	09	27	4C	6F	61	6E	20	41	6D	74	09	34	38
DEC	10	13	10	9	39	76	111	97	110	32	65	109	116	9	52	56
ASC	^J	^M	^J	^I						^`				^I		
ALT	LF	CR	LF	HT						SPC				HT		
SYM					'	L	o	a	n		A	m	t		4	8

← Newline | Tab | L Just | ←——— Label A3 ———→ | Tab | ← Contents B3 →

BYTE	96	97	98	99	100	101	102	103	104	105	106	107	108	109	110	111
HEX	30	30	0D	0A	09	27	49	6E	74	65	72	65	73	74	09	30
DEC	48	48	13	10	9	39	73	110	116	101	114	101	115	116	9	48
ASC			^M	^J	^I										^I	
ALT			CR	LF	HT										HT	
SYM	0	0				'	I	n	t	e	r	e	s	t		0

← B3 → | Newline | Tab | L Just | ←——— Label A4 ———→ | Tab | ← B4 →

BYTE	112	113	114	115	116	117	118	119	120	121	122	123	124	125	126	127
HEX	2E	31	38	35	0D	0A	09	27	4D	6F	20	50	6D	74	09	31
DEC	46	49	56	53	13	10	9	39	77	111	32	80	109	116	9	49
ASC					^M	^J	^I				^`				^I	
ALT					CR	LF	HT				SPC				HT	
SYM	.	1	8	5				'	M	o		P	m	t		1

←——— Contents B4 ———→ | Newline | Tab | LJust | ←——— Label A5 ———→ | Tab | ← B5 →

BYTE	128	129	130	131	132	133	134	135	136	137	138	139	140	141	142	143
HEX	37	34	2E	37	33	0D	0A	09	27	50	65	72	69	6F	64	73
DEC	55	52	46	55	51	13	10	9	39	80	101	114	105	111	100	115
ASC						^M	^J	^I								
ALT						CR	LF	HT								
SYM	7	4	.	7	3				'	P	e	r	i	o	d	s

←——— Contents B5 ———→ | Newline | Tab | L Just | ←——— Label A6 ———→

BYTE	144	145	146	147	148	149	150	151	152	153	154	155	156	157	158	159
HEX	09	33	36	0D	0A	0D	0A	09	2A	2D	09	2A	2D	09	2A	2D
DEC	9	51	54	13	10	13	10	9	42	45	9	42	45	9	42	45
ASC	^I			^M	^J	^M	^J	^I			^I			^I		
ALT	HT			CR	LF	CR	LF	HT			HT			HT		
SYM		3	6						*	–		*	–		*	–

Tab | Contents B6 | Newline | Newline | Tab | Repeat Character A8 | Tab | Repeat Character B8 | Tab | ← C8 →

BYTE	160	161	162	163	164	165	166	167	168	169	170	171	172	173	174	175
HEX	09	2A	2D	09	2A	2D	09	2A	2D	09	2A	2D	0D	0A	09	27
DEC	9	42	45	9	42	45	9	42	45	9	42	45	13	10	9	39
ASC	^I			^I			^I			^I			^M	^J	^I	
ALT	HT			HT			HT			HT			CR	LF	HT	
SYM		*	–		*	–		*	–		*	–				'

Tab | ← D8 → | Tab | ← E8 → | Tab | ← F8 → | Tab | ← G8 → | Newline | Tab | L Just

ABILITY SPREADSHEET

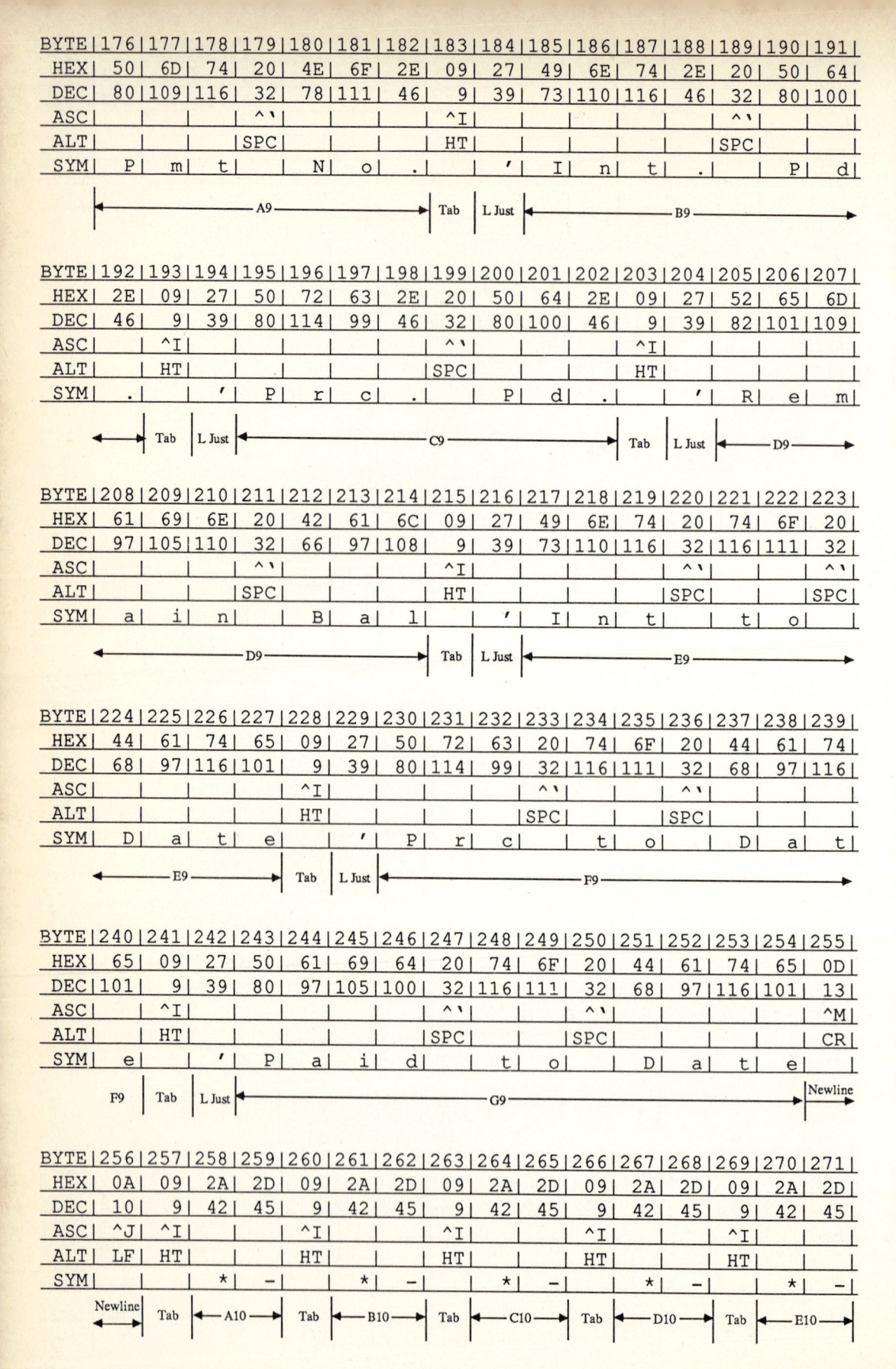

BYTE	176	177	178	179	180	181	182	183	184	185	186	187	188	189	190	191
HEX	50	6D	74	20	4E	6F	2E	09	27	49	6E	74	2E	20	50	64
DEC	80	109	116	32	78	111	46	9	39	73	110	116	46	32	80	100
ASC				^`				^I						^`		
ALT				SPC				HT						SPC		
SYM	P	m	t		N	o	.		'	I	n	t	.		P	d

⟵──────── A9 ────────⟶ | Tab | L Just ⟵──────── B9 ────────⟶

BYTE	192	193	194	195	196	197	198	199	200	201	202	203	204	205	206	207
HEX	2E	09	27	50	72	63	2E	20	50	64	2E	09	27	52	65	6D
DEC	46	9	39	80	114	99	46	32	80	100	46	9	39	82	101	109
ASC		^I						^`				^I				
ALT		HT						SPC				HT				
SYM	.		'	P	r	c	.		P	d	.		'	R	e	m

⟵ Tab | L Just ⟵──────── C9 ────────⟶ | Tab | L Just ⟵──── D9 ────⟶

BYTE	208	209	210	211	212	213	214	215	216	217	218	219	220	221	222	223
HEX	61	69	6E	20	42	61	6C	09	27	49	6E	74	20	74	6F	20
DEC	97	105	110	32	66	97	108	9	39	73	110	116	32	116	111	32
ASC				^`				^I					^`			^`
ALT				SPC				HT					SPC			SPC
SYM	a	i	n		B	a	l		'	I	n	t		t	o	

⟵──────── D9 ────────⟶ | Tab | L Just ⟵──────── E9 ────────⟶

BYTE	224	225	226	227	228	229	230	231	232	233	234	235	236	237	238	239
HEX	44	61	74	65	09	27	50	72	63	20	74	6F	20	44	61	74
DEC	68	97	116	101	9	39	80	114	99	32	116	111	32	68	97	116
ASC					^I					^`			^`			
ALT					HT					SPC			SPC			
SYM	D	a	t	e		'	P	r	c		t	o		D	a	t

⟵──── E9 ────⟶ | Tab | L Just ⟵──────── F9 ────────⟶

BYTE	240	241	242	243	244	245	246	247	248	249	250	251	252	253	254	255
HEX	65	09	27	50	61	69	64	20	74	6F	20	44	61	74	65	0D
DEC	101	9	39	80	97	105	100	32	116	111	32	68	97	116	101	13
ASC		^I						^`			^`					^M
ALT		HT						SPC			SPC					CR
SYM	e		'	P	a	i	d		t	o		D	a	t	e	

F9 | Tab | L Just ⟵──────── G9 ────────⟶ | Newline

BYTE	256	257	258	259	260	261	262	263	264	265	266	267	268	269	270	271
HEX	0A	09	2A	2D	09	2A	2D	09	2A	2D	09	2A	2D	09	2A	2D
DEC	10	9	42	45	9	42	45	9	42	45	9	42	45	9	42	45
ASC	^J	^I		^I		^I		^I		^I		^I		^I		
ALT	LF	HT		HT		HT		HT		HT		HT		HT		
SYM			*	–		*	–		*	–		*	–		*	–

Newline | Tab ⟵ A10 ⟶ Tab ⟵ B10 ⟶ Tab ⟵ C10 ⟶ Tab ⟵ D10 ⟶ Tab ⟵ E10 ⟶

180 ABILITY SPREADSHEET

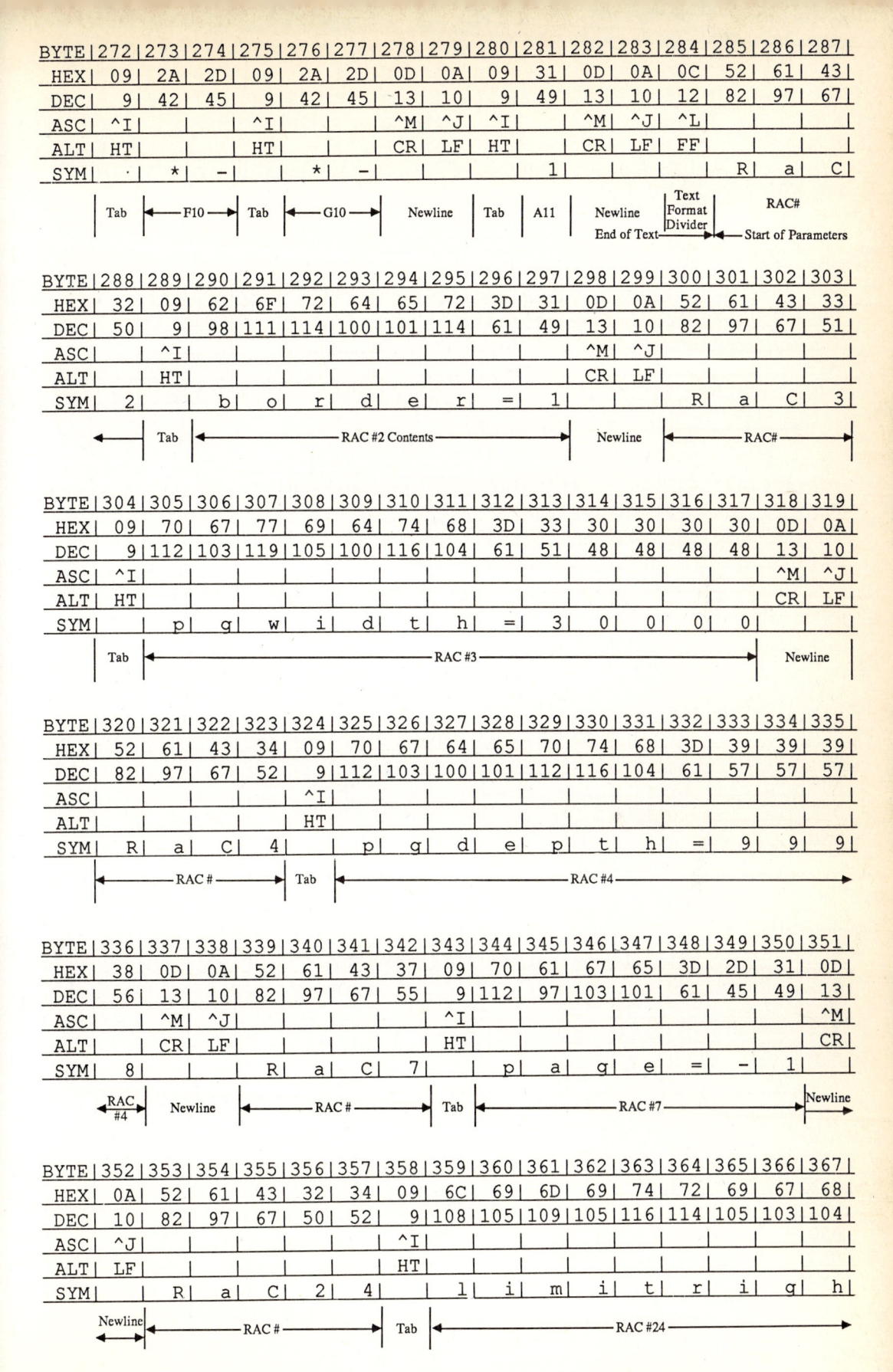

BYTE	272	273	274	275	276	277	278	279	280	281	282	283	284	285	286	287
HEX	09	2A	2D	09	2A	2D	0D	0A	09	31	0D	0A	0C	52	61	43
DEC	9	42	45	9	42	45	13	10	9	49	13	10	12	82	97	67
ASC	^I			^I			^M	^J	^I		^M	^J	^L			
ALT	HT			HT			CR	LF	HT		CR	LF	FF			
SYM		*	−		*	−				1				R	a	C

Tab ←—F10—→ Tab ←—G10—→ Newline Tab A11 Newline Text Format Divider RAC#
                                           End of Text—→ ←—Start of Parameters

BYTE	288	289	290	291	292	293	294	295	296	297	298	299	300	301	302	303
HEX	32	09	62	6F	72	64	65	72	3D	31	0D	0A	52	61	43	33
DEC	50	9	98	111	114	100	101	114	61	49	13	10	82	97	67	51
ASC		^I									^M	^J				
ALT		HT									CR	LF				
SYM	2		b	o	r	d	e	r	=	1			R	a	C	3

←— Tab ←——— RAC #2 Contents ———→ Newline ←——— RAC# ———→

BYTE	304	305	306	307	308	309	310	311	312	313	314	315	316	317	318	319
HEX	09	70	67	77	69	64	74	68	3D	33	30	30	30	30	0D	0A
DEC	9	112	103	119	105	100	116	104	61	51	48	48	48	48	13	10
ASC	^I														^M	^J
ALT	HT														CR	LF
SYM		p	g	w	i	d	t	h	=	3	0	0	0	0		

Tab ←——————— RAC #3 ———————→ Newline

BYTE	320	321	322	323	324	325	326	327	328	329	330	331	332	333	334	335
HEX	52	61	43	34	09	70	67	64	65	70	74	68	3D	39	39	39
DEC	82	97	67	52	9	112	103	100	101	112	116	104	61	57	57	57
ASC					^I											
ALT					HT											
SYM	R	a	C	4		p	g	d	e	p	t	h	=	9	9	9

←— RAC # —→ Tab ←——————— RAC #4 ———————→

BYTE	336	337	338	339	340	341	342	343	344	345	346	347	348	349	350	351
HEX	38	0D	0A	52	61	43	37	09	70	61	67	65	3D	2D	31	0D
DEC	56	13	10	82	97	67	55	9	112	97	103	101	61	45	49	13
ASC		^M	^J					^I								^M
ALT		CR	LF					HT								CR
SYM	8			R	a	C	7		p	a	g	e	=	−	1	

←RAC #4 Newline ←——— RAC # ———→ Tab ←——— RAC #7 ———→ Newline

BYTE	352	353	354	355	356	357	358	359	360	361	362	363	364	365	366	367
HEX	0A	52	61	43	32	34	09	6C	69	6D	69	74	72	69	67	68
DEC	10	82	97	67	50	52	9	108	105	109	105	116	114	105	103	104
ASC	^J						^I									
ALT	LF						HT									
SYM		R	a	C	2	4		l	i	m	i	t	r	i	g	h

Newline ←——— RAC # ———→ Tab ←——————— RAC #24 ———————→

ABILITY SPREADSHEET **181**

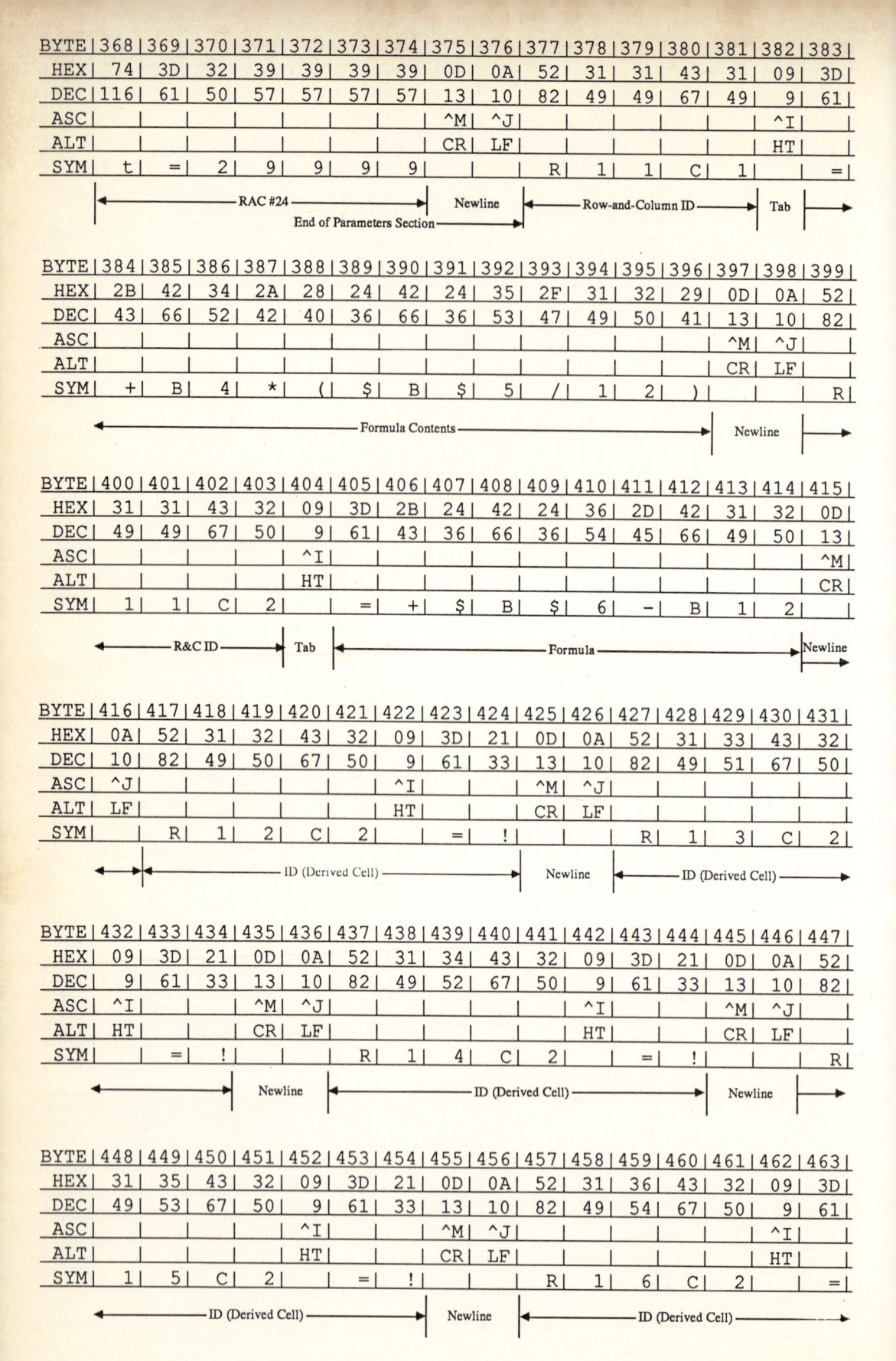

BYTE	368	369	370	371	372	373	374	375	376	377	378	379	380	381	382	383
HEX	74	3D	32	39	39	39	39	0D	0A	52	31	31	43	31	09	3D
DEC	116	61	50	57	57	57	57	13	10	82	49	49	67	49	9	61
ASC								^M	^J						^I	
ALT								CR	LF						HT	
SYM	t	=	2	9	9	9	9			R	1	1	C	1		=

◄────── RAC #24 ──────► ◄─ Newline ─► ◄─ Row-and-Column ID ─► ◄ Tab ►
           End of Parameters Section

BYTE	384	385	386	387	388	389	390	391	392	393	394	395	396	397	398	399
HEX	2B	42	34	2A	28	24	42	24	35	2F	31	32	29	0D	0A	52
DEC	43	66	52	42	40	36	66	36	53	47	49	50	41	13	10	82
ASC														^M	^J	
ALT														CR	LF	
SYM	+	B	4	*	(	$	B	$	5	/	1	2	)			R

◄────────── Formula Contents ──────────► ◄ Newline ►

BYTE	400	401	402	403	404	405	406	407	408	409	410	411	412	413	414	415
HEX	31	31	43	32	09	3D	2B	24	42	24	36	2D	42	31	32	0D
DEC	49	49	67	50	9	61	43	36	66	36	54	45	66	49	50	13
ASC				^I												^M
ALT				HT												CR
SYM	1	1	C	2		=	+	$	B	$	6	-	B	1	2	

◄─── R&C ID ───► ◄ Tab ► ◄─────── Formula ───────► ◄ Newline

BYTE	416	417	418	419	420	421	422	423	424	425	426	427	428	429	430	431
HEX	0A	52	31	32	43	32	09	3D	21	0D	0A	52	31	33	43	32
DEC	10	82	49	50	67	50	9	61	33	13	10	82	49	51	67	50
ASC	^J				^I					^M	^J					
ALT	LF				HT					CR	LF					
SYM		R	1	2	C	2		=	!			R	1	3	C	2

► ◄────── ID (Derived Cell) ──────► ◄ Newline ► ◄── ID (Derived Cell) ──►

BYTE	432	433	434	435	436	437	438	439	440	441	442	443	444	445	446	447
HEX	09	3D	21	0D	0A	52	31	34	43	32	09	3D	21	0D	0A	52
DEC	9	61	33	13	10	82	49	52	67	50	9	61	33	13	10	82
ASC	^I			^M	^J						^I			^M	^J	
ALT	HT			CR	LF						HT			CR	LF	
SYM		=	!			R	1	4	C	2		=	!			R

◄─────── Newline ───────► ◄── ID (Derived Cell) ──► ◄ Newline ►

BYTE	448	449	450	451	452	453	454	455	456	457	458	459	460	461	462	463
HEX	31	35	43	32	09	3D	21	0D	0A	52	31	36	43	32	09	3D
DEC	49	53	67	50	9	61	33	13	10	82	49	54	67	50	9	61
ASC				^I				^M	^J						^I	
ALT				HT				CR	LF						HT	
SYM	1	5	C	2		=	!			R	1	6	C	2		=

◄──── ID (Derived Cell) ────► ◄ Newline ► ◄──── ID (Derived Cell) ────►

182 ABILITY SPREADSHEET

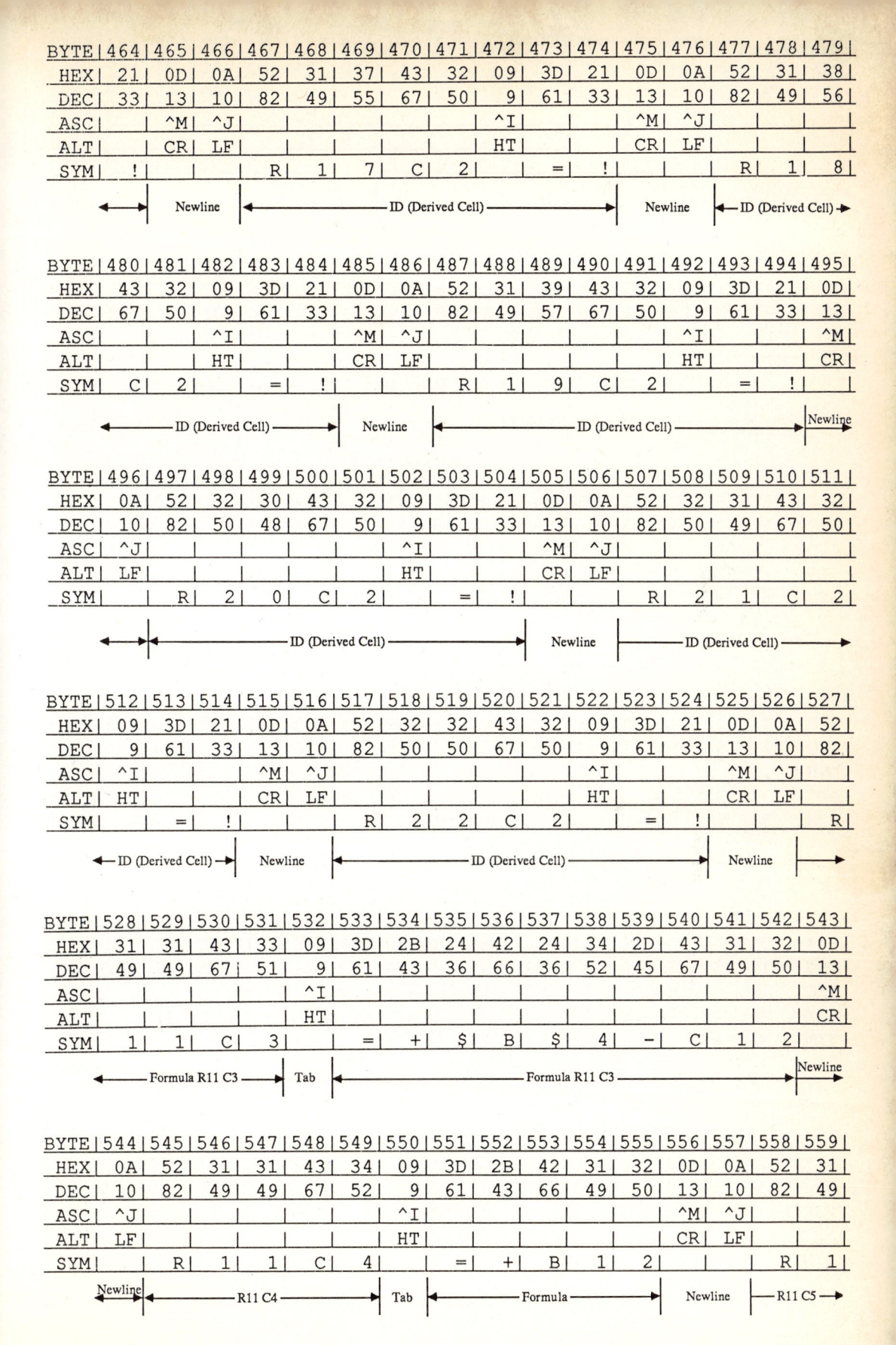

BYTE	464	465	466	467	468	469	470	471	472	473	474	475	476	477	478	479
HEX	21	0D	0A	52	31	37	43	32	09	3D	21	0D	0A	52	31	38
DEC	33	13	10	82	49	55	67	50	9	61	33	13	10	82	49	56
ASC		^M	^J						^I			^M	^J			
ALT		CR	LF						HT			CR	LF			
SYM	!			R	1	7	C	2		=	!			R	1	8

←— Newline —→ ←———— ID (Derived Cell) ————→ ←— Newline —→ ←— ID (Derived Cell) →

BYTE	480	481	482	483	484	485	486	487	488	489	490	491	492	493	494	495
HEX	43	32	09	3D	21	0D	0A	52	31	39	43	32	09	3D	21	0D
DEC	67	50	9	61	33	13	10	82	49	57	67	50	9	61	33	13
ASC			^I			^M	^J						^I			^M
ALT			HT			CR	LF						HT			CR
SYM	C	2		=	!			R	1	9	C	2		=	!	

←——— ID (Derived Cell) ———→ ←— Newline —→ ←——— ID (Derived Cell) ———→ Newline

BYTE	496	497	498	499	500	501	502	503	504	505	506	507	508	509	510	511
HEX	0A	52	32	30	43	32	09	3D	21	0D	0A	52	32	31	43	32
DEC	10	82	50	48	67	50	9	61	33	13	10	82	50	49	67	50
ASC	^J						^I			^M	^J					
ALT	LF						HT			CR	LF					
SYM		R	2	0	C	2		=	!			R	2	1	C	2

←—— ID (Derived Cell) ——→ ←— Newline —→ ←—— ID (Derived Cell) ——→

BYTE	512	513	514	515	516	517	518	519	520	521	522	523	524	525	526	527
HEX	09	3D	21	0D	0A	52	32	32	43	32	09	3D	21	0D	0A	52
DEC	9	61	33	13	10	82	50	50	67	50	9	61	33	13	10	82
ASC	^I			^M	^J						^I			^M	^J	
ALT	HT			CR	LF						HT			CR	LF	
SYM		=	!			R	2	2	C	2		=	!			R

←— ID (Derived Cell) → Newline ←——— ID (Derived Cell) ———→ Newline

BYTE	528	529	530	531	532	533	534	535	536	537	538	539	540	541	542	543
HEX	31	31	43	33	09	3D	2B	24	42	24	34	2D	43	31	32	0D
DEC	49	49	67	51	9	61	43	36	66	36	52	45	67	49	50	13
ASC					^I											^M
ALT					HT											CR
SYM	1	1	C	3		=	+	$	B	$	4	-	C	1	2	

←—— Formula R11 C3 ——→ Tab ←———— Formula R11 C3 ————→ Newline

BYTE	544	545	546	547	548	549	550	551	552	553	554	555	556	557	558	559
HEX	0A	52	31	31	43	34	09	3D	2B	42	31	32	0D	0A	52	31
DEC	10	82	49	49	67	52	9	61	43	66	49	50	13	10	82	49
ASC	^J						^I						^M	^J		
ALT	LF						HT						CR	LF		
SYM		R	1	1	C	4		=	+	B	1	2			R	1

Newline ←—— R11 C4 ——→ Tab ←—— Formula ——→ Newline ←— R11 C5 →

ABILITY SPREADSHEET

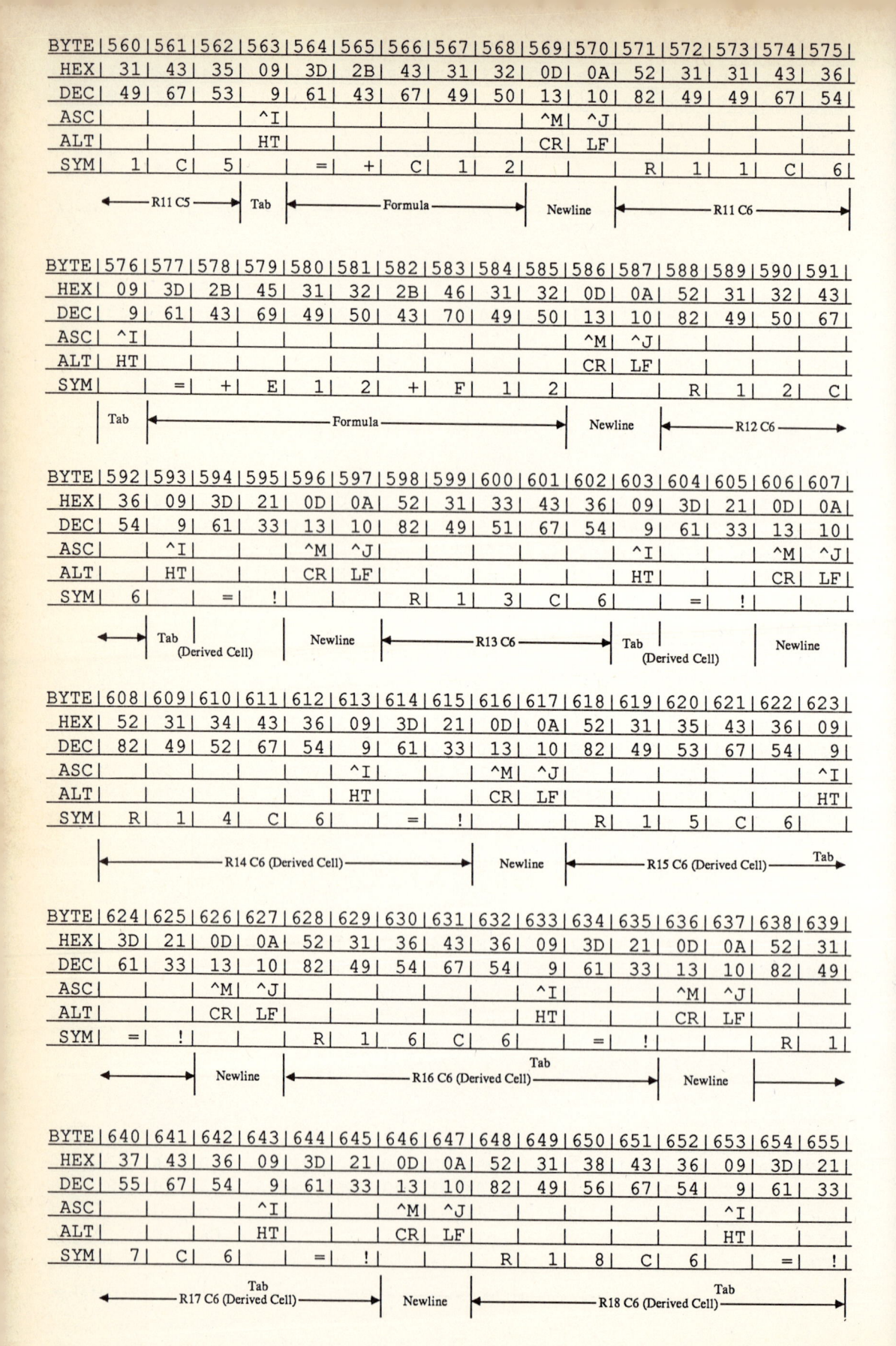

BYTE	560	561	562	563	564	565	566	567	568	569	570	571	572	573	574	575
HEX	31	43	35	09	3D	2B	43	31	32	0D	0A	52	31	31	43	36
DEC	49	67	53	9	61	43	67	49	50	13	10	82	49	49	67	54
ASC				^I						^M	^J					
ALT				HT						CR	LF					
SYM	1	C	5		=	+	C	1	2			R	1	1	C	6

←—— R11 C5 ——→ | Tab | ←———— Formula ————→ | Newline | ←———— R11 C6 ————→

BYTE	576	577	578	579	580	581	582	583	584	585	586	587	588	589	590	591
HEX	09	3D	2B	45	31	32	2B	46	31	32	0D	0A	52	31	32	43
DEC	9	61	43	69	49	50	43	70	49	50	13	10	82	49	50	67
ASC	^I										^M	^J				
ALT	HT										CR	LF				
SYM		=	+	E	1	2	+	F	1	2			R	1	2	C

Tab | ←———————— Formula ————————→ | Newline | ←—— R12 C6 ——→

BYTE	592	593	594	595	596	597	598	599	600	601	602	603	604	605	606	607
HEX	36	09	3D	21	0D	0A	52	31	33	43	36	09	3D	21	0D	0A
DEC	54	9	61	33	13	10	82	49	51	67	54	9	61	33	13	10
ASC		^I			^M	^J						^I			^M	^J
ALT		HT			CR	LF						HT			CR	LF
SYM	6		=	!			R	1	3	C	6		=	!		

←— Tab (Derived Cell) —→ | Newline | ←—— R13 C6 ——→ | Tab (Derived Cell) | Newline

BYTE	608	609	610	611	612	613	614	615	616	617	618	619	620	621	622	623
HEX	52	31	34	43	36	09	3D	21	0D	0A	52	31	35	43	36	09
DEC	82	49	52	67	54	9	61	33	13	10	82	49	53	67	54	9
ASC						^I			^M	^J						^I
ALT						HT			CR	LF						HT
SYM	R	1	4	C	6		=	!			R	1	5	C	6	

←———— R14 C6 (Derived Cell) ————→ | Newline | ←———— R15 C6 (Derived Cell) ————→ | Tab

BYTE	624	625	626	627	628	629	630	631	632	633	634	635	636	637	638	639
HEX	3D	21	0D	0A	52	31	36	43	36	09	3D	21	0D	0A	52	31
DEC	61	33	13	10	82	49	54	67	54	9	61	33	13	10	82	49
ASC			^M	^J						^I			^M	^J		
ALT			CR	LF						HT			CR	LF		
SYM	=	!			R	1	6	C	6		=	!			R	1

Newline | ←———— R16 C6 (Derived Cell) ————→ Tab | Newline

BYTE	640	641	642	643	644	645	646	647	648	649	650	651	652	653	654	655
HEX	37	43	36	09	3D	21	0D	0A	52	31	38	43	36	09	3D	21
DEC	55	67	54	9	61	33	13	10	82	49	56	67	54	9	61	33
ASC				^I			^M	^J						^I		
ALT				HT			CR	LF						HT		
SYM	7	C	6		=	!			R	1	8	C	6		=	!

←—— R17 C6 (Derived Cell) ——→ Tab | Newline | ←—— R18 C6 (Derived Cell) ——→ Tab

184 ABILITY SPREADSHEET

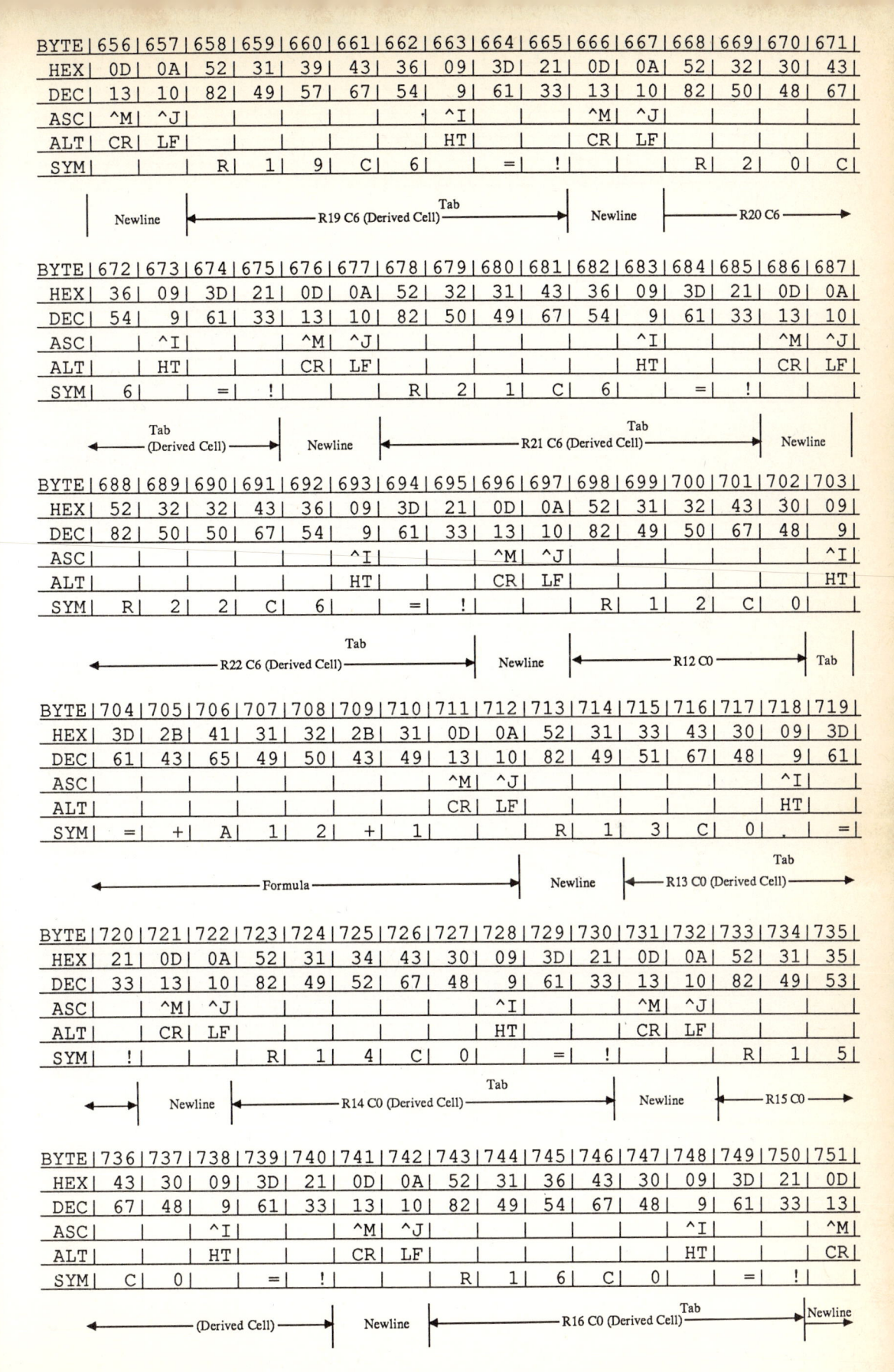

BYTE	656	657	658	659	660	661	662	663	664	665	666	667	668	669	670	671
HEX	0D	0A	52	31	39	43	36	09	3D	21	0D	0A	52	32	30	43
DEC	13	10	82	49	57	67	54	9	61	33	13	10	82	50	48	67
ASC	^M	^J						^I			^M	^J				
ALT	CR	LF						HT			CR	LF				
SYM			R	1	9	C	6		=	!			R	2	0	C

|← Newline | ←——— R19 C6 (Derived Cell) ———→ Tab | Newline | ←——— R20 C6 ———→ |

BYTE	672	673	674	675	676	677	678	679	680	681	682	683	684	685	686	687
HEX	36	09	3D	21	0D	0A	52	32	31	43	36	09	3D	21	0D	0A
DEC	54	9	61	33	13	10	82	50	49	67	54	9	61	33	13	10
ASC		^I			^M	^J						^I			^M	^J
ALT		HT			CR	LF						HT			CR	LF
SYM	6		=	!			R	2	1	C	6		=	!		

| ←— Tab (Derived Cell) —→ | Newline | ←——— Tab R21 C6 (Derived Cell) ———→ | Newline |

BYTE	688	689	690	691	692	693	694	695	696	697	698	699	700	701	702	703
HEX	52	32	32	43	36	09	3D	21	0D	0A	52	31	32	43	30	09
DEC	82	50	50	67	54	9	61	33	13	10	82	49	50	67	48	9
ASC					^I		^M	^J								^I
ALT					HT		CR	LF								HT
SYM	R	2	2	C	6		=	!			R	1	2	C	0	

| ←——— R22 C6 (Derived Cell) ———→ Tab | Newline | ←——— R12 C0 ———→ | Tab |

BYTE	704	705	706	707	708	709	710	711	712	713	714	715	716	717	718	719
HEX	3D	2B	41	31	32	2B	31	0D	0A	52	31	33	43	30	09	3D
DEC	61	43	65	49	50	43	49	13	10	82	49	51	67	48	9	61
ASC								^M	^J						^I	
ALT								CR	LF						HT	
SYM	=	+	A	1	2	+	1			R	1	3	C	0	.	=

| ←——— Formula ———→ | Newline | ←— Tab R13 C0 (Derived Cell) —→ |

BYTE	720	721	722	723	724	725	726	727	728	729	730	731	732	733	734	735
HEX	21	0D	0A	52	31	34	43	30	09	3D	21	0D	0A	52	31	35
DEC	33	13	10	82	49	52	67	48	9	61	33	13	10	82	49	53
ASC		^M	^J						^I			^M	^J			
ALT		CR	LF						HT			CR	LF			
SYM	!			R	1	4	C	0		=	!			R	1	5

| ←— Newline —→ | ←——— R14 C0 (Derived Cell) ———→ Tab | Newline | ←— R15 C0 —→ |

BYTE	736	737	738	739	740	741	742	743	744	745	746	747	748	749	750	751
HEX	43	30	09	3D	21	0D	0A	52	31	36	43	30	09	3D	21	0D
DEC	67	48	9	61	33	13	10	82	49	54	67	48	9	61	33	13
ASC			^I			^M	^J						^I			^M
ALT			HT			CR	LF						HT			CR
SYM	C	0		=	!			R	1	6	C	0		=	!	

| ←——— (Derived Cell) ———→ | Newline | ←——— R16 C0 (Derived Cell) ———→ Tab | Newline |

ABILITY SPREADSHEET 185

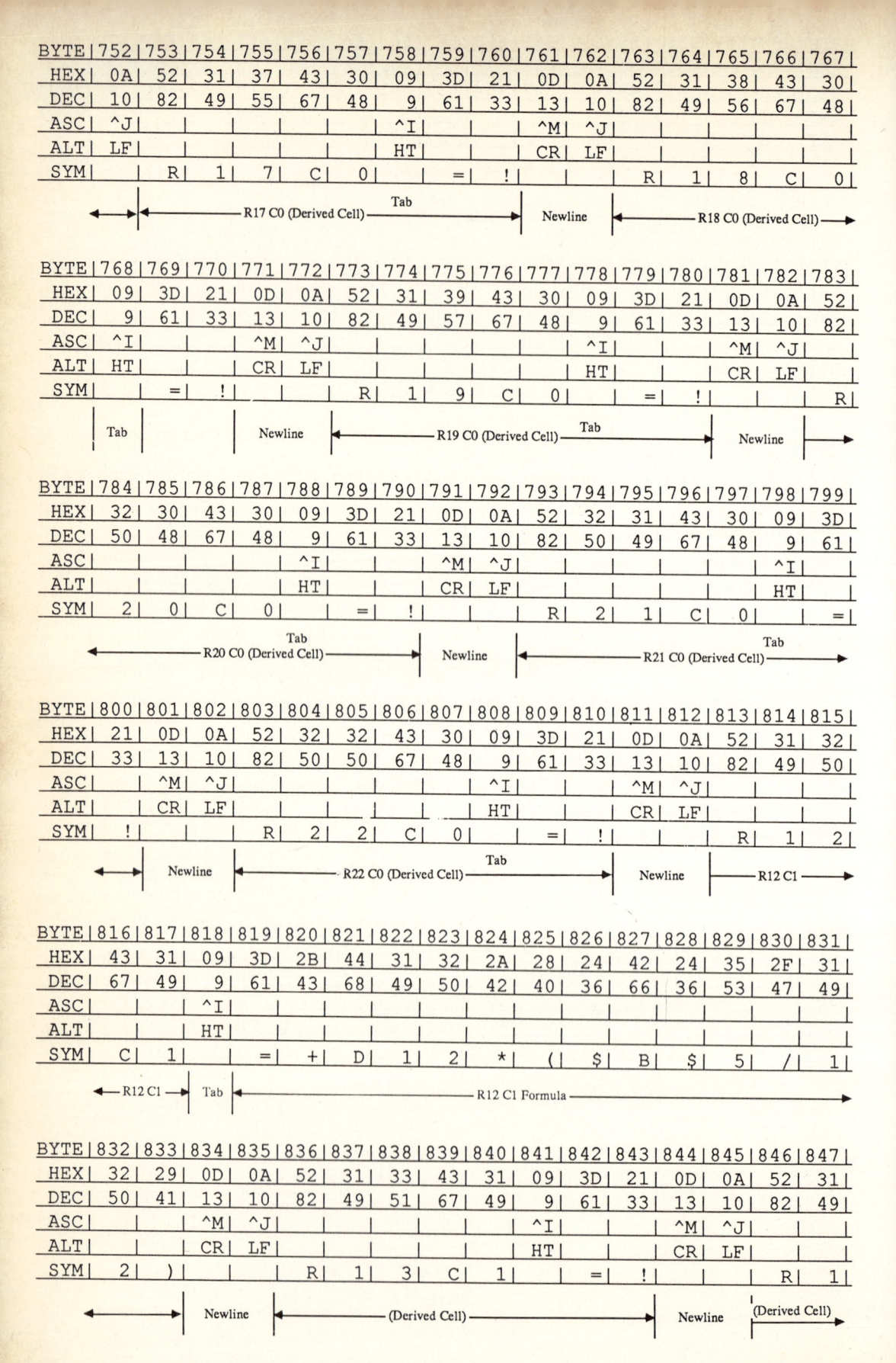

BYTE	752	753	754	755	756	757	758	759	760	761	762	763	764	765	766	767
HEX	0A	52	31	37	43	30	09	3D	21	0D	0A	52	31	38	43	30
DEC	10	82	49	55	67	48	9	61	33	13	10	82	49	56	67	48
ASC	^J						^I			^M	^J					
ALT	LF						HT			CR	LF					
SYM		R	1	7	C	0		=	!			R	1	8	C	0

← R17 C0 (Derived Cell) → Tab → Newline ← R18 C0 (Derived Cell) →

BYTE	768	769	770	771	772	773	774	775	776	777	778	779	780	781	782	783
HEX	09	3D	21	0D	0A	52	31	39	43	30	09	3D	21	0D	0A	52
DEC	9	61	33	13	10	82	49	57	67	48	9	61	33	13	10	82
ASC	^I			^M	^J						^I			^M	^J	
ALT	HT			CR	LF						HT			CR	LF	
SYM		=	!			R	1	9	C	0		=	!			R

Tab ← Newline ← R19 C0 (Derived Cell) → Tab → Newline →

BYTE	784	785	786	787	788	789	790	791	792	793	794	795	796	797	798	799
HEX	32	30	43	30	09	3D	21	0D	0A	52	32	31	43	30	09	3D
DEC	50	48	67	48	9	61	33	13	10	82	50	49	67	48	9	61
ASC				^I		^M	^J							^I		
ALT				HT		CR	LF							HT		
SYM	2	0	C	0		=	!			R	2	1	C	0		=

← R20 C0 (Derived Cell) → Tab → Newline ← R21 C0 (Derived Cell) → Tab →

BYTE	800	801	802	803	804	805	806	807	808	809	810	811	812	813	814	815
HEX	21	0D	0A	52	32	32	43	30	09	3D	21	0D	0A	52	31	32
DEC	33	13	10	82	50	50	67	48	9	61	33	13	10	82	49	50
ASC		^M	^J						^I			^M	^J			
ALT		CR	LF						HT			CR	LF			
SYM	!			R	2	2	C	0		=	!			R	1	2

← Newline ← R22 C0 (Derived Cell) → Tab → Newline ← R12 C1 →

BYTE	816	817	818	819	820	821	822	823	824	825	826	827	828	829	830	831
HEX	43	31	09	3D	2B	44	31	32	2A	28	24	42	24	35	2F	31
DEC	67	49	9	61	43	68	49	50	42	40	36	66	36	53	47	49
ASC			^I													
ALT			HT													
SYM	C	1		=	+	D	1	2	*	(	$	B	$	5	/	1

← R12 C1 → Tab ← R12 C1 Formula →

BYTE	832	833	834	835	836	837	838	839	840	841	842	843	844	845	846	847
HEX	32	29	0D	0A	52	31	33	43	31	09	3D	21	0D	0A	52	31
DEC	50	41	13	10	82	49	51	67	49	9	61	33	13	10	82	49
ASC			^M	^J						^I			^M	^J		
ALT			CR	LF						HT			CR	LF		
SYM	2	)			R	1	3	C	1		=	!			R	1

← Newline ← (Derived Cell) → Newline ← (Derived Cell)

186 ABILITY SPREADSHEET

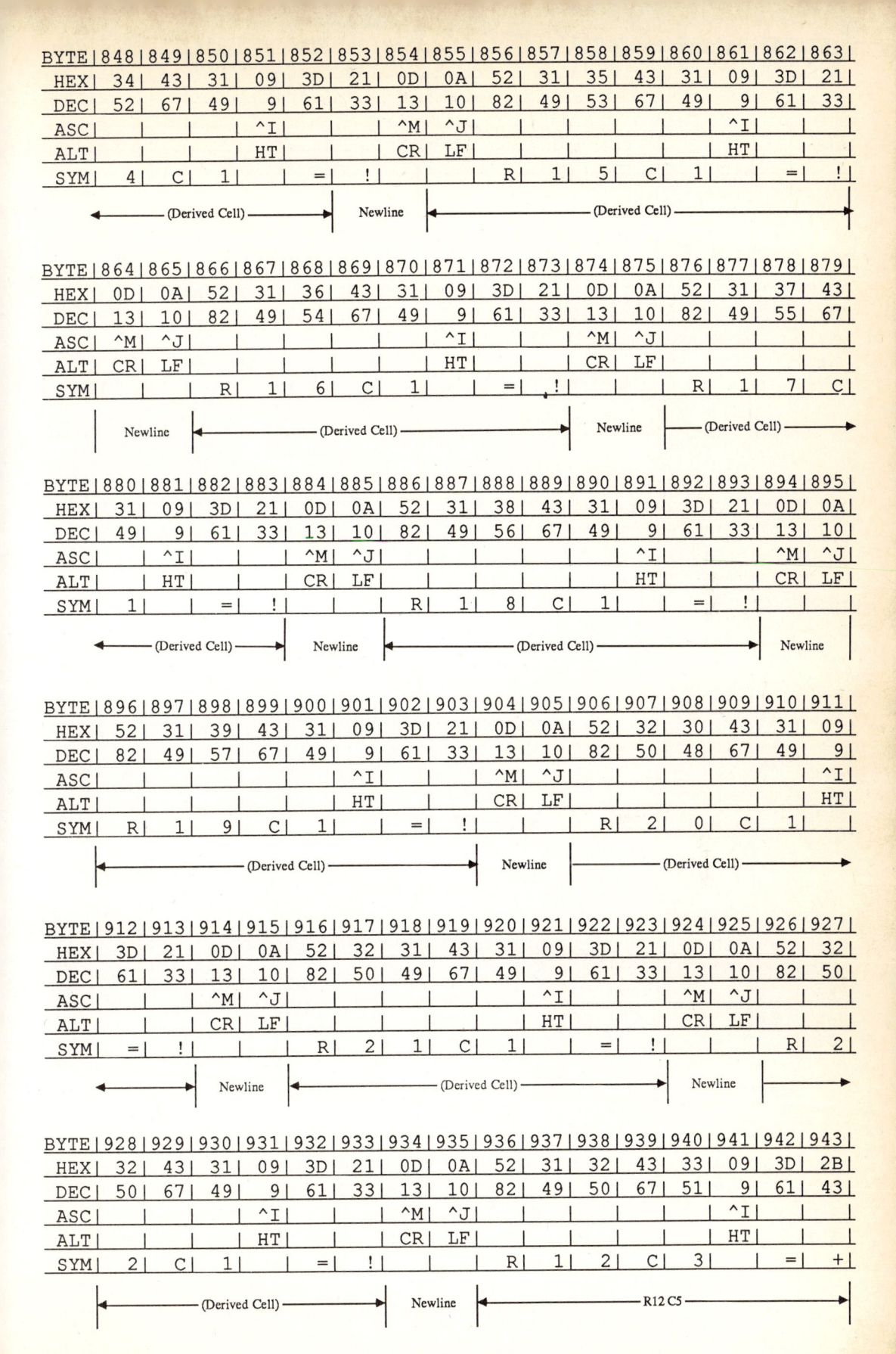

BYTE	848	849	850	851	852	853	854	855	856	857	858	859	860	861	862	863
HEX	34	43	31	09	3D	21	0D	0A	52	31	35	43	31	09	3D	21
DEC	52	67	49	9	61	33	13	10	82	49	53	67	49	9	61	33
ASC				^I			^M	^J						^I		
ALT				HT			CR	LF						HT		
SYM	4	C	1		=	!			R	1	5	C	1		=	!

←——— (Derived Cell) ———→ Newline ←——— (Derived Cell) ———→

BYTE	864	865	866	867	868	869	870	871	872	873	874	875	876	877	878	879
HEX	0D	0A	52	31	36	43	31	09	3D	21	0D	0A	52	31	37	43
DEC	13	10	82	49	54	67	49	9	61	33	13	10	82	49	55	67
ASC	^M	^J						^I			^M	^J				
ALT	CR	LF						HT			CR	LF				
SYM			R	1	6	C	1		=	!			R	1	7	C

Newline ←——— (Derived Cell) ———→ Newline ←——— (Derived Cell) ———→

BYTE	880	881	882	883	884	885	886	887	888	889	890	891	892	893	894	895
HEX	31	09	3D	21	0D	0A	52	31	38	43	31	09	3D	21	0D	0A
DEC	49	9	61	33	13	10	82	49	56	67	49	9	61	33	13	10
ASC		^I			^M	^J						^I			^M	^J
ALT		HT			CR	LF						HT			CR	LF
SYM	1		=	!			R	1	8	C	1		=	!		

←—— (Derived Cell) ——→ Newline ←——— (Derived Cell) ———→ Newline

BYTE	896	897	898	899	900	901	902	903	904	905	906	907	908	909	910	911
HEX	52	31	39	43	31	09	3D	21	0D	0A	52	32	30	43	31	09
DEC	82	49	57	67	49	9	61	33	13	10	82	50	48	67	49	9
ASC						^I			^M	^J						^I
ALT						HT			CR	LF						HT
SYM	R	1	9	C	1		=	!			R	2	0	C	1	

←——— (Derived Cell) ———→ Newline ←——— (Derived Cell) ———→

BYTE	912	913	914	915	916	917	918	919	920	921	922	923	924	925	926	927
HEX	3D	21	0D	0A	52	32	31	43	31	09	3D	21	0D	0A	52	32
DEC	61	33	13	10	82	50	49	67	49	9	61	33	13	10	82	50
ASC			^M	^J						^I			^M	^J		
ALT			CR	LF						HT			CR	LF		
SYM	=	!			R	2	1	C	1		=	!			R	2

←—— Newline ——→ ←——— (Derived Cell) ———→ Newline →

BYTE	928	929	930	931	932	933	934	935	936	937	938	939	940	941	942	943
HEX	32	43	31	09	3D	21	0D	0A	52	31	32	43	33	09	3D	2B
DEC	50	67	49	9	61	33	13	10	82	49	50	67	51	9	61	43
ASC				^I			^M	^J						^I		
ALT				HT			CR	LF						HT		
SYM	2	C	1		=	!			R	1	2	C	3		=	+

←——— (Derived Cell) ———→ Newline ←——— R12 C5 ———→

ABILITY SPREADSHEET 187

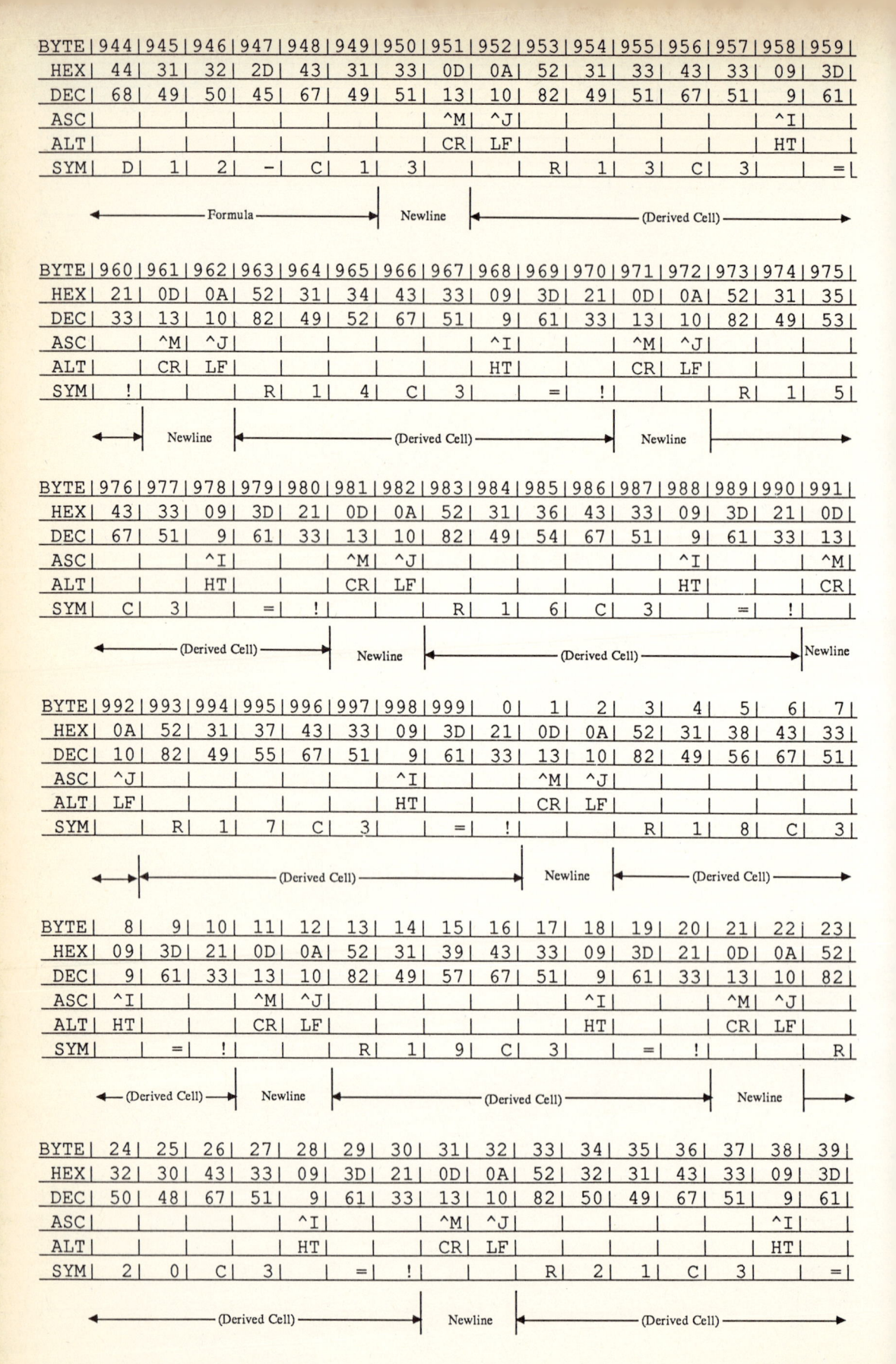

BYTE	944	945	946	947	948	949	950	951	952	953	954	955	956	957	958	959
HEX	44	31	32	2D	43	31	33	0D	0A	52	31	33	43	33	09	3D
DEC	68	49	50	45	67	49	51	13	10	82	49	51	67	51	9	61
ASC								^M	^J						^I	
ALT								CR	LF						HT	
SYM	D	1	2	-	C	1	3			R	1	3	C	3		=

←——— Formula ———→ | ← Newline → | ←———— (Derived Cell) ————→

BYTE	960	961	962	963	964	965	966	967	968	969	970	971	972	973	974	975
HEX	21	0D	0A	52	31	34	43	33	09	3D	21	0D	0A	52	31	35
DEC	33	13	10	82	49	52	67	51	9	61	33	13	10	82	49	53
ASC		^M	^J						^I			^M	^J			
ALT		CR	LF						HT			CR	LF			
SYM	!			R	1	4	C	3		=	!			R	1	5

←— Newline —→ | ←———— (Derived Cell) ————→ | ← Newline →

BYTE	976	977	978	979	980	981	982	983	984	985	986	987	988	989	990	991
HEX	43	33	09	3D	21	0D	0A	52	31	36	43	33	09	3D	21	0D
DEC	67	51	9	61	33	13	10	82	49	54	67	51	9	61	33	13
ASC			^I			^M	^J						^I			^M
ALT			HT			CR	LF						HT			CR
SYM	C	3		=	!			R	1	6	C	3		=	!	

←——— (Derived Cell) ———→ | ← Newline → | ←———— (Derived Cell) ————→ | Newline

BYTE	992	993	994	995	996	997	998	999	0	1	2	3	4	5	6	7
HEX	0A	52	31	37	43	33	09	3D	21	0D	0A	52	31	38	43	33
DEC	10	82	49	55	67	51	9	61	33	13	10	82	49	56	67	51
ASC	^J						^I			^M	^J					
ALT	LF						HT			CR	LF					
SYM		R	1	7	C	3		=	!			R	1	8	C	3

←————— (Derived Cell) —————→ | ← Newline → | ←——— (Derived Cell) ———→

BYTE	8	9	10	11	12	13	14	15	16	17	18	19	20	21	22	23
HEX	09	3D	21	0D	0A	52	31	39	43	33	09	3D	21	0D	0A	52
DEC	9	61	33	13	10	82	49	57	67	51	9	61	33	13	10	82
ASC	^I			^M	^J						^I			^M	^J	
ALT	HT			CR	LF						HT			CR	LF	
SYM		=	!			R	1	9	C	3		=	!			R

←(Derived Cell)→ | Newline | ←——— (Derived Cell) ———→ | Newline

BYTE	24	25	26	27	28	29	30	31	32	33	34	35	36	37	38	39
HEX	32	30	43	33	09	3D	21	0D	0A	52	32	31	43	33	09	3D
DEC	50	48	67	51	9	61	33	13	10	82	50	49	67	51	9	61
ASC					^I			^M	^J						^I	
ALT					HT			CR	LF						HT	
SYM	2	0	C	3		=	!			R	2	1	C	3		=

←——— (Derived Cell) ———→ | ← Newline → | ←——— (Derived Cell) ———→

188 ABILITY SPREADSHEET

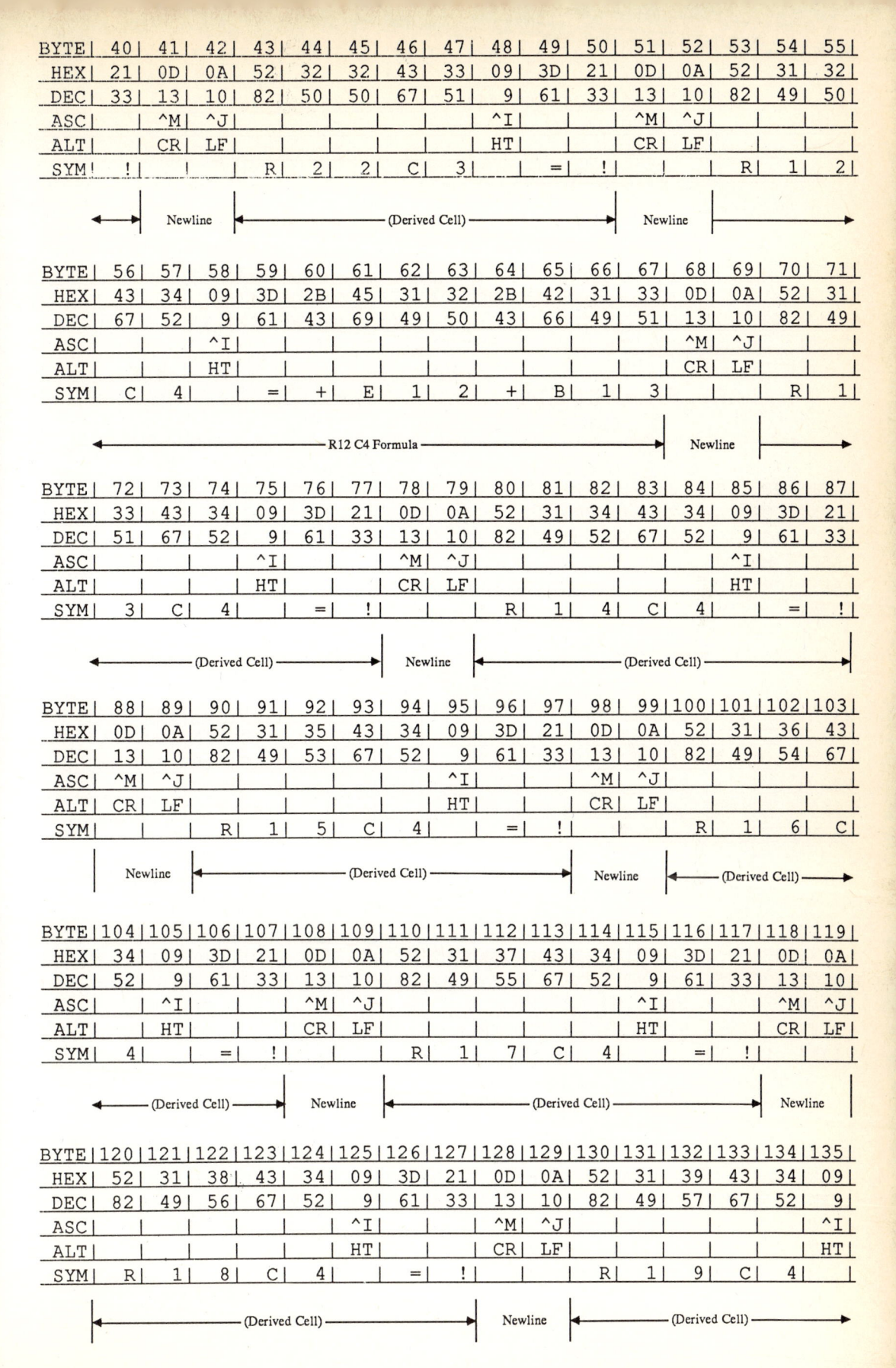

BYTE	40	41	42	43	44	45	46	47	48	49	50	51	52	53	54	55
HEX	21	0D	0A	52	32	32	43	33	09	3D	21	0D	0A	52	31	32
DEC	33	13	10	82	50	50	67	51	9	61	33	13	10	82	49	50
ASC		^M	^J						^I			^M	^J			
ALT		CR	LF						HT			CR	LF			
SYM	!			R	2	2	C	3		=	!			R	1	2

←——— Newline ———←——————— (Derived Cell) ———————→ Newline ———→

BYTE	56	57	58	59	60	61	62	63	64	65	66	67	68	69	70	71
HEX	43	34	09	3D	2B	45	31	32	2B	42	31	33	0D	0A	52	31
DEC	67	52	9	61	43	69	49	50	43	66	49	51	13	10	82	49
ASC			^I										^M	^J		
ALT			HT										CR	LF		
SYM	C	4		=	+	E	1	2	+	B	1	3			R	1

←——————— R12 C4 Formula ———————→ Newline ———→

BYTE	72	73	74	75	76	77	78	79	80	81	82	83	84	85	86	87
HEX	33	43	34	09	3D	21	0D	0A	52	31	34	43	34	09	3D	21
DEC	51	67	52	9	61	33	13	10	82	49	52	67	52	9	61	33
ASC				^I			^M	^J						^I		
ALT				HT			CR	LF						HT		
SYM	3	C	4		=	!			R	1	4	C	4		=	!

←——— (Derived Cell) ———→ Newline ←——— (Derived Cell) ———→

BYTE	88	89	90	91	92	93	94	95	96	97	98	99	100	101	102	103
HEX	0D	0A	52	31	35	43	34	09	3D	21	0D	0A	52	31	36	43
DEC	13	10	82	49	53	67	52	9	61	33	13	10	82	49	54	67
ASC	^M	^J						^I			^M	^J				
ALT	CR	LF						HT			CR	LF				
SYM			R	1	5	C	4		=	!			R	1	6	C

Newline ←——— (Derived Cell) ———→ Newline ←——— (Derived Cell) ———→

BYTE	104	105	106	107	108	109	110	111	112	113	114	115	116	117	118	119
HEX	34	09	3D	21	0D	0A	52	31	37	43	34	09	3D	21	0D	0A
DEC	52	9	61	33	13	10	82	49	55	67	52	9	61	33	13	10
ASC		^I			^M	^J						^I			^M	^J
ALT		HT			CR	LF						HT			CR	LF
SYM	4		=	!			R	1	7	C	4		=	!		

←——— (Derived Cell) ———→ Newline ←——— (Derived Cell) ———→ Newline

BYTE	120	121	122	123	124	125	126	127	128	129	130	131	132	133	134	135
HEX	52	31	38	43	34	09	3D	21	0D	0A	52	31	39	43	34	09
DEC	82	49	56	67	52	9	61	33	13	10	82	49	57	67	52	9
ASC					^I				^M	^J						^I
ALT					HT				CR	LF						HT
SYM	R	1	8	C	4		=	!			R	1	9	C	4	

←——— (Derived Cell) ———→ Newline ←——— (Derived Cell) ———→

ABILITY SPREADSHEET

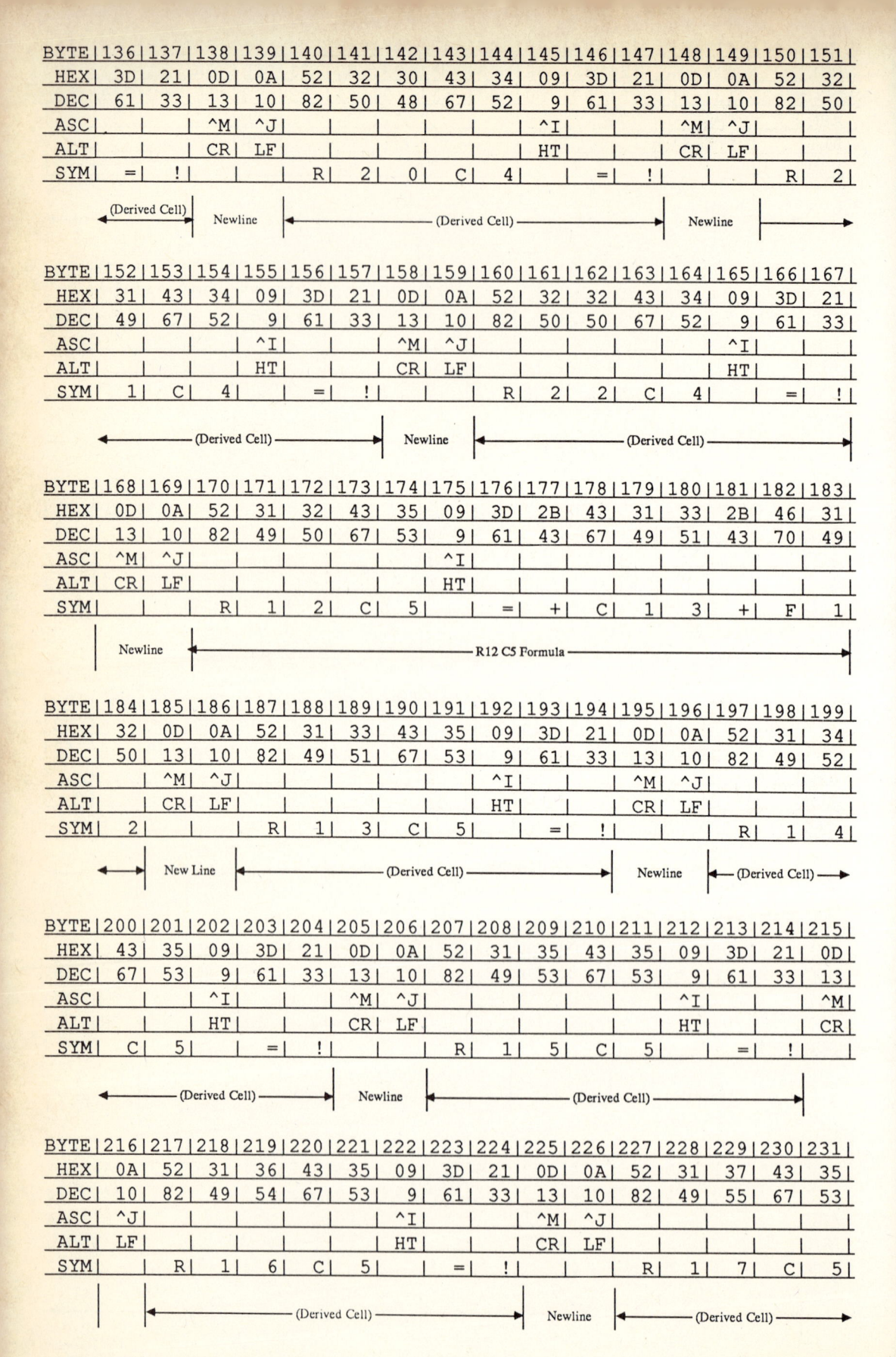

BYTE	136	137	138	139	140	141	142	143	144	145	146	147	148	149	150	151
HEX	3D	21	0D	0A	52	32	30	43	34	09	3D	21	0D	0A	52	32
DEC	61	33	13	10	82	50	48	67	52	9	61	33	13	10	82	50
ASC			^M	^J						^I			^M	^J		
ALT			CR	LF						HT			CR	LF		
SYM	=	!			R	2	0	C	4		=	!			R	2

← (Derived Cell) → | Newline | ← (Derived Cell) → | Newline

BYTE	152	153	154	155	156	157	158	159	160	161	162	163	164	165	166	167
HEX	31	43	34	09	3D	21	0D	0A	52	32	32	43	34	09	3D	21
DEC	49	67	52	9	61	33	13	10	82	50	50	67	52	9	61	33
ASC				^I										^I		
ALT				HT										HT		
SYM	1	C	4		=	!			R	2	2	C	4		=	!

← (Derived Cell) → | Newline | ← (Derived Cell) →

BYTE	168	169	170	171	172	173	174	175	176	177	178	179	180	181	182	183
HEX	0D	0A	52	31	32	43	35	09	3D	2B	43	31	33	2B	46	31
DEC	13	10	82	49	50	67	53	9	61	43	67	49	51	43	70	49
ASC	^M	^J						^I								
ALT	CR	LF						HT								
SYM			R	1	2	C	5		=	+	C	1	3	+	F	1

Newline | ← R12 C5 Formula →

BYTE	184	185	186	187	188	189	190	191	192	193	194	195	196	197	198	199
HEX	32	0D	0A	52	31	33	43	35	09	3D	21	0D	0A	52	31	34
DEC	50	13	10	82	49	51	67	53	9	61	33	13	10	82	49	52
ASC		^M	^J						^I			^M	^J			
ALT		CR	LF						HT			CR	LF			
SYM	2			R	1	3	C	5		=	!			R	1	4

← | New Line | ← (Derived Cell) → | Newline | ← (Derived Cell) →

BYTE	200	201	202	203	204	205	206	207	208	209	210	211	212	213	214	215
HEX	43	35	09	3D	21	0D	0A	52	31	35	43	35	09	3D	21	0D
DEC	67	53	9	61	33	13	10	82	49	53	67	53	9	61	33	13
ASC			^I			^M	^J						^I			^M
ALT			HT			CR	LF						HT			CR
SYM	C	5		=	!			R	1	5	C	5		=	!	

← (Derived Cell) → | Newline | ← (Derived Cell) →

BYTE	216	217	218	219	220	221	222	223	224	225	226	227	228	229	230	231
HEX	0A	52	31	36	43	35	09	3D	21	0D	0A	52	31	37	43	35
DEC	10	82	49	54	67	53	9	61	33	13	10	82	49	55	67	53
ASC	^J						^I			^M	^J					
ALT	LF						HT			CR	LF					
SYM		R	1	6	C	5		=	!			R	1	7	C	5

← (Derived Cell) → | Newline | ← (Derived Cell) →

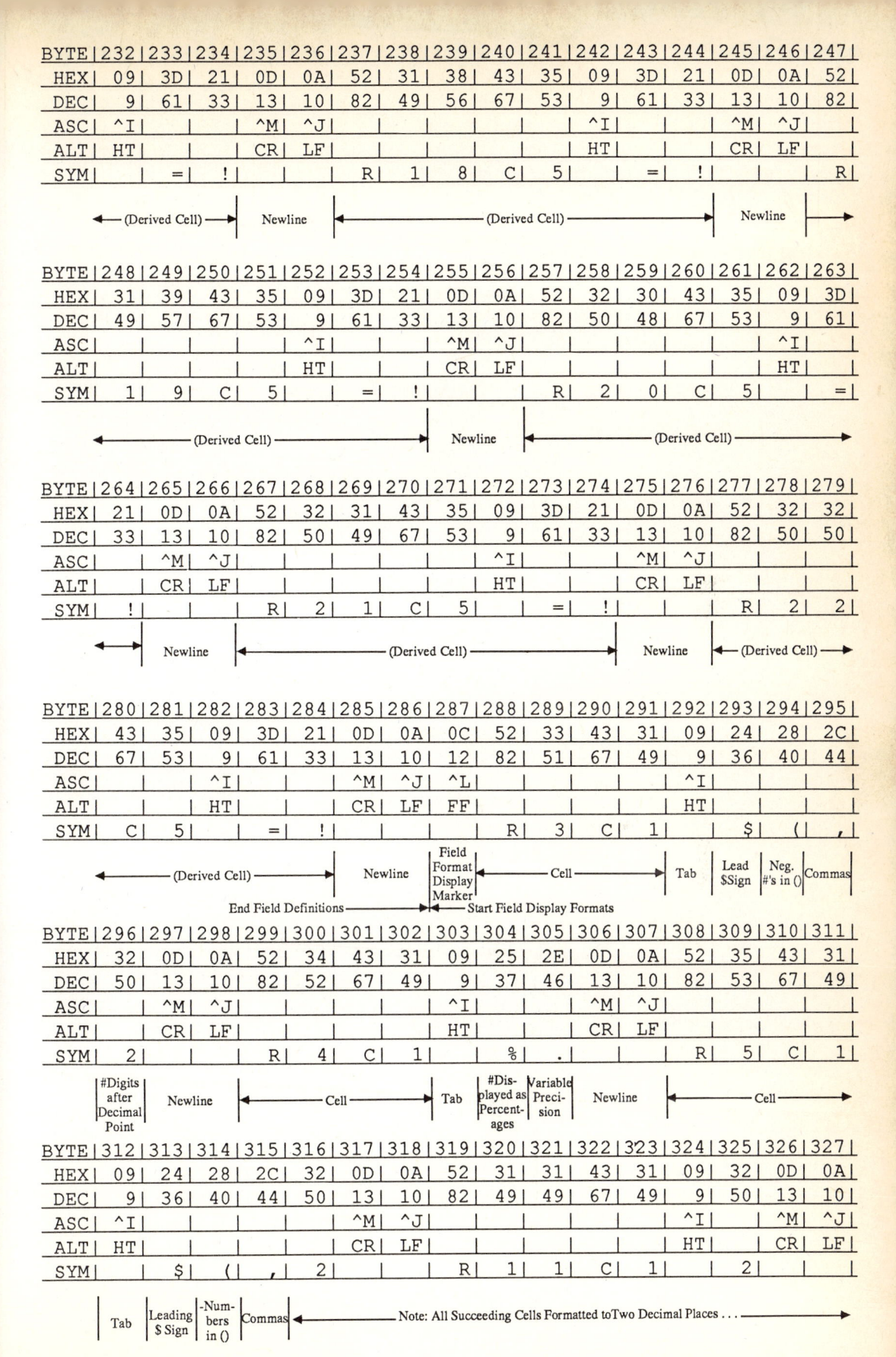

BYTE	232	233	234	235	236	237	238	239	240	241	242	243	244	245	246	247
HEX	09	3D	21	0D	0A	52	31	38	43	35	09	3D	21	0D	0A	52
DEC	9	61	33	13	10	82	49	56	67	53	9	61	33	13	10	82
ASC	^I			^M	^J						^I			^M	^J	
ALT	HT			CR	LF						HT			CR	LF	
SYM		=	!			R	1	8	C	5		=	!			R

⟵— (Derived Cell) —⟶ | Newline | ⟵————— (Derived Cell) —————⟶ | Newline

BYTE	248	249	250	251	252	253	254	255	256	257	258	259	260	261	262	263
HEX	31	39	43	35	09	3D	21	0D	0A	52	32	30	43	35	09	3D
DEC	49	57	67	53	9	61	33	13	10	82	50	48	67	53	9	61
ASC				^I				^M	^J						^I	
ALT				HT				CR	LF						HT	
SYM	1	9	C	5		=	!			R	2	0	C	5		=

⟵———— (Derived Cell) ————⟶ | Newline | ⟵———— (Derived Cell) ————⟶

BYTE	264	265	266	267	268	269	270	271	272	273	274	275	276	277	278	279
HEX	21	0D	0A	52	32	31	43	35	09	3D	21	0D	0A	52	32	32
DEC	33	13	10	82	50	49	67	53	9	61	33	13	10	82	50	50
ASC		^M	^J						^I			^M	^J			
ALT		CR	LF						HT			CR	LF			
SYM	!			R	2	1	C	5		=	!			R	2	2

⟵⟶ | Newline | ⟵———— (Derived Cell) ————⟶ | Newline | ⟵— (Derived Cell) —⟶

BYTE	280	281	282	283	284	285	286	287	288	289	290	291	292	293	294	295
HEX	43	35	09	3D	21	0D	0A	0C	52	33	43	31	09	24	28	2C
DEC	67	53	9	61	33	13	10	12	82	51	67	49	9	36	40	44
ASC			^I			^M	^J	^L					^I			
ALT			HT			CR	LF	FF					HT			
SYM	C	5		=	!				R	3	C	1		$	(	,

⟵—— (Derived Cell) ——⟶ | Newline | Field Format Display Marker | ⟵—— Cell ——⟶ | Tab | Lead $Sign | Neg. #'s in () | Commas

End Field Definitions ———— Start Field Display Formats

BYTE	296	297	298	299	300	301	302	303	304	305	306	307	308	309	310	311
HEX	32	0D	0A	52	34	43	31	09	25	2E	0D	0A	52	35	43	31
DEC	50	13	10	82	52	67	49	9	37	46	13	10	82	53	67	49
ASC		^M	^J					^I			^M	^J				
ALT		CR	LF					HT			CR	LF				
SYM	2			R	4	C	1		%	.			R	5	C	1

#Digits after Decimal Point | Newline | ⟵—— Cell ——⟶ | Tab | #Displayed as Percentages | Variable Precision | Newline | ⟵—— Cell ——⟶

BYTE	312	313	314	315	316	317	318	319	320	321	322	323	324	325	326	327
HEX	09	24	28	2C	32	0D	0A	52	31	31	43	31	09	32	0D	0A
DEC	9	36	40	44	50	13	10	82	49	49	67	49	9	50	13	10
ASC	^I				^M	^J							^I		^M	^J
ALT	HT				CR	LF							HT		CR	LF
SYM		$	(	,	2			R	1	1	C	1		2		

Tab | Leading $ Sign | -Numbers in () | Commas | ⟵———— Note: All Succeeding Cells Formatted to Two Decimal Places . . . ————⟶

ABILITY SPREADSHEET 191

BYTE	328	329	330	331	332	333	334	335	336	337	338	339	340	341	342	343
HEX	52	31	31	43	32	09	32	0D	0A	52	31	31	43	33	09	32
DEC	82	49	49	67	50	9	50	13	10	82	49	49	67	51	9	50
ASC					^I			^M	^J						^I	
ALT					HT			CR	LF						HT	
SYM	R	1	1	C	2		2			R	1	1	C	3		2

←——————————— Note: All Succeeding Cells Formatted to Decimal Places... ———————————→

Ability File Continues . . . (Not Shown)

Gettysburg Address as an Ability File

BYTE	0	1	2	3	4	5	6	7	8	9	10	11	12	13	14	15
HEX	2D	2D	48	44	52	31	2E	30	2D	2D	20	31	33	20	54	58
DEC	45	45	72	68	82	49	46	48	45	45	32	49	51	32	84	88
ASC											^`			^`		
ALT											SPC			SPC		
SYM	-	-	H	D	R	1	.	0	-	-		1	3		T	X

◄──────────── Header & Version # ────────────► │ #Lines in Document │ Document Type

BYTE	16	17	18	19	20	21	22	23	24	25	26	27	28	29	30	31
HEX	3B	0D	0A	20	20	20	20	20	20	20	20	20	20	20	20	20
DEC	59	13	10	32	32	32	32	32	32	32	32	32	32	32	32	32
ASC		^M	^J	^`	^`	^`	^`	^`	^`	^`	^`	^`	^`	^`	^`	^`
ALT		CR	LF	SPC	SPC	SPC	SPC	SPC	SPC	SPC	SPC	SPC	SPC	SPC	SPC	SPC
SYM	;															

│ Newline │ ◄──────── Centered Text Offset Stored as Space Characters ────────►

BYTE	32	33	34	35	36	37	38	39	40	41	42	43	44	45	46	47
HEX	20	20	20	20	20	20	20	20	02	54	68	65	20	47	65	74
DEC	32	32	32	32	32	32	32	32	2	84	104	101	32	71	101	116
ASC	^`	^`	^`	^`	^`	^`	^`	^`	^B				^`			
ALT	SPC	SPC	SPC	SPC	SPC	SPC	SPC	SPC	STX				SPC			
SYM										T	h	e		G	e	t

◄──────────────────────────────────► │Bold Face Toggle│ ◄──── Boldface Title ────►

BYTE	48	49	50	51	52	53	54	55	56	57	58	59	60	61	62	63
HEX	74	79	73	62	75	72	67	20	41	64	64	72	65	73	73	02
DEC	116	121	115	98	117	114	103	32	65	100	100	114	101	115	115	2
ASC							^`									^B
ALT							SPC									STX
SYM	t	y	s	b	u	r	g		A	d	d	r	e	s	s	

◄──────────── Boldface Title ────────────► │Bold Face Toggle│

BYTE	64	65	66	67	68	69	70	71	72	73	74	75	76	77	78	79
HEX	0D	0A	0D	0A	46	6F	75	72	73	63	6F	72	65	20	61	6E
DEC	13	10	13	10	70	111	117	114	115	99	111	114	101	32	97	110
ASC	^M	^J	^M	^J										^`		
ALT	CR	LF	CR	LF										SPC		
SYM					F	o	u	r	s	c	o	r	e		a	n

│ Newline │ Newline │ ◄──────────── Text ────────────►

ABILITY WORD PROCESSING 193

BYTE	80	81	82	83	84	85	86	87	88	89	90	91	92	93	94	95
HEX	64	20	73	65	76	65	6E	20	79	65	61	72	73	20	61	67
DEC	100	32	115	101	118	101	110	32	121	101	97	114	115	32	97	103
ASC		^`						^`						^`		
ALT		SPC						SPC						SPC		
SYM	d		s	e	v	e	n		y	e	a	r	s		a	g

BYTE	96	97	98	99	100	101	102	103	104	105	106	107	108	109	110	111
HEX	6F	20	6F	75	72	20	66	61	74	68	65	72	73	20	62	72
DEC	111	32	111	117	114	32	102	97	116	104	101	114	115	32	98	114
ASC		^`				^`								^`		
ALT		SPC				SPC								SPC		
SYM	o		o	u	r		f	a	t	h	e	r	s		b	r

BYTE	112	113	114	115	116	117	118	119	120	121	122	123	124	125	126	127
HEX	6F	75	67	68	74	20	66	6F	72	74	68	20	6F	6E	20	74
DEC	111	117	103	104	116	32	102	111	114	116	104	32	111	110	32	116
ASC					^`							^`			^`	
ALT					SPC							SPC			SPC	
SYM	o	u	g	h	t		f	o	r	t	h		o	n		t

BYTE	128	129	130	131	132	133	134	135	136	137	138	139	140	141	142	143
HEX	68	69	73	8D	0A	63	6F	6E	74	69	6E	65	6E	74	2C	61
DEC	104	105	115	141	10	99	111	110	116	105	110	101	110	116	44	97
ASC				141	^J											
ALT				141	LF											
SYM	h	i	s			c	o	n	t	i	n	e	n	t	,	a

Soft CR & Linefeed (at byte 131)

BYTE	144	145	146	147	148	149	150	151	152	153	154	155	156	157	158	159
HEX	20	6E	65	77	20	6E	61	74	69	6F	6E	2C	20	63	6F	6E
DEC	32	110	101	119	32	110	97	116	105	111	110	44	32	99	111	110
ASC	^`				^`								^`			
ALT	SPC				SPC								SPC			
SYM		n	e	w		n	a	t	i	o	n	,		c	o	n

BYTE	160	161	162	163	164	165	166	167	168	169	170	171	172	173	174	175
HEX	63	65	69	76	65	64	20	69	6E	20	15	4C	69	62	65	72
DEC	99	101	105	118	101	100	32	105	110	32	21	76	105	98	101	114
ASC						^`			^`	^U						
ALT						SPC			SPC	NAK						
SYM	c	e	i	v	e	d		i	n			L	i	b	e	r

Underline Toggle (at byte 170)

194 ABILITY WORD PROCESSING

BYTE	176	177	178	179	180	181	182	183	184	185	186	187	188	189	190	191
HEX	74	79	15	2C	20	61	6E	64	20	64	65	64	69	63	61	74
DEC	116	121	21	44	32	97	110	100	32	100	101	100	105	99	97	116
ASC			^U		^`				^`							
ALT			NAK		SPC				SPC							
SYM	t	y		,		a	n	d		d	e	d	i	c	a	t

(178: Underline Toggle)

BYTE	192	193	194	195	196	197	198	199	200	201	202	203	204	205	206	207
HEX	65	64	20	74	6F	8D	0A	74	68	65	20	70	72	6F	70	6F
DEC	101	100	32	116	111	141	10	116	104	101	32	112	114	111	112	111
ASC			^`			141	^J				^`					
ALT			SPC			141	LF				SPC					
SYM	e	d		t	o			t	h	e		p	r	o	p	o

(197–198: Soft CR Linefeed)

BYTE	208	209	210	211	212	213	214	215	216	217	218	219	220	221	222	223
HEX	73	69	74	69	6F	6E	20	74	68	61	74	20	61	6C	6C	20
DEC	115	105	116	105	111	110	32	116	104	97	116	32	97	108	108	32
ASC							^`			^`			^`			
ALT							SPC			SPC			SPC			
SYM	s	i	t	i	o	n		t	h	a	t		a	l	l	

BYTE	224	225	226	227	228	229	230	231	232	233	234	235	236	237	238	239
HEX	6D	65	6E	20	61	72	65	20	63	72	65	61	74	65	64	20
DEC	109	101	110	32	97	114	101	32	99	114	101	97	116	101	100	32
ASC				^`			^`									^`
ALT				SPC			SPC									SPC
SYM	m	e	n		a	r	e		c	r	e	a	t	e	d	

BYTE	240	241	242	243	244	245	246	247	248	249	250	251	252	253	254	255
HEX	65	71	75	61	6C	2E	0D	0A	0D	0A	4E	6F	77	20	77	65
DEC	101	113	117	97	108	46	13	10	13	10	78	111	119	32	119	101
ASC							^M	^J	^M	^J				^`		
ALT							CR	LF	CR	LF				SPC		
SYM	e	q	u	a	l	.					N	o	w		w	e

(246–247: Newline; 248–249: Newline)

BYTE	256	257	258	259	260	261	262	263	264	265	266	267	268	269	270	271
HEX	20	61	72	65	20	65	6E	67	61	67	65	64	20	69	6E	20
DEC	32	97	114	101	32	101	110	103	97	103	101	100	32	105	110	32
ASC	^`				^`								^`			^`
ALT	SPC				SPC								SPC			SPC
SYM		a	r	e		e	n	g	a	g	e	d		i	n	

BYTE	272	273	274	275	276	277	278	279	280	281	282	283	284	285	286	287
HEX	61	20	67	72	65	61	74	20	63	69	76	69	6C	20	77	61
DEC	97	32	103	114	101	97	116	32	99	105	118	105	108	32	119	97
ASC		^`						^`						^`		
ALT		SPC						SPC						SPC		
SYM	a		g	r	e	a	t		c	i	v	i	l		w	a

BYTE	288	289	290	291	292	293	294	295	296	297	298	299	300	301	302	303
HEX	72	2C	20	74	65	73	74	69	6E	67	20	77	68	65	74	68
DEC	114	44	32	116	101	115	116	105	110	103	32	119	104	101	116	104
ASC			^`								^`					
ALT			SPC								SPC					
SYM	r	,		t	e	s	t	i	n	g		w	h	e	t	h

BYTE	304	305	306	307	308	309	310	311	312	313	314	315	316	317	318	319
HEX	65	72	20	74	68	61	74	8D	0A	6E	61	74	69	6F	6E	20
DEC	101	114	32	116	104	97	116	141	10	110	97	116	105	111	110	32
ASC			^`					141	^J							^`
ALT			SPC					141	LF							SPC
SYM	e	r		t	h	a	t			n	a	t	i	o	n	

Soft CR Linefeed

BYTE	320	321	322	323	324	325	326	327	328	329	330	331	332	333	334	335
HEX	6F	72	20	61	6E	79	20	6E	61	74	69	6F	6E	20	73	6F
DEC	111	114	32	97	110	121	32	110	97	116	105	111	110	32	115	111
ASC			^`				^`							^`		
ALT			SPC				SPC							SPC		
SYM	o	r		a	n	y		n	a	t	i	o	n		s	o

BYTE	336	337	338	339	340	341	342	343	344	345	346	347	348	349	350	351
HEX	20	63	6F	6E	63	65	69	76	65	64	20	61	6E	64	20	73
DEC	32	99	111	110	99	101	105	118	101	100	32	97	110	100	32	115
ASC	^`										^`				^`	
ALT	SPC										SPC				SPC	
SYM		c	o	n	c	e	i	v	e	d		a	n	d		s

BYTE	352	353	354	355	356	357	358	359	360	361	362	363	364	365	366	367
HEX	6F	20	64	65	64	69	63	61	74	65	64	20	63	61	6E	20
DEC	111	32	100	101	100	105	99	97	116	101	100	32	99	97	110	32
ASC		^`										^`				^`
ALT		SPC										SPC				SPC
SYM	o		d	e	d	i	c	a	t	e	d		c	a	n	

BYTE	368	369	370	371	372	373	374	375	376	377	378	379	380	381	382	383
HEX	6C	6F	6E	67	8D	0A	65	6E	64	75	72	65	2E	20	20	57
DEC	108	111	110	103	141	10	101	110	100	117	114	101	46	32	32	87
ASC					141	^J								^`	^`	
ALT					141	LF								SPC	SPC	
SYM	l	o	n	g			e	n	d	u	r	e	.			W

Soft CR Linefeed

BYTE	384	385	386	387	388	389	390	391	392	393	394	395	396	397	398	399
HEX	65	20	61	72	65	20	6D	65	74	20	6F	6E	20	61	20	67
DEC	101	32	97	114	101	32	109	101	116	32	111	110	32	97	32	103
ASC		^`				^`				^`			^`		^`	
ALT		SPC				SPC				SPC			SPC		SPC	
SYM	e		a	r	e		m	e	t		o	n		a		g

BYTE	400	401	402	403	404	405	406	407	408	409	410	411	412	413	414	415
HEX	72	65	61	74	20	62	61	74	74	6C	65	66	69	65	6C	64
DEC	114	101	97	116	32	98	97	116	116	108	101	102	105	101	108	100
ASC					^`											
ALT					SPC											
SYM	r	e	a	t		b	a	t	t	l	e	f	i	e	l	d

BYTE	416	417	418	419	420	421	422	423	424	425	426	427	428	429	430	431
HEX	20	6F	66	20	74	68	61	74	20	77	61	72	2E	20	20	57
DEC	32	111	102	32	116	104	97	116	32	119	97	114	46	32	32	87
ASC	^`			^`					^`					^`	^`	
ALT	SPC			SPC					SPC					SPC	SPC	
SYM		o	f		t	h	a	t		w	a	r	.			W

BYTE	432	433	434	435	436	437	438	439	440	441	442	443	444	445	446	447
HEX	65	20	68	61	76	65	8D	0A	63	6F	6D	65	20	74	6F	20
DEC	101	32	104	97	118	101	141	10	99	111	109	101	32	116	111	32
ASC		^`					141	^J					^`			^`
ALT		SPC					141	LF					SPC			SPC
SYM	e		h	a	v	e			c	o	m	e		t	o	

Soft CR Linefeed

BYTE	448	449	450	451	452	453	454	455	456	457	458	459	460	461	462	463
HEX	64	65	64	69	63	61	74	65	20	61	20	70	6F	72	74	69
DEC	100	101	100	105	99	97	116	101	32	97	32	112	111	114	116	105
ASC									^`		^`					
ALT									SPC		SPC					
SYM	d	e	d	i	c	a	t	e		a		p	o	r	t	i

ABILITY WORD PROCESSING **197**

BYTE	464	465	466	467	468	469	470	471	472	473	474	475	476	477	478	479
HEX	6F	6E	20	6F	66	20	74	68	61	74	20	66	69	65	6C	64
DEC	111	110	32	111	102	32	116	104	97	116	32	102	105	101	108	100
ASC			^`		^`						^`					
ALT			SPC		SPC						SPC					
SYM	o	n		o	f		t	h	a	t		f	i	e	l	d

BYTE	480	481	482	483	484	485	486	487	488	489	490	491	492	493	494	495
HEX	2C	20	61	73	20	61	20	66	69	6E	61	6C	20	72	65	73
DEC	44	32	97	115	32	97	32	102	105	110	97	108	32	114	101	115
ASC		^`			^`		^`						^`			
ALT		SPC			SPC		SPC						SPC			
SYM	,		a	s		a		f	i	n	a	l		r	e	s

BYTE	496	497	498	499	500	501	502	503	504	505	506	507	508	509	510	511
HEX	74	69	6E	67	8D	0A	70	6C	61	63	65	20	66	6F	72	20
DEC	116	105	110	103	141	10	112	108	97	99	101	32	102	111	114	32
ASC					141	^J						^`				^`
ALT					141	LF						SPC				SPC
SYM	t	i	n	g			p	l	a	c	e		f	o	r	

                        Soft CR
                        Linefeed

BYTE	512	513	514	515	516	517	518	519	520	521	522	523	524	525	526	527
HEX	74	68	6F	73	65	20	77	68	6F	20	68	65	72	65	20	67
DEC	116	104	111	115	101	32	119	104	111	32	104	101	114	101	32	103
ASC						^`				^`					^`	
ALT						SPC				SPC					SPC	
SYM	t	h	o	s	e		w	h	o		h	e	r	e		g

BYTE	528	529	530	531	532	533	534	535	536	537	538	539	540	541	542	543
HEX	61	76	65	20	74	68	65	69	72	20	6C	69	76	65	73	20
DEC	97	118	101	32	116	104	101	105	114	32	108	105	118	101	115	32
ASC				^`						^`						^`
ALT				SPC						SPC						SPC
SYM	a	v	e		t	h	e	i	r		l	i	v	e	s	

BYTE	544	545	546	547	548	549	550	551	552	553	554	555	556	557	558	559
HEX	74	68	61	74	20	74	68	61	74	20	6E	61	74	69	6F	6E
DEC	116	104	97	116	32	116	104	97	116	32	110	97	116	105	111	110
ASC					^`					^`						
ALT					SPC					SPC						
SYM	t	h	a	t		t	h	a	t		n	a	t	i	o	n

198   ABILITY WORD PROCESSING

BYTE	560	561	562	563	564	565	566	567	568	569	570	571	572	573	574	575
HEX	20	6D	69	67	68	74	8D	0A	6C	69	76	65	2E	20	20	49
DEC	32	109	105	103	104	116	141	10	108	105	118	101	46	32	32	73
ASC	^'						141	^J						^'	^'	
ALT	SPC						141	LF						SPC	SPC	
SYM		m	i	g	h	t			l	i	v	e	.			I

Soft CR Linefeed (between bytes 566/567)

BYTE	576	577	578	579	580	581	582	583	584	585	586	587	588	589	590	591
HEX	74	20	69	73	20	61	6C	74	6F	67	65	74	68	65	72	20
DEC	116	32	105	115	32	97	108	116	111	103	101	116	104	101	114	32
ASC		^'			^'											^'
ALT		SPC			SPC											SPC
SYM	t		i	s		a	l	t	o	g	e	t	h	e	r	

BYTE	592	593	594	595	596	597	598	599	600	601	602	603	604	605	606	607
HEX	66	69	74	74	69	6E	67	20	61	6E	64	20	70	72	6F	70
DEC	102	105	116	116	105	110	103	32	97	110	100	32	112	114	111	112
ASC								^'				^'				
ALT								SPC				SPC				
SYM	f	i	t	t	i	n	g		a	n	d		p	r	o	p

BYTE	608	609	610	611	612	613	614	615	616	617	618	619	620	621	622	623
HEX	65	72	20	74	68	61	74	20	77	65	20	73	68	6F	75	6C
DEC	101	114	32	116	104	97	116	32	119	101	32	115	104	111	117	108
ASC			^'					^'			^'					
ALT			SPC					SPC			SPC					
SYM	e	r		t	h	a	t		w	e		s	h	o	u	l

BYTE	624	625	626	627	628	629	630	631	632	633	634	635	636	637	638	639
HEX	64	20	64	6F	8D	0A	74	68	69	73	2E	0D	0A	0C	52	61
DEC	100	32	100	111	141	10	116	104	105	115	46	13	10	12	82	97
ASC		^'			141	^J						^M	^J	^L		
ALT		SPC			141	LF						CR	LF	FF		
SYM	d		d	o			t	h	i	s	.				R	a

Soft CR Linefeed · Newline · Format Divider · Parameters Section
◀── Text Section ──▶

BYTE	640	641	642	643	644	645	646	647	648	649	650	651	652	653	654	655
HEX	43	32	09	62	6F	72	64	65	72	3D	32	0D	0A	52	61	43
DEC	67	50	9	98	111	114	100	101	114	61	50	13	10	82	97	67
ASC			^I									^M	^J			
ALT			HT									CR	LF			
SYM	C	2		b	o	r	d	e	r	=	2			R	a	C

◀── Uses Borders (Borders = 2) ──▶ Newline ◀──

ABILITY WORD PROCESSING   199

BYTE	656	657	658	659	660	661	662	663	664	665	666	667	668	669	670	671
HEX	31	34	09	70	67	68	65	61	64	31	3D	27	4C	69	6E	63
DEC	49	52	9	112	103	104	101	97	100	49	61	39	76	105	110	99
ASC			^I													
ALT			HT													
SYM	1	4		p	g	h	e	a	d	1	=	'	L	i	n	c

Pageheader 1 = Center of Headerline ⟶ Text ⟶

BYTE	672	673	674	675	676	677	678	679	680	681	682	683	684	685	686	687
HEX	6F	6C	6E	27	73	20	47	65	74	74	79	73	62	75	72	67
DEC	111	108	110	39	115	32	71	101	116	116	121	115	98	117	114	103
ASC						^`										
ALT						SPC										
SYM	o	l	n	'	s		G	e	t	t	y	s	b	u	r	g

⟵ Text of Header ⟶

BYTE	688	689	690	691	692	693	694	695	696	697	698	0	0	0	0	0
HEX	20	41	64	64	72	65	73	73	0D	0A	1A	XX	XX	XX	XX	XX
DEC	32	65	100	100	114	101	115	115	13	10	26	0	0	0	0	0
ASC	^`								^M	^J	^Z	XXX	XXX	XXX	XXX	XXX
ALT	SPC								CR	LF	SUB	XXX	XXX	XXX	XXX	XXX
SYM		A	d	d	r	e	s	s								

Newline | EOF

End of Gettysburg Address as an Ability File

Lincoln's Gettysburg Address as a MultiMate File

BYTE	0	1	2	3	4	5	6	7	8	9	10	11	12	13	14	15
HEX	47	41	4D	4D	20	20	20	20	20	20	20	20	20	20	20	20
DEC	71	65	77	77	32	32	32	32	32	32	32	32	32	32	32	32
ASC					^\	^\	^\	^\	^\	^\	^\	^\	^\	^\	^\	^\
ALT					SPC	SPC	SPC	SPC	SPC	SPC	SPC	SPC	SPC	SPC	SPC	SPC
SYM	G	A	M	M												

←———————————————— Filename ————————————————→

BYTE	16	17	18	19	20	21	22	23	24	25	26	27	28	29	30	31
HEX	20	20	20	20	41	2E	20	4C	69	6E	63	6F	6C	6E	00	00
DEC	32	32	32	32	65	46	32	76	105	110	99	111	108	110	0	0
ASC	^\	^\	^\	^\		^\									^@	^@
ALT	SPC	SPC	SPC	SPC		SPC									NUL	NUL
SYM					A	.		L	i	n	c	o	l	n		

←—— Filename ——→ ←———— Author -- Library Entry Field ————→

BYTE	32	33	34	35	36	37	38	39	40	41	42	43	44	45	46	47
HEX	00	00	00	00	00	00	00	00	54	72	6F	6F	70	73	00	00
DEC	0	0	0	0	0	0	0	0	84	114	111	111	112	115	0	0
ASC	^@	^@	^@	^@	^@	^@	^@	^@							^@	^@
ALT	NUL	NUL	NUL	NUL	NUL	NUL	NUL	NUL							NUL	NUL
SYM									T	r	o	o	p	s		

←———— Author ————→ ←———— Addressee -- Library Entry Field ————→

BYTE	48	49	50	51	52	53	54	55	56	57	58	59	60	61	62	63
HEX	00	00	00	00	00	00	00	00	00	00	00	00	4A	42	57	00
DEC	0	0	0	0	0	0	0	0	0	0	0	0	74	66	87	0
ASC	^@	^@	^@	^@	^@	^@	^@	^@	^@	^@	^@	^@				^@
ALT	NUL	NUL	NUL	NUL	NUL	NUL	NUL	NUL	NUL	NUL	NUL	NUL				NUL
SYM													J	B	W	

←———— Addressee -- Library Entry Field ————→ ←———— Operator ————→

BYTE	64	65	66	67	68	69	70	71	72	73	74	75	76	77	78	79
HEX	00	00	00	00	00	00	00	00	00	00	00	00	00	00	00	00
DEC	0	0	0	0	0	0	0	0	0	0	0	0	0	0	0	0
ASC	^@	^@	^@	^@	^@	^@	^@	^@	^@	^@	^@	^@	^@	^@	^@	^@
ALT	NUL	NUL	NUL	NUL	NUL	NUL	NUL	NUL	NUL	NUL	NUL	NUL	NUL	NUL	NUL	NUL
SYM																

←———————————————— Operator ————————————————→

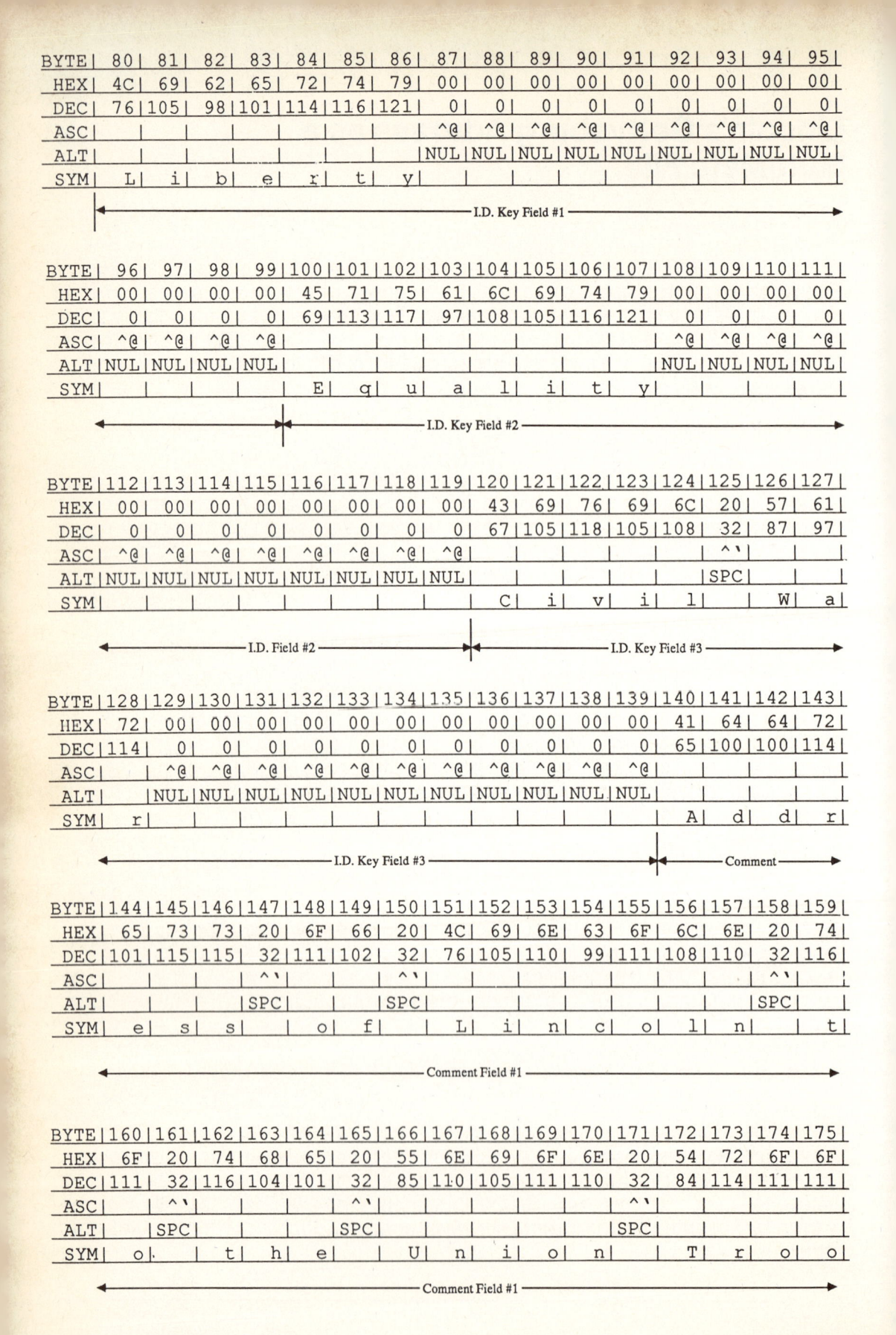

BYTE	80	81	82	83	84	85	86	87	88	89	90	91	92	93	94	95
HEX	4C	69	62	65	72	74	79	00	00	00	00	00	00	00	00	00
DEC	76	105	98	101	114	116	121	0	0	0	0	0	0	0	0	0
ASC								^@	^@	^@	^@	^@	^@	^@	^@	^@
ALT								NUL	NUL	NUL	NUL	NUL	NUL	NUL	NUL	NUL
SYM	L	i	b	e	r	t	y									

←——————————————— I.D. Key Field #1 ———————————————→

BYTE	96	97	98	99	100	101	102	103	104	105	106	107	108	109	110	111
HEX	00	00	00	00	45	71	75	61	6C	69	74	79	00	00	00	00
DEC	0	0	0	0	69	113	117	97	108	105	116	121	0	0	0	0
ASC	^@	^@	^@	^@									^@	^@	^@	^@
ALT	NUL	NUL	NUL	NUL									NUL	NUL	NUL	NUL
SYM					E	q	u	a	l	i	t	y				

←——————————————— I.D. Key Field #2 ———————————————→

BYTE	112	113	114	115	116	117	118	119	120	121	122	123	124	125	126	127
HEX	00	00	00	00	00	00	00	00	43	69	76	69	6C	20	57	61
DEC	0	0	0	0	0	0	0	0	67	105	118	105	108	32	87	97
ASC	^@	^@	^@	^@	^@	^@	^@	^@						^`		
ALT	NUL	NUL	NUL	NUL	NUL	NUL	NUL	NUL						SPC		
SYM									C	i	v	i	l		W	a

←——— I.D. Field #2 ———→←——————— I.D. Key Field #3 ———————→

BYTE	128	129	130	131	132	133	134	135	136	137	138	139	140	141	142	143
HEX	72	00	00	00	00	00	00	00	00	00	00	00	41	64	64	72
DEC	114	0	0	0	0	0	0	0	0	0	0	0	65	100	100	114
ASC		^@	^@	^@	^@	^@	^@	^@	^@	^@	^@	^@				
ALT		NUL	NUL	NUL	NUL	NUL	NUL	NUL	NUL	NUL	NUL	NUL				
SYM	r												A	d	d	r

←——————— I.D. Key Field #3 ———————→←——— Comment ———→

BYTE	144	145	146	147	148	149	150	151	152	153	154	155	156	157	158	159
HEX	65	73	73	20	6F	66	20	4C	69	6E	63	6F	6C	6E	20	74
DEC	101	115	115	32	111	102	32	76	105	110	99	111	108	110	32	116
ASC				^`			^`								^`	
ALT				SPC			SPC								SPC	
SYM	e	s	s		o	f		L	i	n	c	o	l	n		t

←——————————————— Comment Field #1 ———————————————→

BYTE	160	161	162	163	164	165	166	167	168	169	170	171	172	173	174	175
HEX	6F	20	74	68	65	20	55	6E	69	6F	6E	20	54	72	6F	6F
DEC	111	32	116	104	101	32	85	110	105	111	110	32	84	114	111	111
ASC		^`				^`						^`				
ALT		SPC				SPC						SPC				
SYM	o		t	h	e		U	n	i	o	n		T	r	o	o

←——————————————— Comment Field #1 ———————————————→

202 MULTIMATE

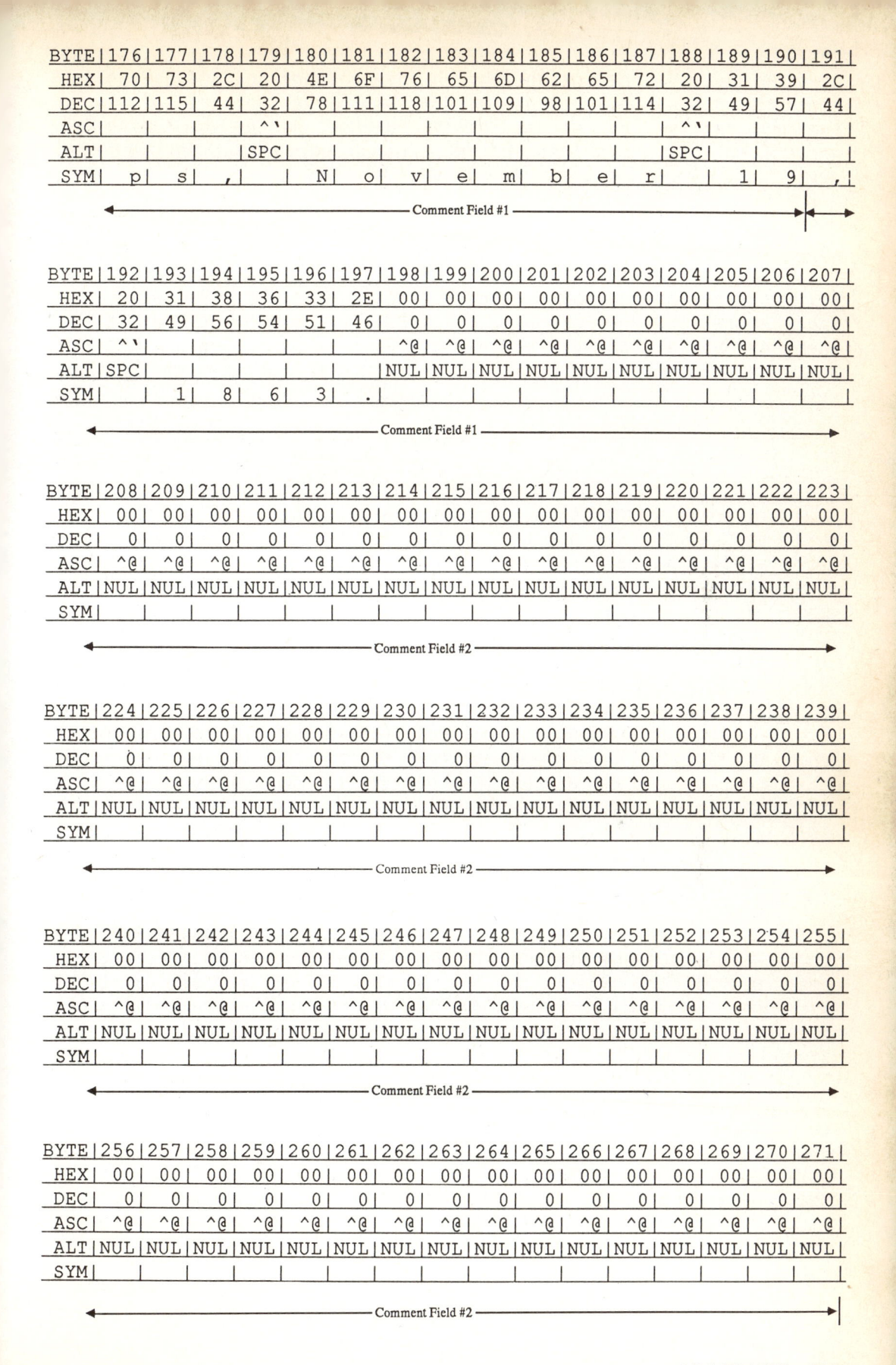

BYTE	176	177	178	179	180	181	182	183	184	185	186	187	188	189	190	191
HEX	70	73	2C	20	4E	6F	76	65	6D	62	65	72	20	31	39	2C
DEC	112	115	44	32	78	111	118	101	109	98	101	114	32	49	57	44
ASC				^`									^`			
ALT				SPC									SPC			
SYM	p	s	,		N	o	v	e	m	b	e	r		1	9	,

◄──────────────── Comment Field #1 ────────────────►

BYTE	192	193	194	195	196	197	198	199	200	201	202	203	204	205	206	207
HEX	20	31	38	36	33	2E	00	00	00	00	00	00	00	00	00	00
DEC	32	49	56	54	51	46	0	0	0	0	0	0	0	0	0	0
ASC	^`						^@	^@	^@	^@	^@	^@	^@	^@	^@	^@
ALT	SPC						NUL	NUL	NUL	NUL	NUL	NUL	NUL	NUL	NUL	NUL
SYM		1	8	6	3	.										

◄──────────────── Comment Field #1 ────────────────►

BYTE	208	209	210	211	212	213	214	215	216	217	218	219	220	221	222	223
HEX	00	00	00	00	00	00	00	00	00	00	00	00	00	00	00	00
DEC	0	0	0	0	0	0	0	0	0	0	0	0	0	0	0	0
ASC	^@	^@	^@	^@	^@	^@	^@	^@	^@	^@	^@	^@	^@	^@	^@	^@
ALT	NUL	NUL	NUL	NUL	NUL	NUL	NUL	NUL	NUL	NUL	NUL	NUL	NUL	NUL	NUL	NUL
SYM																

◄──────────────── Comment Field #2 ────────────────►

BYTE	224	225	226	227	228	229	230	231	232	233	234	235	236	237	238	239
HEX	00	00	00	00	00	00	00	00	00	00	00	00	00	00	00	00
DEC	0	0	0	0	0	0	0	0	0	0	0	0	0	0	0	0
ASC	^@	^@	^@	^@	^@	^@	^@	^@	^@	^@	^@	^@	^@	^@	^@	^@
ALT	NUL	NUL	NUL	NUL	NUL	NUL	NUL	NUL	NUL	NUL	NUL	NUL	NUL	NUL	NUL	NUL
SYM																

◄──────────────── Comment Field #2 ────────────────►

BYTE	240	241	242	243	244	245	246	247	248	249	250	251	252	253	254	255
HEX	00	00	00	00	00	00	00	00	00	00	00	00	00	00	00	00
DEC	0	0	0	0	0	0	0	0	0	0	0	0	0	0	0	0
ASC	^@	^@	^@	^@	^@	^@	^@	^@	^@	^@	^@	^@	^@	^@	^@	^@
ALT	NUL	NUL	NUL	NUL	NUL	NUL	NUL	NUL	NUL	NUL	NUL	NUL	NUL	NUL	NUL	NUL
SYM																

◄──────────────── Comment Field #2 ────────────────►

BYTE	256	257	258	259	260	261	262	263	264	265	266	267	268	269	270	271
HEX	00	00	00	00	00	00	00	00	00	00	00	00	00	00	00	00
DEC	0	0	0	0	0	0	0	0	0	0	0	0	0	0	0	0
ASC	^@	^@	^@	^@	^@	^@	^@	^@	^@	^@	^@	^@	^@	^@	^@	^@
ALT	NUL	NUL	NUL	NUL	NUL	NUL	NUL	NUL	NUL	NUL	NUL	NUL	NUL	NUL	NUL	NUL
SYM																

◄──────────────── Comment Field #2 ────────────────►

MULTIMATE

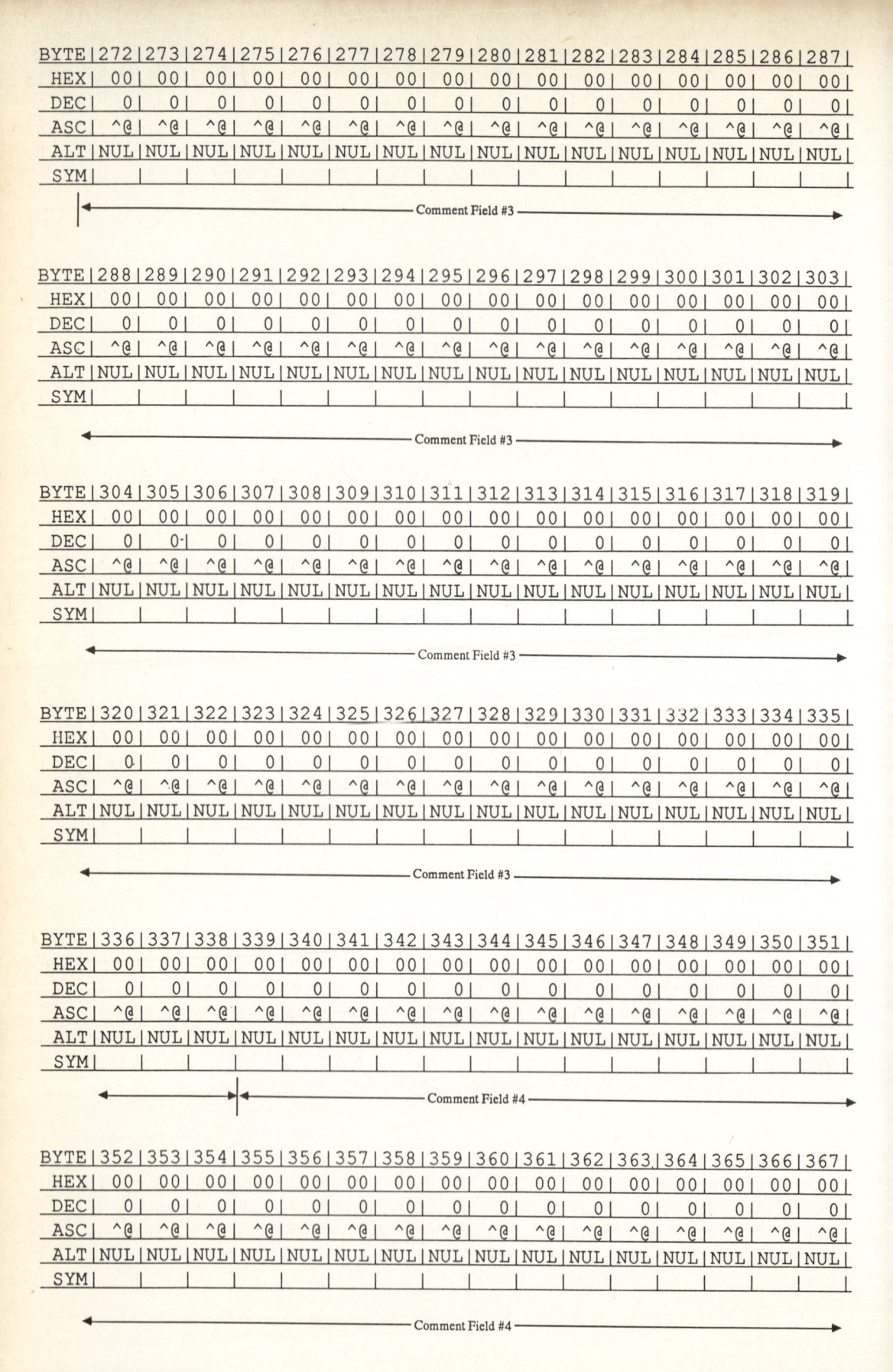

BYTE	272	273	274	275	276	277	278	279	280	281	282	283	284	285	286	287
HEX	00	00	00	00	00	00	00	00	00	00	00	00	00	00	00	00
DEC	0	0	0	0	0	0	0	0	0	0	0	0	0	0	0	0
ASC	^@	^@	^@	^@	^@	^@	^@	^@	^@	^@	^@	^@	^@	^@	^@	^@
ALT	NUL	NUL	NUL	NUL	NUL	NUL	NUL	NUL	NUL	NUL	NUL	NUL	NUL	NUL	NUL	NUL
SYM																

←——————————— Comment Field #3 ———————————→

BYTE	288	289	290	291	292	293	294	295	296	297	298	299	300	301	302	303
HEX	00	00	00	00	00	00	00	00	00	00	00	00	00	00	00	00
DEC	0	0	0	0	0	0	0	0	0	0	0	0	0	0	0	0
ASC	^@	^@	^@	^@	^@	^@	^@	^@	^@	^@	^@	^@	^@	^@	^@	^@
ALT	NUL	NUL	NUL	NUL	NUL	NUL	NUL	NUL	NUL	NUL	NUL	NUL	NUL	NUL	NUL	NUL
SYM																

←——————————— Comment Field #3 ———————————→

BYTE	304	305	306	307	308	309	310	311	312	313	314	315	316	317	318	319
HEX	00	00	00	00	00	00	00	00	00	00	00	00	00	00	00	00
DEC	0	0	0	0	0	0	0	0	0	0	0	0	0	0	0	0
ASC	^@	^@	^@	^@	^@	^@	^@	^@	^@	^@	^@	^@	^@	^@	^@	^@
ALT	NUL	NUL	NUL	NUL	NUL	NUL	NUL	NUL	NUL	NUL	NUL	NUL	NUL	NUL	NUL	NUL
SYM																

←——————————— Comment Field #3 ———————————→

BYTE	320	321	322	323	324	325	326	327	328	329	330	331	332	333	334	335
HEX	00	00	00	00	00	00	00	00	00	00	00	00	00	00	00	00
DEC	0	0	0	0	0	0	0	0	0	0	0	0	0	0	0	0
ASC	^@	^@	^@	^@	^@	^@	^@	^@	^@	^@	^@	^@	^@	^@	^@	^@
ALT	NUL	NUL	NUL	NUL	NUL	NUL	NUL	NUL	NUL	NUL	NUL	NUL	NUL	NUL	NUL	NUL
SYM																

←——————————— Comment Field #3 ———————————→

BYTE	336	337	338	339	340	341	342	343	344	345	346	347	348	349	350	351
HEX	00	00	00	00	00	00	00	00	00	00	00	00	00	00	00	00
DEC	0	0	0	0	0	0	0	0	0	0	0	0	0	0	0	0
ASC	^@	^@	^@	^@	^@	^@	^@	^@	^@	^@	^@	^@	^@	^@	^@	^@
ALT	NUL	NUL	NUL	NUL	NUL	NUL	NUL	NUL	NUL	NUL	NUL	NUL	NUL	NUL	NUL	NUL
SYM																

←——————————— Comment Field #4 ———————————→

BYTE	352	353	354	355	356	357	358	359	360	361	362	363	364	365	366	367
HEX	00	00	00	00	00	00	00	00	00	00	00	00	00	00	00	00
DEC	0	0	0	0	0	0	0	0	0	0	0	0	0	0	0	0
ASC	^@	^@	^@	^@	^@	^@	^@	^@	^@	^@	^@	^@	^@	^@	^@	^@
ALT	NUL	NUL	NUL	NUL	NUL	NUL	NUL	NUL	NUL	NUL	NUL	NUL	NUL	NUL	NUL	NUL
SYM																

←——————————— Comment Field #4 ———————————→

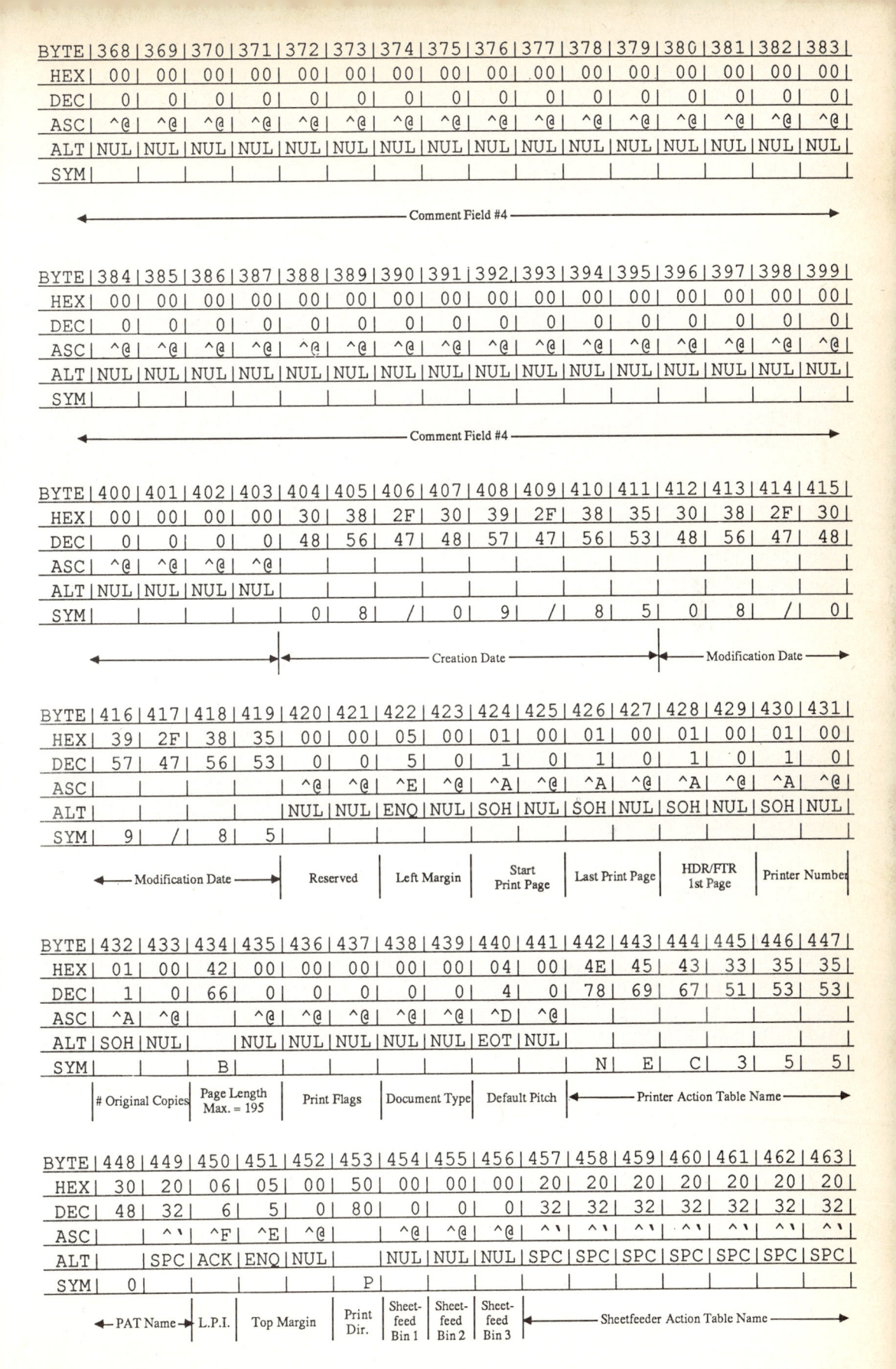

BYTE	368	369	370	371	372	373	374	375	376	377	378	379	380	381	382	383
HEX	00	00	00	00	00	00	00	00	00	00	00	00	00	00	00	00
DEC	0	0	0	0	0	0	0	0	0	0	0	0	0	0	0	0
ASC	^@	^@	^@	^@	^@	^@	^@	^@	^@	^@	^@	^@	^@	^@	^@	^@
ALT	NUL	NUL	NUL	NUL	NUL	NUL	NUL	NUL	NUL	NUL	NUL	NUL	NUL	NUL	NUL	NUL
SYM																

◄──────────────── Comment Field #4 ────────────────►

BYTE	384	385	386	387	388	389	390	391	392	393	394	395	396	397	398	399
HEX	00	00	00	00	00	00	00	00	00	00	00	00	00	00	00	00
DEC	0	0	0	0	0	0	0	0	0	0	0	0	0	0	0	0
ASC	^@	^@	^@	^@	^@	^@	^@	^@	^@	^@	^@	^@	^@	^@	^@	^@
ALT	NUL	NUL	NUL	NUL	NUL	NUL	NUL	NUL	NUL	NUL	NUL	NUL	NUL	NUL	NUL	NUL
SYM																

◄──────────────── Comment Field #4 ────────────────►

BYTE	400	401	402	403	404	405	406	407	408	409	410	411	412	413	414	415
HEX	00	00	00	00	30	38	2F	30	39	2F	38	35	30	38	2F	30
DEC	0	0	0	0	48	56	47	48	57	47	56	53	48	56	47	48
ASC	^@	^@	^@	^@												
ALT	NUL	NUL	NUL	NUL												
SYM					0	8	/	0	9	/	8	5	0	8	/	0

◄──────────────┤◄──── Creation Date ────►◄──── Modification Date ────►

BYTE	416	417	418	419	420	421	422	423	424	425	426	427	428	429	430	431
HEX	39	2F	38	35	00	00	05	00	01	00	01	00	01	00	01	00
DEC	57	47	56	53	0	0	5	0	1	0	1	0	1	0	1	0
ASC					^@	^@	^E	^@	^A	^@	^A	^@	^A	^@	^A	^@
ALT					NUL	NUL	ENQ	NUL	SOH	NUL	SOH	NUL	SOH	NUL	SOH	NUL
SYM	9	/	8	5												

◄── Modification Date ──► | Reserved | Left Margin | Start Print Page | Last Print Page | HDR/FTR 1st Page | Printer Number

BYTE	432	433	434	435	436	437	438	439	440	441	442	443	444	445	446	447
HEX	01	00	42	00	00	00	00	00	04	00	4E	45	43	33	35	35
DEC	1	0	66	0	0	0	0	0	4	0	78	69	67	51	53	53
ASC	^A	^@		^@	^@	^@	^@	^@	^D	^@						
ALT	SOH	NUL		NUL	NUL	NUL	NUL	NUL	EOT	NUL						
SYM			B								N	E	C	3	5	5

| # Original Copies | Page Length Max. = 195 | Print Flags | Document Type | Default Pitch | ◄── Printer Action Table Name ──► |

BYTE	448	449	450	451	452	453	454	455	456	457	458	459	460	461	462	463
HEX	30	20	06	05	00	50	00	00	00	20	20	20	20	20	20	20
DEC	48	32	6	5	0	80	0	0	0	32	32	32	32	32	32	32
ASC		^\	^F	^E	^@		^@	^@	^@	^\	^\	^\	^\	^\	^\	^\
ALT		SPC	ACK	ENQ	NUL		NUL	NUL	NUL	SPC	SPC	SPC	SPC	SPC	SPC	SPC
SYM	0					P										

◄─ PAT Name ─► | L.P.I. | Top Margin | Print Dir. | Sheet-feed Bin 1 | Sheet-feed Bin 2 | Sheet-feed Bin 3 | ◄── Sheetfeeder Action Table Name ──►

MULTIMATE **205**

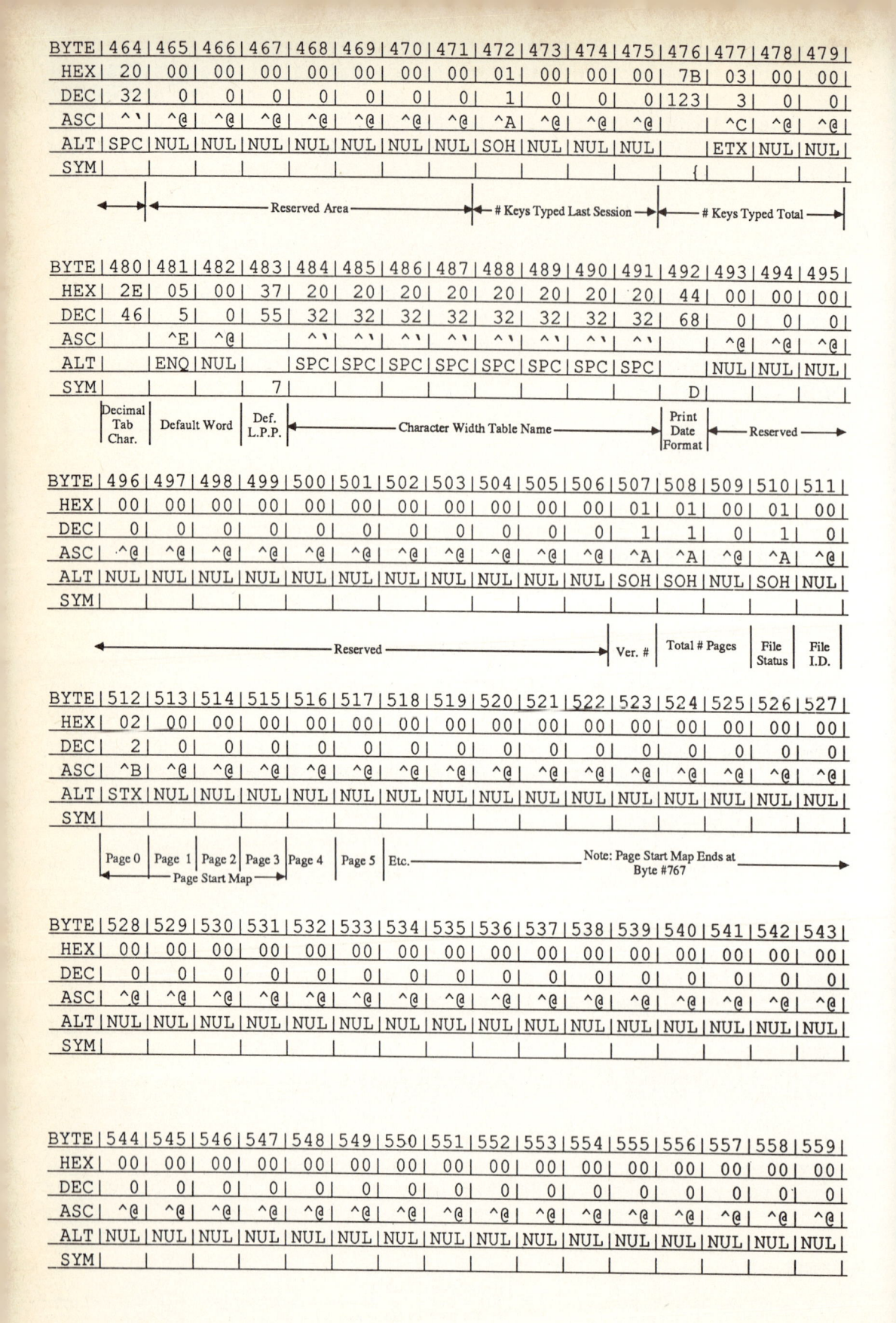

BYTE	464	465	466	467	468	469	470	471	472	473	474	475	476	477	478	479
HEX	20	00	00	00	00	00	00	00	01	00	00	00	7B	03	00	00
DEC	32	0	0	0	0	0	0	0	1	0	0	0	123	3	0	0
ASC	^`	^@	^@	^@	^@	^@	^@	^@	^A	^@	^@	^@		^C	^@	^@
ALT	SPC	NUL	NUL	NUL	NUL	NUL	NUL	NUL	SOH	NUL	NUL	NUL		ETX	NUL	NUL
SYM													{			

←———————— Reserved Area ————————→ ←— # Keys Typed Last Session —→ ←— # Keys Typed Total —→

BYTE	480	481	482	483	484	485	486	487	488	489	490	491	492	493	494	495
HEX	2E	05	00	37	20	20	20	20	20	20	20	20	44	00	00	00
DEC	46	5	0	55	32	32	32	32	32	32	32	32	68	0	0	0
ASC	.	^E	^@		^`	^`	^`	^`	^`	^`	^`	^`		^@	^@	^@
ALT		ENQ	NUL		SPC	SPC	SPC	SPC	SPC	SPC	SPC	SPC		NUL	NUL	NUL
SYM				7									D			

| Decimal Tab Char. | Default Word | Def. L.P.P. | ←———— Character Width Table Name ————→ | Print Date Format | ←— Reserved —→ |

BYTE	496	497	498	499	500	501	502	503	504	505	506	507	508	509	510	511
HEX	00	00	00	00	00	00	00	00	00	00	00	00	01	01	00	01	00
DEC	0	0	0	0	0	0	0	0	0	0	0	0	1	1	0	1	0
ASC	^@	^@	^@	^@	^@	^@	^@	^@	^@	^@	^@	^@	^A	^A	^@	^A	^@
ALT	NUL	NUL	NUL	NUL	NUL	NUL	NUL	NUL	NUL	NUL	NUL	NUL	SOH	SOH	NUL	SOH	NUL
SYM																	

←———————————— Reserved ————————————→ | Ver. # | Total # Pages | File Status | File I.D. |

BYTE	512	513	514	515	516	517	518	519	520	521	522	523	524	525	526	527
HEX	02	00	00	00	00	00	00	00	00	00	00	00	00	00	00	00
DEC	2	0	0	0	0	0	0	0	0	0	0	0	0	0	0	0
ASC	^B	^@	^@	^@	^@	^@	^@	^@	^@	^@	^@	^@	^@	^@	^@	^@
ALT	STX	NUL	NUL	NUL	NUL	NUL	NUL	NUL	NUL	NUL	NUL	NUL	NUL	NUL	NUL	NUL
SYM																

| Page 0 | Page 1 | Page 2 | Page 3 | Page 4 | Page 5 | Etc. ————— | Note: Page Start Map Ends at Byte #767 |
←— Page Start Map —→

BYTE	528	529	530	531	532	533	534	535	536	537	538	539	540	541	542	543
HEX	00	00	00	00	00	00	00	00	00	00	00	00	00	00	00	00
DEC	0	0	0	0	0	0	0	0	0	0	0	0	0	0	0	0
ASC	^@	^@	^@	^@	^@	^@	^@	^@	^@	^@	^@	^@	^@	^@	^@	^@
ALT	NUL	NUL	NUL	NUL	NUL	NUL	NUL	NUL	NUL	NUL	NUL	NUL	NUL	NUL	NUL	NUL
SYM																

BYTE	544	545	546	547	548	549	550	551	552	553	554	555	556	557	558	559
HEX	00	00	00	00	00	00	00	00	00	00	00	00	00	00	00	00
DEC	0	0	0	0	0	0	0	0	0	0	0	0	0	0	0	0
ASC	^@	^@	^@	^@	^@	^@	^@	^@	^@	^@	^@	^@	^@	^@	^@	^@
ALT	NUL	NUL	NUL	NUL	NUL	NUL	NUL	NUL	NUL	NUL	NUL	NUL	NUL	NUL	NUL	NUL
SYM																

BYTE	560	561	562	563	564	565	566	567	568	569	570	571	572	573	574	575
HEX	00	00	00	00	00	00	00	00	00	00	00	00	00	00	00	00
DEC	0	0	0	0	0	0	0	0	0	0	0	0	0	0	0	0
ASC	^@	^@	^@	^@	^@	^@	^@	^@	^@	^@	^@	^@	^@	^@	^@	^@
ALT	NUL	NUL	NUL	NUL	NUL	NUL	NUL	NUL	NUL	NUL	NUL	NUL	NUL	NUL	NUL	NUL
SYM																

BYTE	576	577	578	579	580	581	582	583	584	585	586	587	588	589	590	591
HEX	00	00	00	00	00	00	00	00	00	00	00	00	00	00	00	00
DEC	0	0	0	0	0	0	0	0	0	0	0	0	0	0	0	0
ASC	^@	^@	^@	^@	^@	^@	^@	^@	^@	^@	^@	^@	^@	^@	^@	^@
ALT	NUL	NUL	NUL	NUL	NUL	NUL	NUL	NUL	NUL	NUL	NUL	NUL	NUL	NUL	NUL	NUL
SYM																

BYTE	592	593	594	595	596	597	598	599	600	601	602	603	604	605	606	607
HEX	00	00	00	00	00	00	00	00	00	00	00	00	00	00	00	00
DEC	0	0	0	0	0	0	0	0	0	0	0	0	0	0	0	0
ASC	^@	^@	^@	^@	^@	^@	^@	^@	^@	^@	^@	^@	^@	^@	^@	^@
ALT	NUL	NUL	NUL	NUL	NUL	NUL	NUL	NUL	NUL	NUL	NUL	NUL	NUL	NUL	NUL	NUL
SYM																

BYTE	608	609	610	611	612	613	614	615	616	617	618	619	620	621	622	623
HEX	00	00	00	00	00	00	00	00	00	00	00	00	00	00	00	00
DEC	0	0	0	0	0	0	0	0	0	0	0	0	0	0	0	0
ASC	^@	^@	^@	^@	^@	^@	^@	^@	^@	^@	^@	^@	^@	^@	^@	^@
ALT	NUL	NUL	NUL	NUL	NUL	NUL	NUL	NUL	NUL	NUL	NUL	NUL	NUL	NUL	NUL	NUL
SYM																

BYTE	624	625	626	627	628	629	630	631	632	633	634	635	636	637	638	639
HEX	00	00	00	00	00	00	00	00	00	00	00	00	00	00	00	00
DEC	0	0	0	0	0	0	0	0	0	0	0	0	0	0	0	0
ASC	^@	^@	^@	^@	^@	^@	^@	^@	^@	^@	^@	^@	^@	^@	^@	^@
ALT	NUL	NUL	NUL	NUL	NUL	NUL	NUL	NUL	NUL	NUL	NUL	NUL	NUL	NUL	NUL	NUL
SYM																

BYTE	640	641	642	643	644	645	646	647	648	649	650	651	652	653	654	655
HEX	00	00	00	00	00	00	00	00	00	00	00	00	00	00	00	00
DEC	0	0	0	0	0	0	0	0	0	0	0	0	0	0	0	0
ASC	^@	^@	^@	^@	^@	^@	^@	^@	^@	^@	^@	^@	^@	^@	^@	^@
ALT	NUL	NUL	NUL	NUL	NUL	NUL	NUL	NUL	NUL	NUL	NUL	NUL	NUL	NUL	NUL	NUL
SYM																

BYTE	656	657	658	659	660	661	662	663	664	665	666	667	668	669	670	671
HEX	00	00	00	00	00	00	00	00	00	00	00	00	00	00	00	00
DEC	0	0	0	0	0	0	0	0	0	0	0	0	0	0	0	0
ASC	^@	^@	^@	^@	^@	^@	^@	^@	^@	^@	^@	^@	^@	^@	^@	^@
ALT	NUL	NUL	NUL	NUL	NUL	NUL	NUL	NUL	NUL	NUL	NUL	NUL	NUL	NUL	NUL	NUL
SYM																

BYTE	672	673	674	675	676	677	678	679	680	681	682	683	684	685	686	687
HEX	00	00	00	00	00	00	00	00	00	00	00	00	00	00	00	00
DEC	0	0	0	0	0	0	0	0	0	0	0	0	0	0	0	0
ASC	^@	^@	^@	^@	^@	^@	^@	^@	^@	^@	^@	^@	^@	^@	^@	^@
ALT	NUL	NUL	NUL	NUL	NUL	NUL	NUL	NUL	NUL	NUL	NUL	NUL	NUL	NUL	NUL	NUL
SYM																

BYTE	688	689	690	691	692	693	694	695	696	697	698	699	700	701	702	703
HEX	00	00	00	00	00	00	00	00	00	00	00	00	00	00	00	00
DEC	0	0	0	0	0	0	0	0	0	0	0	0	0	0	0	0
ASC	^@	^@	^@	^@	^@	^@	^@	^@	^@	^@	^@	^@	^@	^@	^@	^@
ALT	NUL	NUL	NUL	NUL	NUL	NUL	NUL	NUL	NUL	NUL	NUL	NUL	NUL	NUL	NUL	NUL
SYM																

BYTE	704	705	706	707	708	709	710	711	712	713	714	715	716	717	718	719
HEX	00	00	00	00	00	00	00	00	00	00	00	00	00	00	00	00
DEC	0	0	0	0	0	0	0	0	0	0	0	0	0	0	0	0
ASC	^@	^@	^@	^@	^@	^@	^@	^@	^@	^@	^@	^@	^@	^@	^@	^@
ALT	NUL	NUL	NUL	NUL	NUL	NUL	NUL	NUL	NUL	NUL	NUL	NUL	NUL	NUL	NUL	NUL
SYM																

BYTE	720	721	722	723	724	725	726	727	728	729	730	731	732	733	734	735
HEX	00	00	00	00	00	00	00	00	00	00	00	00	00	00	00	00
DEC	0	0	0	0	0	0	0	0	0	0	0	0	0	0	0	0
ASC	^@	^@	^@	^@	^@	^@	^@	^@	^@	^@	^@	^@	^@	^@	^@	^@
ALT	NUL	NUL	NUL	NUL	NUL	NUL	NUL	NUL	NUL	NUL	NUL	NUL	NUL	NUL	NUL	NUL
SYM																

BYTE	736	737	738	739	740	741	742	743	744	745	746	747	748	749	750	751
HEX	00	00	00	00	00	00	00	00	00	00	00	00	00	00	00	00
DEC	0	0	0	0	0	0	0	0	0	0	0	0	0	0	0	0
ASC	^@	^@	^@	^@	^@	^@	^@	^@	^@	^@	^@	^@	^@	^@	^@	^@
ALT	NUL	NUL	NUL	NUL	NUL	NUL	NUL	NUL	NUL	NUL	NUL	NUL	NUL	NUL	NUL	NUL
SYM																

BYTE	752	753	754	755	756	757	758	759	760	761	762	763	764	765	766	767
HEX	00	00	00	00	00	00	00	00	00	00	00	00	00	00	00	00
DEC	0	0	0	0	0	0	0	0	0	0	0	0	0	0	0	0
ASC	^@	^@	^@	^@	^@	^@	^@	^@	^@	^@	^@	^@	^@	^@	^@	^@
ALT	NUL	NUL	NUL	NUL	NUL	NUL	NUL	NUL	NUL	NUL	NUL	NUL	NUL	NUL	NUL	NUL
SYM																

Page Start Map ⟶ | Unused
End Page Start Map ⟶

BYTE	768	769	770	771	772	773	774	775	776	777	778	779	780	781	782	783
HEX	01	01	03	01	00	00	00	00	00	00	00	00	00	00	00	00
DEC	1	1	3	1	0	0	0	0	0	0	0	0	0	0	0	0
ASC	^A	^A	^C	^A	^@	^@	^@	^@	^@	^@	^@	^@	^@	^@	^@	^@
ALT	SOH	SOH	ETX	SOH	NUL	NUL	NUL	NUL	NUL	NUL	NUL	NUL	NUL	NUL	NUL	NUL
SYM																

Must Be 1 | Must Be 1 | Rel. Rec. 2 | Rel. Rec. 3 | Rel. Rec. 4 | Etc. ⟶ Note: Record Allocation Table Continues to Byte 1023 ⟶
⟵ Start Record Allocation Table

BYTE	784	785	786	787	788	789	790	791	792	793	794	795	796	797	798	799
HEX	00	00	00	00	00	00	00	00	00	00	00	00	00	00	00	00
DEC	0	0	0	0	0	0	0	0	0	0	0	0	0	0	0	0
ASC	^@	^@	^@	^@	^@	^@	^@	^@	^@	^@	^@	^@	^@	^@	^@	^@
ALT	NUL	NUL	NUL	NUL	NUL	NUL	NUL	NUL	NUL	NUL	NUL	NUL	NUL	NUL	NUL	NUL
SYM																

BYTE	800	801	802	803	804	805	806	807	808	809	810	811	812	813	814	815
HEX	00	00	00	00	00	00	00	00	00	00	00	00	00	00	00	00
DEC	0	0	0	0	0	0	0	0	0	0	0	0	0	0	0	0
ASC	^@	^@	^@	^@	^@	^@	^@	^@	^@	^@	^@	^@	^@	^@	^@	^@
ALT	NUL	NUL	NUL	NUL	NUL	NUL	NUL	NUL	NUL	NUL	NUL	NUL	NUL	NUL	NUL	NUL
SYM																

BYTE	816	817	818	819	820	821	822	823	824	825	826	827	828	829	830	831
HEX	00	00	00	00	00	00	00	00	00	00	00	00	00	00	00	00
DEC	0	0	0	0	0	0	0	0	0	0	0	0	0	0	0	0
ASC	^@	^@	^@	^@	^@	^@	^@	^@	^@	^@	^@	^@	^@	^@	^@	^@
ALT	NUL	NUL	NUL	NUL	NUL	NUL	NUL	NUL	NUL	NUL	NUL	NUL	NUL	NUL	NUL	NUL
SYM																

BYTE	832	833	834	835	836	837	838	839	840	841	842	843	844	845	846	847
HEX	00	00	00	00	00	00	00	00	00	00	00	00	00	00	00	00
DEC	0	0	0	0	0	0	0	0	0	0	0	0	0	0	0	0
ASC	^@	^@	^@	^@	^@	^@	^@	^@	^@	^@	^@	^@	^@	^@	^@	^@
ALT	NUL	NUL	NUL	NUL	NUL	NUL	NUL	NUL	NUL	NUL	NUL	NUL	NUL	NUL	NUL	NUL
SYM																

BYTE	848	849	850	851	852	853	854	855	856	857	858	859	860	861	862	863
HEX	00	00	00	00	00	00	00	00	00	00	00	00	00	00	00	00
DEC	0	0	0	0	0	0	0	0	0	0	0	0	0	0	0	0
ASC	^@	^@	^@	^@	^@	^@	^@	^@	^@	^@	^@	^@	^@	^@	^@	^@
ALT	NUL	NUL	NUL	NUL	NUL	NUL	NUL	NUL	NUL	NUL	NUL	NUL	NUL	NUL	NUL	NUL
SYM																

BYTE	864	865	866	867	868	869	870	871	872	873	874	875	876	877	878	879
HEX	00	00	00	00	00	00	00	00	00	00	00	00	00	00	00	00
DEC	0	0	0	0	0	0	0	0	0	0	0	0	0	0	0	0
ASC	^@	^@	^@	^@	^@	^@	^@	^@	^@	^@	^@	^@	^@	^@	^@	^@
ALT	NUL	NUL	NUL	NUL	NUL	NUL	NUL	NUL	NUL	NUL	NUL	NUL	NUL	NUL	NUL	NUL
SYM																

BYTE	880	881	882	883	884	885	886	887	888	889	890	891	892	893	894	895
HEX	00	00	00	00	00	00	00	00	00	00	00	00	00	00	00	00
DEC	0	0	0	0	0	0	0	0	0	0	0	0	0	0	0	0
ASC	^@	^@	^@	^@	^@	^@	^@	^@	^@	^@	^@	^@	^@	^@	^@	^@
ALT	NUL	NUL	NUL	NUL	NUL	NUL	NUL	NUL	NUL	NUL	NUL	NUL	NUL	NUL	NUL	NUL
SYM																

BYTE	896	897	898	899	900	901	902	903	904	905	906	907	908	909	910	911
HEX	00	00	00	00	00	00	00	00	00	00	00	00	00	00	00	00
DEC	0	0	0	0	0	0	0	0	0	0	0	0	0	0	0	0
ASC	^@	^@	^@	^@	^@	^@	^@	^@	^@	^@	^@	^@	^@	^@	^@	^@
ALT	NUL	NUL	NUL	NUL	NUL	NUL	NUL	NUL	NUL	NUL	NUL	NUL	NUL	NUL	NUL	NUL
SYM																

BYTE	912	913	914	915	916	917	918	919	920	921	922	923	924	925	926	927
HEX	00	00	00	00	00	00	00	00	00	00	00	00	00	00	00	00
DEC	0	0	0	0	0	0	0	0	0	0	0	0	0	0	0	0
ASC	^@	^@	^@	^@	^@	^@	^@	^@	^@	^@	^@	^@	^@	^@	^@	^@
ALT	NUL	NUL	NUL	NUL	NUL	NUL	NUL	NUL	NUL	NUL	NUL	NUL	NUL	NUL	NUL	NUL
SYM																

BYTE	928	929	930	931	932	933	934	935	936	937	938	939	940	941	942	943
HEX	00	00	00	00	00	00	00	00	00	00	00	00	00	00	00	00
DEC	0	0	0	0	0	0	0	0	0	0	0	0	0	0	0	0
ASC	^@	^@	^@	^@	^@	^@	^@	^@	^@	^@	^@	^@	^@	^@	^@	^@
ALT	NUL	NUL	NUL	NUL	NUL	NUL	NUL	NUL	NUL	NUL	NUL	NUL	NUL	NUL	NUL	NUL
SYM																

BYTE	944	945	946	947	948	949	950	951	952	953	954	955	956	957	958	959
HEX	00	00	00	00	00	00	00	00	00	00	00	00	00	00	00	00
DEC	0	0	0	0	0	0	0	0	0	0	0	0	0	0	0	0
ASC	^@	^@	^@	^@	^@	^@	^@	^@	^@	^@	^@	^@	^@	^@	^@	^@
ALT	NUL	NUL	NUL	NUL	NUL	NUL	NUL	NUL	NUL	NUL	NUL	NUL	NUL	NUL	NUL	NUL
SYM																

BYTE	960	961	962	963	964	965	966	967	968	969	970	971	972	973	974	975
HEX	00	00	00	00	00	00	00	00	00	00	00	00	00	00	00	00
DEC	0	0	0	0	0	0	0	0	0	0	0	0	0	0	0	0
ASC	^@	^@	^@	^@	^@	^@	^@	^@	^@	^@	^@	^@	^@	^@	^@	^@
ALT	NUL	NUL	NUL	NUL	NUL	NUL	NUL	NUL	NUL	NUL	NUL	NUL	NUL	NUL	NUL	NUL
SYM																

BYTE	976	977	978	979	980	981	982	983	984	985	986	987	988	989	990	991
HEX	00	00	00	00	00	00	00	00	00	00	00	00	00	00	00	00
DEC	0	0	0	0	0	0	0	0	0	0	0	0	0	0	0	0
ASC	^@	^@	^@	^@	^@	^@	^@	^@	^@	^@	^@	^@	^@	^@	^@	^@
ALT	NUL	NUL	NUL	NUL	NUL	NUL	NUL	NUL	NUL	NUL	NUL	NUL	NUL	NUL	NUL	NUL
SYM																

BYTE	992	993	994	995	996	997	998	999	0	1	2	3	4	5	6	7
HEX	00	00	00	00	00	00	00	00	00	00	00	00	00	00	00	00
DEC	0	0	0	0	0	0	0	0	0	0	0	0	0	0	0	0
ASC	^@	^@	^@	^@	^@	^@	^@	^@	^@	^@	^@	^@	^@	^@	^@	^@
ALT	NUL	NUL	NUL	NUL	NUL	NUL	NUL	NUL	NUL	NUL	NUL	NUL	NUL	NUL	NUL	NUL
SYM																

BYTE	8	9	10	11	12	13	14	15	16	17	18	19	20	21	22	23
HEX	00	00	00	00	00	00	00	00	00	00	00	00	00	00	00	00
DEC	0	0	0	0	0	0	0	0	0	0	0	0	0	0	0	0
ASC	^@	^@	^@	^@	^@	^@	^@	^@	^@	^@	^@	^@	^@	^@	^@	^@
ALT	NUL	NUL	NUL	NUL	NUL	NUL	NUL	NUL	NUL	NUL	NUL	NUL	NUL	NUL	NUL	NUL
SYM																

End of Record Allocation Table ──────────▶

BYTE	24	25	26	27	28	29	30	31	32	33	34	35	36	37	38	39
HEX	03	00	FF	03	B3	31	2E	2E	AF	2E	2E	2E	2E	AF	2E	2E
DEC	3	0	255	3	179	49	46	46	175	46	46	46	46	175	46	46
ASC	^C	^@	255	^C	179				175					175		
ALT	ETX	NUL	255	ETX	179				175					175		
SYM						1	.	.		.	.	.	.		.	.

Fwd. Pointer | Bkwd. Pointer | Attrib. Change | Attrib. Norm. | Format Char. | Line Spacing | Tab Stop | Tab Stop

◀──── Data Section ────▶ ◀──────── Format Line ────────▶

MULTIMATE **211**

BYTE	40	41	42	43	44	45	46	47	48	49	50	51	52	53	54	55
HEX	2E	2E	AF	2E	2E	2E	2E	2E	2E	2E	2E	2E	2E	2E	2E	2E
DEC	46	46	175	46	46	46	46	46	46	46	46	46	46	46	46	46
ASC			175													
ALT			175													
SYM	.	.		.	.	.	.	.	.	.	.	.	.	.	.	.

            Tab
            Stop

←─────────────────────── Format Line ───────────────────────→

BYTE	56	57	58	59	60	61	62	63	64	65	66	67	68	69	70	71
HEX	2E	2E	2E	2E	2E	2E	2E	2E	2E	2E	2E	2E	2E	2E	2E	2E
DEC	46	46	46	46	46	46	46	46	46	46	46	46	46	46	46	46
ASC																
ALT																
SYM	.	.	.	.	.	.	.	.	.	.	.	.	.	.	.	.

←─────────────────────── Format Line ───────────────────────→

BYTE	72	73	74	75	76	77	78	79	80	81	82	83	84	85	86	87
HEX	2E	2E	2E	2E	2E	2E	2E	2E	2E	2E	2E	2E	2E	2E	2E	2E
DEC	46	46	46	46	46	46	46	46	46	46	46	46	46	46	46	46
ASC																
ALT																
SYM	.	.	.	.	.	.	.	.	.	.	.	.	.	.	.	.

←─────────────────────── Format Line ───────────────────────→

BYTE	88	89	90	91	92	93	94	95	96	97	98	99	100	101	102	103
HEX	2E	2E	2E	2E	AE	1D	D7	4C	69	6E	63	6F	6C	6E	27	73
DEC	46	46	46	46	174	29	215	76	105	110	99	111	108	110	39	115
ASC					174	^]	215									
ALT					174	GS	215									
SYM	.	.	.	.				L	i	n	c	o	l	n	'	s

                                                                Carriage | Center | Header
                                                                Return | Char. | ←────── Text of Header ──────→

BYTE	104	105	106	107	108	109	110	111	112	113	114	115	116	117	118	119
HEX	20	47	65	74	74	79	73	62	75	72	67	20	41	64	64	72
DEC	32	71	101	116	116	121	115	98	117	114	103	32	65	100	100	114
ASC	^`											^`				
ALT	SPC											SPC				
SYM		G	e	t	t	y	s	b	u	r	g		A	d	d	r

BYTE	120	121	122	123	124	125	126	127	128	129	130	131	132	133	134	135
HEX	65	73	73	D7	AE	AE	1D	B2	54	68	65	20	47	65	74	74
DEC	101	115	115	215	174	174	29	178	84	104	101	32	71	101	116	116
ASC				215	174	174	^]	178				^`				
ALT				215	174	174	GS	178				SPC				
SYM	e	s	s						T	h	e		G	e	t	t

                            Header | Carriage | Carriage | Center | Bold
                                         Return | Return | | Toggle

BYTE	136	137	138	139	140	141	142	143	144	145	146	147	148	149	150	151
HEX	79	73	62	75	72	67	20	41	64	64	72	65	73	73	B2	AE
DEC	121	115	98	117	114	103	32	65	100	100	114	101	115	115	178	174
ASC							^`								178	174
ALT							SPC								178	174
SYM	y	s	b	u	r	g		A	d	d	r	e	s	s	Bold Toggle	Carriage Return

BYTE	152	153	154	155	156	157	158	159	160	161	162	163	164	165	166	167
HEX	AE	46	6F	75	72	73	63	6F	72	65	20	61	6E	64	20	73
DEC	174	70	111	117	114	115	99	111	114	101	32	97	110	100	32	115
ASC	174										^`				^`	
ALT	174										SPC				SPC	
SYM	Carriage Return	F	o	u	r	s	c	o	r	e		a	n	d		s

BYTE	168	169	170	171	172	173	174	175	176	177	178	179	180	181	182	183
HEX	65	76	65	6E	20	79	65	61	72	73	20	61	67	6F	20	6F
DEC	101	118	101	110	32	121	101	97	114	115	32	97	103	111	32	111
ASC					^`						^`				^`	
ALT					SPC						SPC				SPC	
SYM	e	v	e	n		y	e	a	r	s		a	g	o		o

BYTE	184	185	186	187	188	189	190	191	192	193	194	195	196	197	198	199
HEX	75	72	20	66	61	74	68	65	72	73	20	62	72	6F	75	67
DEC	117	114	32	102	97	116	104	101	114	115	32	98	114	111	117	103
ASC			^`								^`					
ALT			SPC								SPC					
SYM	u	r		f	a	t	h	e	r	s		b	r	o	u	g

BYTE	200	201	202	203	204	205	206	207	208	209	210	211	212	213	214	215
HEX	68	74	20	66	6F	72	74	68	20	6F	6E	20	74	68	69	73
DEC	104	116	32	102	111	114	116	104	32	111	110	32	116	104	105	115
ASC			^`						^`			^`				
ALT			SPC						SPC			SPC				
SYM	h	t		f	o	r	t	h		o	n		t	h	i	s

BYTE	216	217	218	219	220	221	222	223	224	225	226	227	228	229	230	231
HEX	20	63	6F	6E	74	69	6E	65	6E	74	2C	20	61	20	6E	65
DEC	32	99	111	110	116	105	110	101	110	116	44	32	97	32	110	101
ASC	^`											^`		^`		
ALT	SPC											SPC		SPC		
SYM		c	o	n	t	i	n	e	n	t	,		a		n	e

MULTIMATE   213

BYTE	232	233	234	235	236	237	238	239	240	241	242	243	244	245	246	247
HEX	77	20	6E	61	74	69	6F	6E	2C	20	63	6F	6E	63	65	69
DEC	119	32	110	97	116	105	111	110	44	32	99	111	110	99	101	105
ASC		^`							^`							
ALT		SPC							SPC							
SYM	w		n	a	t	i	o	n	,		c	o	n	c	e	i

BYTE	248	249	250	251	252	253	254	255	256	257	258	259	260	261	262	263
HEX	76	65	64	20	69	6E	20	FF	01	4C	69	62	65	72	74	79
DEC	118	101	100	32	105	110	32	255	1	76	105	98	101	114	116	121
ASC				^`		^`	255	^A								
ALT				SPC		SPC	255	SOH								
SYM	v	e	d		i	n				L	i	b	e	r	t	y

Format Change / Underscore

BYTE	264	265	266	267	268	269	270	271	272	273	274	275	276	277	278	279
HEX	FF	03	2C	20	61	6E	64	20	64	65	64	69	63	61	74	65
DEC	255	3	44	32	97	110	100	32	100	101	100	105	99	97	116	101
ASC	255	^C	^`				^`									
ALT	255	ETX	SPC				SPC									
SYM			,		a	n	d		d	e	d	i	c	a	t	e

Format Change / Normal Text

BYTE	280	281	282	283	284	285	286	287	288	289	290	291	292	293	294	295
HEX	64	20	74	6F	20	74	68	65	20	70	72	6F	70	6F	73	69
DEC	100	32	116	111	32	116	104	101	32	112	114	111	112	111	115	105
ASC		^`		^`				^`								
ALT		SPC		SPC				SPC								
SYM	d		t	o		t	h	e		p	r	o	p	o	s	i

BYTE	296	297	298	299	300	301	302	303	304	305	306	307	308	309	310	311
HEX	74	69	6F	6E	20	74	68	61	74	20	61	6C	6C	20	6D	65
DEC	116	105	111	110	32	116	104	97	116	32	97	108	108	32	109	101
ASC				^`				^`					^`			
ALT				SPC				SPC					SPC			
SYM	t	i	o	n		t	h	a	t		a	l	l		m	e

BYTE	312	313	314	315	316	317	318	319	320	321	322	323	324	325	326	327
HEX	6E	20	61	72	65	20	63	72	65	61	74	65	64	20	65	71
DEC	110	32	97	114	101	32	99	114	101	97	116	101	100	32	101	113
ASC		^`			^`								^`			
ALT		SPC			SPC								SPC			
SYM	n		a	r	e		c	r	e	a	t	e	d		e	q

BYTE	328	329	330	331	332	333	334	335	336	337	338	339	340	341	342	343
HEX	75	61	6C	2E	AE	AE	4E	6F	77	20	77	65	20	61	72	65
DEC	117	97	108	46	174	174	78	111	119	32	119	101	32	97	114	101
ASC					174	174				^`			^`			
ALT					174	174				SPC			SPC			
SYM	u	a	l	.			N	o	w		w	e		a	r	e
					Carriage Return	Carriage Return										

BYTE	344	345	346	347	348	349	350	351	352	353	354	355	356	357	358	359
HEX	20	65	6E	67	61	67	65	64	20	69	6E	20	61	20	67	72
DEC	32	101	110	103	97	103	101	100	32	105	110	32	97	32	103	114
ASC	^`								^`			^`		^`		
ALT	SPC								SPC			SPC		SPC		
SYM		e	n	g	a	g	e	d		i	n		a		g	r

Fwd. Pointer | Bkwd. Pointer — Text Continues →
← Begin Relative Record 3 →

BYTE	360	361	362	363	364	365	366	367	368	369	370	371	372	373	374	375
HEX	65	61	74	20	63	69	76	69	6C	20	77	61	72	2C	20	74
DEC	101	97	116	32	99	105	118	105	108	32	119	97	114	44	32	116
ASC				^`						^`					^`	
ALT				SPC						SPC					SPC	
SYM	e	a	t		c	i	v	i	l		w	a	r	,		t

BYTE	376	377	378	379	380	381	382	383	384	385	386	387	388	389	390	391
HEX	65	73	74	69	6E	67	20	77	68	65	74	68	65	72	20	74
DEC	101	115	116	105	110	103	32	119	104	101	116	104	101	114	32	116
ASC							^`								^`	
ALT							SPC								SPC	
SYM	e	s	t	i	n	g		w	h	e	t	h	e	r		t

BYTE	392	393	394	395	396	397	398	399	400	401	402	403	404	405	406	407
HEX	68	61	74	20	6E	61	74	69	6F	6E	20	6F	72	20	61	6E
DEC	104	97	116	32	110	97	116	105	111	110	32	111	114	32	97	110
ASC				^`							^`			^`		
ALT				SPC							SPC			SPC		
SYM	h	a	t		n	a	t	i	o	n		o	r		a	n

BYTE	408	409	410	411	412	413	414	415	416	417	418	419	420	421	422	423
HEX	79	20	6E	61	74	69	6F	6E	20	73	6F	20	63	6F	6E	63
DEC	121	32	110	97	116	105	111	110	32	115	111	32	99	111	110	99
ASC		^`							^`			^`				
ALT		SPC							SPC			SPC				
SYM	y		n	a	t	i	o	n		s	o		c	o	n	c

MULTIMATE 215

BYTE	424	425	426	427	428	429	430	431	432	433	434	435	436	437	438	439
HEX	65	69	76	65	64	20	61	6E	64	20	73	6F	20	64	65	64
DEC	101	105	118	101	100	32	97	110	100	32	115	111	32	100	101	100
ASC						^`				^`			^`			
ALT						SPC				SPC			SPC			
SYM	e	i	v	e	d		a	n	d		s	o		d	e	d

BYTE	440	441	442	443	444	445	446	447	448	449	450	451	452	453	454	455
HEX	69	63	61	74	65	64	20	63	61	6E	20	6C	6F	6E	67	20
DEC	105	99	97	116	101	100	32	99	97	110	32	108	111	110	103	32
ASC							^`			^`						^`
ALT							SPC			SPC						SPC
SYM	i	c	a	t	e	d		c	a	n		l	o	n	g	

BYTE	456	457	458	459	460	461	462	463	464	465	466	467	468	469	470	471
HEX	65	6E	64	75	72	65	2E	20	20	57	65	20	61	72	65	20
DEC	101	110	100	117	114	101	46	32	32	87	101	32	97	114	101	32
ASC							^`	^`		^`						^`
ALT								SPC	SPC		SPC					SPC
SYM	e	n	d	u	r	e	.			W	e		a	r	e	

BYTE	472	473	474	475	476	477	478	479	480	481	482	483	484	485	486	487
HEX	6D	65	74	20	6F	6E	20	61	20	67	72	65	61	74	20	62
DEC	109	101	116	32	111	110	32	97	32	103	114	101	97	116	32	98
ASC				^`		^`		^`							^`	
ALT				SPC		SPC		SPC							SPC	
SYM	m	e	t		o	n		a		g	r	e	a	t		b

BYTE	488	489	490	491	492	493	494	495	496	497	498	499	500	501	502	503
HEX	61	74	74	6C	65	66	69	65	6C	64	20	6F	66	20	74	68
DEC	97	116	116	108	101	102	105	101	108	100	32	111	102	32	116	104
ASC											^`		^`			
ALT											SPC		SPC			
SYM	a	t	t	l	e	f	i	e	l	d		o	f		t	h

BYTE	504	505	506	507	508	509	510	511	512	513	514	515	516	517	518	519
HEX	61	74	20	77	61	72	2E	20	20	57	65	20	68	61	76	65
DEC	97	116	32	119	97	114	46	32	32	87	101	32	104	97	118	101
ASC			^`			^`	^`		^`							
ALT			SPC			SPC	SPC		SPC							
SYM	a	t		w	a	r	.			W	e		h	a	v	e

216   MULTIMATE

BYTE	520	521	522	523	524	525	526	527	528	529	530	531	532	533	534	535
HEX	20	63	6F	6D	65	20	74	6F	20	64	65	64	69	63	61	74
DEC	32	99	111	109	101	32	116	111	32	100	101	100	105	99	97	116
ASC	^`					^`			^`							
ALT	SPC					SPC			SPC							
SYM		c	o	m	e		t	o		d	e	d	i	c	a	t

← End Relative Record 2 →

BYTE	536	537	538	539	540	541	542	543	544	545	546	547	548	549	550	551
HEX	01	02	65	20	61	20	70	6F	72	74	69	6F	6E	20	6F	66
DEC	1	2	101	32	97	32	112	111	114	116	105	111	110	32	111	102
ASC	^A	^B		^`		^`								^`		
ALT	SOH	STX		SPC		SPC								SPC		
SYM			e		a		p	o	r	t	i	o	n		o	f

Fwd. Pattern | Bkwd. Pattern | ← Text Continues →
← Begin Relative Record 3 →

BYTE	552	553	554	555	556	557	558	559	560	561	562	563	564	565	566	567
HEX	20	74	68	61	74	20	66	69	65	6C	64	2C	20	61	73	20
DEC	32	116	104	97	116	32	102	105	101	108	100	44	32	97	115	32
ASC	^`					^`						^`				^`
ALT	SPC					SPC						SPC				SPC
SYM		t	h	a	t		f	i	e	l	d	,		a	s	

BYTE	568	569	570	571	572	573	574	575	576	577	578	579	580	581	582	583
HEX	61	20	66	69	6E	61	6C	20	72	65	73	74	69	6E	67	20
DEC	97	32	102	105	110	97	108	32	114	101	115	116	105	110	103	32
ASC		^`						^`								^`
ALT		SPC						SPC								SPC
SYM	a		f	i	n	a	l		r	e	s	t	i	n	g	

BYTE	584	585	586	587	588	589	590	591	592	593	594	595	596	597	598	599
HEX	70	6C	61	63	65	20	66	6F	72	20	74	68	6F	73	65	20
DEC	112	108	97	99	101	32	102	111	114	32	116	104	111	115	101	32
ASC						^`				^`						^`
ALT						SPC				SPC						SPC
SYM	p	l	a	c	e		f	o	r		t	h	o	s	e	

BYTE	600	601	602	603	604	605	606	607	608	609	610	611	612	613	614	615
HEX	77	68	6F	20	68	65	72	65	20	67	61	76	65	20	74	68
DEC	119	104	111	32	104	101	114	101	32	103	97	118	101	32	116	104
ASC				^`					^`					^`		
ALT				SPC					SPC					SPC		
SYM	w	h	o		h	e	r	e		g	a	v	e		t	h

MULTIMATE **217**

BYTE	616	617	618	619	620	621	622	623	624	625	626	627	628	629	630	631
HEX	65	69	72	20	6C	69	76	65	73	20	74	68	61	74	20	74
DEC	101	105	114	32	108	105	118	101	115	32	116	104	97	116	32	116
ASC				^'						^'					^'	
ALT				SPC						SPC					SPC	
SYM	e	i	r		l	i	v	e	s		t	h	a	t		t

BYTE	632	633	634	635	636	637	638	639	640	641	642	643	644	645	646	647
HEX	68	61	74	20	6E	61	74	69	6F	6E	20	6D	69	67	68	74
DEC	104	97	116	32	110	97	116	105	111	110	32	109	105	103	104	116
ASC				^'							^'					
ALT				SPC							SPC					
SYM	h	a	t		n	a	t	i	o	n		m	i	g	h	t

BYTE	648	649	650	651	652	653	654	655	656	657	658	659	660	661	662	663
HEX	20	6C	69	76	65	2E	20	20	49	74	20	69	73	20	61	6C
DEC	32	108	105	118	101	46	32	32	73	116	32	105	115	32	97	108
ASC	^'					^'	^'		^'					^'		
ALT	SPC					SPC	SPC		SPC					SPC		
SYM		l	i	v	e	.			I	t		i	s		a	l

BYTE	664	665	666	667	668	669	670	671	672	673	674	675	676	677	678	679
HEX	74	6F	67	65	74	68	65	72	20	66	69	74	74	69	6E	67
DEC	116	111	103	101	116	104	101	114	32	102	105	116	116	105	110	103
ASC									^'							
ALT									SPC							
SYM	t	o	g	e	t	h	e	r		f	i	t	t	i	n	g

BYTE	680	681	682	683	684	685	686	687	688	689	690	691	692	693	694	695
HEX	20	61	6E	64	20	70	72	6F	70	65	72	20	74	68	61	74
DEC	32	97	110	100	32	112	114	111	112	101	114	32	116	104	97	116
ASC	^'				^'							^'				
ALT	SPC				SPC							SPC				
SYM		a	n	d		p	r	o	p	e	r		t	h	a	t

BYTE	696	697	698	699	700	701	702	703	704	705	706	707	708	709	710	711
HEX	20	77	65	20	73	68	6F	75	6C	64	20	64	6F	20	74	68
DEC	32	119	101	32	115	104	111	117	108	100	32	100	111	32	116	104
ASC	^'			^'							^'			^'		
ALT	SPC			SPC							SPC			SPC		
SYM		w	e		s	h	o	u	l	d		d	o		t	h

BYTE	712	713	714	715	716	717	718	719	720	721	722	723	724	725	726	727
HEX	69	73	2E	00	00	00	00	00	00	00	00	00	00	00	00	00
DEC	105	115	46	0	0	0	0	0	0	0	0	0	0	0	0	0
ASC				^@	^@	^@	^@	^@	^@	^@	^@	^@	^@	^@	^@	^@
ALT				NUL	NUL	NUL	NUL	NUL	NUL	NUL	NUL	NUL	NUL	NUL	NUL	NUL
SYM	i	s	.													

Note: Balance of Record Null-Filled

BYTE	728	729	730	731	732	733	734	735	736	737	738	739	740	741	742	743
HEX	00	00	00	00	00	00	00	00	00	00	00	00	00	00	00	00
DEC	0	0	0	0	0	0	0	0	0	0	0	0	0	0	0	0
ASC	^@	^@	^@	^@	^@	^@	^@	^@	^@	^@	^@	^@	^@	^@	^@	^@
ALT	NUL	NUL	NUL	NUL	NUL	NUL	NUL	NUL	NUL	NUL	NUL	NUL	NUL	NUL	NUL	NUL
SYM																

BYTE	744	745	746	747	748	749	750	751	752	753	754	755	756	757	758	759
HEX	00	00	00	00	00	00	00	00	00	00	00	00	00	00	00	00
DEC	0	0	0	0	0	0	0	0	0	0	0	0	0	0	0	0
ASC	^@	^@	^@	^@	^@	^@	^@	^@	^@	^@	^@	^@	^@	^@	^@	^@
ALT	NUL	NUL	NUL	NUL	NUL	NUL	NUL	NUL	NUL	NUL	NUL	NUL	NUL	NUL	NUL	NUL
SYM																

BYTE	760	761	762	763	764	765	766	767	768	769	770	771	772	773	774	775
HEX	00	00	00	00	00	00	00	00	00	00	00	00	00	00	00	00
DEC	0	0	0	0	0	0	0	0	0	0	0	0	0	0	0	0
ASC	^@	^@	^@	^@	^@	^@	^@	^@	^@	^@	^@	^@	^@	^@	^@	^@
ALT	NUL	NUL	NUL	NUL	NUL	NUL	NUL	NUL	NUL	NUL	NUL	NUL	NUL	NUL	NUL	NUL
SYM																

BYTE	776	777	778	779	780	781	782	783	784	785	786	787	788	789	790	791
HEX	00	00	00	00	00	00	00	00	00	00	00	00	00	00	00	00
DEC	0	0	0	0	0	0	0	0	0	0	0	0	0	0	0	0
ASC	^@	^@	^@	^@	^@	^@	^@	^@	^@	^@	^@	^@	^@	^@	^@	^@
ALT	NUL	NUL	NUL	NUL	NUL	NUL	NUL	NUL	NUL	NUL	NUL	NUL	NUL	NUL	NUL	NUL
SYM																

BYTE	792	793	794	795	796	797	798	799	800	801	802	803	804	805	806	807
HEX	00	00	00	00	00	00	00	00	00	00	00	00	00	00	00	00
DEC	0	0	0	0	0	0	0	0	0	0	0	0	0	0	0	0
ASC	^@	^@	^@	^@	^@	^@	^@	^@	^@	^@	^@	^@	^@	^@	^@	^@
ALT	NUL	NUL	NUL	NUL	NUL	NUL	NUL	NUL	NUL	NUL	NUL	NUL	NUL	NUL	NUL	NUL
SYM																

BYTE	808	809	810	811	812	813	814	815	816	817	818	819	820	821	822	823
HEX	00	00	00	00	00	00	00	00	00	00	00	00	00	00	00	00
DEC	0	0	0	0	0	0	0	0	0	0	0	0	0	0	0	0
ASC	^@	^@	^@	^@	^@	^@	^@	^@	^@	^@	^@	^@	^@	^@	^@	^@
ALT	NUL	NUL	NUL	NUL	NUL	NUL	NUL	NUL	NUL	NUL	NUL	NUL	NUL	NUL	NUL	NUL
SYM																

BYTE	824	825	826	827	828	829	830	831	832	833	834	835	836	837	838	839
HEX	00	00	00	00	00	00	00	00	00	00	00	00	00	00	00	00
DEC	0	0	0	0	0	0	0	0	0	0	0	0	0	0	0	0
ASC	^@	^@	^@	^@	^@	^@	^@	^@	^@	^@	^@	^@	^@	^@	^@	^@
ALT	NUL	NUL	NUL	NUL	NUL	NUL	NUL	NUL	NUL	NUL	NUL	NUL	NUL	NUL	NUL	NUL
SYM																

BYTE	840	841	842	843	844	845	846	847	848	849	850	851	852	853	854	855
HEX	00	00	00	00	00	00	00	00	00	00	00	00	00	00	00	00
DEC	0	0	0	0	0	0	0	0	0	0	0	0	0	0	0	0
ASC	^@	^@	^@	^@	^@	^@	^@	^@	^@	^@	^@	^@	^@	^@	^@	^@
ALT	NUL	NUL	NUL	NUL	NUL	NUL	NUL	NUL	NUL	NUL	NUL	NUL	NUL	NUL	NUL	NUL
SYM																

BYTE	856	857	858	859	860	861	862	863	864	865	866	867	868	869	870	871
HEX	00	00	00	00	00	00	00	00	00	00	00	00	00	00	00	00
DEC	0	0	0	0	0	0	0	0	0	0	0	0	0	0	0	0
ASC	^@	^@	^@	^@	^@	^@	^@	^@	^@	^@	^@	^@	^@	^@	^@	^@
ALT	NUL	NUL	NUL	NUL	NUL	NUL	NUL	NUL	NUL	NUL	NUL	NUL	NUL	NUL	NUL	NUL
SYM																

BYTE	872	873	874	875	876	877	878	879	880	881	882	883	884	885	886	887
HEX	00	00	00	00	00	00	00	00	00	00	00	00	00	00	00	00
DEC	0	0	0	0	0	0	0	0	0	0	0	0	0	0	0	0
ASC	^@	^@	^@	^@	^@	^@	^@	^@	^@	^@	^@	^@	^@	^@	^@	^@
ALT	NUL	NUL	NUL	NUL	NUL	NUL	NUL	NUL	NUL	NUL	NUL	NUL	NUL	NUL	NUL	NUL
SYM																

BYTE	888	889	890	891	892	893	894	895	896	897	898	899	900	901	902	903
HEX	00	00	00	00	00	00	00	00	00	00	00	00	00	00	00	00
DEC	0	0	0	0	0	0	0	0	0	0	0	0	0	0	0	0
ASC	^@	^@	^@	^@	^@	^@	^@	^@	^@	^@	^@	^@	^@	^@	^@	^@
ALT	NUL	NUL	NUL	NUL	NUL	NUL	NUL	NUL	NUL	NUL	NUL	NUL	NUL	NUL	NUL	NUL
SYM																

BYTE	904	905	906	907	908	909	910	911	912	913	914	915	916	917	918	919
HEX	00	00	00	00	00	00	00	00	00	00	00	00	00	00	00	00
DEC	0	0	0	0	0	0	0	0	0	0	0	0	0	0	0	0
ASC	^@	^@	^@	^@	^@	^@	^@	^@	^@	^@	^@	^@	^@	^@	^@	^@
ALT	NUL	NUL	NUL	NUL	NUL	NUL	NUL	NUL	NUL	NUL	NUL	NUL	NUL	NUL	NUL	NUL
SYM																

BYTE	920	921	922	923	924	925	926	927	928	929	930	931	932	933	934	935
HEX	00	00	00	00	00	00	00	00	00	00	00	00	00	00	00	00
DEC	0	0	0	0	0	0	0	0	0	0	0	0	0	0	0	0
ASC	^@	^@	^@	^@	^@	^@	^@	^@	^@	^@	^@	^@	^@	^@	^@	^@
ALT	NUL	NUL	NUL	NUL	NUL	NUL	NUL	NUL	NUL	NUL	NUL	NUL	NUL	NUL	NUL	NUL
SYM																

BYTE	936	937	938	939	940	941	942	943	944	945	946	947	948	949	950	951
HEX	00	00	00	00	00	00	00	00	00	00	00	00	00	00	00	00
DEC	0	0	0	0	0	0	0	0	0	0	0	0	0	0	0	0
ASC	^@	^@	^@	^@	^@	^@	^@	^@	^@	^@	^@	^@	^@	^@	^@	^@
ALT	NUL	NUL	NUL	NUL	NUL	NUL	NUL	NUL	NUL	NUL	NUL	NUL	NUL	NUL	NUL	NUL
SYM																

BYTE	952	953	954	955	956	957	958	959	960	961	962	963	964	965	966	967
HEX	00	00	00	00	00	00	00	00	00	00	00	00	00	00	00	00
DEC	0	0	0	0	0	0	0	0	0	0	0	0	0	0	0	0
ASC	^@	^@	^@	^@	^@	^@	^@	^@	^@	^@	^@	^@	^@	^@	^@	^@
ALT	NUL	NUL	NUL	NUL	NUL	NUL	NUL	NUL	NUL	NUL	NUL	NUL	NUL	NUL	NUL	NUL
SYM																

BYTE	968	969	970	971	972	973	974	975	976	977	978	979	980	981	982	983
HEX	00	00	00	00	00	00	00	00	00	00	00	00	00	00	00	00
DEC	0	0	0	0	0	0	0	0	0	0	0	0	0	0	0	0
ASC	^@	^@	^@	^@	^@	^@	^@	^@	^@	^@	^@	^@	^@	^@	^@	^@
ALT	NUL	NUL	NUL	NUL	NUL	NUL	NUL	NUL	NUL	NUL	NUL	NUL	NUL	NUL	NUL	NUL
SYM																

BYTE	984	985	986	987	988	989	990	991	992	993	994	995	996	997	998	999
HEX	00	00	00	00	00	00	00	00	00	00	00	00	00	00	00	00
DEC	0	0	0	0	0	0	0	0	0	0	0	0	0	0	0	0
ASC	^@	^@	^@	^@	^@	^@	^@	^@	^@	^@	^@	^@	^@	^@	^@	^@
ALT	NUL	NUL	NUL	NUL	NUL	NUL	NUL	NUL	NUL	NUL	NUL	NUL	NUL	NUL	NUL	NUL
SYM																

BYTE	0	1	2	3	4	5	6	7	8	9	10	11	12	13	14	15
HEX	00	00	00	00	00	00	00	00	00	00	00	00	00	00	00	00
DEC	0	0	0	0	0	0	0	0	0	0	0	0	0	0	0	0
ASC	^@	^@	^@	^@	^@	^@	^@	^@	^@	^@	^@	^@	^@	^@	^@	^@
ALT	NUL	NUL	NUL	NUL	NUL	NUL	NUL	NUL	NUL	NUL	NUL	NUL	NUL	NUL	NUL	NUL
SYM																

BYTE	16	17	18	19	20	21	22	23	24	25	26	27	28	29	30	31
HEX	00	00	00	00	00	00	00	00	00	00	00	00	00	00	00	00
DEC	0	0	0	0	0	0	0	0	0	0	0	0	0	0	0	0
ASC	^@	^@	^@	^@	^@	^@	^@	^@	^@	^@	^@	^@	^@	^@	^@	^@
ALT	NUL	NUL	NUL	NUL	NUL	NUL	NUL	NUL	NUL	NUL	NUL	NUL	NUL	NUL	NUL	NUL
SYM																

BYTE	32	33	34	35	36	37	38	39	40	41	42	43	44	45	46	47
HEX	00	00	00	00	00	00	00	00	00	00	00	00	00	00	00	00
DEC	0	0	0	0	0	0	0	0	0	0	0	0	0	0	0	0
ASC	^@	^@	^@	^@	^@	^@	^@	^@	^@	^@	^@	^@	^@	^@	^@	^@
ALT	NUL	NUL	NUL	NUL	NUL	NUL	NUL	NUL	NUL	NUL	NUL	NUL	NUL	NUL	NUL	NUL
SYM																

End of MultiMate Gettysburg Address File

Sample File in SYLK Format as an ASCII Dump

```
ID;PMP ──────────────── Id Field - Name of Program: MultiPlan
F;K;DG0G10  ⎫          Format of worksheet. Commas used; default format is general,
F;W4 4 11   ⎬ ──       no decimals, general alignment, 10-character wide columns.
F;W5 8 13   ⎭          Column 4 is 11 characters wide. Columns 5 thru 8 are 13.
B;Y13;X8 ⎬── Worksheet Bounds
C;Y1;X4;K"PAYMENT ANA"
C;X5;K"LYSIS WORKSHE"
C;X6;K"ET"
C;Y2;X4;K"============";G
C;X5;K"==============="
C;X6;K"=="
C;Y3;X1;K"LOAN AMT"
C;X2;K4800    ⎫ __ Cell uses commas; Formatted for 2 fixed decimal places, leading
F;F$2D        ⎭    $ sign.
C;Y4;X1;K"INTEREST"
C;X2;K0.185   ⎫
F;F%2D        ⎭ ── Cell formatted for leading % sign and 2 fixed decimal places
C;Y5;X1;K"MO PMT"
C;X2;K174.73
F;F$2D
C;Y6;X1;K"PERIODS"
C;X2;K36
C;Y8;X1;K"----------";G
C;X2;S;R8;C1;K"----------"
C;X3;S;K"----------"
C;X4;K"--------------";G
C;X5;S;C4;K"--------------"
C;X6;S;K"--------------"
C;X7;S;K"--------------"
C;X8;S;K"--------------"
C;Y9;X1;K"PMT NO"
C;X2;K"INT PD"
C;X3;K"PRC PD"
C;X4;K"REMAIN BAL"
C;X5;K"INT TO DATE"
C;X6;K"PRC TO DATE"
C;X7;K"PAID TO DATE"
C;Y10;X1;K"----------";G
C;X2;S;R10;C1;K"----------"
C;X3;S;K"----------"
```

```
C;X4;K"-------------";G
C;X5;S;C4;K"-------------"
C;X6;S;K"-------------"
C;X7;S;K"-------------"
C;X8;S;K"-------------"
C;Y11;X1;K1
C;X2;E+R[-8]C*(R[-7]C/12);K74.000000000002
F;F$2D
C;X3;E+R[-6]C[-1]-RC[-1];K100.73
F;F$2D
C;X4;E+R[-8]C[-2]-RC[-1];K4699.27
F;F$2D
C;X5;E+RC[-3];K74.000000000002
F;F$2D
C;X6;E+RC[-3];K100.73
F;F$2D
C;X7;E+RC[-2]+RC[-1];K174.73
F;F$2D
C;Y12;X1;E+R[-1]C+1;D;K2
C;Y13;S;R12;C1;K3
C;Y12;X2;E+R[-1]C[+2]*(R[-8]C/12);K72.447079166668
F;F$2D
C;X3;E+R[-7]C[-1]-RC[-1];K102.28292083333
F;F$2D
C;X4;E+R[-1]C-RC[-1];K4596.9870791667
F;F$2D
C;X5;E+R[-1]C+RC[-3];K146.44707916667
F;F$2D
C;X6;E+R[-1]C+RC[-3];K203.01292083333
F;F$2D
C;X7;E+R[-1]C+RC[-5]+RC[-4];K349.46
F;F$2D
C;Y13;X2;E+R[-1]C[+2]*(R[-9]C/12);K70.870217470488
F;F$2D
C;X3;E+R[-8]C[-1]-RC[-1];K103.85978252951
F;F$2D
C;X4;E+R[-1]C-RC[-1];K4493.1272966372
F;F$2D
C;X5;E+R[-1]C+RC[-3];K217.31729663716
F;F$2D
C;X6;E+R[-1]C+RC[-3];K306.87270336284
F;F$2D
C;X7;E+R[-1]C+RC[-5]+RC[-4];K524.19
F;F$2D
W;N1;A1 1;C7 0 7   } Window - Window 1, R1C1 is in upper left corner
E } End of File
```

— Formula
— Result When Saved

Sample Spreadsheet as an IBM Plans+ . ~MD File

BYTE	0	1	2	3	4	5	6	7	8	9	10	11	12	13	14	15
HEX	31	30	3C	3C	53	50	44	44	45	46	3E	3E	00	00	1D	54
DEC	49	48	60	60	83	80	68	68	69	70	62	62	0	0	29	84
ASC													^@	^@	^]	
ALT													NUL	NUL	GS	
SYM	1	0	<	<	S	P	D	D	E	F	>	>				T

Record Type | SPD.ID | Free Chain Record # | Len.

BYTE	16	17	18	19	20	21	22	23	24	25	26	27	28	29	30	31
HEX	68	69	72	64	20	74	65	73	74	20	6F	66	20	50	44	53
DEC	104	105	114	100	32	116	101	115	116	32	111	102	32	80	68	83
ASC					^`					^`			^`			
ALT					SPC					SPC			SPC			
SYM	h	i	r	d		t	e	s	t		o	f		P	D	S

Spreadsheet Description

BYTE	32	33	34	35	36	37	38	39	40	41	42	43	44	45	46	47
HEX	20	73	70	72	65	61	64	73	68	65	65	74	20	20	20	20
DEC	32	115	112	114	101	97	100	115	104	101	101	116	32	32	32	32
ASC	^`												^`	^`	^`	^`
ALT	SPC												SPC	SPC	SPC	SPC
SYM		s	p	r	e	a	d	s	h	e	e	t				

Spreadsheet Description

BYTE	48	49	50	51	52	53	54	55	56	57	58	59	60	61	62	63
HEX	20	20	20	20	20	20	20	00	05	53	53	50	44	53	00	00
DEC	32	32	32	32	32	32	32	0	5	83	83	80	68	83	0	0
ASC	^`	^`	^`	^`	^`	^`	^`	^@	^E						^@	^@
ALT	SPC	SPC	SPC	SPC	SPC	SPC	SPC	NUL	ENQ						NUL	NUL
SYM										S	S	P	D	S		

Spreadsheet Description | Len. | Last Data

BYTE	64	65	66	67	68	69	70	71	72	73	74	75	76	77	78	79
HEX	00	42	51	30	30	2E	45	58	45	00	00	00	00	00	00	00
DEC	0	66	81	48	48	46	69	88	69	0	0	0	0	0	0	0
ASC	^@									^@	^@	^@	^@	^@	^@	^@
ALT	NUL									NUL	NUL	NUL	NUL	NUL	NUL	NUL
SYM		B	Q	0	0	.	E	X	E							

Last Data DOS File Identification

SYLK FORMAT

BYTE	80	81	82	83	84	85	86	87	88	89	90	91	92	93	94	95
HEX	00	00	00	00	00	00	51	01	00	00	00	00	00	00	00	00
DEC	0	0	0	0	0	0	81	1	0	0	0	0	0	0	0	0
ASC	^@	^@	^@	^@	^@	^@		^A	^@	^@	^@	^@	^@	^@	^@	^@
ALT	NUL	NUL	NUL	NUL	NUL	NUL		SOH	NUL	NUL	NUL	NUL	NUL	NUL	NUL	NUL
SYM							Q									

◄─────────────────── Last Data DOS File Identification ───────────────────►

BYTE	96	97	98	99	100	101	102	103	104	105	106	107	108	109	110	111
HEX	00	00	00	00	41	54	41	33	00	00	00	00	00	00	00	00
DEC	0	0	0	0	65	84	65	51	0	0	0	0	0	0	0	0
ASC	^@	^@	^@	^@					^@	^@	^@	^@	^@	^@	^@	^@
ALT	NUL	NUL	NUL	NUL					NUL	NUL	NUL	NUL	NUL	NUL	NUL	NUL
SYM					A	T	A	3								

◄─ Last Data ─►◄─────────────────── Reserved ───────────────────►

BYTE	112	113	114	115	116	117	118	119	120	121	122	123	124	125	126	127
HEX	00	00	00	00	00	00	00	00	00	00	00	00	00	00	00	00
DEC	0	0	0	0	0	0	0	0	0	0	0	0	0	0	0	0
ASC	^@	^@	^@	^@	^@	^@	^@	^@	^@	^@	^@	^@	^@	^@	^@	^@
ALT	NUL	NUL	NUL	NUL	NUL	NUL	NUL	NUL	NUL	NUL	NUL	NUL	NUL	NUL	NUL	NUL
SYM																

◄─────────────────── Reserved ───────────────────►

BYTE	128	129	130	131	132	133	134	135	136	137	138	139	140	141	142	143
HEX	08	50	44	53	53	2E	45	58	45	00	00	00	00	00	00	00
DEC	8	80	68	83	83	46	69	88	69	0	0	0	0	0	0	0
ASC	^H									^@	^@	^@	^@	^@	^@	^@
ALT	BS									NUL	NUL	NUL	NUL	NUL	NUL	NUL
SYM		P	D	S	S	.	E	X	E							

◄─────────────────── Reserved ───────────────────►

BYTE	144	145	146	147	148	149	150	151	152	153	154	155	156	157	158	159
HEX	00	00	00	00	00	00	20	00	00	00	00	00	00	00	00	00
DEC	0	0	0	0	0	0	32	0	0	0	0	0	0	0	0	0
ASC	^@	^@	^@	^@	^@	^@	^`	^@	^@	^@	^@	^@	^@	^@	^@	^@
ALT	NUL	NUL	NUL	NUL	NUL	NUL	SPC	NUL	NUL	NUL	NUL	NUL	NUL	NUL	NUL	NUL
SYM																

◄─────────────────── Reserved ───────────────────►

BYTE	160	161	162	163	164	165	166	167	168	169	170	171	172	173	174	175
HEX	00	00	05	44	41	54	41	31	00	00	00	00	00	00	00	00
DEC	0	0	5	68	65	84	65	49	0	0	0	0	0	0	0	0
ASC	^@	^@	^E						^@	^@	^@	^@	^@	^@	^@	^@
ALT	NUL	NUL	ENQ						NUL	NUL	NUL	NUL	NUL	NUL	NUL	NUL
SYM				D	A	T	A	1								

◄─────────────────── Reserved ───────────────────►

226 IBM PLANS+.~MD

BYTE	176	177	178	179	180	181	182	183	184	185	186	187	188	189	190	191
HEX	00	00	00	00	00	00	00	00	00	00	00	00	00	00	00	00
DEC	0	0	0	0	0	0	0	0	0	0	0	0	0	0	0	0
ASC	^@	^@	^@	^@	^@	^@	^@	^@	^@	^@	^@	^@	^@	^@	^@	^@
ALT	NUL	NUL	NUL	NUL	NUL	NUL	NUL	NUL	NUL	NUL	NUL	NUL	NUL	NUL	NUL	NUL
SYM																

◄──────────────── Reserved ────────────────►

BYTE	192	193	194	195	196	197	198	199	200	201	202	203	204	205	206	207
HEX	08	50	44	53	58	2E	45	58	45	00	00	00	00	00	00	00
DEC	8	80	68	83	88	46	69	88	69	0	0	0	0	0	0	0
ASC	^H									^@	^@	^@	^@	^@	^@	^@
ALT	BS									NUL	NUL	NUL	NUL	NUL	NUL	NUL
SYM		P	D	S	X	.	E	X	E							

◄──────────────── Reserved ────────────────►

BYTE	208	209	210	211	212	213	214	215	216	217	218	219	220	221	222	223
HEX	00	00	00	00	00	00	20	00	00	00	00	00	00	00	00	00
DEC	0	0	0	0	0	0	32	0	0	0	0	0	0	0	0	0
ASC	^@	^@	^@	^@	^@	^@	^`	^@	^@	^@	^@	^@	^@	^@	^@	^@
ALT	NUL	NUL	NUL	NUL	NUL	NUL	SPC	NUL	NUL	NUL	NUL	NUL	NUL	NUL	NUL	NUL
SYM																

◄──────────────── Reserved ────────────────►

BYTE	224	225	226	227	228	229	230	231	232	233	234	235	236	237	238	239
HEX	00	00	05	44	41	54	41	31	00	00	00	00	00	00	00	00
DEC	0	0	5	68	65	84	65	49	0	0	0	0	0	0	0	0
ASC	^@	^@	^E						^@	^@	^@	^@	^@	^@	^@	^@
ALT	NUL	NUL	ENQ						NUL	NUL	NUL	NUL	NUL	NUL	NUL	NUL
SYM				D	A	T	A	1								

◄──────────────── Reserved ────────────────►

BYTE	240	241	242	243	244	245	246	247	248	249	250	251	252	253	254	255
HEX	00	00	00	00	00	00	00	00	00	00	00	00	00	00	00	00
DEC	0	0	0	0	0	0	0	0	0	0	0	0	0	0	0	0
ASC	^@	^@	^@	^@	^@	^@	^@	^@	^@	^@	^@	^@	^@	^@	^@	^@
ALT	NUL	NUL	NUL	NUL	NUL	NUL	NUL	NUL	NUL	NUL	NUL	NUL	NUL	NUL	NUL	NUL
SYM																

◄──────────────── Reserved ────────────────►

BYTE	256	257	258	259	260	261	262	263	264	265	266	267	268	269	270	271
HEX	18	28	14	00	06	00	0A	00	0A	00	0A	00	0A	00	0A	00
DEC	24	40	20	0	6	0	10	0	10	0	10	0	10	0	10	0
ASC	^X		^T	^@	^F	^@	^J	^@	^J	^@	^J	^@	^J	^@	^J	^@
ALT	CAN		DC4	NUL	ACK	NUL	LF	NUL	LF	NUL	LF	NUL	LF	NUL	LF	NUL
SYM		(														

| Cell Global | Global Format Def. | Reserved | Width Column 1 | Width Column 2 | Width Column 3 | 4 | 5 |

IBM PLANS+.~MD

BYTE	272	273	274	275	276	277	278	279	280	281	282	283	284	285	286	287
HEX	0A	00	0A	00	0A	00	0A	00	0A	00	0A	00	0A	00	0A	00
DEC	10	0	10	0	10	0	10	0	10	0	10	0	10	0	10	0
ASC	^J	^@	^J	^@	^J	^@	^J	^@	^J	^@	^J	^@	^J	^@	^J	^@
ALT	LF	NUL	LF	NUL	LF	NUL	LF	NUL	LF	NUL	LF	NUL	LF	NUL	LF	NUL
SYM																

Width Column 6 | 7 | 8 | 9 | 10 | 11 | 12 | 13

BYTE	288	289	290	291	292	293	294	295	296	297	298	299	300	301	302	303
HEX	0A	00	0A	00	0A	00	0A	00	0A	00	0A	00	0A	00	0A	00
DEC	10	0	10	0	10	0	10	0	10	0	10	0	10	0	10	0
ASC	^J	^@	^J	^@	^J	^@	^J	^@	^J	^@	^J	^@	^J	^@	^J	^@
ALT	LF	NUL	LF	NUL	LF	NUL	LF	NUL	LF	NUL	LF	NUL	LF	NUL	LF	NUL
SYM																

14 | 15 | 16 | 17 | 18 | 19 | 20 | 21

BYTE	304	305	306	307	308	309	310	311	312	313	314	315	316	317	318	319
HEX	0A	00	0A	00	0A	00	0A	00	0A	00	0A	00	0A	00	0A	00
DEC	10	0	10	0	10	0	10	0	10	0	10	0	10	0	10	0
ASC	^J	^@	^J	^@	^J	^@	^J	^@	^J	^@	^J	^@	^J	^@	^J	^@
ALT	LF	NUL	LF	NUL	LF	NUL	LF	NUL	LF	NUL	LF	NUL	LF	NUL	LF	NUL
SYM																

22 | 23 | 24 | 25 | 26 | 27 | 28 | 29

BYTE	320	321	322	323	324	325	326	327	328	329	330	331	332	333	334	335
HEX	0A	00	0A	00	0A	00	0A	00	0A	00	0A	00	0A	00	0A	00
DEC	10	0	10	0	10	0	10	0	10	0	10	0	10	0	10	0
ASC	^J	^@	^J	^@	^J	^@	^J	^@	^J	^@	^J	^@	^J	^@	^J	^@
ALT	LF	NUL	LF	NUL	LF	NUL	LF	NUL	LF	NUL	LF	NUL	LF	NUL	LF	NUL
SYM																

30 | 31 | 32 | 33 | 34 | 35 | 36 | 37

BYTE	336	337	338	339	340	341	342	343	344	345	346	347	348	349	350	351
HEX	0A	00	0A	00	0A	00	0A	00	0A	00	0A	00	0A	00	0A	00
DEC	10	0	10	0	10	0	10	0	10	0	10	0	10	0	10	0
ASC	^J	^@	^J	^@	^J	^@	^J	^@	^J	^@	^J	^@	^J	^@	^J	^@
ALT	LF	NUL	LF	NUL	LF	NUL	LF	NUL	LF	NUL	LF	NUL	LF	NUL	LF	NUL
SYM																

38 | 39 | 40 | 41 | 42 | 43 | 44 | 45

BYTE	352	353	354	355	356	357	358	359	360	361	362	363	364	365	366	367
HEX	0A	00	0A	00	0A	00	0A	00	0A	00	0A	00	0A	00	0A	00
DEC	10	0	10	0	10	0	10	0	10	0	10	0	10	0	10	0
ASC	^J	^@	^J	^@	^J	^@	^J	^@	^J	^@	^J	^@	^J	^@	^J	^@
ALT	LF	NUL	LF	NUL	LF	NUL	LF	NUL	LF	NUL	LF	NUL	LF	NUL	LF	NUL
SYM																

46 | 47 | 48 | 49 | 50 | 51 | 52 | 53

BYTE	368	369	370	371	372	373	374	375	376	377	378	379	380	381	382	383
HEX	0A	00	0A	00	0A	00	0A	00	0A	00	0A	00	0A	00	0A	00
DEC	10	0	10	0	10	0	10	0	10	0	10	0	10	0	10	0
ASC	^J	^@	^J	^@	^J	^@	^J	^@	^J	^@	^J	^@	^J	^@	^J	^@
ALT	LF	NUL	LF	NUL	LF	NUL	LF	NUL	LF	NUL	LF	NUL	LF	NUL	LF	NUL
SYM																

| Width Column 54 | 55 | 56 | 57 | 58 | 59 | 60 | 61 |

BYTE	384	385	386	387	388	389	390	391	392	393	394	395	396	397	398	399
HEX	0A	00	0A	00	0A	00	0A	00	0A	00	0A	00	0A	00	0A	00
DEC	10	0	10	0	10	0	10	0	10	0	10	0	10	0	10	0
ASC	^J	^@	^J	^@	^J	^@	^J	^@	^J	^@	^J	^@	^J	^@	^J	^@
ALT	LF	NUL	LF	NUL	LF	NUL	LF	NUL	LF	NUL	LF	NUL	LF	NUL	LF	NUL
SYM																

| 62 | 63 | 64 | 65 | 66 | 67 | 68 | 69 |

BYTE	400	401	402	403	404	405	406	407	408	409	410	411	412	413	414	415
HEX	0A	00	0A	00	0A	00	0A	00	0A	00	0A	00	0A	00	0A	00
DEC	10	0	10	0	10	0	10	0	10	0	10	0	10	0	10	0
ASC	^J	^@	^J	^@	^J	^@	^J	^@	^J	^@	^J	^@	^J	^@	^J	^@
ALT	LF	NUL	LF	NUL	LF	NUL	LF	NUL	LF	NUL	LF	NUL	LF	NUL	LF	NUL
SYM																

| 70 | 71 | 72 | 73 | 74 | 75 | 76 | 77 |

BYTE	416	417	418	419	420	421	422	423	424	425	426	427	428	429	430	431
HEX	0A	00	0A	00	0A	00	0A	00	0A	00	0A	00	0A	00	0A	00
DEC	10	0	10	0	10	0	10	0	10	0	10	0	10	0	10	0
ASC	^J	^@	^J	^@	^J	^@	^J	^@	^J	^@	^J	^@	^J	^@	^J	^@
ALT	LF	NUL	LF	NUL	LF	NUL	LF	NUL	LF	NUL	LF	NUL	LF	NUL	LF	NUL
SYM																

| 78 | 79 | 80 | 81 | 82 | 83 | 84 | 85 |

BYTE	432	433	434	435	436	437	438	439	440	441	442	443	444	445	446	447
HEX	0A	00	0A	00	0A	00	0A	00	0A	00	0A	00	0A	00	0A	00
DEC	10	0	10	0	10	0	10	0	10	0	10	0	10	0	10	0
ASC	^J	^@	^J	^@	^J	^@	^J	^@	^J	^@	^J	^@	^J	^@	^J	^@
ALT	LF	NUL	LF	NUL	LF	NUL	LF	NUL	LF	NUL	LF	NUL	LF	NUL	LF	NUL
SYM																

| 86 | 87 | 88 | 89 | 90 | 91 | 92 | 93 |

BYTE	448	449	450	451	452	453	454	455	456	457	458	459	460	461	462	463
HEX	0A	00	0A	00	0A	00	0A	00	0A	00	0A	00	01	00	01	00
DEC	10	0	10	0	10	0	10	0	10	0	10	0	1	0	1	0
ASC	^J	^@	^J	^@	^J	^@	^J	^@	^J	^@	^J	^@	^A	^@	^A	^@
ALT	LF	NUL	LF	NUL	LF	NUL	LF	NUL	LF	NUL	LF	NUL	SOH	NUL	SOH	NUL
SYM																

| 94 | 95 | 96 | 97 | 98 | 99 | Current Window | # Windows |

IBM PLANS+.~MD **229**

BYTE	464	465	466	467	468	469	470	471	472	473	474	475	476	477	478	479
HEX	63	00	00	00	50	00	00	00	00	00	00	00	FF	FF	01	00
DEC	99	0	0	0	80	0	0	0	0	0	0	0	255	255	1	0
ASC		^@	^@	^@		^@	^@	^@	^@	^@	^@	^@	255	255	^A	^@
ALT		NUL	NUL	NUL		NUL	NUL	NUL	NUL	NUL	NUL	NUL	255	255	SOH	NUL
SYM	c				P											
	Right Column Margin			Title			# Characters in Window		T-FIRST-INST Instance of First Title Row		T-OCCUR # of Title Instances		T-FIRST-COL # of First Column Title Displayed		T-LAST-COL # of Last Title Column Displayed		S-FIRST-INST Instance of First Scrollable Row	

BYTE	480	481	482	483	484	485	486	487	488	489	490	491	492	493	494	495
HEX	0D	00	01	00	07	00	0A	00	01	00	01	00	07	00	0A	00
DEC	13	0	1	0	7	0	10	0	1	0	1	0	7	0	10	0
ASC	^M	^@	^A	^@	^G	^@	^J	^@	^A	^@	^A	^@	^G	^@	^J	^@
ALT	CR	NUL	SOH	NUL	BEL	NUL	LF	NUL	SOH	NUL	SOH	NUL	BEL	NUL	LF	NUL
SYM																
	S-OCCUR # of Scrollable Instances		# of First Scrollable Column Display		# of Last Scrollable Column Display		Current Row		Current Column		Cursor Pointer Instance		Cursor Pointer Change Position		Current Cell Cursor Width	

BYTE	496	497	498	499	500	501	502	503	504	505	506	507	508	509	510	511
HEX	01	00	01	00	00	00	50	00	00	00	00	00	00	00	FF	FF
DEC	1	0	1	0	0	0	80	0	0	0	0	0	0	0	255	255
ASC	^A	^@	^A	^@	^@	^@		^@	^@	^@	^@	^@	^@	^@	255	255
ALT	SOH	NUL	SOH	NUL	NUL	NUL		NUL	NUL	NUL	NUL	NUL	NUL	NUL	255	255
SYM							P									
	Left Character Edge of Data Window		Top Border Edge of Data Window		Title Window 2		# Characters in Window 2		Instance of First Title Row		# of Title Instances		# of First Column Title Displayed		# of Last Title Column Displayed	

BYTE	512	513	514	515	516	517	518	519	520	521	522	523	524	525	526	527
HEX	01	00	0D	00	01	00	07	00	0A	00	01	00	01	00	07	00
DEC	1	0	13	0	1	0	7	0	10	0	1	0	1	0	7	0
ASC	^A	^@	^M	^@	^A	^@	^G	^@	^J	^@	^A	^@	^A	^@	^G	^@
ALT	SOH	NUL	CR	NUL	SOH	NUL	BEL	NUL	LF	NUL	SOH	NUL	SOH	NUL	BEL	NUL
SYM																
	Instance of First Scrollable Row		# of Scrollable Instances		# of First Scrollable Column Display		# of Last Scrollable Column Display		Current Row		Current Column		Cursor Pointer Instance		Cursor Pointer Character Position	

BYTE	528	529	530	531	532	533	534	535	536	537	538	539	540	541	542	543
HEX	0A	00	01	00	01	00	40	00	00	00	00	00	00	00	00	00
DEC	10	0	1	0	1	0	64	0	0	0	0	0	0	0	0	0
ASC	^J	^@	^A	^@	^A	^@		^@	^@	^@	^@	^@	^@	^@	^@	^@
ALT	LF	NUL	SOH	NUL	SOH	NUL		NUL	NUL	NUL	NUL	NUL	NUL	NUL	NUL	NUL
SYM							@									
	Current Cell Cursor Width		Left Character Edge of Data Window		Top Edge of Data Window		Data Scroll Direction Flag		Data Windows Synched		←――― Header Text ―――→					

BYTE	544	545	546	547	548	549	550	551	552	553	554	555	556	557	558	559
HEX	00	00	00	00	00	00	00	00	00	00	00	00	00	00	00	00
DEC	0	0	0	0	0	0	0	0	0	0	0	0	0	0	0	0
ASC	^@	^@	^@	^@	^@	^@	^@	^@	^@	^@	^@	^@	^@	^@	^@	^@
ALT	NUL	NUL	NUL	NUL	NUL	NUL	NUL	NUL	NUL	NUL	NUL	NUL	NUL	NUL	NUL	NUL
SYM																

←――――――――――――― Header Text ―――――――――――――→

BYTE	560	561	562	563	564	565	566	567	568	569	570	571	572	573	574	575
HEX	00	00	00	00	00	00	00	00	00	00	00	00	00	00	00	00
DEC	0	0	0	0	0	0	0	0	0	0	0	0	0	0	0	0
ASC	^@	^@	^@	^@	^@	^@	^@	^@	^@	^@	^@	^@	^@	^@	^@	^@
ALT	NUL	NUL	NUL	NUL	NUL	NUL	NUL	NUL	NUL	NUL	NUL	NUL	NUL	NUL	NUL	NUL
SYM																

◄──────────────────── Header Text ────────────────────►

BYTE	576	577	578	579	580	581	582	583	584	585	586	587	588	589	590	591
HEX	00	00	00	00	00	00	00	00	00	00	00	00	00	00	00	00
DEC	0	0	0	0	0	0	0	0	0	0	0	0	0	0	0	0
ASC	^@	^@	^@	^@	^@	^@	^@	^@	^@	^@	^@	^@	^@	^@	^@	^@
ALT	NUL	NUL	NUL	NUL	NUL	NUL	NUL	NUL	NUL	NUL	NUL	NUL	NUL	NUL	NUL	NUL
SYM																

◄──────────────────── Header Text ────────────────────►

BYTE	592	593	594	595	596	597	598	599	600	601	602	603	604	605	606	607
HEX	00	00	00	00	00	00	00	00	00	00	00	00	00	00	00	00
DEC	0	0	0	0	0	0	0	0	0	0	0	0	0	0	0	0
ASC	^@	^@	^@	^@	^@	^@	^@	^@	^@	^@	^@	^@	^@	^@	^@	^@
ALT	NUL	NUL	NUL	NUL	NUL	NUL	NUL	NUL	NUL	NUL	NUL	NUL	NUL	NUL	NUL	NUL
SYM																

◄──────────────────── Header Text ────────────────────►

BYTE	608	609	610	611	612	613	614	615	616	617	618	619	620	621	622	623
HEX	00	00	00	00	00	00	00	00	00	00	00	00	00	00	00	00
DEC	0	0	0	0	0	0	0	0	0	0	0	0	0	0	0	0
ASC	^@	^@	^@	^@	^@	^@	^@	^@	^@	^@	^@	^@	^@	^@	^@	^@
ALT	NUL	NUL	NUL	NUL	NUL	NUL	NUL	NUL	NUL	NUL	NUL	NUL	NUL	NUL	NUL	NUL
SYM																

◄──────────────────── Header Text ────────────────────►

BYTE	624	625	626	627	628	629	630	631	632	633	634	635	636	637	638	639
HEX	00	00	00	00	00	00	00	00	00	00	00	00	00	00	00	00
DEC	0	0	0	0	0	0	0	0	0	0	0	0	0	0	0	0
ASC	^@	^@	^@	^@	^@	^@	^@	^@	^@	^@	^@	^@	^@	^@	^@	^@
ALT	NUL	NUL	NUL	NUL	NUL	NUL	NUL	NUL	NUL	NUL	NUL	NUL	NUL	NUL	NUL	NUL
SYM																

◄──────────────────── Header Text ────────────────────►

BYTE	640	641	642	643	644	645	646	647	648	649	650	651	652	653	654	655
HEX	00	00	00	00	00	00	00	00	00	00	00	00	00	00	00	00
DEC	0	0	0	0	0	0	0	0	0	0	0	0	0	0	0	0
ASC	^@	^@	^@	^@	^@	^@	^@	^@	^@	^@	^@	^@	^@	^@	^@	^@
ALT	NUL	NUL	NUL	NUL	NUL	NUL	NUL	NUL	NUL	NUL	NUL	NUL	NUL	NUL	NUL	NUL
SYM																

◄──────────────────── Header Text ────────────────────►

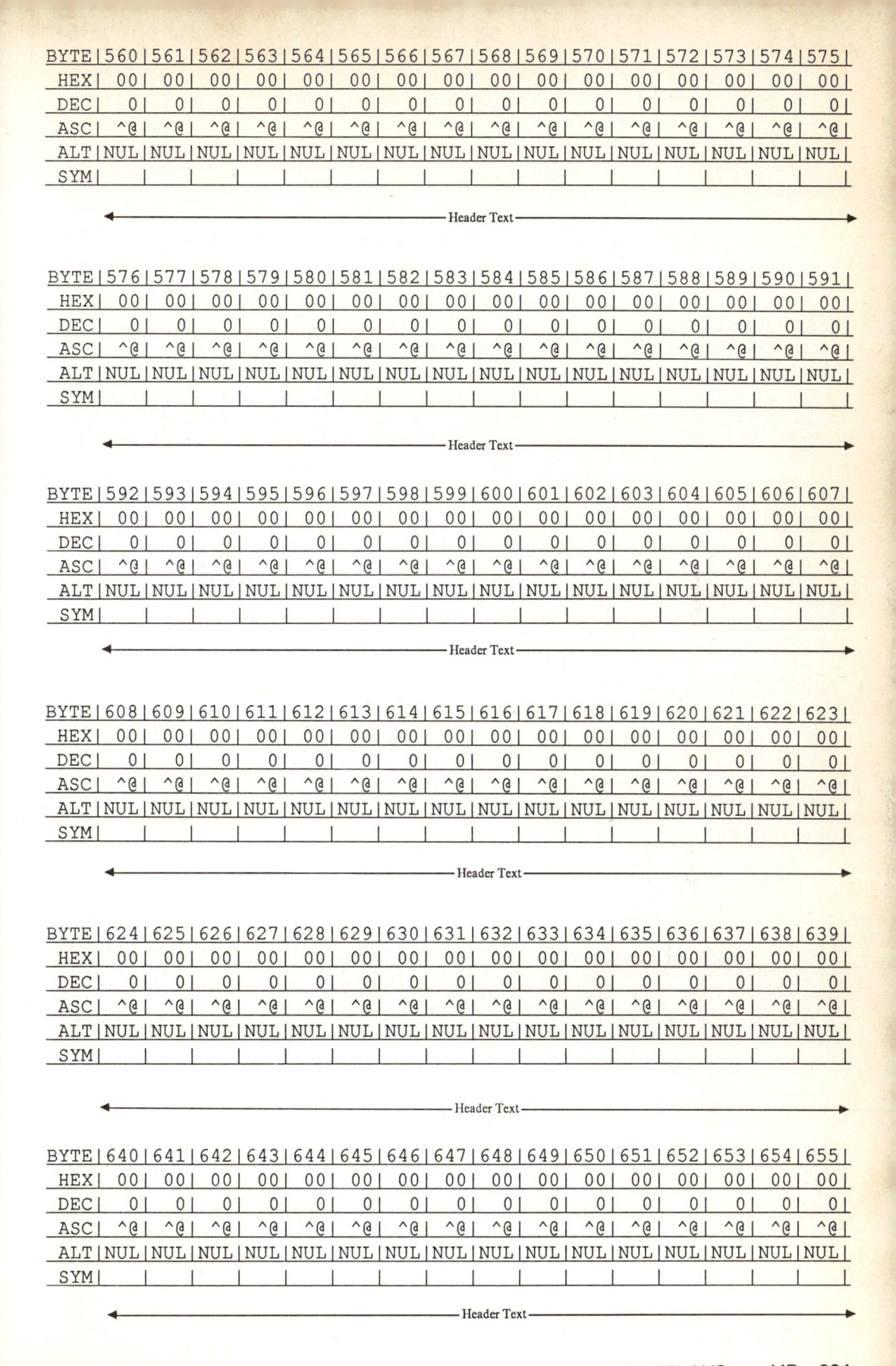

```
BYTE|656|657|658|659|660|661|662|663|664|665|666|667|668|669|670|671|
HEX| 00| 00| 00| 00| 00| 00| 00| 00| 00| 00| 00| 00| 00| 00| 00| 00|
DEC|  0|  0|  0|  0|  0|  0|  0|  0|  0|  0|  0|  0|  0|  0|  0|  0|
ASC| ^@| ^@| ^@| ^@| ^@| ^@| ^@| ^@| ^@| ^@| ^@| ^@| ^@| ^@| ^@| ^@|
ALT|NUL|NUL|NUL|NUL|NUL|NUL|NUL|NUL|NUL|NUL|NUL|NUL|NUL|NUL|NUL|NUL|
SYM|   |   |   |   |   |   |   |   |   |   |   |   |   |   |   |   |
       ◄─────────────────────── Header Text ───────────────────────►

BYTE|672|673|674|675|676|677|678|679|680|681|682|683|684|685|686|687|
HEX| 00| 00| 00| 00| 00| 00| 00| 00| 00| 00| 00| 00| 00| 00| 00| 00|
DEC|  0|  0|  0|  0|  0|  0|  0|  0|  0|  0|  0|  0|  0|  0|  0|  0|
ASC| ^@| ^@| ^@| ^@| ^@| ^@| ^@| ^@| ^@| ^@| ^@| ^@| ^@| ^@| ^@| ^@|
ALT|NUL|NUL|NUL|NUL|NUL|NUL|NUL|NUL|NUL|NUL|NUL|NUL|NUL|NUL|NUL|NUL|
SYM|   |   |   |   |   |   |   |   |   |   |   |   |   |   |   |   |
       ◄─────────────────────── Footer Text ───────────────────────►

BYTE|688|689|690|691|692|693|694|695|696|697|698|699|700|701|702|703|
HEX| 00| 00| 00| 00| 00| 00| 00| 00| 00| 00| 00| 00| 00| 00| 00| 00|
DEC|  0|  0|  0|  0|  0|  0|  0|  0|  0|  0|  0|  0|  0|  0|  0|  0|
ASC| ^@| ^@| ^@| ^@| ^@| ^@| ^@| ^@| ^@| ^@| ^@| ^@| ^@| ^@| ^@| ^@|
ALT|NUL|NUL|NUL|NUL|NUL|NUL|NUL|NUL|NUL|NUL|NUL|NUL|NUL|NUL|NUL|NUL|
SYM|   |   |   |   |   |   |   |   |   |   |   |   |   |   |   |   |
       ◄─────────────────────── Footer Text ───────────────────────►

BYTE|704|705|706|707|708|709|710|711|712|713|714|715|716|717|718|719|
HEX| 00| 00| 00| 00| 00| 00| 00| 00| 00| 00| 00| 00| 00| 00| 00| 00|
DEC|  0|  0|  0|  0|  0|  0|  0|  0|  0|  0|  0|  0|  0|  0|  0|  0|
ASC| ^@| ^@| ^@| ^@| ^@| ^@| ^@| ^@| ^@| ^@| ^@| ^@| ^@| ^@| ^@| ^@|
ALT|NUL|NUL|NUL|NUL|NUL|NUL|NUL|NUL|NUL|NUL|NUL|NUL|NUL|NUL|NUL|NUL|
SYM|   |   |   |   |   |   |   |   |   |   |   |   |   |   |   |   |
       ◄─────────────────────── Footer Text ───────────────────────►

BYTE|720|721|722|723|724|725|726|727|728|729|730|731|732|733|734|735|
HEX| 00| 00| 00| 00| 00| 00| 00| 00| 00| 00| 00| 00| 00| 00| 00| 00|
DEC|  0|  0|  0|  0|  0|  0|  0|  0|  0|  0|  0|  0|  0|  0|  0|  0|
ASC| ^@| ^@| ^@| ^@| ^@| ^@| ^@| ^@| ^@| ^@| ^@| ^@| ^@| ^@| ^@| ^@|
ALT|NUL|NUL|NUL|NUL|NUL|NUL|NUL|NUL|NUL|NUL|NUL|NUL|NUL|NUL|NUL|NUL|
SYM|   |   |   |   |   |   |   |   |   |   |   |   |   |   |   |   |
       ◄─────────────────────── Footer Text ───────────────────────►

BYTE|736|737|738|739|740|741|742|743|744|745|746|747|748|749|750|751|
HEX| 00| 00| 00| 00| 00| 00| 00| 00| 00| 00| 00| 00| 00| 00| 00| 00|
DEC|  0|  0|  0|  0|  0|  0|  0|  0|  0|  0|  0|  0|  0|  0|  0|  0|
ASC| ^@| ^@| ^@| ^@| ^@| ^@| ^@| ^@| ^@| ^@| ^@| ^@| ^@| ^@| ^@| ^@|
ALT|NUL|NUL|NUL|NUL|NUL|NUL|NUL|NUL|NUL|NUL|NUL|NUL|NUL|NUL|NUL|NUL|
SYM|   |   |   |   |   |   |   |   |   |   |   |   |   |   |   |   |
       ◄─────────────────────── Footer Text ───────────────────────►
```

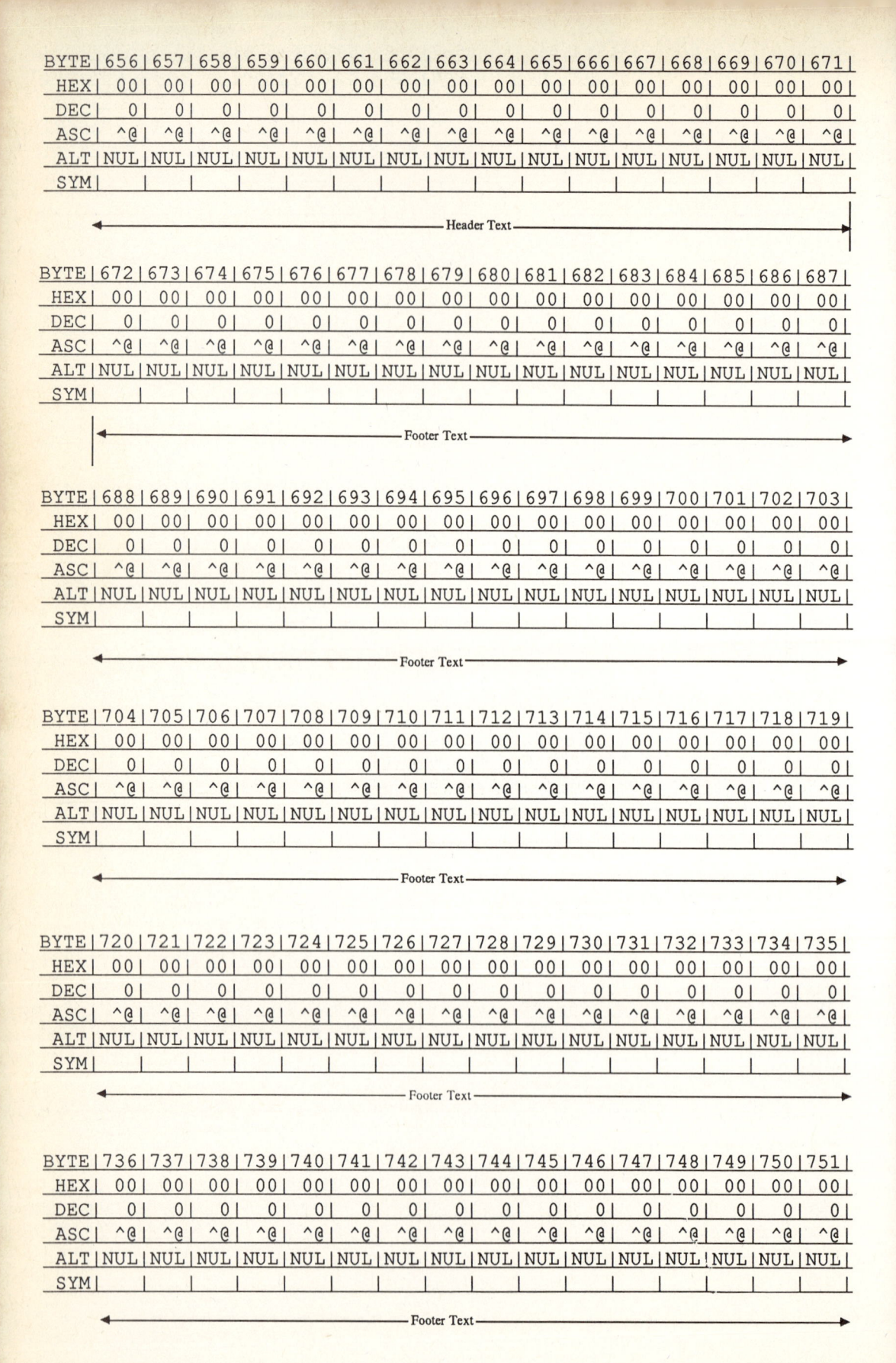

BYTE	752	753	754	755	756	757	758	759	760	761	762	763	764	765	766	767
HEX	00	00	00	00	00	00	00	00	00	00	00	00	00	00	00	00
DEC	0	0	0	0	0	0	0	0	0	0	0	0	0	0	0	0
ASC	^@	^@	^@	^@	^@	^@	^@	^@	^@	^@	^@	^@	^@	^@	^@	^@
ALT	NUL	NUL	NUL	NUL	NUL	NUL	NUL	NUL	NUL	NUL	NUL	NUL	NUL	NUL	NUL	NUL
SYM																

←─────────────────────── Footer Text ───────────────────────→

BYTE	768	769	770	771	772	773	774	775	776	777	778	779	780	781	782	783
HEX	00	00	00	00	00	00	00	00	00	00	00	00	00	00	00	00
DEC	0	0	0	0	0	0	0	0	0	0	0	0	0	0	0	0
ASC	^@	^@	^@	^@	^@	^@	^@	^@	^@	^@	^@	^@	^@	^@	^@	^@
ALT	NUL	NUL	NUL	NUL	NUL	NUL	NUL	NUL	NUL	NUL	NUL	NUL	NUL	NUL	NUL	NUL
SYM																

←─────────────────────── Footer Text ───────────────────────→

BYTE	784	785	786	787	788	789	790	791	792	793	794	795	796	797	798	799
HEX	00	00	00	00	00	00	00	00	00	00	00	00	00	00	00	00
DEC	0	0	0	0	0	0	0	0	0	0	0	0	0	0	0	0
ASC	^@	^@	^@	^@	^@	^@	^@	^@	^@	^@	^@	^@	^@	^@	^@	^@
ALT	NUL	NUL	NUL	NUL	NUL	NUL	NUL	NUL	NUL	NUL	NUL	NUL	NUL	NUL	NUL	NUL
SYM																

←─────────────────────── Footer Text ───────────────────────→

BYTE	800	801	802	803	804	805	806	807	808	809	810	811	812	813	814	815
HEX	00	00	00	00	00	00	00	00	00	00	00	00	00	00	00	00
DEC	0	0	0	0	0	0	0	0	0	0	0	0	0	0	0	0
ASC	^@	^@	^@	^@	^@	^@	^@	^@	^@	^@	^@	^@	^@	^@	^@	^@
ALT	NUL	NUL	NUL	NUL	NUL	NUL	NUL	NUL	NUL	NUL	NUL	NUL	NUL	NUL	NUL	NUL
SYM																

←─────── Footer Text ───────→ | PR 1   PR 2   PR 3   PR 4   PR 5
                                ←──────── Print Range ────────→

BYTE	816	817	818	819	820	821	822	823	824	825	826	827	828	829	830	831
HEX	00	00	00	00	00	00	05	4C	50	54	31	3A	00	00	00	00
DEC	0	0	0	0	0	0	5	76	80	84	49	58	0	0	0	0
ASC	^@	^@	^@	^@	^@	^@	^E						^@	^@	^@	^@
ALT	NUL	NUL	NUL	NUL	NUL	NUL	ENQ						NUL	NUL	NUL	NUL
SYM								L	P	T	1	:				

  PR 6   PR 7   PR 8   ←──────── Print Name ────────→
←─── Print Range ───→

BYTE	832	833	834	835	836	837	838	839	840	841	842	843	844	845	846	847
HEX	00	00	00	00	01	00	06	00	42	00	3A	00	50	00	04	00
DEC	0	0	0	0	1	0	6	0	66	0	58	0	80	0	4	0
ASC	^@	^@	^@	^@	^A	^@	^F	^@		^@		^@		^@	^D	^@
ALT	NUL	NUL	NUL	NUL	SOH	NUL	ACK	NUL		NUL		NUL		NUL	EOT	NUL
SYM									B		:		P			

←── Print Name ──→│Page Numbering│Lines Per Inch│Form Length in Lines│Lines Per Page│Maximum Line Width│Formatted/ Unformatted

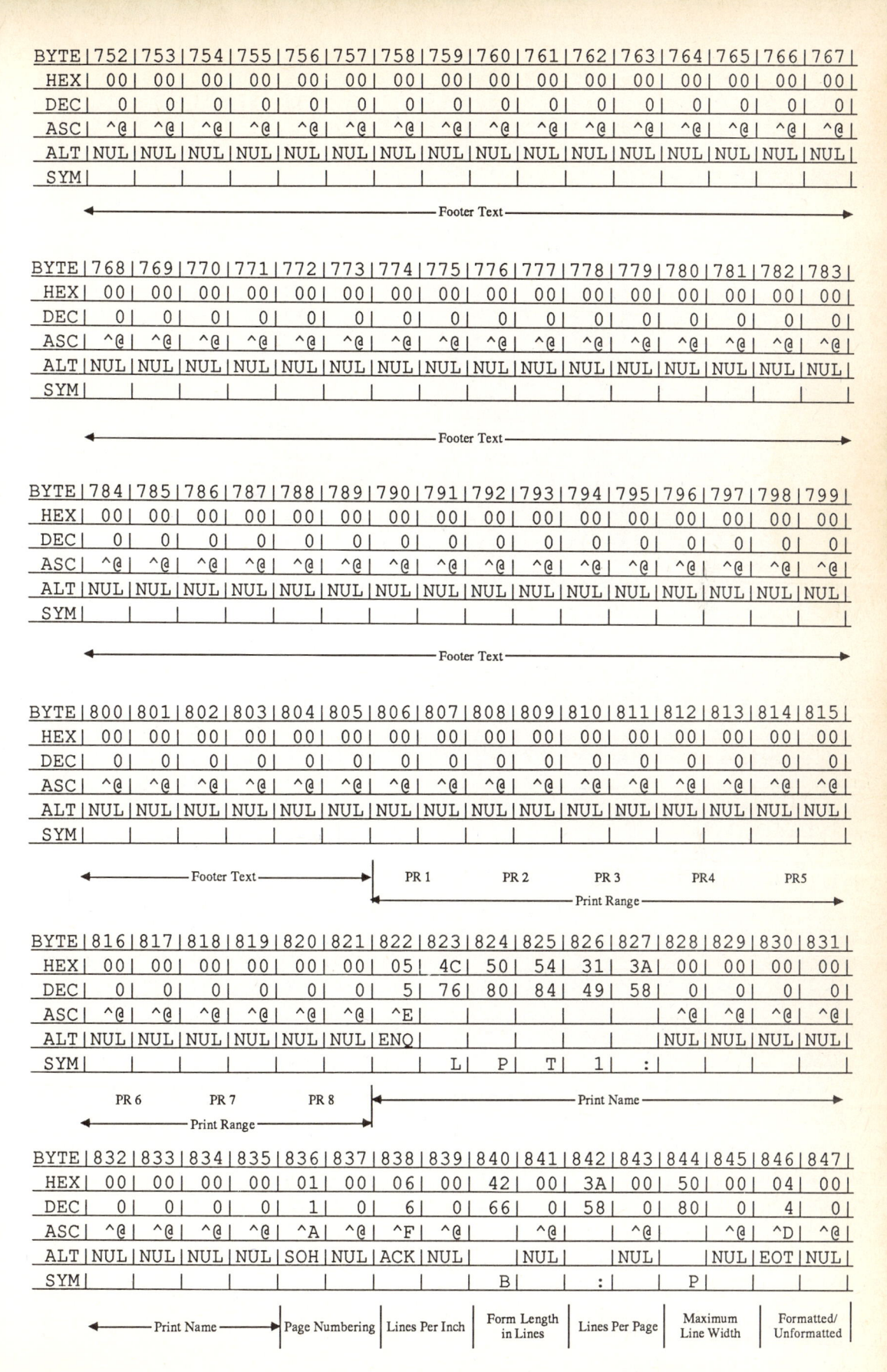

IBM PLANS+.~MD   233

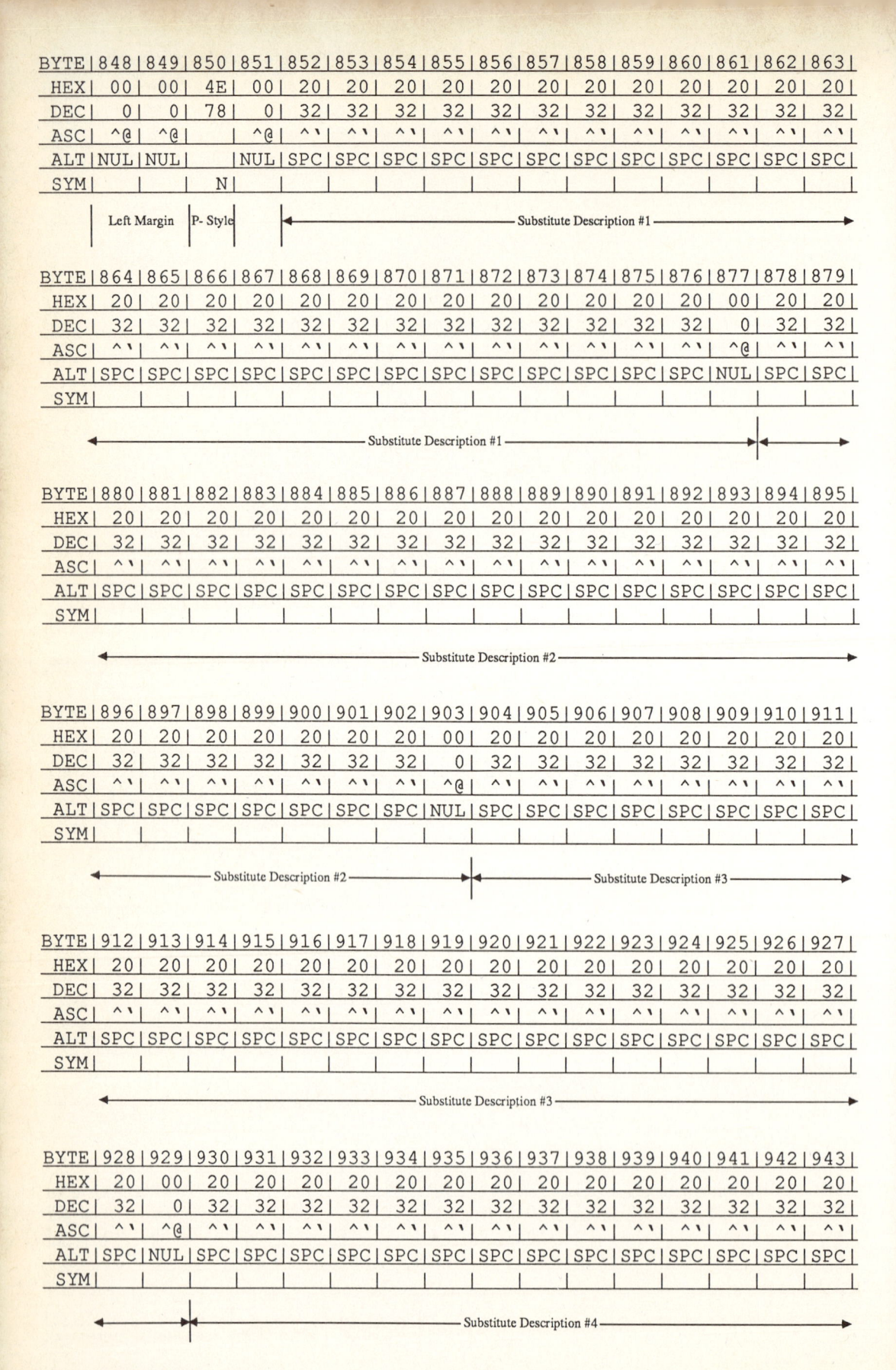

BYTE	848	849	850	851	852	853	854	855	856	857	858	859	860	861	862	863
HEX	00	00	4E	00	20	20	20	20	20	20	20	20	20	20	20	20
DEC	0	0	78	0	32	32	32	32	32	32	32	32	32	32	32	32
ASC	^@	^@		^@	^ `	^ `	^ `	^ `	^ `	^ `	^ `	^ `	^ `	^ `	^ `	^ `
ALT	NUL	NUL		NUL	SPC	SPC	SPC	SPC	SPC	SPC	SPC	SPC	SPC	SPC	SPC	SPC
SYM			N													

|Left Margin|P-Style|←─────────── Substitute Description #1 ───────────→|

BYTE	864	865	866	867	868	869	870	871	872	873	874	875	876	877	878	879
HEX	20	20	20	20	20	20	20	20	20	20	20	20	20	00	20	20
DEC	32	32	32	32	32	32	32	32	32	32	32	32	32	0	32	32
ASC	^ `	^ `	^ `	^ `	^ `	^ `	^ `	^ `	^ `	^ `	^ `	^ `	^ `	^@	^ `	^ `
ALT	SPC	SPC	SPC	SPC	SPC	SPC	SPC	SPC	SPC	SPC	SPC	SPC	SPC	NUL	SPC	SPC
SYM																

←─────────── Substitute Description #1 ───────────→|←──→

BYTE	880	881	882	883	884	885	886	887	888	889	890	891	892	893	894	895
HEX	20	20	20	20	20	20	20	20	20	20	20	20	20	20	20	20
DEC	32	32	32	32	32	32	32	32	32	32	32	32	32	32	32	32
ASC	^ `	^ `	^ `	^ `	^ `	^ `	^ `	^ `	^ `	^ `	^ `	^ `	^ `	^ `	^ `	^ `
ALT	SPC	SPC	SPC	SPC	SPC	SPC	SPC	SPC	SPC	SPC	SPC	SPC	SPC	SPC	SPC	SPC
SYM																

←─────────── Substitute Description #2 ───────────→

BYTE	896	897	898	899	900	901	902	903	904	905	906	907	908	909	910	911
HEX	20	20	20	20	20	20	20	00	20	20	20	20	20	20	20	20
DEC	32	32	32	32	32	32	32	0	32	32	32	32	32	32	32	32
ASC	^ `	^ `	^ `	^ `	^ `	^ `	^ `	^@	^ `	^ `	^ `	^ `	^ `	^ `	^ `	^ `
ALT	SPC	SPC	SPC	SPC	SPC	SPC	SPC	NUL	SPC	SPC	SPC	SPC	SPC	SPC	SPC	SPC
SYM																

←─── Substitute Description #2 ───→|←─── Substitute Description #3 ───→

BYTE	912	913	914	915	916	917	918	919	920	921	922	923	924	925	926	927
HEX	20	20	20	20	20	20	20	20	20	20	20	20	20	20	20	20
DEC	32	32	32	32	32	32	32	32	32	32	32	32	32	32	32	32
ASC	^ `	^ `	^ `	^ `	^ `	^ `	^ `	^ `	^ `	^ `	^ `	^ `	^ `	^ `	^ `	^ `
ALT	SPC	SPC	SPC	SPC	SPC	SPC	SPC	SPC	SPC	SPC	SPC	SPC	SPC	SPC	SPC	SPC
SYM																

←─────────── Substitute Description #3 ───────────→

BYTE	928	929	930	931	932	933	934	935	936	937	938	939	940	941	942	943
HEX	20	00	20	20	20	20	20	20	20	20	20	20	20	20	20	20
DEC	32	0	32	32	32	32	32	32	32	32	32	32	32	32	32	32
ASC	^ `	^@	^ `	^ `	^ `	^ `	^ `	^ `	^ `	^ `	^ `	^ `	^ `	^ `	^ `	^ `
ALT	SPC	NUL	SPC	SPC	SPC	SPC	SPC	SPC	SPC	SPC	SPC	SPC	SPC	SPC	SPC	SPC
SYM																

←──→|←─────────── Substitute Description #4 ───────────→

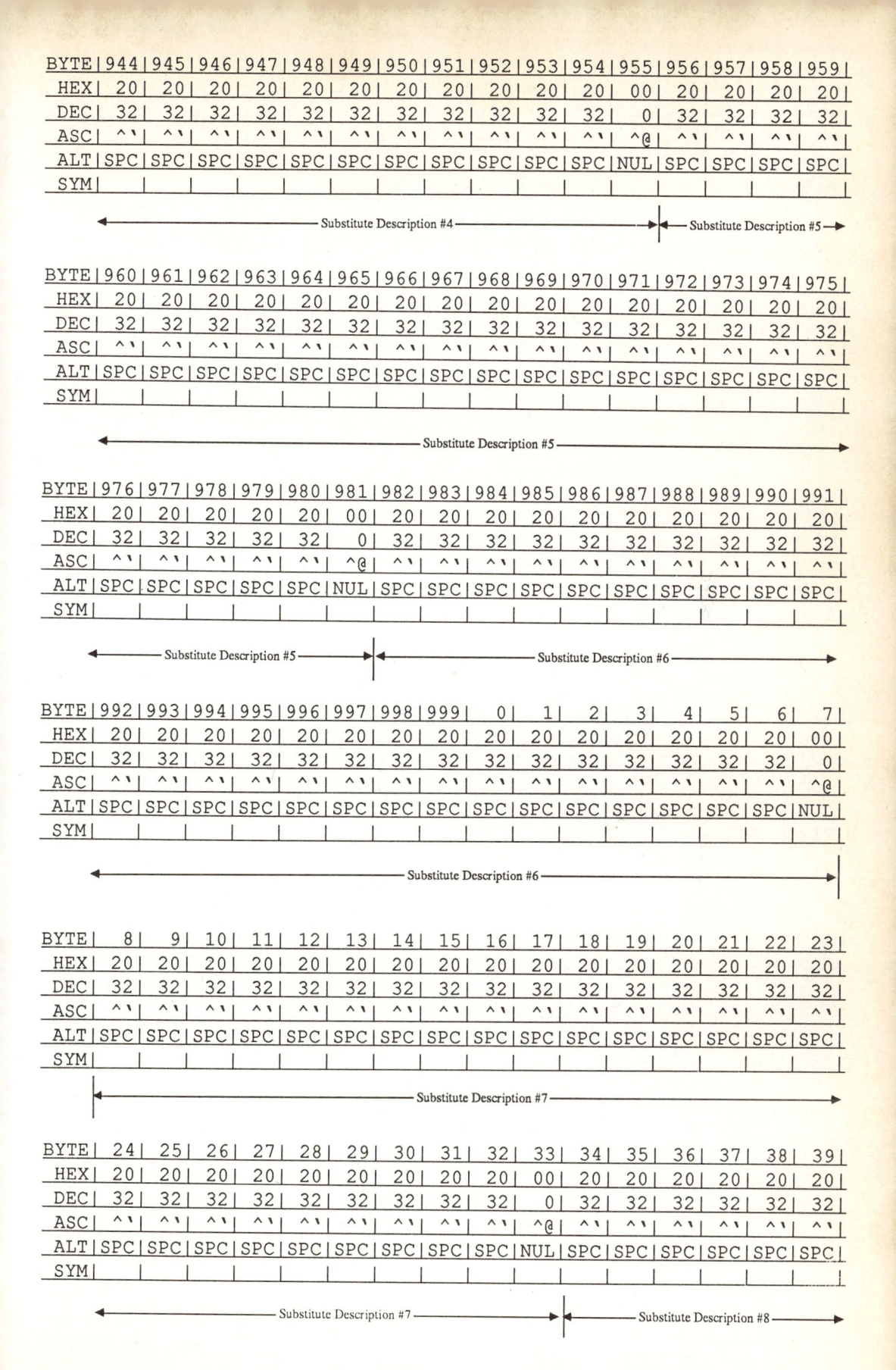

BYTE	944	945	946	947	948	949	950	951	952	953	954	955	956	957	958	959
HEX	20	20	20	20	20	20	20	20	20	20	20	00	20	20	20	20
DEC	32	32	32	32	32	32	32	32	32	32	32	0	32	32	32	32
ASC	^\	^\	^\	^\	^\	^\	^\	^\	^\	^\	^\	^@	^\	^\	^\	^\
ALT	SPC	SPC	SPC	SPC	SPC	SPC	SPC	SPC	SPC	SPC	SPC	NUL	SPC	SPC	SPC	SPC
SYM																

◄─────── Substitute Description #4 ───────►│◄─ Substitute Description #5 ─►

BYTE	960	961	962	963	964	965	966	967	968	969	970	971	972	973	974	975
HEX	20	20	20	20	20	20	20	20	20	20	20	20	20	20	20	20
DEC	32	32	32	32	32	32	32	32	32	32	32	32	32	32	32	32
ASC	^\	^\	^\	^\	^\	^\	^\	^\	^\	^\	^\	^\	^\	^\	^\	^\
ALT	SPC	SPC	SPC	SPC	SPC	SPC	SPC	SPC	SPC	SPC	SPC	SPC	SPC	SPC	SPC	SPC
SYM																

◄─────────────── Substitute Description #5 ───────────────►

BYTE	976	977	978	979	980	981	982	983	984	985	986	987	988	989	990	991
HEX	20	20	20	20	20	00	20	20	20	20	20	20	20	20	20	20
DEC	32	32	32	32	32	0	32	32	32	32	32	32	32	32	32	32
ASC	^\	^\	^\	^\	^\	^@	^\	^\	^\	^\	^\	^\	^\	^\	^\	^\
ALT	SPC	SPC	SPC	SPC	SPC	NUL	SPC	SPC	SPC	SPC	SPC	SPC	SPC	SPC	SPC	SPC
SYM																

◄── Substitute Description #5 ──►│◄─────── Substitute Description #6 ───────►

BYTE	992	993	994	995	996	997	998	999	0	1	2	3	4	5	6	7
HEX	20	20	20	20	20	20	20	20	20	20	20	20	20	20	20	00
DEC	32	32	32	32	32	32	32	32	32	32	32	32	32	32	32	0
ASC	^\	^\	^\	^\	^\	^\	^\	^\	^\	^\	^\	^\	^\	^\	^\	^@
ALT	SPC	SPC	SPC	SPC	SPC	SPC	SPC	SPC	SPC	SPC	SPC	SPC	SPC	SPC	SPC	NUL
SYM																

◄─────────────── Substitute Description #6 ───────────────►

BYTE	8	9	10	11	12	13	14	15	16	17	18	19	20	21	22	23
HEX	20	20	20	20	20	20	20	20	20	20	20	20	20	20	20	20
DEC	32	32	32	32	32	32	32	32	32	32	32	32	32	32	32	32
ASC	^\	^\	^\	^\	^\	^\	^\	^\	^\	^\	^\	^\	^\	^\	^\	^\
ALT	SPC	SPC	SPC	SPC	SPC	SPC	SPC	SPC	SPC	SPC	SPC	SPC	SPC	SPC	SPC	SPC
SYM																

◄─────────────── Substitute Description #7 ───────────────►

BYTE	24	25	26	27	28	29	30	31	32	33	34	35	36	37	38	39
HEX	20	20	20	20	20	20	20	20	20	00	20	20	20	20	20	20
DEC	32	32	32	32	32	32	32	32	32	0	32	32	32	32	32	32
ASC	^\	^\	^\	^\	^\	^\	^\	^\	^\	^@	^\	^\	^\	^\	^\	^\
ALT	SPC	SPC	SPC	SPC	SPC	SPC	SPC	SPC	SPC	NUL	SPC	SPC	SPC	SPC	SPC	SPC
SYM																

◄─────── Substitute Description #7 ───────►│◄─────── Substitute Description #8 ───────►

IBM PLANS+ . ~ MD   **235**

BYTE	40	41	42	43	44	45	46	47	48	49	50	51	52	53	54	55
HEX	20	20	20	20	20	20	20	20	20	20	20	20	20	20	20	20
DEC	32	32	32	32	32	32	32	32	32	32	32	32	32	32	32	32
ASC	^'	^'	^'	^'	^'	^'	^'	^'	^'	^'	^'	^'	^'	^'	^'	^'
ALT	SPC	SPC	SPC	SPC	SPC	SPC	SPC	SPC	SPC	SPC	SPC	SPC	SPC	SPC	SPC	SPC
SYM																

◀──────────────── Substitute Description #8 ────────────────▶

BYTE	56	57	58	59	60	61	62	63	64	65	66	67	68	69	70	71
HEX	20	20	20	00	20	20	20	20	20	20	20	20	20	20	20	20
DEC	32	32	32	0	32	32	32	32	32	32	32	32	32	32	32	32
ASC	^'	^'	^'	^@	^'	^'	^'	^'	^'	^'	^'	^'	^'	^'	^'	^'
ALT	SPC	SPC	SPC	NUL	SPC	SPC	SPC	SPC	SPC	SPC	SPC	SPC	SPC	SPC	SPC	SPC
SYM																

◀── Substitute Description #8 ──▶◀──────── Substitute Description #9 ────────▶

BYTE	72	73	74	75	76	77	78	79	80	81	82	83	84	85	86	87
HEX	20	20	20	20	20	20	20	20	20	20	20	20	20	00	20	20
DEC	32	32	32	32	32	32	32	32	32	32	32	32	32	0	32	32
ASC	^'	^'	^'	^'	^'	^'	^'	^'	^'	^'	^'	^'	^'	^@	^'	^'
ALT	SPC	SPC	SPC	SPC	SPC	SPC	SPC	SPC	SPC	SPC	SPC	SPC	SPC	NUL	SPC	SPC
SYM																

◀──────────────── Substitute Description #9 ────────────────▶

BYTE	88	89	90	91	92	93	94	95	96	97	98	99	100	101	102	103
HEX	20	20	20	20	20	20	20	20	20	20	20	20	20	20	20	20
DEC	32	32	32	32	32	32	32	32	32	32	32	32	32	32	32	32
ASC	^'	^'	^'	^'	^'	^'	^'	^'	^'	^'	^'	^'	^'	^'	^'	^'
ALT	SPC	SPC	SPC	SPC	SPC	SPC	SPC	SPC	SPC	SPC	SPC	SPC	SPC	SPC	SPC	SPC
SYM																

◀──────────────── Substitute Description #10 ────────────────▶

BYTE	104	105	106	107	108	109	110	111	112	113	114	115	116	117	118	119
HEX	20	20	20	20	20	20	20	00	3F	31	20	20	20	20	20	20
DEC	32	32	32	32	32	32	32	0	63	49	32	32	32	32	32	32
ASC	^'	^'	^'	^'	^'	^'	^'	^@			^'	^'	^'	^'	^'	^'
ALT	SPC	SPC	SPC	SPC	SPC	SPC	SPC	NUL			SPC	SPC	SPC	SPC	SPC	SPC
SYM									?	1						

◀──────── Substitute Description #10 ────────▶◀──────── Substitute Value #1 ────────▶

BYTE	120	121	122	123	124	125	126	127	128	129	130	131	132	133	134	135
HEX	20	20	20	20	20	20	20	20	20	20	20	20	20	20	20	20
DEC	32	32	32	32	32	32	32	32	32	32	32	32	32	32	32	32
ASC	^'	^'	^'	^'	^'	^'	^'	^'	^'	^'	^'	^'	^'	^'	^'	^'
ALT	SPC	SPC	SPC	SPC	SPC	SPC	SPC	SPC	SPC	SPC	SPC	SPC	SPC	SPC	SPC	SPC
SYM																

◀──────────────── Substitute Value #1 ────────────────▶

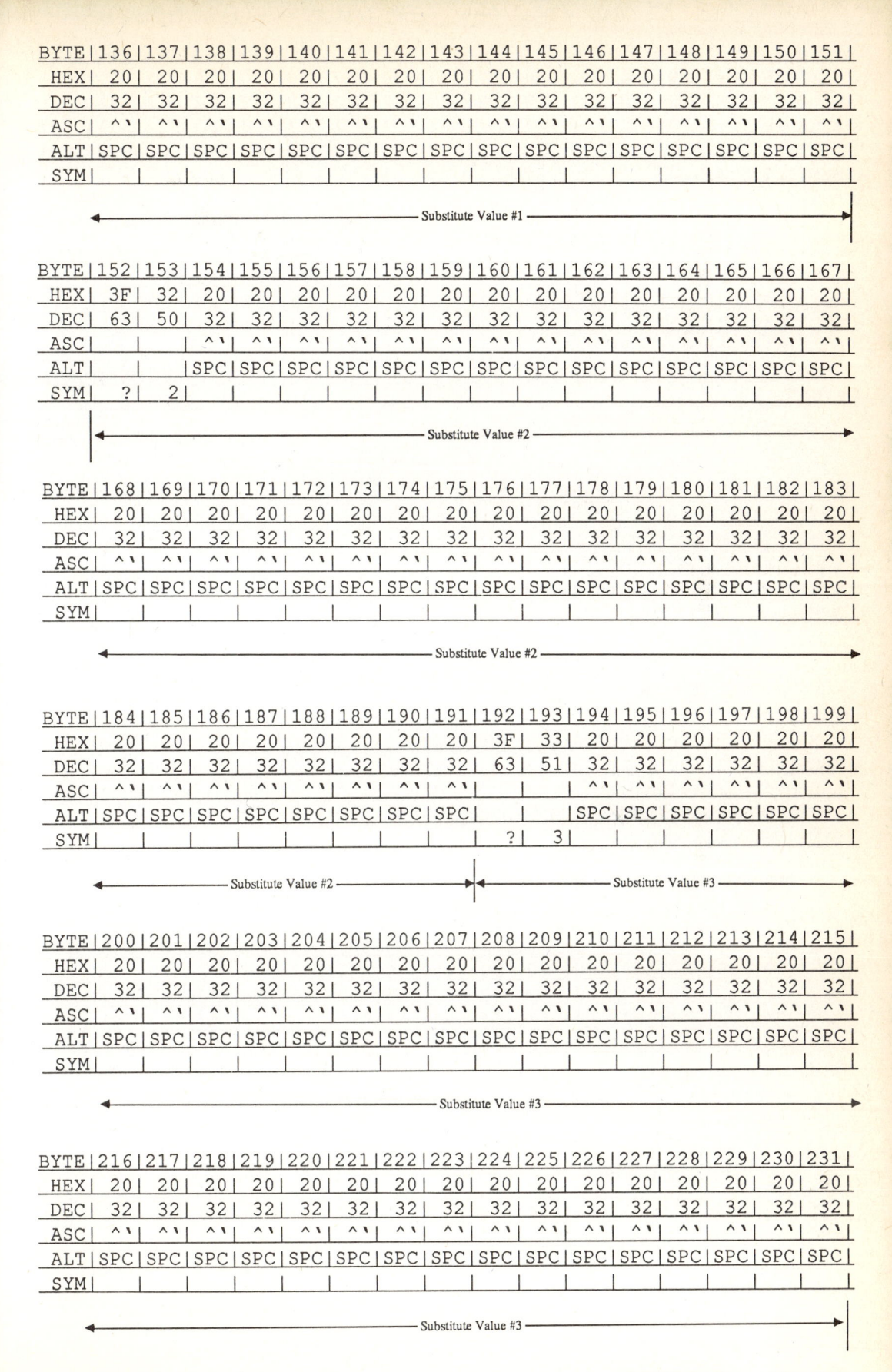

BYTE	136	137	138	139	140	141	142	143	144	145	146	147	148	149	150	151
HEX	20	20	20	20	20	20	20	20	20	20	20	20	20	20	20	20
DEC	32	32	32	32	32	32	32	32	32	32	32	32	32	32	32	32
ASC	^'	^'	^'	^'	^'	^'	^'	^'	^'	^'	^'	^'	^'	^'	^'	^'
ALT	SPC	SPC	SPC	SPC	SPC	SPC	SPC	SPC	SPC	SPC	SPC	SPC	SPC	SPC	SPC	SPC
SYM																

◄──────────────── Substitute Value #1 ────────────────►

BYTE	152	153	154	155	156	157	158	159	160	161	162	163	164	165	166	167
HEX	3F	32	20	20	20	20	20	20	20	20	20	20	20	20	20	20
DEC	63	50	32	32	32	32	32	32	32	32	32	32	32	32	32	32
ASC			^'	^'	^'	^'	^'	^'	^'	^'	^'	^'	^'	^'	^'	^'
ALT			SPC	SPC	SPC	SPC	SPC	SPC	SPC	SPC	SPC	SPC	SPC	SPC	SPC	SPC
SYM	?	2														

◄──────────────── Substitute Value #2 ────────────────►

BYTE	168	169	170	171	172	173	174	175	176	177	178	179	180	181	182	183
HEX	20	20	20	20	20	20	20	20	20	20	20	20	20	20	20	20
DEC	32	32	32	32	32	32	32	32	32	32	32	32	32	32	32	32
ASC	^'	^'	^'	^'	^'	^'	^'	^'	^'	^'	^'	^'	^'	^'	^'	^'
ALT	SPC	SPC	SPC	SPC	SPC	SPC	SPC	SPC	SPC	SPC	SPC	SPC	SPC	SPC	SPC	SPC
SYM																

◄──────────────── Substitute Value #2 ────────────────►

BYTE	184	185	186	187	188	189	190	191	192	193	194	195	196	197	198	199
HEX	20	20	20	20	20	20	20	20	3F	33	20	20	20	20	20	20
DEC	32	32	32	32	32	32	32	32	63	51	32	32	32	32	32	32
ASC	^'	^'	^'	^'	^'	^'	^'	^'			^'	^'	^'	^'	^'	^'
ALT	SPC	SPC	SPC	SPC	SPC	SPC	SPC	SPC			SPC	SPC	SPC	SPC	SPC	SPC
SYM									?	3						

◄─── Substitute Value #2 ───┼─── Substitute Value #3 ───►

BYTE	200	201	202	203	204	205	206	207	208	209	210	211	212	213	214	215
HEX	20	20	20	20	20	20	20	20	20	20	20	20	20	20	20	20
DEC	32	32	32	32	32	32	32	32	32	32	32	32	32	32	32	32
ASC	^'	^'	^'	^'	^'	^'	^'	^'	^'	^'	^'	^'	^'	^'	^'	^'
ALT	SPC	SPC	SPC	SPC	SPC	SPC	SPC	SPC	SPC	SPC	SPC	SPC	SPC	SPC	SPC	SPC
SYM																

◄──────────────── Substitute Value #3 ────────────────►

BYTE	216	217	218	219	220	221	222	223	224	225	226	227	228	229	230	231
HEX	20	20	20	20	20	20	20	20	20	20	20	20	20	20	20	20
DEC	32	32	32	32	32	32	32	32	32	32	32	32	32	32	32	32
ASC	^'	^'	^'	^'	^'	^'	^'	^'	^'	^'	^'	^'	^'	^'	^'	^'
ALT	SPC	SPC	SPC	SPC	SPC	SPC	SPC	SPC	SPC	SPC	SPC	SPC	SPC	SPC	SPC	SPC
SYM																

◄──────────────── Substitute Value #3 ────────────────►

IBM PLANS+.~MD

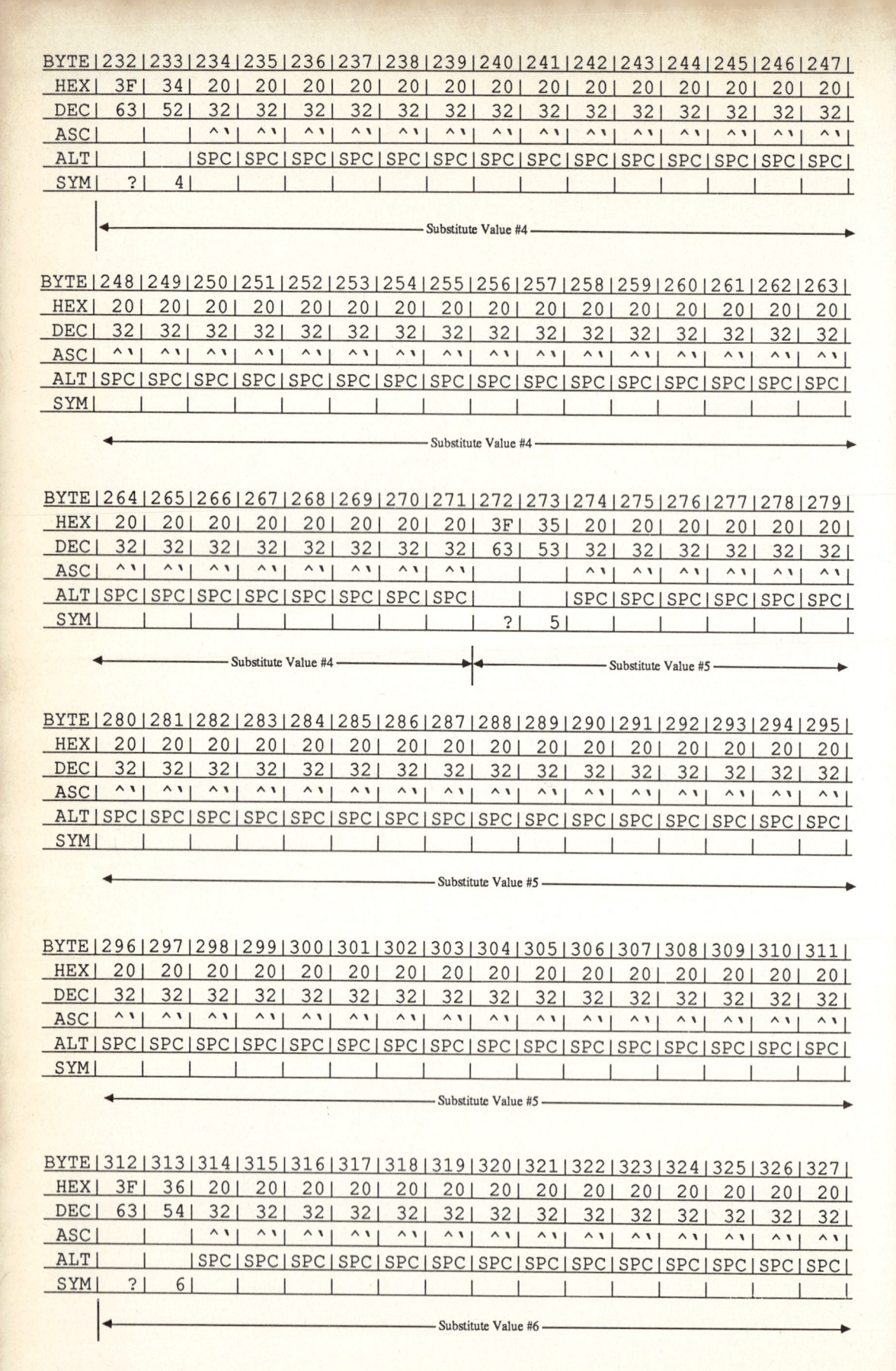

BYTE	232	233	234	235	236	237	238	239	240	241	242	243	244	245	246	247
HEX	3F	34	20	20	20	20	20	20	20	20	20	20	20	20	20	20
DEC	63	52	32	32	32	32	32	32	32	32	32	32	32	32	32	32
ASC			^'	^'	^'	^'	^'	^'	^'	^'	^'	^'	^'	^'	^'	^'
ALT			SPC	SPC	SPC	SPC	SPC	SPC	SPC	SPC	SPC	SPC	SPC	SPC	SPC	SPC
SYM	?	4														

◄──────────── Substitute Value #4 ────────────►

BYTE	248	249	250	251	252	253	254	255	256	257	258	259	260	261	262	263
HEX	20	20	20	20	20	20	20	20	20	20	20	20	20	20	20	20
DEC	32	32	32	32	32	32	32	32	32	32	32	32	32	32	32	32
ASC	^'	^'	^'	^'	^'	^'	^'	^'	^'	^'	^'	^'	^'	^'	^'	^'
ALT	SPC	SPC	SPC	SPC	SPC	SPC	SPC	SPC	SPC	SPC	SPC	SPC	SPC	SPC	SPC	SPC
SYM																

◄──────────── Substitute Value #4 ────────────►

BYTE	264	265	266	267	268	269	270	271	272	273	274	275	276	277	278	279
HEX	20	20	20	20	20	20	20	20	3F	35	20	20	20	20	20	20
DEC	32	32	32	32	32	32	32	32	63	53	32	32	32	32	32	32
ASC	^'	^'	^'	^'	^'	^'	^'	^'			^'	^'	^'	^'	^'	^'
ALT	SPC	SPC	SPC	SPC	SPC	SPC	SPC	SPC			SPC	SPC	SPC	SPC	SPC	SPC
SYM									?	5						

◄──── Substitute Value #4 ────►◄──── Substitute Value #5 ────►

BYTE	280	281	282	283	284	285	286	287	288	289	290	291	292	293	294	295
HEX	20	20	20	20	20	20	20	20	20	20	20	20	20	20	20	20
DEC	32	32	32	32	32	32	32	32	32	32	32	32	32	32	32	32
ASC	^'	^'	^'	^'	^'	^'	^'	^'	^'	^'	^'	^'	^'	^'	^'	^'
ALT	SPC	SPC	SPC	SPC	SPC	SPC	SPC	SPC	SPC	SPC	SPC	SPC	SPC	SPC	SPC	SPC
SYM																

◄──────────── Substitute Value #5 ────────────►

BYTE	296	297	298	299	300	301	302	303	304	305	306	307	308	309	310	311
HEX	20	20	20	20	20	20	20	20	20	20	20	20	20	20	20	20
DEC	32	32	32	32	32	32	32	32	32	32	32	32	32	32	32	32
ASC	^'	^'	^'	^'	^'	^'	^'	^'	^'	^'	^'	^'	^'	^'	^'	^'
ALT	SPC	SPC	SPC	SPC	SPC	SPC	SPC	SPC	SPC	SPC	SPC	SPC	SPC	SPC	SPC	SPC
SYM																

◄──────────── Substitute Value #5 ────────────►

BYTE	312	313	314	315	316	317	318	319	320	321	322	323	324	325	326	327
HEX	3F	36	20	20	20	20	20	20	20	20	20	20	20	20	20	20
DEC	63	54	32	32	32	32	32	32	32	32	32	32	32	32	32	32
ASC			^'	^'	^'	^'	^'	^'	^'	^'	^'	^'	^'	^'	^'	^'
ALT			SPC	SPC	SPC	SPC	SPC	SPC	SPC	SPC	SPC	SPC	SPC	SPC	SPC	SPC
SYM	?	6														

◄──────────── Substitute Value #6 ────────────►

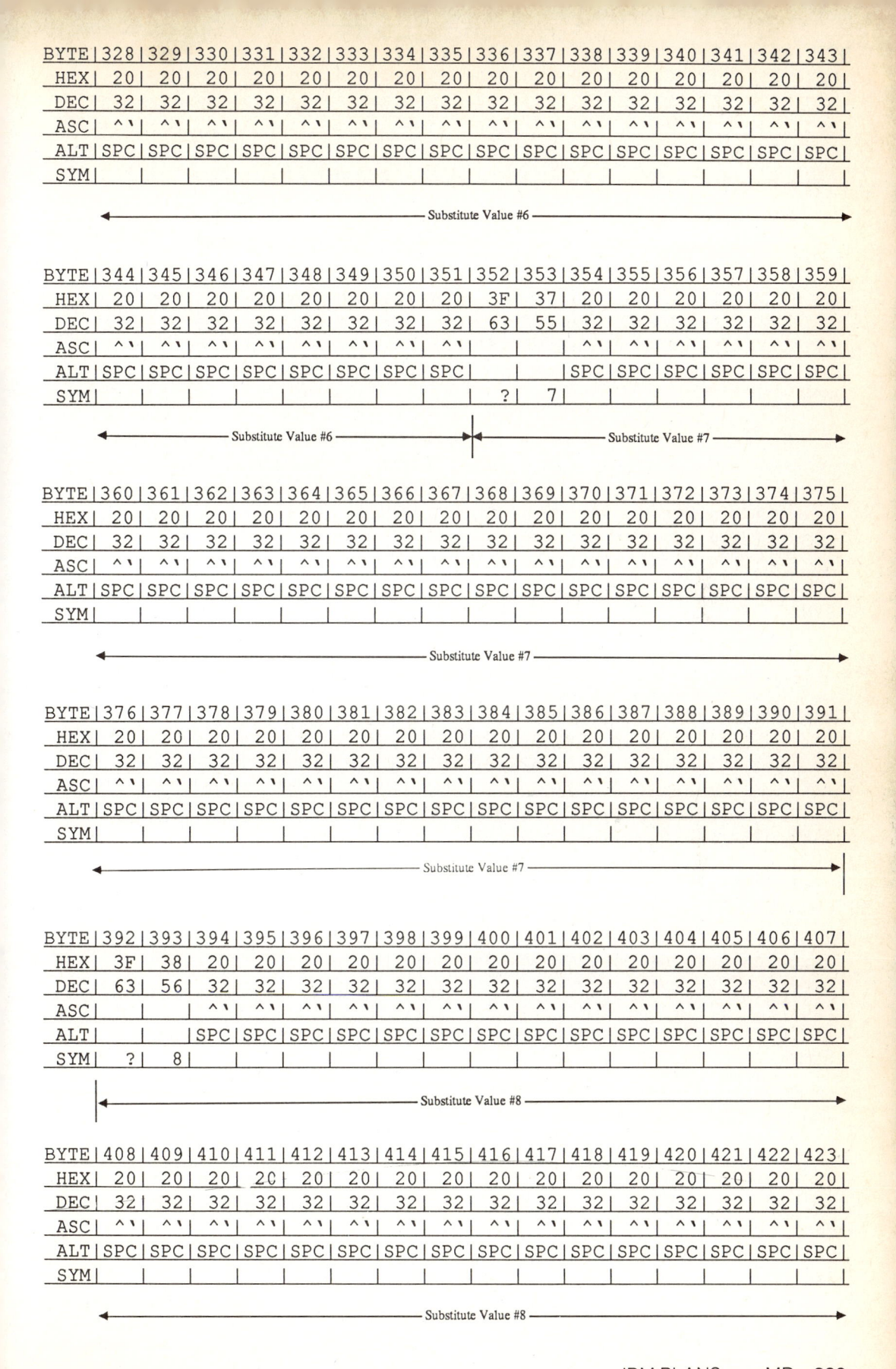

```
BYTE|328|329|330|331|332|333|334|335|336|337|338|339|340|341|342|343|
HEX | 20| 20| 20| 20| 20| 20| 20| 20| 20| 20| 20| 20| 20| 20| 20| 20|
DEC | 32| 32| 32| 32| 32| 32| 32| 32| 32| 32| 32| 32| 32| 32| 32| 32|
ASC | ^'| ^'| ^'| ^'| ^'| ^'| ^'| ^'| ^'| ^'| ^'| ^'| ^'| ^'| ^'| ^'|
ALT |SPC|SPC|SPC|SPC|SPC|SPC|SPC|SPC|SPC|SPC|SPC|SPC|SPC|SPC|SPC|SPC|
SYM |   |   |   |   |   |   |   |   |   |   |   |   |   |   |   |   |
```

◄──────────────── Substitute Value #6 ────────────────►

```
BYTE|344|345|346|347|348|349|350|351|352|353|354|355|356|357|358|359|
HEX | 20| 20| 20| 20| 20| 20| 20| 20| 3F| 37| 20| 20| 20| 20| 20| 20|
DEC | 32| 32| 32| 32| 32| 32| 32| 32| 63| 55| 32| 32| 32| 32| 32| 32|
ASC | ^'| ^'| ^'| ^'| ^'| ^'| ^'| ^'|   |   | ^'| ^'| ^'| ^'| ^'| ^'|
ALT |SPC|SPC|SPC|SPC|SPC|SPC|SPC|SPC|   |   |SPC|SPC|SPC|SPC|SPC|SPC|
SYM |   |   |   |   |   |   |   |   | ? | 7 |   |   |   |   |   |   |
```

◄────── Substitute Value #6 ──────►◄────── Substitute Value #7 ──────►

```
BYTE|360|361|362|363|364|365|366|367|368|369|370|371|372|373|374|375|
HEX | 20| 20| 20| 20| 20| 20| 20| 20| 20| 20| 20| 20| 20| 20| 20| 20|
DEC | 32| 32| 32| 32| 32| 32| 32| 32| 32| 32| 32| 32| 32| 32| 32| 32|
ASC | ^'| ^'| ^'| ^'| ^'| ^'| ^'| ^'| ^'| ^'| ^'| ^'| ^'| ^'| ^'| ^'|
ALT |SPC|SPC|SPC|SPC|SPC|SPC|SPC|SPC|SPC|SPC|SPC|SPC|SPC|SPC|SPC|SPC|
SYM |   |   |   |   |   |   |   |   |   |   |   |   |   |   |   |   |
```

◄──────────────── Substitute Value #7 ────────────────►

```
BYTE|376|377|378|379|380|381|382|383|384|385|386|387|388|389|390|391|
HEX | 20| 20| 20| 20| 20| 20| 20| 20| 20| 20| 20| 20| 20| 20| 20| 20|
DEC | 32| 32| 32| 32| 32| 32| 32| 32| 32| 32| 32| 32| 32| 32| 32| 32|
ASC | ^'| ^'| ^'| ^'| ^'| ^'| ^'| ^'| ^'| ^'| ^'| ^'| ^'| ^'| ^'| ^'|
ALT |SPC|SPC|SPC|SPC|SPC|SPC|SPC|SPC|SPC|SPC|SPC|SPC|SPC|SPC|SPC|SPC|
SYM |   |   |   |   |   |   |   |   |   |   |   |   |   |   |   |   |
```

◄──────────────── Substitute Value #7 ────────────────►

```
BYTE|392|393|394|395|396|397|398|399|400|401|402|403|404|405|406|407|
HEX | 3F| 38| 20| 20| 20| 20| 20| 20| 20| 20| 20| 20| 20| 20| 20| 20|
DEC | 63| 56| 32| 32| 32| 32| 32| 32| 32| 32| 32| 32| 32| 32| 32| 32|
ASC |   |   | ^'| ^'| ^'| ^'| ^'| ^'| ^'| ^'| ^'| ^'| ^'| ^'| ^'| ^'|
ALT |   |   |SPC|SPC|SPC|SPC|SPC|SPC|SPC|SPC|SPC|SPC|SPC|SPC|SPC|SPC|
SYM | ? | 8 |   |   |   |   |   |   |   |   |   |   |   |   |   |   |
```

◄──────────────── Substitute Value #8 ────────────────►

```
BYTE|408|409|410|411|412|413|414|415|416|417|418|419|420|421|422|423|
HEX | 20| 20| 20| 20| 20| 20| 20| 20| 20| 20| 20| 20| 20| 20| 20| 20|
DEC | 32| 32| 32| 32| 32| 32| 32| 32| 32| 32| 32| 32| 32| 32| 32| 32|
ASC | ^'| ^'| ^'| ^'| ^'| ^'| ^'| ^'| ^'| ^'| ^'| ^'| ^'| ^'| ^'| ^'|
ALT |SPC|SPC|SPC|SPC|SPC|SPC|SPC|SPC|SPC|SPC|SPC|SPC|SPC|SPC|SPC|SPC|
SYM |   |   |   |   |   |   |   |   |   |   |   |   |   |   |   |   |
```

◄──────────────── Substitute Value #8 ────────────────►

BYTE	424	425	426	427	428	429	430	431	432	433	434	435	436	437	438	439
HEX	20	20	20	20	20	20	20	20	3F	39	20	20	20	20	20	20
DEC	32	32	32	32	32	32	32	32	63	57	32	32	32	32	32	32
ASC	^`	^`	^`	^`	^`	^`	^`	^`			^`	^`	^`	^`	^`	^`
ALT	SPC	SPC	SPC	SPC	SPC	SPC	SPC	SPC			SPC	SPC	SPC	SPC	SPC	SPC
SYM									?	9						

◄──────── Substitute Value #8 ────────┤├──────── Substitute Value #9 ────────►

BYTE	440	441	442	443	444	445	446	447	448	449	450	451	452	453	454	455
HEX	20	20	20	20	20	20	20	20	20	20	20	20	20	20	20	20
DEC	32	32	32	32	32	32	32	32	32	32	32	32	32	32	32	32
ASC	^`	^`	^`	^`	^`	^`	^`	^`	^`	^`	^`	^`	^`	^`	^`	^`
ALT	SPC	SPC	SPC	SPC	SPC	SPC	SPC	SPC	SPC	SPC	SPC	SPC	SPC	SPC	SPC	SPC
SYM																

◄──────────────────── Substitute Value #9 ────────────────────►

BYTE	456	457	458	459	460	461	462	463	464	465	466	467	468	469	470	471
HEX	20	20	20	20	20	20	20	20	20	20	20	20	20	20	20	20
DEC	32	32	32	32	32	32	32	32	32	32	32	32	32	32	32	32
ASC	^`	^`	^`	^`	^`	^`	^`	^`	^`	^`	^`	^`	^`	^`	^`	^`
ALT	SPC	SPC	SPC	SPC	SPC	SPC	SPC	SPC	SPC	SPC	SPC	SPC	SPC	SPC	SPC	SPC
SYM																

◄──────────────────── Substitute Value #9 ────────────────────┤

BYTE	472	473	474	475	476	477	478	479	480	481	482	483	484	485	486	487
HEX	3F	31	30	20	20	20	20	20	20	20	20	20	20	20	20	20
DEC	63	49	48	32	32	32	32	32	32	32	32	32	32	32	32	32
ASC				^`	^`	^`	^`	^`	^`	^`	^`	^`	^`	^`	^`	^`
ALT				SPC	SPC	SPC	SPC	SPC	SPC	SPC	SPC	SPC	SPC	SPC	SPC	SPC
SYM	?	1	0													

├──────────────────── Substitute Value #10 ────────────────────►

BYTE	488	489	490	491	492	493	494	495	496	497	498	499	500	501	502	503
HEX	20	20	20	20	20	20	20	20	20	20	20	20	20	20	20	20
DEC	32	32	32	32	32	32	32	32	32	32	32	32	32	32	32	32
ASC	^`	^`	^`	^`	^`	^`	^`	^`	^`	^`	^`	^`	^`	^`	^`	^`
ALT	SPC	SPC	SPC	SPC	SPC	SPC	SPC	SPC	SPC	SPC	SPC	SPC	SPC	SPC	SPC	SPC
SYM																

◄──────────────────── Substitute Value #10 ────────────────────►

BYTE	504	505	506	507	508	509	510	511	512	513	514	515	516	517	518	519
HEX	20	20	20	20	20	20	20	20	01	2A	00	00	00	00	00	00
DEC	32	32	32	32	32	32	32	32	1	42	0	0	0	0	0	0
ASC	^`	^`	^`	^`	^`	^`	^`	^`	^A		^@	^@	^@	^@	^@	^@
ALT	SPC	SPC	SPC	SPC	SPC	SPC	SPC	SPC	SOH		NUL	NUL	NUL	NUL	NUL	NUL
SYM										*						

◄──── Substitute Value #10 ────┤├──────── Graph Name ────────►
├──── Begin Graph Format ────►

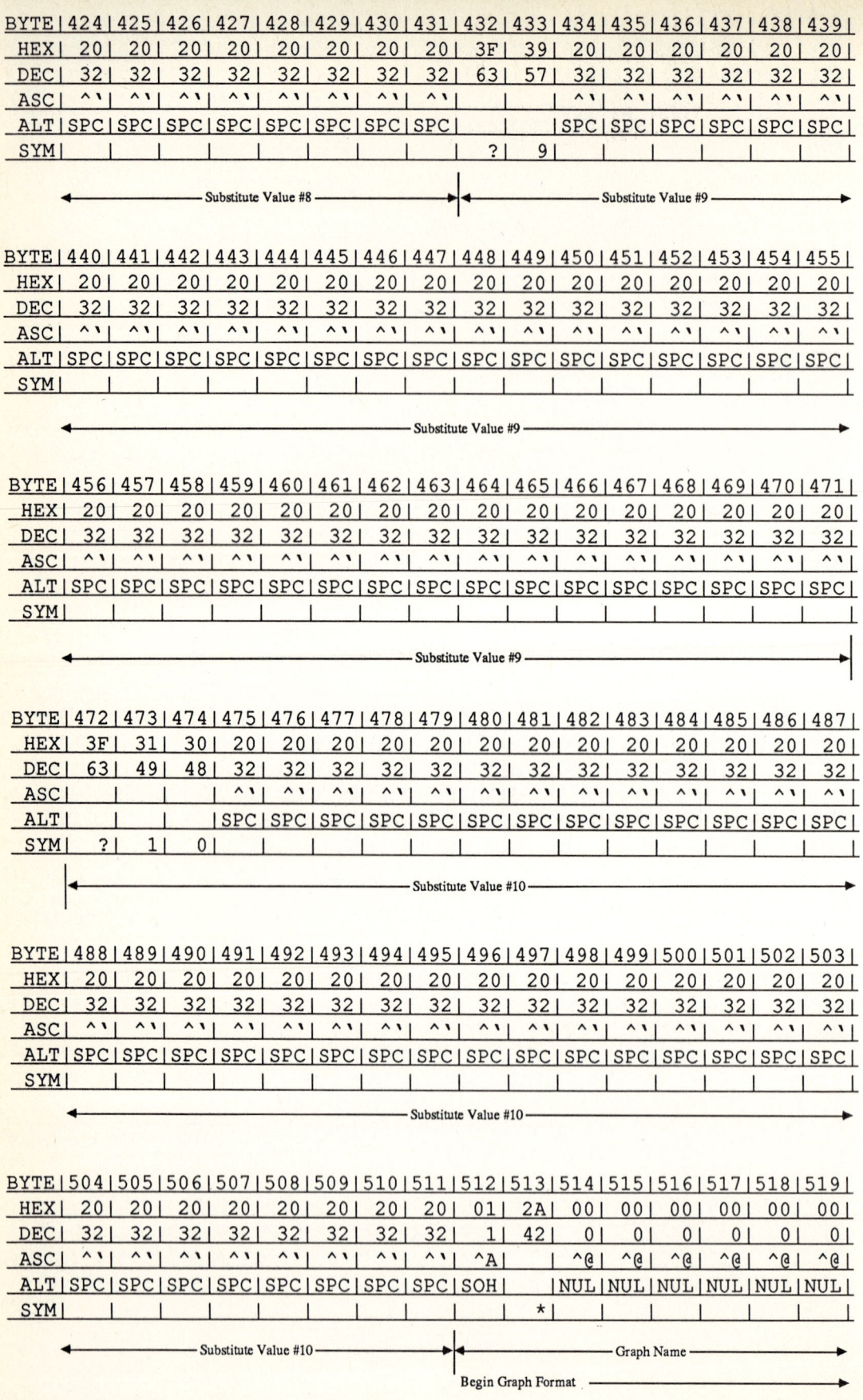

BYTE	520	521	522	523	524	525	526	527	528	529	530	531	532	533	534	535
HEX	00	00	09	00	01	20	00	00	00	00	00	00	00	00	00	00
DEC	0	0	9	0	1	32	0	0	0	0	0	0	0	0	0	0
ASC	^@	^@	^I	^@	^A	^`	^@	^@	^@	^@	^@	^@	^@	^@	^@	^@
ALT	NUL	NUL	HT	NUL	SOH	SPC	NUL	NUL	NUL	NUL	NUL	NUL	NUL	NUL	NUL	NUL
SYM																

←――――→|― Graph Type ―|←―――――――――― First Graph Title ――――――――――→

BYTE	536	537	538	539	540	541	542	543	544	545	546	547	548	549	550	551
HEX	00	00	00	00	00	00	00	00	00	00	00	00	00	00	00	00
DEC	0	0	0	0	0	0	0	0	0	0	0	0	0	0	0	0
ASC	^@	^@	^@	^@	^@	^@	^@	^@	^@	^@	^@	^@	^@	^@	^@	^@
ALT	NUL	NUL	NUL	NUL	NUL	NUL	NUL	NUL	NUL	NUL	NUL	NUL	NUL	NUL	NUL	NUL
SYM																

←――――――――――――――― First Graph Title ―――――――――――――――→

BYTE	552	553	554	555	556	557	558	559	560	561	562	563	564	565	566	567
HEX	00	00	00	00	00	00	00	00	00	00	00	00	01	20	00	00
DEC	0	0	0	0	0	0	0	0	0	0	0	0	1	32	0	0
ASC	^@	^@	^@	^@	^@	^@	^@	^@	^@	^@	^@	^@	^A	^`	^@	^@
ALT	NUL	NUL	NUL	NUL	NUL	NUL	NUL	NUL	NUL	NUL	NUL	NUL	SOH	SPC	NUL	NUL
SYM																

←―――――――――― First Graph Title ――――――――――→|←― Second Graph Title ―→

BYTE	568	569	570	571	572	573	574	575	576	577	578	579	580	581	582	583
HEX	00	00	00	00	00	00	00	00	00	00	00	00	00	00	00	00
DEC	0	0	0	0	0	0	0	0	0	0	0	0	0	0	0	0
ASC	^@	^@	^@	^@	^@	^@	^@	^@	^@	^@	^@	^@	^@	^@	^@	^@
ALT	NUL	NUL	NUL	NUL	NUL	NUL	NUL	NUL	NUL	NUL	NUL	NUL	NUL	NUL	NUL	NUL
SYM																

←――――――――――――――― Second Graph Title ―――――――――――――――→

BYTE	584	585	586	587	588	589	590	591	592	593	594	595	596	597	598	599
HEX	00	00	00	00	00	00	00	00	00	00	00	00	00	00	00	00
DEC	0	0	0	0	0	0	0	0	0	0	0	0	0	0	0	0
ASC	^@	^@	^@	^@	^@	^@	^@	^@	^@	^@	^@	^@	^@	^@	^@	^@
ALT	NUL	NUL	NUL	NUL	NUL	NUL	NUL	NUL	NUL	NUL	NUL	NUL	NUL	NUL	NUL	NUL
SYM																

←――――――――――――― Second Graph Title ―――――――――――――→

BYTE	600	601	602	603	604	605	606	607	608	609	610	611	612	613	614	615
HEX	00	00	00	00	01	20	00	00	00	00	00	00	00	00	00	00
DEC	0	0	0	0	1	32	0	0	0	0	0	0	0	0	0	0
ASC	^@	^@	^@	^@	^A	^`	^@	^@	^@	^@	^@	^@	^@	^@	^@	^@
ALT	NUL	NUL	NUL	NUL	SOH	SPC	NUL	NUL	NUL	NUL	NUL	NUL	NUL	NUL	NUL	NUL
SYM																

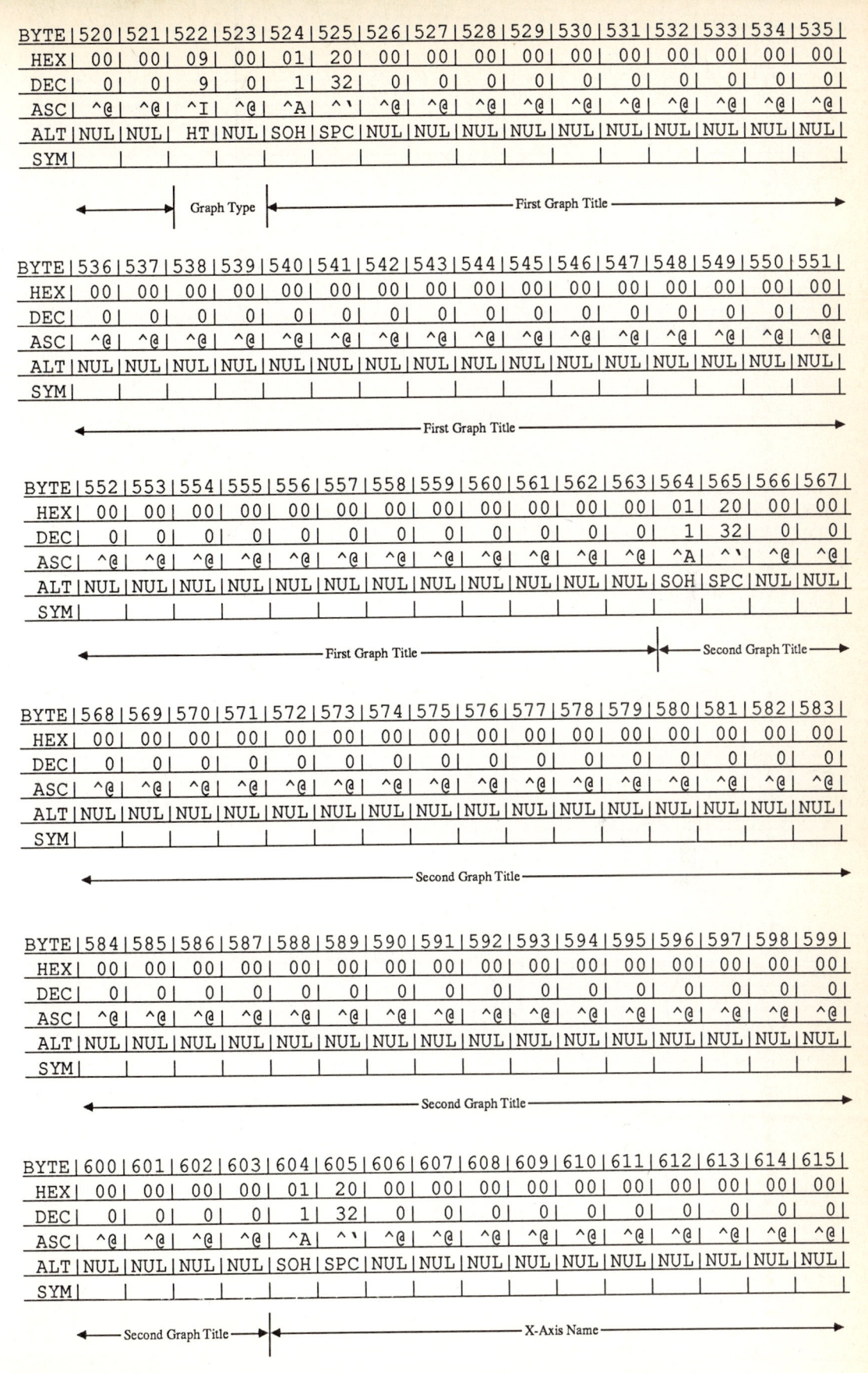

←― Second Graph Title ―→|←――――――――― X-Axis Name ―――――――――→

BYTE	616	617	618	619	620	621	622	623	624	625	626	627	628	629	630	631
HEX	00	00	00	00	00	00	00	00	01	20	00	00	00	00	00	00
DEC	0	0	0	0	0	0	0	0	1	32	0	0	0	0	0	0
ASC	^@	^@	^@	^@	^@	^@	^@	^@	^A	^`	^@	^@	^@	^@	^@	^@
ALT	NUL	NUL	NUL	NUL	NUL	NUL	NUL	NUL	SOH	SPC	NUL	NUL	NUL	NUL	NUL	NUL
SYM																

←——— X-Axis Name ———→←——— Y-Axis Name ———→

BYTE	632	633	634	635	636	637	638	639	640	641	642	643	644	645	646	647
HEX	00	00	00	00	00	00	00	00	00	00	00	00	6E	6E	00	00
DEC	0	0	0	0	0	0	0	0	0	0	0	0	110	110	0	0
ASC	^@	^@	^@	^@	^@	^@	^@	^@	^@	^@	^@	^@			^@	^@
ALT	NUL	NUL	NUL	NUL	NUL	NUL	NUL	NUL	NUL	NUL	NUL	NUL			NUL	NUL
SYM													n	n		

←——— Y-Axis Name ———→ | Grid Type | Label Type | Start Value

BYTE	648	649	650	651	652	653	654	655	656	657	658	659	660	661	662	663
HEX	00	00	79	00	00	00	00	00	00	00	00	00	6E	00	00	00
DEC	0	0	121	0	0	0	0	0	0	0	0	0	110	0	0	0
ASC	^@	^@		^@	^@	^@	^@	^@	^@	^@	^@	^@		^@	^@	^@
ALT	NUL	NUL		NUL	NUL	NUL	NUL	NUL	NUL	NUL	NUL	NUL		NUL	NUL	NUL
SYM			y										n			

End Value | Scale Type | ←— Lower Scale (Real) —→ | ←— Upper Scale (Real) —→ | Reference Line | Reference Value

BYTE	664	665	666	667	668	669	670	671	672	673	674	675	676	677	678	679
HEX	00	00	6E	79	6E	00	00	00	00	00	6E	6E	01	00	03	00
DEC	0	0	110	121	110	0	0	0	0	0	110	110	1	0	3	0
ASC	^@	^@			^@	^@	^@	^@	^@				^A	^@	^C	^@
ALT	NUL	NUL			NUL	NUL	NUL	NUL	NUL				SOH	NUL	ETX	NUL
SYM			n	y	n						n	n				

Reference Value | Float Bar | Marked Line | Scatter Gram | # of Data Sets | Pallette | Save File | View Print | LPTx: (1-3) | PRCODES (Bkg. Color)

BYTE	680	681	682	683	684	685	686	687	688	689	690	691	692	693	694	695
HEX	01	00	6E	00	00	00	00	00	00	00	00	00	00	00	00	00
DEC	1	0	110	0	0	0	0	0	0	0	0	0	0	0	0	0
ASC	^A	^@		^@	^@	^@	^@	^@	^@	^@	^@	^@	^@	^@	^@	^@
ALT	SOH	NUL		NUL	NUL	NUL	NUL	NUL	NUL	NUL	NUL	NUL	NUL	NUL	NUL	NUL
SYM			n													

PRCODED (Printer Type) | View Display | ←— Real 4 —→ | ←— Real 4 —→ | ←— Real 4 —→
←———————— Point Value 1 ————————→

BYTE	696	697	698	699	700	701	702	703	704	705	706	707	708	709	710	711
HEX	00	00	00	00	00	00	00	00	00	00	00	00	00	00	00	00
DEC	0	0	0	0	0	0	0	0	0	0	0	0	0	0	0	0
ASC	^@	^@	^@	^@	^@	^@	^@	^@	^@	^@	^@	^@	^@	^@	^@	^@
ALT	NUL	NUL	NUL	NUL	NUL	NUL	NUL	NUL	NUL	NUL	NUL	NUL	NUL	NUL	NUL	NUL
SYM																

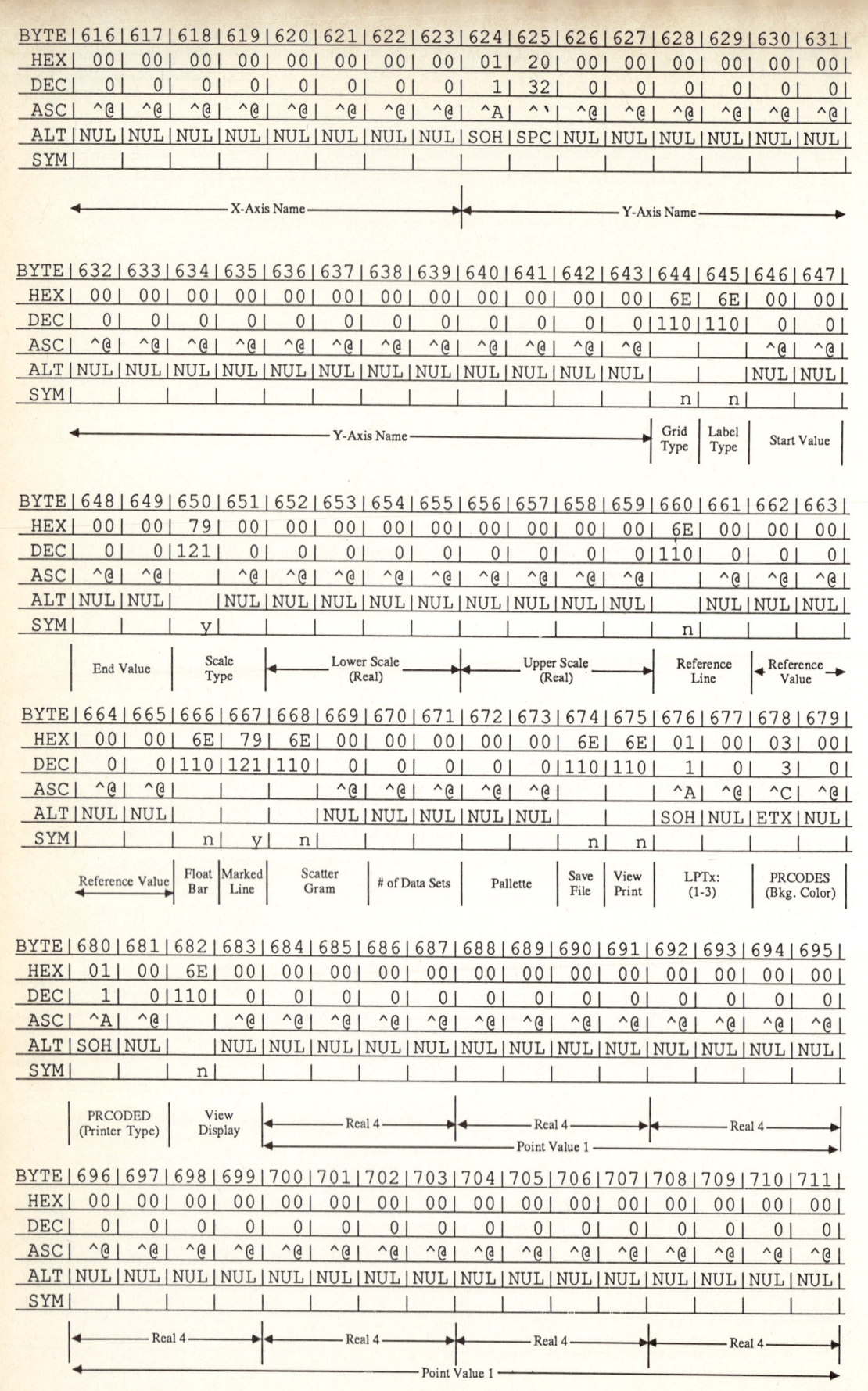

←— Real 4 —→ | ←— Real 4 —→ | ←— Real 4 —→ | ←— Real 4 —→
←———————————————— Point Value 1 ————————————————→

BYTE	712	713	714	715	716	717	718	719	720	721	722	723	724	725	726	727
HEX	00	00	00	00	00	00	00	00	00	00	00	00	00	00	00	00
DEC	0	0	0	0	0	0	0	0	0	0	0	0	0	0	0	0
ASC	^@	^@	^@	^@	^@	^@	^@	^@	^@	^@	^@	^@	^@	^@	^@	^@
ALT	NUL	NUL	NUL	NUL	NUL	NUL	NUL	NUL	NUL	NUL	NUL	NUL	NUL	NUL	NUL	NUL
SYM																

|←——— Real 4 ———→|←——— Real 4 ———→|←——— Real 4 ———→|←——— Real 4 ———→|
|←————————————————————— Point Value 2 —————————————————————→|

BYTE	728	729	730	731	732	733	734	735	736	737	738	739	740	741	742	743
HEX	00	00	00	00	00	00	00	00	00	00	00	00	00	00	00	00
DEC	0	0	0	0	0	0	0	0	0	0	0	0	0	0	0	0
ASC	^@	^@	^@	^@	^@	^@	^@	^@	^@	^@	^@	^@	^@	^@	^@	^@
ALT	NUL	NUL	NUL	NUL	NUL	NUL	NUL	NUL	NUL	NUL	NUL	NUL	NUL	NUL	NUL	NUL
SYM																

|←——— Real 4 ———→|←——— Real 4 ———→|←——— Real 4 ———→|←——— Real 4 ———→|
|←————————— Point Value 2 —————————→|←——— Point Value 3 ———→|

BYTE	744	745	746	747	748	749	750	751	752	753	754	755	756	757	758	759
HEX	00	00	00	00	00	00	00	00	00	00	00	00	00	00	00	00
DEC	0	0	0	0	0	0	0	0	0	0	0	0	0	0	0	0
ASC	^@	^@	^@	^@	^@	^@	^@	^@	^@	^@	^@	^@	^@	^@	^@	^@
ALT	NUL	NUL	NUL	NUL	NUL	NUL	NUL	NUL	NUL	NUL	NUL	NUL	NUL	NUL	NUL	NUL
SYM																

|←——— Real 4 ———→|←——— Real 4 ———→|←——— Real 4 ———→|←——— Real 4 ———→|

BYTE	760	761	762	763	764	765	766	767	768	769	770	771	772	773	774	775
HEX	00	00	00	00	00	00	00	00	00	00	00	00	00	00	00	00
DEC	0	0	0	0	0	0	0	0	0	0	0	0	0	0	0	0
ASC	^@	^@	^@	^@	^@	^@	^@	^@	^@	^@	^@	^@	^@	^@	^@	^@
ALT	NUL	NUL	NUL	NUL	NUL	NUL	NUL	NUL	NUL	NUL	NUL	NUL	NUL	NUL	NUL	NUL
SYM																

|←——— Real 4 ———→|←——— Real 4 ———→|←——— Real 4 ———→|←——— Real 4 ———→|
|←——— Point Value 3 ———→|←——— Point Value 4 ———→|

BYTE	776	777	778	779	780	781	782	783	784	785	786	787	788	789	790	791
HEX	00	00	00	00	00	00	00	00	00	00	00	00	00	00	00	00
DEC	0	0	0	0	0	0	0	0	0	0	0	0	0	0	0	0
ASC	^@	^@	^@	^@	^@	^@	^@	^@	^@	^@	^@	^@	^@	^@	^@	^@
ALT	NUL	NUL	NUL	NUL	NUL	NUL	NUL	NUL	NUL	NUL	NUL	NUL	NUL	NUL	NUL	NUL
SYM																

|←——— Real 4 ———→|←——— Real 4 ———→|←——— Real 4 ———→|←——— Real 4 ———→|

BYTE	792	793	794	795	796	797	798	799	800	801	802	803	804	805	806	807
HEX	00	00	00	00	00	00	00	00	00	00	00	00	00	00	00	00
DEC	0	0	0	0	0	0	0	0	0	0	0	0	0	0	0	0
ASC	^@	^@	^@	^@	^@	^@	^@	^@	^@	^@	^@	^@	^@	^@	^@	^@
ALT	NUL	NUL	NUL	NUL	NUL	NUL	NUL	NUL	NUL	NUL	NUL	NUL	NUL	NUL	NUL	NUL
SYM																

|←——— Real 4 ———→|←——— Real 4 ———→|←——— Real 4 ———→|←——— Real 4 ———→|
|←——— Point Value 4 ———→|←————— Point Value 5 —————→|

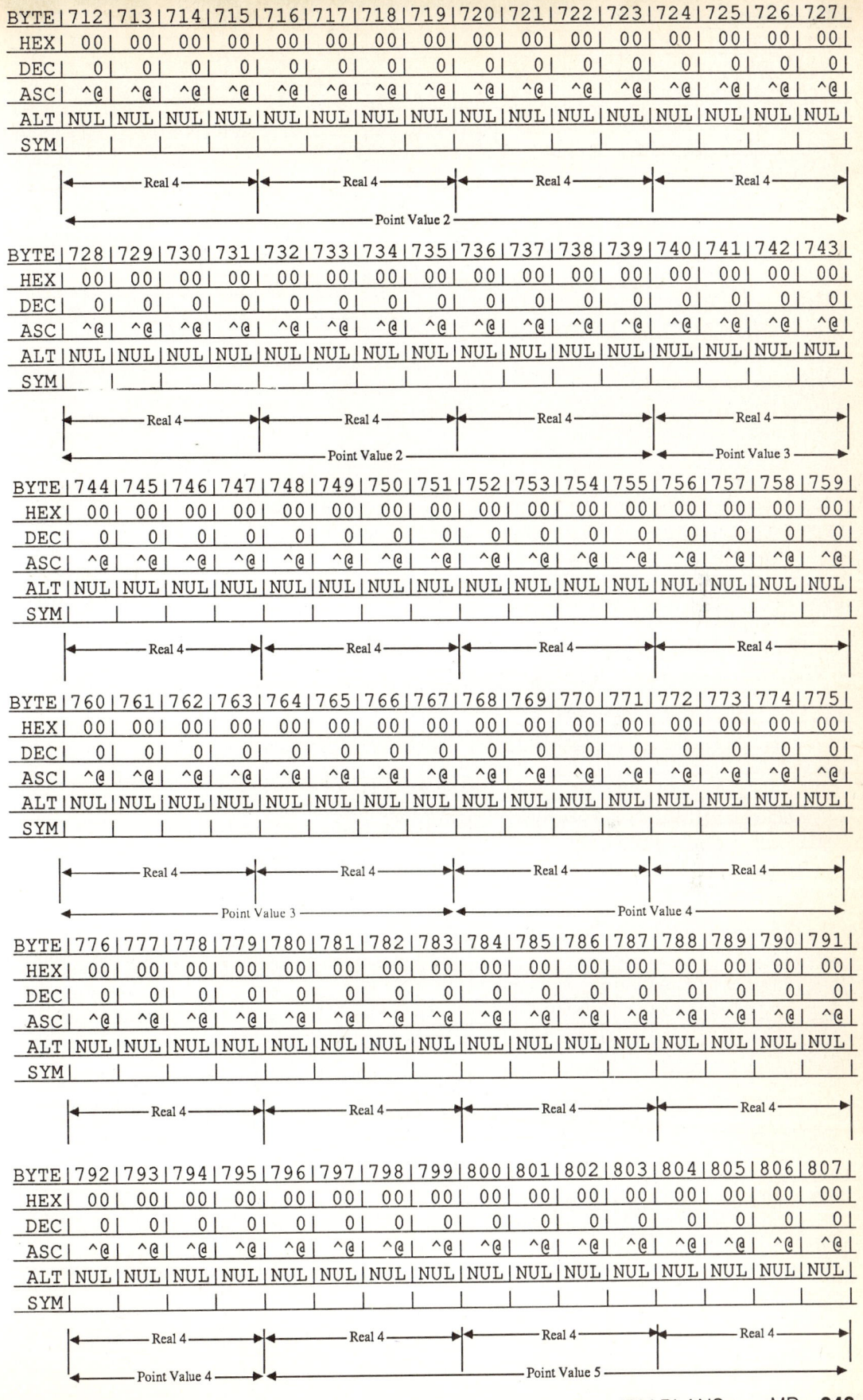

BYTE	808	809	810	811	812	813	814	815	816	817	818	819	820	821	822	823
HEX	00	00	00	00	00	00	00	00	00	00	00	00	00	00	00	00
DEC	0	0	0	0	0	0	0	0	0	0	0	0	0	0	0	0
ASC	^@	^@	^@	^@	^@	^@	^@	^@	^@	^@	^@	^@	^@	^@	^@	^@
ALT	NUL	NUL	NUL	NUL	NUL	NUL	NUL	NUL	NUL	NUL	NUL	NUL	NUL	NUL	NUL	NUL
SYM																

|←——— Real 4 ———→|←——— Real 4 ———→|←——— Real 4 ———→|←——— Real 4 ———→|
|←——————————————————— Point Value 5 ———————————————————→|

BYTE	824	825	826	827	828	829	830	831	832	833	834	835	836	837	838	839
HEX	00	00	00	00	00	00	00	00	00	00	00	00	00	00	00	00
DEC	0	0	0	0	0	0	0	0	0	0	0	0	0	0	0	0
ASC	^@	^@	^@	^@	^@	^@	^@	^@	^@	^@	^@	^@	^@	^@	^@	^@
ALT	NUL	NUL	NUL	NUL	NUL	NUL	NUL	NUL	NUL	NUL	NUL	NUL	NUL	NUL	NUL	NUL
SYM																

|←——— Real 4 ———→|←——— Real 4 ———→|←——— Real 4 ———→|←——— Real 4 ———→|
|←——————————————————— Point Value 6 ———————————————————→|

BYTE	840	841	842	843	844	845	846	847	848	849	850	851	852	853	854	855
HEX	00	00	00	00	00	00	00	00	00	00	00	00	00	00	00	00
DEC	0	0	0	0	0	0	0	0	0	0	0	0	0	0	0	0
ASC	^@	^@	^@	^@	^@	^@	^@	^@	^@	^@	^@	^@	^@	^@	^@	^@
ALT	NUL	NUL	NUL	NUL	NUL	NUL	NUL	NUL	NUL	NUL	NUL	NUL	NUL	NUL	NUL	NUL
SYM																

|←——— Real 4 ———→|←——— Real 4 ———→|←——— Real 4 ———→|←——— Real 4 ———→|
|←————————— Point Value 6 —————————→|←————— Point Value 7 —————→|

BYTE	856	857	858	859	860	861	862	863	864	865	866	867	868	869	870	871
HEX	00	00	00	00	00	00	00	00	00	00	00	00	00	00	00	00
DEC	0	0	0	0	0	0	0	0	0	0	0	0	0	0	0	0
ASC	^@	^@	^@	^@	^@	^@	^@	^@	^@	^@	^@	^@	^@	^@	^@	^@
ALT	NUL	NUL	NUL	NUL	NUL	NUL	NUL	NUL	NUL	NUL	NUL	NUL	NUL	NUL	NUL	NUL
SYM																

|←——— Real 4 ———→|←——— Real 4 ———→|←——— Real 4 ———→|←——— Real 4 ———→|

BYTE	872	873	874	875	876	877	878	879	880	881	882	883	884	885	886	887
HEX	00	00	00	00	00	00	00	00	00	00	00	00	00	00	00	00
DEC	0	0	0	0	0	0	0	0	0	0	0	0	0	0	0	0
ASC	^@	^@	^@	^@	^@	^@	^@	^@	^@	^@	^@	^@	^@	^@	^@	^@
ALT	NUL	NUL	NUL	NUL	NUL	NUL	NUL	NUL	NUL	NUL	NUL	NUL	NUL	NUL	NUL	NUL
SYM																

|←——— Real 4 ———→|←——— Real 4 ———→|←——— Real 4 ———→|←——— Real 4 ———→|
|←————— Point Value 7 —————→|←————————— Point Value 8 —————————→|

BYTE	888	889	890	891	892	893	894	895	896	897	898	899	900	901	902	903
HEX	00	00	00	00	00	00	00	00	00	00	00	00	00	00	00	00
DEC	0	0	0	0	0	0	0	0	0	0	0	0	0	0	0	0
ASC	^@	^@	^@	^@	^@	^@	^@	^@	^@	^@	^@	^@	^@	^@	^@	^@
ALT	NUL	NUL	NUL	NUL	NUL	NUL	NUL	NUL	NUL	NUL	NUL	NUL	NUL	NUL	NUL	NUL
SYM																

|←——— Real 4 ———→|←——— Real 4 ———→|←——— Real 4 ———→|←——— Real 4 ———→|

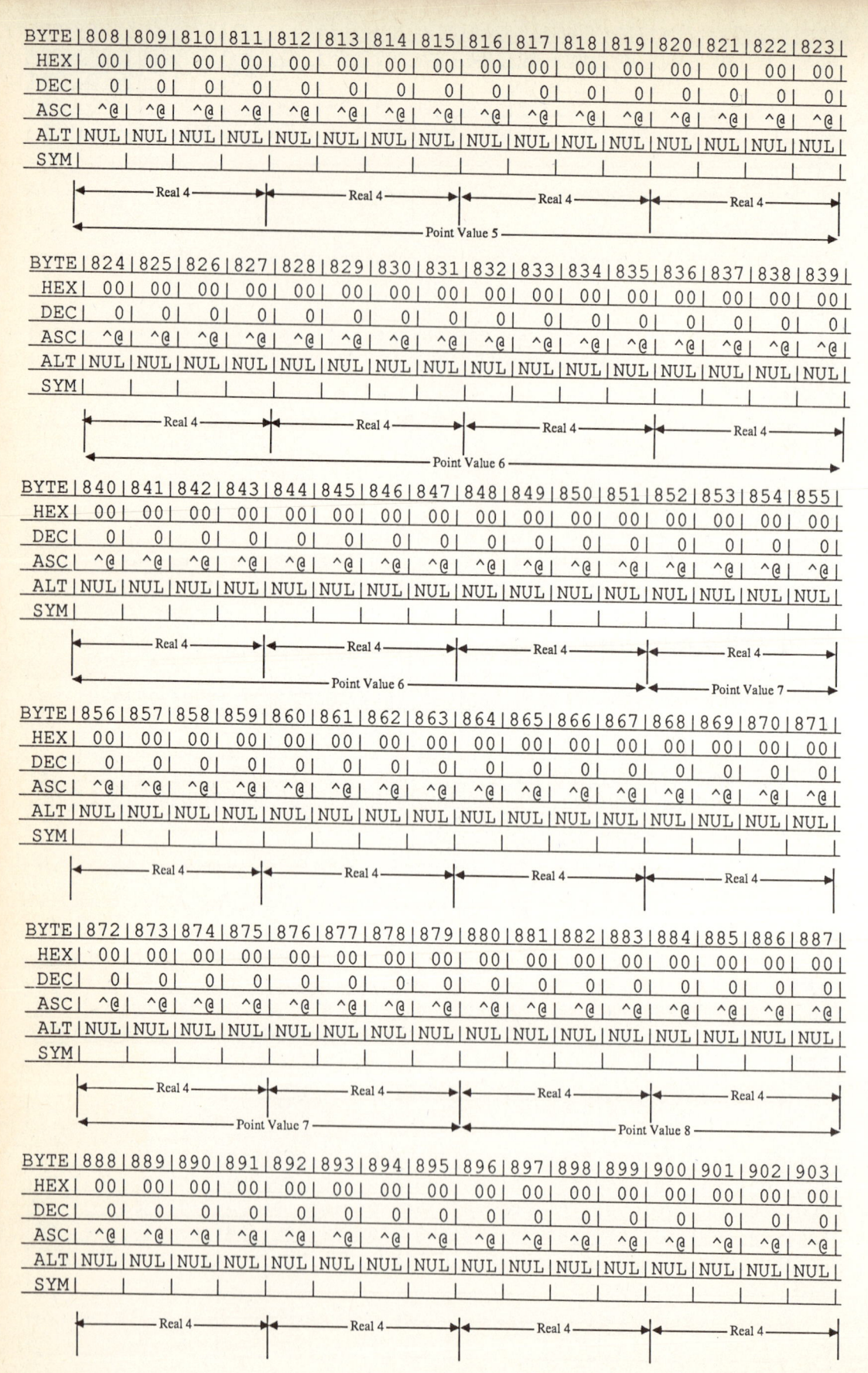

BYTE	904	905	906	907	908	909	910	911	912	913	914	915	916	917	918	919
HEX	00	00	00	00	00	00	00	00	00	00	00	00	00	00	00	00
DEC	0	0	0	0	0	0	0	0	0	0	0	0	0	0	0	0
ASC	^@	^@	^@	^@	^@	^@	^@	^@	^@	^@	^@	^@	^@	^@	^@	^@
ALT	NUL	NUL	NUL	NUL	NUL	NUL	NUL	NUL	NUL	NUL	NUL	NUL	NUL	NUL	NUL	NUL
SYM																

|←——— Real 4 ———→|←——— Real 4 ———→|←——— Real 4 ———→|←——— Real 4 ———→|
|←——— Point Value 8 ———→|←——————— Point Value 9 ———————————————→|

BYTE	920	921	922	923	924	925	926	927	928	929	930	931	932	933	934	935
HEX	00	00	00	00	00	00	00	00	00	00	00	00	00	00	00	00
DEC	0	0	0	0	0	0	0	0	0	0	0	0	0	0	0	0
ASC	^@	^@	^@	^@	^@	^@	^@	^@	^@	^@	^@	^@	^@	^@	^@	^@
ALT	NUL	NUL	NUL	NUL	NUL	NUL	NUL	NUL	NUL	NUL	NUL	NUL	NUL	NUL	NUL	NUL
SYM																

|←——— Real 4 ———→|←——— Real 4 ———→|←——— Real 4 ———→|←——— Real 4 ———→|
|←——————— Point Value 9 ———————————————→|

BYTE	936	937	938	939	940	941	942	943	944	945	946	947	948	949	950	951
HEX	00	00	00	00	00	00	00	00	00	00	00	00	00	00	00	00
DEC	0	0	0	0	0	0	0	0	0	0	0	0	0	0	0	0
ASC	^@	^@	^@	^@	^@	^@	^@	^@	^@	^@	^@	^@	^@	^@	^@	^@
ALT	NUL	NUL	NUL	NUL	NUL	NUL	NUL	NUL	NUL	NUL	NUL	NUL	NUL	NUL	NUL	NUL
SYM																

|←——— Real 4 ———→|←——— Real 4 ———→|←——— Real 4 ———→|←——— Real 4 ———→|
|←——————— Point Value 10 ———————————————→|

BYTE	952	953	954	955	956	957	958	959	960	961	962	963	964	965	966	967
HEX	00	00	00	00	00	00	00	00	00	00	00	00	00	00	00	00
DEC	0	0	0	0	0	0	0	0	0	0	0	0	0	0	0	0
ASC	^@	^@	^@	^@	^@	^@	^@	^@	^@	^@	^@	^@	^@	^@	^@	^@
ALT	NUL	NUL	NUL	NUL	NUL	NUL	NUL	NUL	NUL	NUL	NUL	NUL	NUL	NUL	NUL	NUL
SYM																

|←——— Real 4 ———→|←——— Real 4 ———→|←——— Real 4 ———→|←——— Real 4 ———→|
|←——————— Point Value 10 ———————————→|←——— Point Value 11 ———→|

BYTE	968	969	970	971	972	973	974	975	976	977	978	979	980	981	982	983
HEX	00	00	00	00	00	00	00	00	00	00	00	00	00	00	00	00
DEC	0	0	0	0	0	0	0	0	0	0	0	0	0	0	0	0
ASC	^@	^@	^@	^@	^@	^@	^@	^@	^@	^@	^@	^@	^@	^@	^@	^@
ALT	NUL	NUL	NUL	NUL	NUL	NUL	NUL	NUL	NUL	NUL	NUL	NUL	NUL	NUL	NUL	NUL
SYM																

|←——— Real 4 ———→|←——— Real 4 ———→|←——— Real 4 ———→|←——— Real 4 ———→|

BYTE	984	985	986	987	988	989	990	991	992	993	994	995	996	997	998	999
HEX	00	00	00	00	00	00	00	00	00	00	00	00	00	00	00	00
DEC	0	0	0	0	0	0	0	0	0	0	0	0	0	0	0	0
ASC	^@	^@	^@	^@	^@	^@	^@	^@	^@	^@	^@	^@	^@	^@	^@	^@
ALT	NUL	NUL	NUL	NUL	NUL	NUL	NUL	NUL	NUL	NUL	NUL	NUL	NUL	NUL	NUL	NUL
SYM																

|←——— Real 4 ———→|←——— Real 4 ———→|←——— Real 4 ———→|←——— Real 4 ———→|
|←——— Point Value 11 ———————————→|←——— Point Value 12 ———————————→|

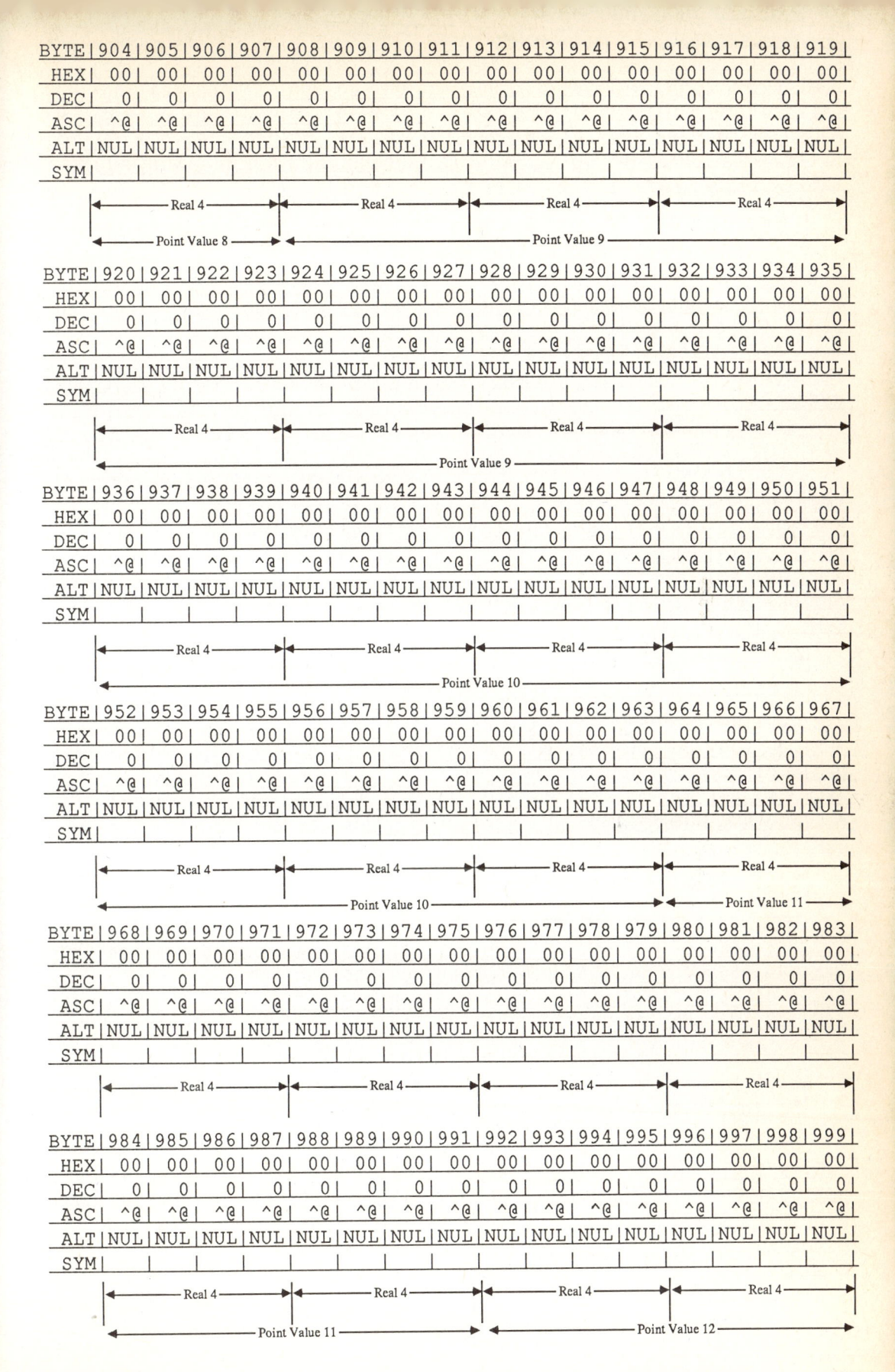

BYTE	0	1	2	3	4	5	6	7	8	9	10	11	12	13	14	15
HEX	00	00	00	00	00	00	00	00	00	00	00	00	00	00	00	00
DEC	0	0	0	0	0	0	0	0	0	0	0	0	0	0	0	0
ASC	^@	^@	^@	^@	^@	^@	^@	^@	^@	^@	^@	^@	^@	^@	^@	^@
ALT	NUL	NUL	NUL	NUL	NUL	NUL	NUL	NUL	NUL	NUL	NUL	NUL	NUL	NUL	NUL	NUL
SYM																

|←—— Real 4 ——→|←—— Real 4 ——→|←—— Real 4 ——→|←—— Real 4 ——→|

BYTE	16	17	18	19	20	21	22	23	24	25	26	27	28	29	30	31
HEX	00	00	00	00	00	00	00	00	00	00	00	00	00	00	00	00
DEC	0	0	0	0	0	0	0	0	0	0	0	0	0	0	0	0
ASC	^@	^@	^@	^@	^@	^@	^@	^@	^@	^@	^@	^@	^@	^@	^@	^@
ALT	NUL	NUL	NUL	NUL	NUL	NUL	NUL	NUL	NUL	NUL	NUL	NUL	NUL	NUL	NUL	NUL
SYM																

|←—— Real 4 ——→|←—— Real 4 ——→|←—— Real 4 ——→|←—— Real 4 ——→|
|←—— Point Value 12 ——→|←——————— Point Value 13 ———————————————→|

BYTE	32	33	34	35	36	37	38	39	40	41	42	43	44	45	46	47
HEX	00	00	00	00	00	00	00	00	00	00	00	00	00	00	00	00
DEC	0	0	0	0	0	0	0	0	0	0	0	0	0	0	0	0
ASC	^@	^@	^@	^@	^@	^@	^@	^@	^@	^@	^@	^@	^@	^@	^@	^@
ALT	NUL	NUL	NUL	NUL	NUL	NUL	NUL	NUL	NUL	NUL	NUL	NUL	NUL	NUL	NUL	NUL
SYM																

|←—— Real 4 ——→|←—— Real 4 ——→|←—— Real 4 ——→|←—— Real 4 ——→|
|←——————— Point Value 13 ———————→|

BYTE	48	49	50	51	52	53	54	55	56	57	58	59	60	61	62	63
HEX	00	00	00	00	00	00	00	00	00	00	00	00	00	00	00	00
DEC	0	0	0	0	0	0	0	0	0	0	0	0	0	0	0	0
ASC	^@	^@	^@	^@	^@	^@	^@	^@	^@	^@	^@	^@	^@	^@	^@	^@
ALT	NUL	NUL	NUL	NUL	NUL	NUL	NUL	NUL	NUL	NUL	NUL	NUL	NUL	NUL	NUL	NUL
SYM																

|←—— Real 4 ——→|←—— Real 4 ——→|←—— Real 4 ——→|←—— Real 4 ——→|
|←——————— Point Value 14 ———————→|

BYTE	64	65	66	67	68	69	70	71	72	73	74	75	76	77	78	79
HEX	00	00	00	00	00	00	00	00	00	00	00	00	00	00	00	00
DEC	0	0	0	0	0	0	0	0	0	0	0	0	0	0	0	0
ASC	^@	^@	^@	^@	^@	^@	^@	^@	^@	^@	^@	^@	^@	^@	^@	^@
ALT	NUL	NUL	NUL	NUL	NUL	NUL	NUL	NUL	NUL	NUL	NUL	NUL	NUL	NUL	NUL	NUL
SYM																

|←—— Real 4 ——→|←—— Real 4 ——→|←—— Real 4 ——→|←—— Real 4 ——→|
|←——— Point Value 14 ———→|←——— Point Value 15 ———→|

BYTE	80	81	82	83	84	85	86	87	88	89	90	91	92	93	94	95
HEX	00	00	00	00	00	00	00	00	00	00	00	00	00	00	00	00
DEC	0	0	0	0	0	0	0	0	0	0	0	0	0	0	0	0
ASC	^@	^@	^@	^@	^@	^@	^@	^@	^@	^@	^@	^@	^@	^@	^@	^@
ALT	NUL	NUL	NUL	NUL	NUL	NUL	NUL	NUL	NUL	NUL	NUL	NUL	NUL	NUL	NUL	NUL
SYM																

|←—— Real 4 ——→|←—— Real 4 ——→|←—— Real 4 ——→|←—— Real 4 ——→|

IBM PLANS+.~MD

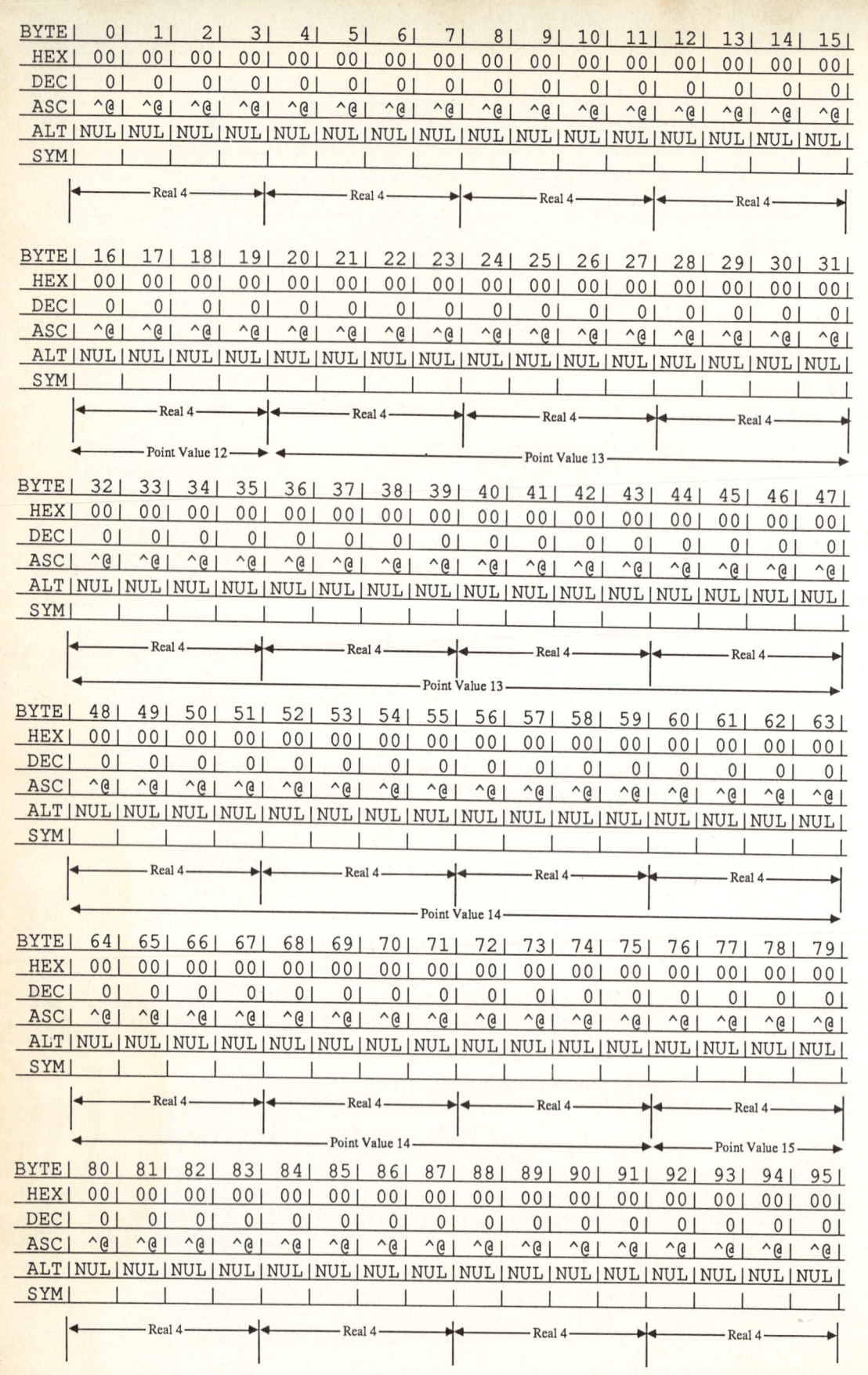

BYTE	96	97	98	99	100	101	102	103	104	105	106	107	108	109	110	111
HEX	00	00	00	00	00	00	00	00	00	00	00	00	00	00	00	00
DEC	0	0	0	0	0	0	0	0	0	0	0	0	0	0	0	0
ASC	^@	^@	^@	^@	^@	^@	^@	^@	^@	^@	^@	^@	^@	^@	^@	^@
ALT	NUL	NUL	NUL	NUL	NUL	NUL	NUL	NUL	NUL	NUL	NUL	NUL	NUL	NUL	NUL	NUL
SYM																

|←——— Real 4 ———→|←——— Real 4 ———→|←——— Real 4 ———→|←——— Real 4 ———→|
|←——————— Point Value 15 ———————→|←——————— Point Value 16 ———————→|

BYTE	112	113	114	115	116	117	118	119	120	121	122	123	124	125	126	127
HEX	00	00	00	00	00	00	00	00	00	00	00	00	00	00	00	00
DEC	0	0	0	0	0	0	0	0	0	0	0	0	0	0	0	0
ASC	^@	^@	^@	^@	^@	^@	^@	^@	^@	^@	^@	^@	^@	^@	^@	^@
ALT	NUL	NUL	NUL	NUL	NUL	NUL	NUL	NUL	NUL	NUL	NUL	NUL	NUL	NUL	NUL	NUL
SYM																

|←——— Real 4 ———→|←——— Real 4 ———→|←——— Real 4 ———→|←——— Real 4 ———→|

BYTE	128	129	130	131	132	133	134	135	136	137	138	139	140	141	142	143
HEX	00	00	00	00	00	00	00	00	00	00	00	00	00	00	00	00
DEC	0	0	0	0	0	0	0	0	0	0	0	0	0	0	0	0
ASC	^@	^@	^@	^@	^@	^@	^@	^@	^@	^@	^@	^@	^@	^@	^@	^@
ALT	NUL	NUL	NUL	NUL	NUL	NUL	NUL	NUL	NUL	NUL	NUL	NUL	NUL	NUL	NUL	NUL
SYM																

|←——— Real 4 ———→|←——— Real 4 ———→|←——— Real 4 ———→|←——— Real 4 ———→|
|←——— Point Value 16 ———→|←——————— Point Value 17 ———————————→

BYTE	144	145	146	147	148	149	150	151	152	153	154	155	156	157	158	159
HEX	00	00	00	00	00	00	00	00	00	00	00	00	00	00	00	00
DEC	0	0	0	0	0	0	0	0	0	0	0	0	0	0	0	0
ASC	^@	^@	^@	^@	^@	^@	^@	^@	^@	^@	^@	^@	^@	^@	^@	^@
ALT	NUL	NUL	NUL	NUL	NUL	NUL	NUL	NUL	NUL	NUL	NUL	NUL	NUL	NUL	NUL	NUL
SYM																

|←——— Real 4 ———→|←——— Real 4 ———→|←——— Real 4 ———→|←——— Real 4 ———→|
|←————————————— Point Value 17 —————————————→|

BYTE	160	161	162	163	164	165	166	167	168	169	170	171	172	173	174	175
HEX	00	00	00	00	00	00	00	00	00	00	00	00	00	00	00	00
DEC	0	0	0	0	0	0	0	0	0	0	0	0	0	0	0	0
ASC	^@	^@	^@	^@	^@	^@	^@	^@	^@	^@	^@	^@	^@	^@	^@	^@
ALT	NUL	NUL	NUL	NUL	NUL	NUL	NUL	NUL	NUL	NUL	NUL	NUL	NUL	NUL	NUL	NUL
SYM																

|←——— Real 4 ———→|←——— Real 4 ———→|←——— Real 4 ———→|←——— Real 4 ———→|
|←——————————— Point Value 18 ———————————→|

BYTE	176	177	178	179	180	181	182	183	184	185	186	187	188	189	190	191
HEX	00	00	00	00	00	00	00	00	00	00	00	00	00	00	00	00
DEC	0	0	0	0	0	0	0	0	0	0	0	0	0	0	0	0
ASC	^@	^@	^@	^@	^@	^@	^@	^@	^@	^@	^@	^@	^@	^@	^@	^@
ALT	NUL	NUL	NUL	NUL	NUL	NUL	NUL	NUL	NUL	NUL	NUL	NUL	NUL	NUL	NUL	NUL
SYM																

|←——— Real 4 ———→|←——— Real 4 ———→|←——— Real 4 ———→|←——— Real 4 ———→|
|←——————— Point Value 18 ———————→|←——— Point Value 19 ———→|

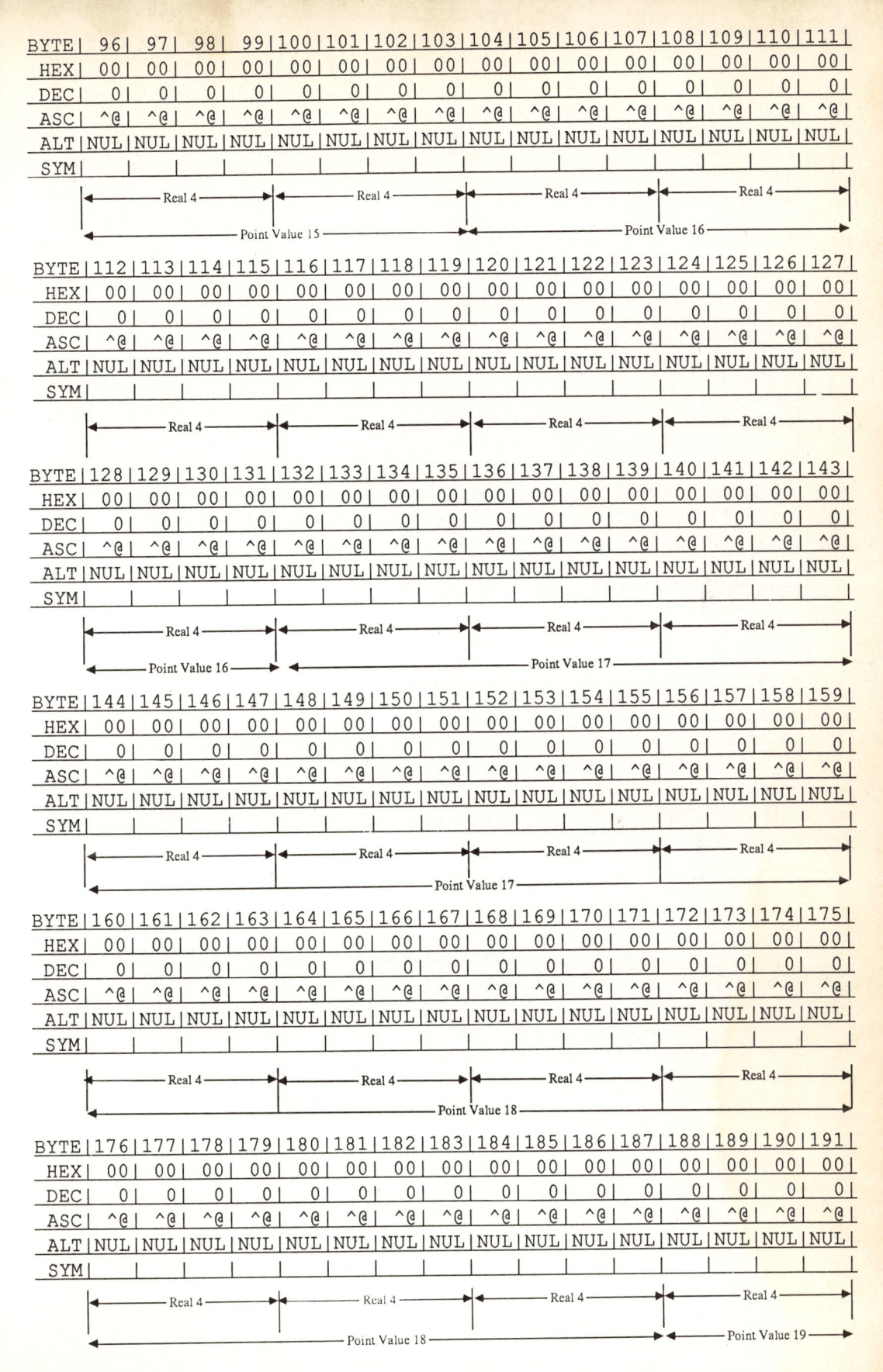

```
BYTE|192|193|194|195|196|197|198|199|200|201|202|203|204|205|206|207|
 HEX| 00| 00| 00| 00| 00| 00| 00| 00| 00| 00| 00| 00| 00| 00| 00| 00|
 DEC|  0|  0|  0|  0|  0|  0|  0|  0|  0|  0|  0|  0|  0|  0|  0|  0|
 ASC| ^@| ^@| ^@| ^@| ^@| ^@| ^@| ^@| ^@| ^@| ^@| ^@| ^@| ^@| ^@| ^@|
 ALT|NUL|NUL|NUL|NUL|NUL|NUL|NUL|NUL|NUL|NUL|NUL|NUL|NUL|NUL|NUL|NUL|
 SYM|   |   |   |   |   |   |   |   |   |   |   |   |   |   |   |   |
     |◄──── Real 4 ────►|◄──── Real 4 ────►|◄──── Real 4 ────►|◄──── Real 4 ────►|
     |◄──────────────────────── Point Value 19 ────────────────────────►|

BYTE|208|209|210|211|212|213|214|215|216|217|218|219|220|221|222|223|
 HEX| 00| 00| 00| 00| 00| 00| 00| 00| 00| 00| 00| 00| 00| 00| 00| 00|
 DEC|  0|  0|  0|  0|  0|  0|  0|  0|  0|  0|  0|  0|  0|  0|  0|  0|
 ASC| ^@| ^@| ^@| ^@| ^@| ^@| ^@| ^@| ^@| ^@| ^@| ^@| ^@| ^@| ^@| ^@|
 ALT|NUL|NUL|NUL|NUL|NUL|NUL|NUL|NUL|NUL|NUL|NUL|NUL|NUL|NUL|NUL|NUL|
 SYM|   |   |   |   |   |   |   |   |   |   |   |   |   |   |   |   |
     |◄──── Real 4 ────►|◄──── Real 4 ────►|◄──── Real 4 ────►|◄──── Real 4 ────►|
     |◄──────── Point Value 19 ────────►|◄──────── Point Value 20 ────────►|

BYTE|224|225|226|227|228|229|230|231|232|233|234|235|236|237|238|239|
 HEX| 00| 00| 00| 00| 00| 00| 00| 00| 00| 00| 00| 00| 00| 00| 00| 00|
 DEC|  0|  0|  0|  0|  0|  0|  0|  0|  0|  0|  0|  0|  0|  0|  0|  0|
 ASC| ^@| ^@| ^@| ^@| ^@| ^@| ^@| ^@| ^@| ^@| ^@| ^@| ^@| ^@| ^@| ^@|
 ALT|NUL|NUL|NUL|NUL|NUL|NUL|NUL|NUL|NUL|NUL|NUL|NUL|NUL|NUL|NUL|NUL|
 SYM|   |   |   |   |   |   |   |   |   |   |   |   |   |   |   |   |
     |◄──── Real 4 ────►|◄──── Real 4 ────►|◄──── Real 4 ────►|◄──── Real 4 ────►|
     |◄──────────────────────── Point Value 20 ────────────────────────►|

BYTE|240|241|242|243|244|245|246|247|248|249|250|251|252|253|254|255|
 HEX| 00| 00| 00| 00| 01| 20| 00| 00| 00| 00| 01| 20| 00| 00| 00| 0C|
 DEC|  0|  0|  0|  0|  1| 32|  0|  0|  0|  0|  1| 32|  0|  0|  0|  0|
 ASC| ^@| ^@| ^@| ^@| ^A| ^`| ^@| ^@| ^@| ^@| ^A| ^`| ^@| ^@| ^@| ^@|
 ALT|NUL|NUL|NUL|NUL|SOH|SPC|NUL|NUL|NUL|NUL|SOH|SPC|NUL|NUL|NUL|NUL|
 SYM|   |   |   |   |   |   |   |   |   |   |   |   |   |   |   |   |
     |◄──── Real 4 ────►|◄──── Point Label 1 ────►|◄──── Point Label 2 ────►|
     |◄── Point Value 20 ──►|

BYTE|256|257|258|259|260|261|262|263|264|265|266|267|268|269|270|271|
 HEX| 01| 20| 00| 00| 00| 00| 01| 20| 00| 00| 00| 00| 01| 20| 00| 00|
 DEC|  1| 32|  0|  0|  0|  0|  1| 32|  0|  0|  0|  0|  1| 32|  0|  0|
 ASC| ^A| ^`| ^@| ^@| ^@| ^@| ^A| ^`| ^@| ^@| ^@| ^@| ^A| ^`| ^@| ^@|
 ALT|SOH|SPC|NUL|NUL|NUL|NUL|SOH|SPC|NUL|NUL|NUL|NUL|SOH|SPC|NUL|NUL|
 SYM|   |   |   |   |   |   |   |   |   |   |   |   |   |   |   |   |
     |◄──── Point Label 3 ────►|◄──── Point Label 4 ────►|◄──── Point Label 5 ────►|

BYTE|272|273|274|275|276|277|278|279|280|281|282|283|284|285|286|287|
 HEX| 00| 00| 01| 20| 00| 00| 00| 00| 01| 20| 00| 00| 00| 00| 01| 20|
 DEC|  0|  0|  1| 32|  0|  0|  0|  0|  1| 32|  0|  0|  0|  0|  1| 32|
 ASC| ^@| ^@| ^A| ^`| ^@| ^@| ^@| ^@| ^A| ^`| ^@| ^@| ^@| ^@| ^A| ^`|
 ALT|NUL|NUL|SOH|SPC|NUL|NUL|NUL|NUL|SOH|SPC|NUL|NUL|NUL|NUL|SOH|SPC|
 SYM|   |   |   |   |   |   |   |   |   |   |   |   |   |   |   |   |
     |◄──── Point Label 6 ────►|◄──── Point Label 7 ────►|
```

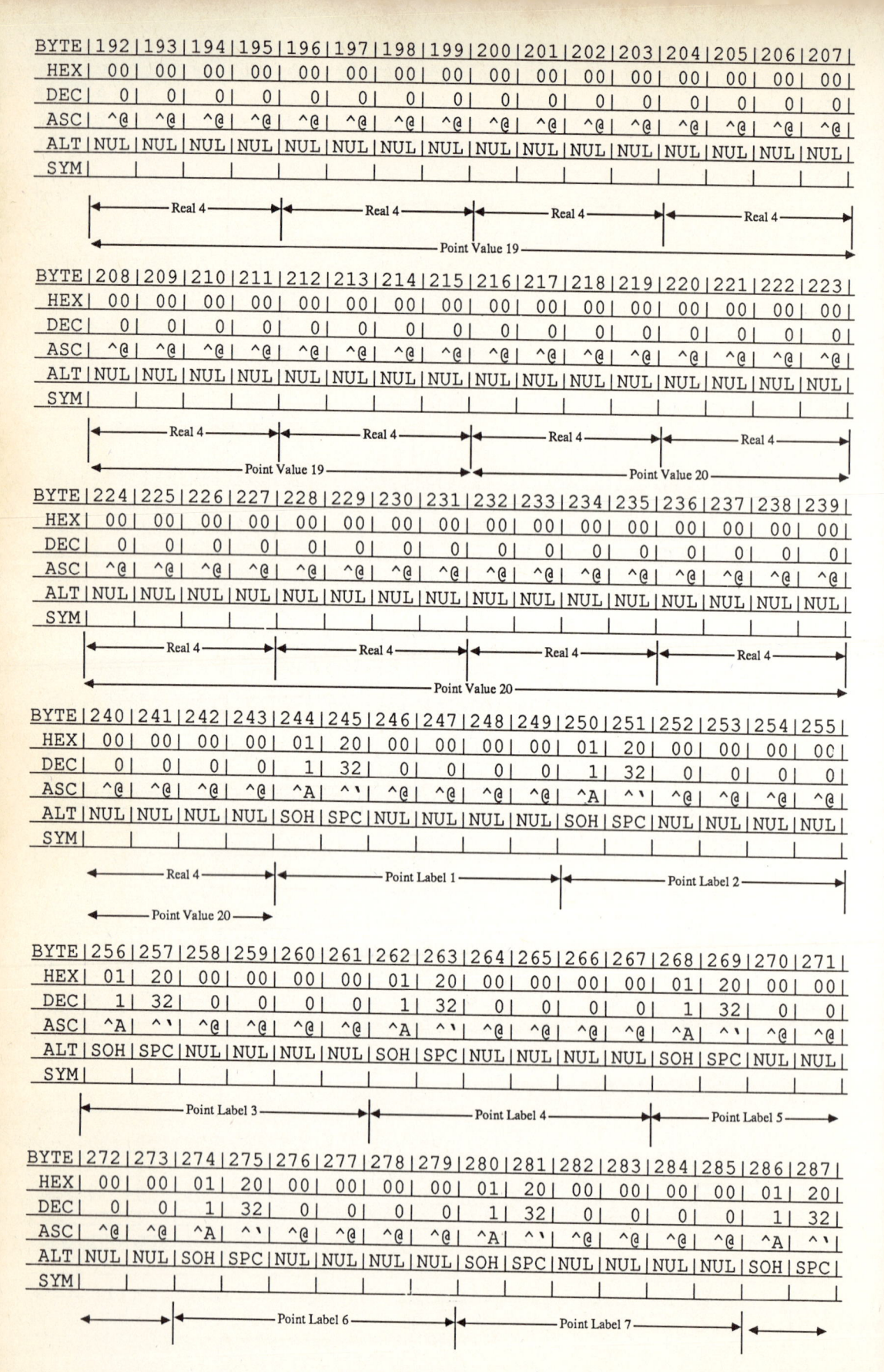

BYTE	288	289	290	291	292	293	294	295	296	297	298	299	300	301	302	303
HEX	00	00	00	00	01	20	00	00	00	00	01	20	00	00	00	00
DEC	0	0	0	0	1	32	0	0	0	0	1	32	0	0	0	0
ASC	^@	^@	^@	^@	^A	^`	^@	^@	^@	^@	^A	^`	^@	^@	^@	^@
ALT	NUL	NUL	NUL	NUL	SOH	SPC	NUL	NUL	NUL	NUL	SOH	SPC	NUL	NUL	NUL	NUL
SYM																

◄──── Point Label 8 ────►◄──── Point Label 9 ────►◄──── Point Label 10 ────►

BYTE	304	305	306	307	308	309	310	311	312	313	314	315	316	317	318	319
HEX	01	20	00	00	00	00	01	20	00	00	00	00	01	20	00	00
DEC	1	32	0	0	0	0	1	32	0	0	0	0	1	32	0	0
ASC	^A	^`	^@	^@	^@	^@	^A	^`	^@	^@	^@	^@	^A	^`	^@	^@
ALT	SOH	SPC	NUL	NUL	NUL	NUL	SOH	SPC	NUL	NUL	NUL	NUL	SOH	SPC	NUL	NUL
SYM																

◄──── Point Label 11 ────►◄──── Point Label 12 ────►◄──── Point Label 13 ────►

BYTE	320	321	322	323	324	325	326	327	328	329	330	331	332	333	334	335
HEX	00	00	01	20	00	00	00	00	01	20	00	00	00	00	01	20
DEC	0	0	1	32	0	0	0	0	1	32	0	0	0	0	1	32
ASC	^@	^@	^A	^`	^@	^@	^@	^@	^A	^`	^@	^@	^@	^@	^A	^`
ALT	NUL	NUL	SOH	SPC	NUL	NUL	NUL	NUL	SOH	SPC	NUL	NUL	NUL	NUL	SOH	SPC
SYM																

◄──►◄──── Point Label 14 ────►◄──── Point Label 15 ────►◄──►

BYTE	336	337	338	339	340	341	342	343	344	345	346	347	348	349	350	351
HEX	00	00	00	00	01	20	00	00	00	00	01	20	00	00	00	00
DEC	0	0	0	0	1	32	0	0	0	0	1	32	0	0	0	0
ASC	^@	^@	^@	^@	^A	^`	^@	^@	^@	^@	^A	^`	^@	^@	^@	^@
ALT	NUL	NUL	NUL	NUL	SOH	SPC	NUL	NUL	NUL	NUL	SOH	SPC	NUL	NUL	NUL	NUL
SYM																

◄──── Point Label 16 ────►◄──── Point Label 17 ────►◄──── Point Label 18 ────►

BYTE	352	353	354	355	356	357	358	359	360	361	362	363	364	365	366	367
HEX	01	20	00	00	00	00	01	20	00	00	00	00	01	20	00	00
DEC	1	32	0	0	0	0	1	32	0	0	0	0	1	32	0	0
ASC	^A	^`	^@	^@	^@	^@	^A	^`	^@	^@	^@	^@	^A	^`	^@	^@
ALT	SOH	SPC	NUL	NUL	NUL	NUL	SOH	SPC	NUL	NUL	NUL	NUL	SOH	SPC	NUL	NUL
SYM																

◄──── Point Label 19 ────►◄──── Point Label 20 ────►◄──── Data Set 1 ────►

BYTE	368	369	370	371	372	373	374	375	376	377	378	379	380	381	382	383
HEX	00	00	01	20	00	00	00	00	01	20	00	00	00	00	01	20
DEC	0	0	1	32	0	0	0	0	1	32	0	0	0	0	1	32
ASC	^@	^@	^A	^`	^@	^@	^@	^@	^A	^`	^@	^@	^@	^@	^A	^`
ALT	NUL	NUL	SOH	SPC	NUL	NUL	NUL	NUL	SOH	SPC	NUL	NUL	NUL	NUL	SOH	SPC
SYM																

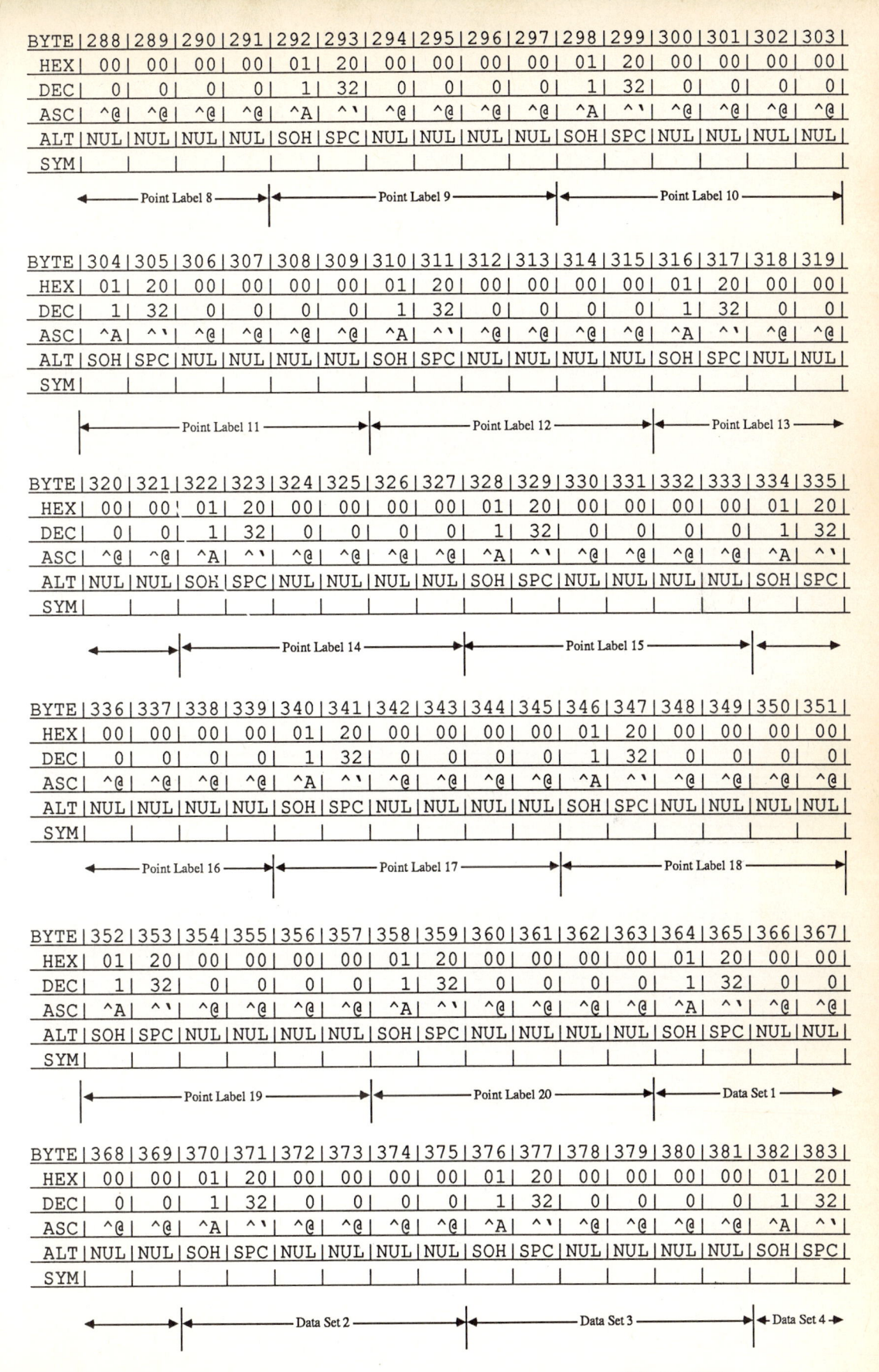

◄──►◄──── Data Set 2 ────►◄──── Data Set 3 ────►◄── Data Set 4 ──►

BYTE	384	385	386	387	388	389	390	391	392	393	394	395	396	397	398	399
HEX	00	00	00	00	01	20	00	00	00	00	01	20	00	00	00	00
DEC	0	0	0	0	1	32	0	0	0	0	1	32	0	0	0	0
ASC	^@	^@	^@	^@	^A	^`	^@	^@	^@	^@	^A	^`	^@	^@	^@	^@
ALT	NUL	NUL	NUL	NUL	SOH	SPC	NUL	NUL	NUL	NUL	SOH	SPC	NUL	NUL	NUL	NUL
SYM																

◄──── Data Set 4 ────►◄──── Data Set 5 ────►◄──── Data Set 6 ────►

BYTE	400	401	402	403	404	405	406	407	408	409	410	411	412	413	414	415
HEX	01	20	00	00	00	00	00	00	00	00	00	00	00	00	00	00
DEC	1	32	0	0	0	0	0	0	0	0	0	0	0	0	0	0
ASC	^A	^`	^@	^@	^@	^@	^@	^@	^@	^@	^@	^@	^@	^@	^@	^@
ALT	SOH	SPC	NUL	NUL	NUL	NUL	NUL	NUL	NUL	NUL	NUL	NUL	NUL	NUL	NUL	NUL
SYM																

◄──── Data Set 7 ────► | Data Set Points 1 | Data Set Points 2 | Data Set Points 3 | Data Set Points 4 | Data Set Points 5 |

BYTE	416	417	418	419	420	421	422	423	424	425	426	427	428	429	430	431
HEX	00	00	00	00	00	00	00	00	00	00	00	00	00	00	00	00
DEC	0	0	0	0	0	0	0	0	0	0	0	0	0	0	0	0
ASC	^@	^@	^@	^@	^@	^@	^@	^@	^@	^@	^@	^@	^@	^@	^@	^@
ALT	NUL	NUL	NUL	NUL	NUL	NUL	NUL	NUL	NUL	NUL	NUL	NUL	NUL	NUL	NUL	NUL
SYM																

| Data Set Points 6 | Data Set Points 7 | ◄──── Data Range 1 ────► | ◄──── Data Range 2 ────► |

BYTE	432	433	434	435	436	437	438	439	440	441	442	443	444	445	446	447
HEX	00	00	00	00	00	00	00	00	00	00	00	00	00	00	00	00
DEC	0	0	0	0	0	0	0	0	0	0	0	0	0	0	0	0
ASC	^@	^@	^@	^@	^@	^@	^@	^@	^@	^@	^@	^@	^@	^@	^@	^@
ALT	NUL	NUL	NUL	NUL	NUL	NUL	NUL	NUL	NUL	NUL	NUL	NUL	NUL	NUL	NUL	NUL
SYM																

◄──── Data Range 2 ────►◄──── Data Range 3 ────►◄──── Data Range 4 ────►

BYTE	448	449	450	451	452	453	454	455	456	457	458	459	460	461	462	463
HEX	00	00	00	00	00	00	00	00	00	00	00	00	00	00	00	00
DEC	0	0	0	0	0	0	0	0	0	0	0	0	0	0	0	0
ASC	^@	^@	^@	^@	^@	^@	^@	^@	^@	^@	^@	^@	^@	^@	^@	^@
ALT	NUL	NUL	NUL	NUL	NUL	NUL	NUL	NUL	NUL	NUL	NUL	NUL	NUL	NUL	NUL	NUL
SYM																

◄──── Data Range 4 ────►◄──── Data Range 5 ────►◄──── Data Range 6 ────►

BYTE	464	465	466	467	468	469	470	471	472	473	474	475	476	477	478	479
HEX	00	00	00	00	00	00	00	00	00	00	00	00	00	00	00	00
DEC	0	0	0	0	0	0	0	0	0	0	0	0	0	0	0	0
ASC	^@	^@	^@	^@	^@	^@	^@	^@	^@	^@	^@	^@	^@	^@	^@	^@
ALT	NUL	NUL	NUL	NUL	NUL	NUL	NUL	NUL	NUL	NUL	NUL	NUL	NUL	NUL	NUL	NUL
SYM																

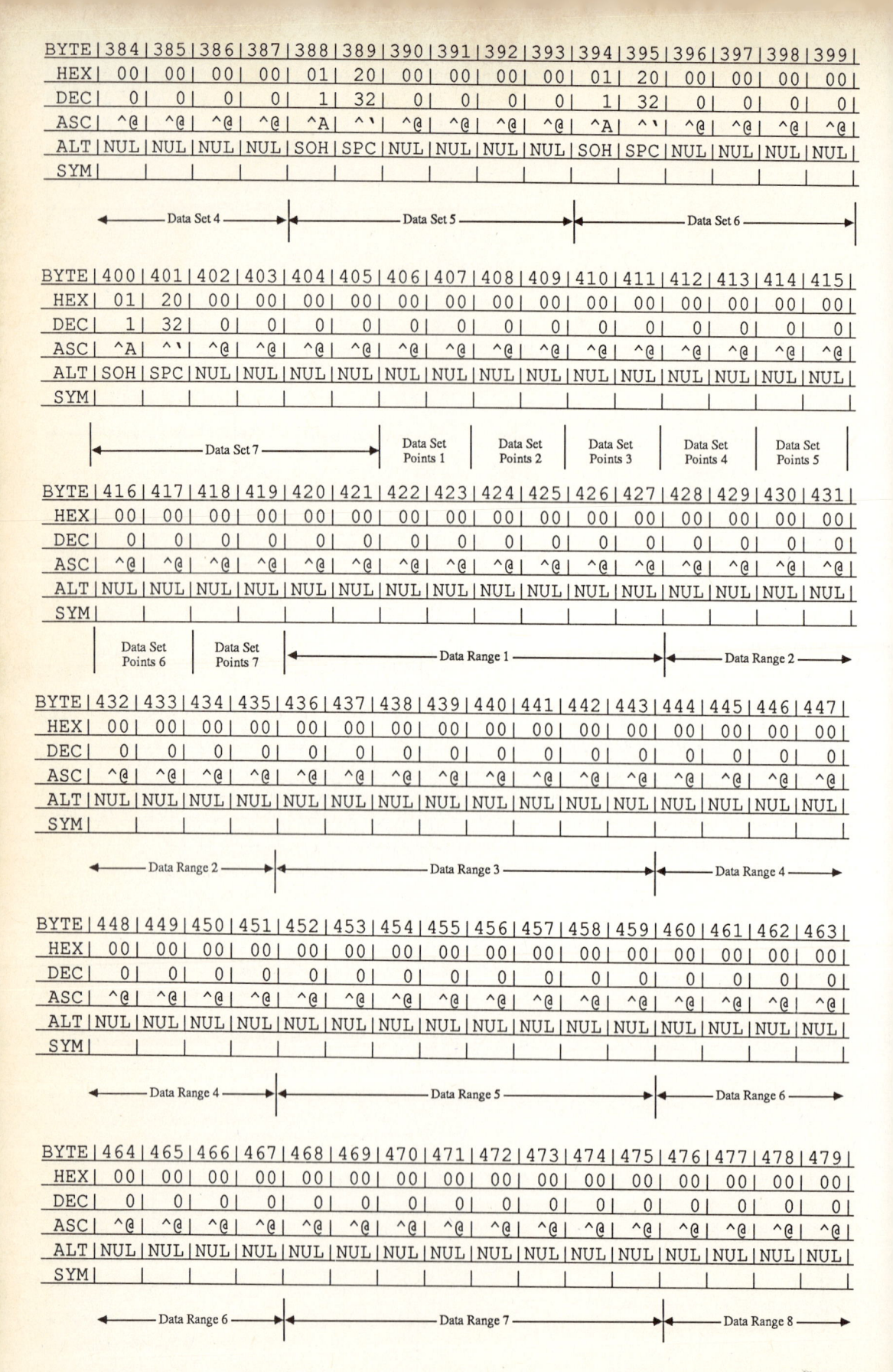

◄──── Data Range 6 ────►◄──── Data Range 7 ────►◄──── Data Range 8 ────►

BYTE	480	481	482	483	484	485	486	487	488	489	490	491	492	493	494	495
HEX	00	00	00	00	20	20	20	20	20	20	20	20	20	20	20	20
DEC	0	0	0	0	32	32	32	32	32	32	32	32	32	32	32	32
ASC	^@	^@	^@	^@	^`	^`	^`	^`	^`	^`	^`	^`	^`	^`	^`	^`
ALT	NUL	NUL	NUL	NUL	SPC	SPC	SPC	SPC	SPC	SPC	SPC	SPC	SPC	SPC	SPC	SPC
SYM																

←—— Data Range 8 ——→|←———————— PUTGDAT (Reserved) ————————→

BYTE	496	497	498	499	500	501	502	503	504	505	506	507	508	509	510	511
HEX	20	20	20	20	20	20	20	20	20	20	20	20	20	20	20	20
DEC	32	32	32	32	32	32	32	32	32	32	32	32	32	32	32	32
ASC	^`	^`	^`	^`	^`	^`	^`	^`	^`	^`	^`	^`	^`	^`	^`	^`
ALT	SPC	SPC	SPC	SPC	SPC	SPC	SPC	SPC	SPC	SPC	SPC	SPC	SPC	SPC	SPC	SPC
SYM																

←————————— PUTGDAT (Reserved) —————————→

BYTE	512	513	514	515	516	517	518	519	520	521	522	523	524	525	526	527
HEX	20	00	00	00	00	00	00	00	00	00	00	00	01	00	01	00
DEC	32	0	0	0	0	0	0	0	0	0	0	0	1	0	1	0
ASC	^`	^@	^@	^@	^@	^@	^@	^@	^@	^@	^@	^@	^A	^@	^A	^@
ALT	SPC	NUL	NUL	NUL	NUL	NUL	NUL	NUL	NUL	NUL	NUL	NUL	SOH	NUL	SOH	NUL
SYM																

| | 1 | 2 | 3 | 4 | 5 | First Calc. on Screen | Current Calculation |

←——————————— Sort Range ———————————→

BYTE	528	529	530	531	532	533	534	535	536	537	538	539	540	541	542	543
HEX	06	00	00	00	09	00	19	79	01	C0	00	01	2A	09	00	1A
DEC	6	0	0	0	9	0	25	121	1	192	0	1	42	9	0	26
ASC	^F	^@	^@	^@	^I	^@	^Y		^A	192	^@	^A		^I	^@	^Z
ALT	ACK	NUL	NUL	NUL	HT	NUL	EM		SOH	192	NUL	SOH		HT	NUL	SUB
SYM								y					*			

| Last Calc. on Screen | Highest Calc. Defined | ←——— Graph Record 1 ———→ | ←— Graph Record 2 —→ |

BYTE	544	545	546	547	548	549	550	551	552	553	554	555	556	557	558	559
HEX	79	01	C0	00	01	2A	09	00	1B	79	01	C0	00	01	2A	09
DEC	121	1	192	0	1	42	9	0	27	121	1	192	0	1	42	9
ASC		^A	192	^@	^A		^I	^@	^[		^A	192	^@	^A		^I
ALT		SOH	192	NUL	SOH		HT	NUL	ESC		SOH	192	NUL	SOH		HT
SYM	y				*					y					*	

←——— Graph Record 2 ———→|← Length of Row →|← Row # →|← # Cells →|← Length of Text in Calculation →|←
←——————————— Graph Record 3 ———————————→

BYTE	560	561	562	563	564	565	566	567	568	569	570	571	572	573	574	575
HEX	00	1C	79	01	C0	00	01	2A	09	00	1D	79	01	C0	00	01
DEC	0	28	121	1	192	0	1	42	9	0	29	121	1	192	0	1
ASC	^@	^\		^A	192	^@	^A		^I	^@	^]		^A	192	^@	^A
ALT	NUL	FS		SOH	192	NUL	SOH		HT	NUL	GS		SOH	192	NUL	SOH
SYM			y				*					y				

←——— Graph Record 4 ———→|←——— Graph Record 5 ———→

IBM PLANS+.~MD 251

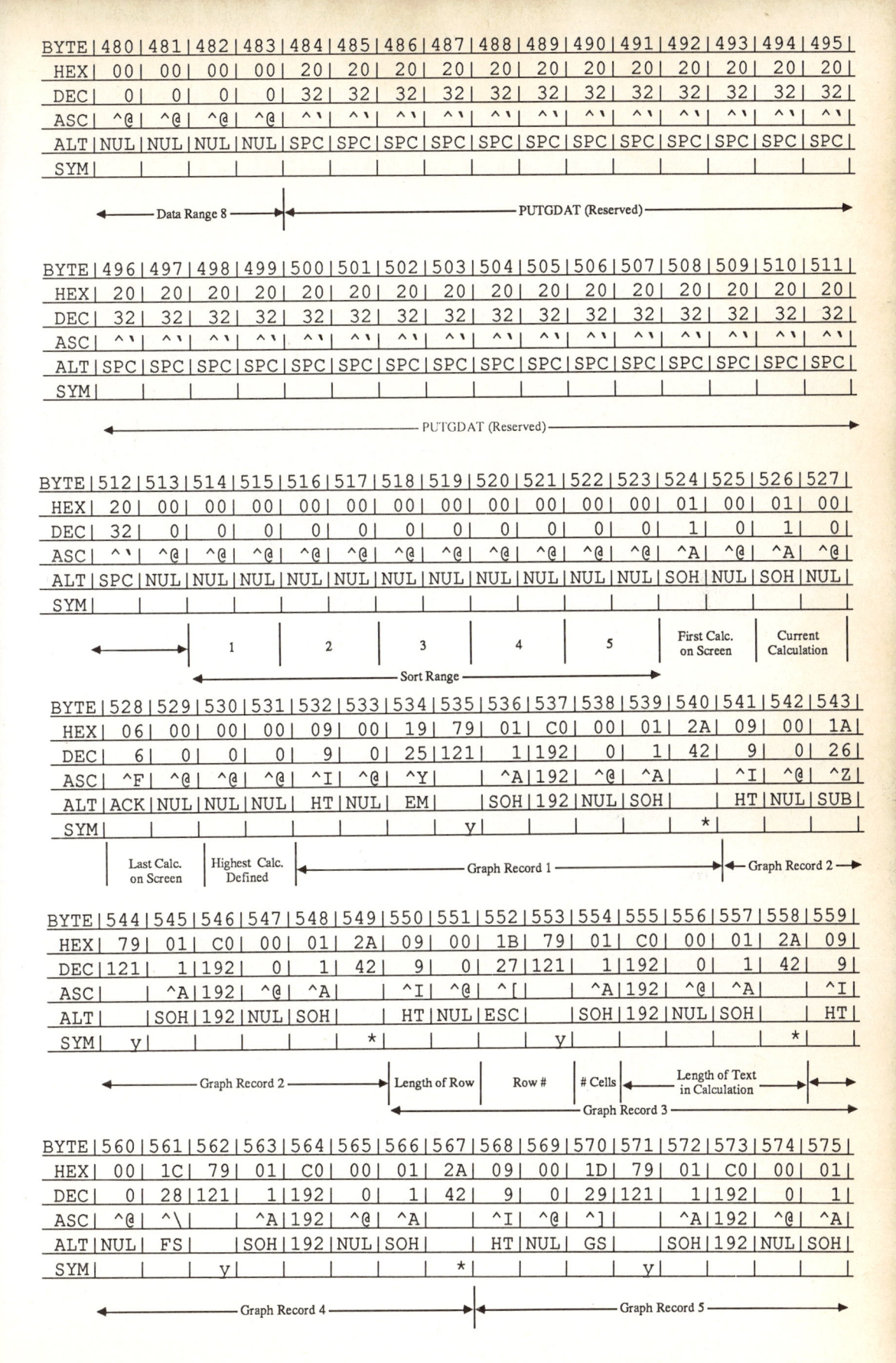

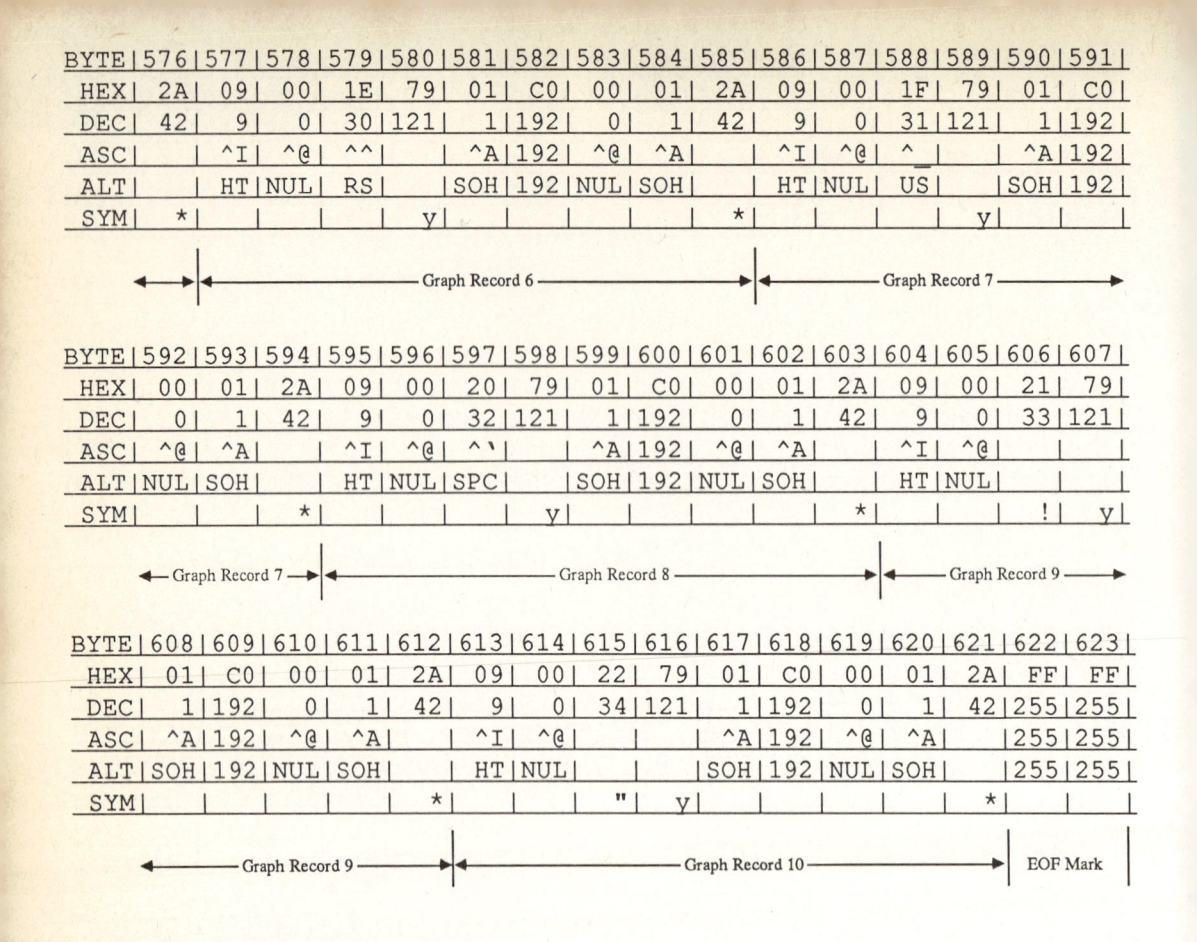

BYTE	576	577	578	579	580	581	582	583	584	585	586	587	588	589	590	591
HEX	2A	09	00	1E	79	01	C0	00	01	2A	09	00	1F	79	01	C0
DEC	42	9	0	30	121	1	192	0	1	42	9	0	31	121	1	192
ASC		^I	^@	^^		^A	192	^@	^A		^I	^@	^_		^A	192
ALT		HT	NUL	RS		SOH	192	NUL	SOH		HT	NUL	US		SOH	192
SYM	*				y					*				y		

←——→|←———————— Graph Record 6 ————————→|←———————— Graph Record 7 ————————→

BYTE	592	593	594	595	596	597	598	599	600	601	602	603	604	605	606	607
HEX	00	01	2A	09	00	20	79	01	C0	00	01	2A	09	00	21	79
DEC	0	1	42	9	0	32	121	1	192	0	1	42	9	0	33	121
ASC	^@	^A		^I	^@	^`		^A	192	^@	^A		^I	^@		
ALT	NUL	SOH		HT	NUL	SPC		SOH	192	NUL	SOH		HT	NUL		
SYM			*				y					*			!	y

←— Graph Record 7 —→|←———————— Graph Record 8 ————————→|←— Graph Record 9 —→

BYTE	608	609	610	611	612	613	614	615	616	617	618	619	620	621	622	623
HEX	01	C0	00	01	2A	09	00	22	79	01	C0	00	01	2A	FF	FF
DEC	1	192	0	1	42	9	0	34	121	1	192	0	1	42	255	255
ASC	^A	192	^@	^A		^I	^@		^A	192	^@	^A			255	255
ALT	SOH	192	NUL	SOH		HT	NUL		SOH	192	NUL	SOH			255	255
SYM					*			"	y					*		

←—— Graph Record 9 ——→|←———————— Graph Record 10 ————————→| EOF Mark

End of Plans+.~MD File

252 IBM PLANS+.~MD

Sample Spreadsheet as an IBM Plans+.~MF File

BYTE	0	1	2	3	4	5	6	7	8	9	10	11	12	13	14	15
HEX	28	00	0A	00	04	84	00	84	00	84	00	80	00	1A	50	41
DEC	40	0	10	0	4	132	0	132	0	132	0	128	0	26	80	65
ASC	(	^@	^J	^@	^D	132	^@	132	^@	132	^@	128	^@	^Z		
ALT		NUL	LF	NUL	EOT	132	NUL	132	NUL	132	NUL	128	NUL	SUB		
SYM	(														P	A

Length Row | Row # | # Cols. This Row | Flag Null Cell | Flag Null Cell | Flag Null Cell | Flags Text Cell | Text Length | ←Text→
← Row Header →

BYTE	16	17	18	19	20	21	22	23	24	25	26	27	28	29	30	31
HEX	59	4D	45	4E	54	20	41	4E	41	4C	59	53	49	53	20	57
DEC	89	77	69	78	84	32	65	78	65	76	89	83	73	83	32	87
ASC						^\									^\	
ALT						SPC									SPC	
SYM	Y	M	E	N	T		A	N	A	L	Y	S	I	S		W

←————————————————— Text —————————————————→

BYTE	32	33	34	35	36	37	38	39	40	41	42	43	44	45	46	47
HEX	4F	52	4B	53	48	45	45	54	3E	00	14	00	06	84	00	84
DEC	79	82	75	83	72	69	69	84	62	0	20	0	6	132	0	132
ASC										^@	^T	^@	^F	132	^@	132
ALT										NUL	DC4	NUL	ACK	132	NUL	132
SYM	O	R	K	S	H	E	E	T	>							

←————— Text —————→ | Length Row | Row # | # Cols. This Row | Flag Null Cell | Flag Null Cell
← Row Header →

BYTE	48	49	50	51	52	53	54	55	56	57	58	59	60	61	62	63
HEX	00	84	00	80	00	0E	3D	3D	3D	3D	3D	3D	3D	3D	3D	3D
DEC	0	132	0	128	0	14	61	61	61	61	61	61	61	61	61	61
ASC	^@	132	^@	128	^@	^N										
ALT	NUL	132	NUL	128	NUL	SO										
SYM							=	=	=	=	=	=	=	=	=	=

← Flag Null Cell | Flag Text Cell | Length Text | ←————————— Text —————————→

BYTE	64	65	66	67	68	69	70	71	72	73	74	75	76	77	78	79
HEX	3D	3D	3D	3D	80	00	0E	3D	3D	3D	3D	3D	3D	3D	3D	3D
DEC	61	61	61	61	128	0	14	61	61	61	61	61	61	61	61	61
ASC					128	^@	^N									
ALT					128	NUL	SO									
SYM	=	=	=	=				=	=	=	=	=	=	=	=	=

←— Text —→ | Text Cell | Length Text | ←————— Text —————→

BYTE	80	81	82	83	84	85	86	87	88	89	90	91	92	93	94	95
HEX	3D	3D	3D	3D	3D	80	00	0E	3D	3D	3D	3D	3D	3D	3D	3D
DEC	61	61	61	61	61	128	0	14	61	61	61	61	61	61	61	61
ASC						128	^@	^N								
ALT						128	NUL	SO								
SYM	=	=	=	=	=				=	=	=	=	=	=	=	=

←——— Text ———→ | Text Cell | Length Text | ←——————— Text ———————→

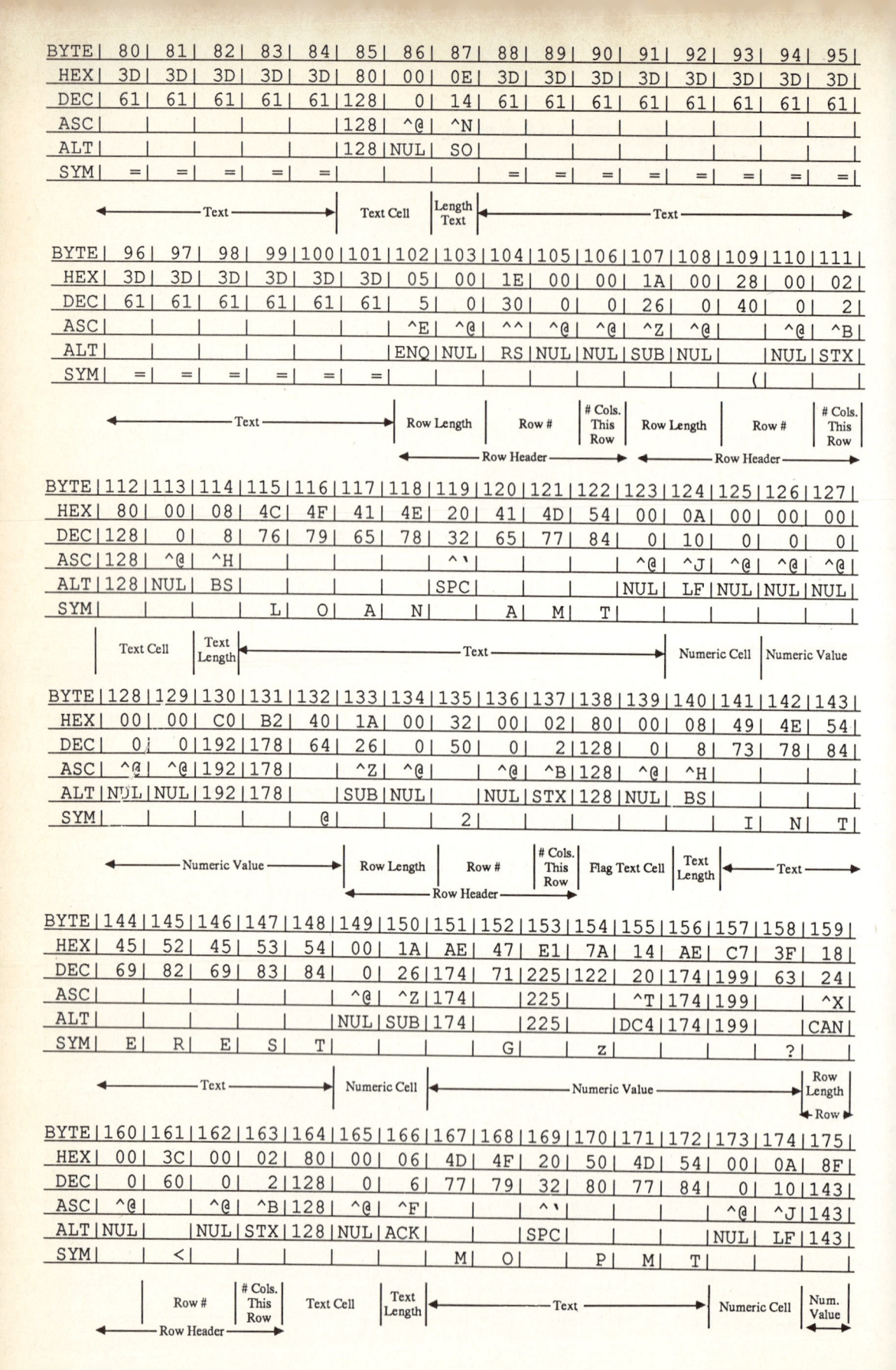

BYTE	96	97	98	99	100	101	102	103	104	105	106	107	108	109	110	111
HEX	3D	3D	3D	3D	3D	3D	05	00	1E	00	00	1A	00	28	00	02
DEC	61	61	61	61	61	61	5	0	30	0	0	26	0	40	0	2
ASC							^E	^@	^^	^@	^@	^Z	^@		^@	^B
ALT							ENQ	NUL	RS	NUL	NUL	SUB	NUL		NUL	STX
SYM	=	=	=	=	=	=								(		

←——— Text ———→ | Row Length | Row # | # Cols. This Row | Row Length | Row # | # Cols. This Row |
                 ←——— Row Header ———→   ←——— Row Header ———→

BYTE	112	113	114	115	116	117	118	119	120	121	122	123	124	125	126	127
HEX	80	00	08	4C	4F	41	4E	20	41	4D	54	00	0A	00	00	00
DEC	128	0	8	76	79	65	78	32	65	77	84	0	10	0	0	0
ASC	128	^@	^H					^'				^@	^J	^@	^@	^@
ALT	128	NUL	BS					SPC				NUL	LF	NUL	NUL	NUL
SYM				L	O	A	N		A	M	T					

| Text Cell | Text Length | ←——————— Text ———————→ | Numeric Cell | Numeric Value |

BYTE	128	129	130	131	132	133	134	135	136	137	138	139	140	141	142	143
HEX	00	00	C0	B2	40	1A	00	32	00	02	80	00	08	49	4E	54
DEC	0	0	192	178	64	26	0	50	0	2	128	0	8	73	78	84
ASC	^@	^@	192	178		^Z	^@		^@	^B	128	^@	^H			
ALT	NUL	NUL	192	178		SUB	NUL		NUL	STX	128	NUL	BS			
SYM					@			2						I	N	T

←——— Numeric Value ———→ | Row Length | Row # | # Cols. This Row | Flag Text Cell | Text Length | ←——— Text ———→
                          ←——— Row Header ———→

BYTE	144	145	146	147	148	149	150	151	152	153	154	155	156	157	158	159
HEX	45	52	45	53	54	00	1A	AE	47	E1	7A	14	AE	C7	3F	18
DEC	69	82	69	83	84	0	26	174	71	225	122	20	174	199	63	24
ASC						^@	^Z	174		225		^T	174	199		^X
ALT						NUL	SUB	174		225		DC4	174	199		CAN
SYM	E	R	E	S	T				G		z				?	

←——— Text ———→ | Numeric Cell | ←——— Numeric Value ———→ | Row Length |
                                                            ←— Row —→

BYTE	160	161	162	163	164	165	166	167	168	169	170	171	172	173	174	175
HEX	00	3C	00	02	80	00	06	4D	4F	20	50	4D	54	00	0A	8F
DEC	0	60	0	2	128	0	6	77	79	32	80	77	84	0	10	143
ASC	^@		^@	^B	128	^@	^F			^'				^@	^J	143
ALT	NUL		NUL	STX	128	NUL	ACK			SPC				NUL	LF	143
SYM		<						M	O		P	M	T			

| Row # | # Cols. This Row | Text Cell | Text Length | ←——— Text ———→ | Numeric Cell | Num. Value |
←— Row Header —→

254   IBM PLANS+.~MF

BYTE	176	177	178	179	180	181	182	183	184	185	186	187	188	189	190	191
HEX	C2	F5	28	5C	D7	65	40	19	00	46	00	02	80	00	07	50
DEC	194	245	40	92	215	101	64	25	0	70	0	2	128	0	7	80
ASC	194	245			215			^Y	^@		^@	^B	128	^@	^G	
ALT	194	245			215			EM	NUL		NUL	STX	128	NUL	BEL	
SYM			(	\		e	@			F						P

```
<──────────── Numeric Value ────────────>│ Row Length │ Row # │ # Cols. This Row │ Text Cell │ Text Length │──>
                                         <──────── Row Header ────────>
```

IBM PLANS +.~MF

Gettysburg Address as a WordStar File

BYTE	0	1	2	3	4	5	6	7	8	9	10	11	12	13	14	15
HEX	20	20	20	20	20	20	20	20	20	20	20	20	20	20	20	20
DEC	32	32	32	32	32	32	32	32	32	32	32	32	32	32	32	32
ASC	^`	^`	^`	^`	^`	^`	^`	^`	^`	^`	^`	^`	^`	^`	^`	^`
ALT	SPC	SPC	SPC	SPC	SPC	SPC	SPC	SPC	SPC	SPC	SPC	SPC	SPC	SPC	SPC	SPC
SYM																

← File Padded With Spaces By Centering Command →
← Document Begins

BYTE	16	17	18	19	20	21	22	23	24	25	26	27	28	29	30	31
HEX	2E	48	45	20	4C	69	6E	63	6F	6C	6E	27	73	20	47	65
DEC	46	72	69	32	76	105	110	99	111	108	110	39	115	32	71	101
ASC				^`										^`		
ALT				SPC										SPC		
SYM	.	H	E		L	i	n	c	o	l	n	'	s		G	e

← Header → ← Header Text →

BYTE	32	33	34	35	36	37	38	39	40	41	42	43	44	45	46	47
HEX	74	74	79	73	62	75	72	67	20	41	64	64	72	65	73	73
DEC	116	116	121	115	98	117	114	103	32	65	100	100	114	101	115	115
ASC									^`							
ALT									SPC							
SYM	t	t	y	s	b	u	r	g		A	d	d	r	e	s	s

← Header Text →

BYTE	48	49	50	51	52	53	54	55	56	57	58	59	60	61	62	63
HEX	0D	0A	0D	0A	20	20	20	20	20	20	20	20	20	20	20	20
DEC	13	10	13	10	32	32	32	32	32	32	32	32	32	32	32	32
ASC	^M	^J	^M	^J	^`	^`	^`	^`	^`	^`	^`	^`	^`	^`	^`	^`
ALT	CR	LF	CR	LF	SPC	SPC	SPC	SPC	SPC	SPC	SPC	SPC	SPC	SPC	SPC	SPC
SYM																

| Newline | Newline | ← Space-Padded To Center →

BYTE	64	65	66	67	68	69	70	71	72	73	74	75	76	77	78	79
HEX	20	20	20	20	20	20	20	20	20	02	54	68	65	20	47	65
DEC	32	32	32	32	32	32	32	32	32	2	84	104	101	32	71	101
ASC	^`	^`	^`	^`	^`	^`	^`	^`	^`	^B				^`		
ALT	SPC	SPC	SPC	SPC	SPC	SPC	SPC	SPC	SPC	STX				SPC		
SYM											T	h	e		G	e

← Space-Padded to Center → | Bold Face Toggle |

256 WORDSTAR

BYTE	80	81	82	83	84	85	86	87	88	89	90	91	92	93	94	95
HEX	74	74	79	73	62	75	72	67	20	41	64	64	72	65	73	73
DEC	116	116	121	115	98	117	114	103	32	65	100	100	114	101	115	115
ASC								^'								
ALT								SPC								
SYM	t	t	y	s	b	u	r	g		A	d	d	r	e	s	s

BYTE	96	97	98	99	100	101	102	103	104	105	106	107	108	109	110	111
HEX	02	0D	0A	0D	0A	46	6F	75	72	73	63	6F	72	E5	A0	20
DEC	2	13	10	13	10	70	111	117	114	115	99	111	114	229	160	32
ASC	^B	^M	^J	^M	^J									229	160	^'
ALT	STX	CR	LF	CR	LF									229	160	SPC
SYM						F	o	u	r	s	c	o	r			

| Bold Face Toggle | Newline | Newline | ◄─────────── Text ───────────► | HIBIT E | Phantom Space |

BYTE	112	113	114	115	116	117	118	119	120	121	122	123	124	125	126	127
HEX	61	6E	E4	20	73	65	76	65	EE	20	79	65	61	72	F3	20
DEC	97	110	228	32	115	101	118	101	238	32	121	101	97	114	243	32
ASC			228	^'					238	^'					243	^'
ALT			228	SPC					238	SPC					243	SPC
SYM	a	n			s	e	v	e			y	e	a	r		

d   n   s

BYTE	128	129	130	131	132	133	134	135	136	137	138	139	140	141	142	143
HEX	61	67	EF	20	6F	75	F2	20	66	61	74	68	65	72	F3	20
DEC	97	103	239	32	111	117	242	32	102	97	116	104	101	114	243	32
ASC			239	^'			242	^'							243	^'
ALT			239	SPC			242	SPC							243	SPC
SYM	a	g			o	u			f	a	t	h	e	r		

o   r   s

BYTE	144	145	146	147	148	149	150	151	152	153	154	155	156	157	158	159
HEX	62	72	6F	75	67	68	F4	20	66	6F	72	74	E8	20	6F	EE
DEC	98	114	111	117	103	104	244	32	102	111	114	116	232	32	111	238
ASC							244	^'					232	^'		238
ALT							244	SPC					232	SPC		238
SYM	b	r	o	u	g	h			f	o	r	t			o	

t   h   n

BYTE	160	161	162	163	164	165	166	167	168	169	170	171	172	173	174	175
HEX	A0	20	74	68	69	F3	20	8D	0A	63	6F	6E	74	69	6E	65
DEC	160	32	116	104	105	243	32	141	10	99	111	110	116	105	110	101
ASC	160	^'				243	^'	141	^J							
ALT	160	SPC				243	SPC	141	LF							
SYM			t	h	i					c	o	n	t	i	n	e

| Phantom Space | | | s | "Soft" CR | |

WORDSTAR   **257**

BYTE	176	177	178	179	180	181	182	183	184	185	186	187	188	189	190	191
HEX	6E	74	AC	A0	20	E1	20	6E	65	F7	20	6E	61	74	69	6F
DEC	110	116	172	160	32	225	32	110	101	247	32	110	97	116	105	111
ASC			172	160	^`	225	^`			247		^`				
ALT			172	160	SPC	225	SPC			247		SPC				
SYM	n	t						n	e			n	a	t	i	o

, Phantom Space   a   w

BYTE	192	193	194	195	196	197	198	199	200	201	202	203	204	205	206	207
HEX	6E	AC	A0	20	63	6F	6E	63	65	69	76	65	E4	20	69	EE
DEC	110	172	160	32	99	111	110	99	101	105	118	101	228	32	105	238
ASC		172	160	^`									228	^`		238
ALT		172	160	SPC									228	SPC		238
SYM	n				c	o	n	c	e	i	v	e			i	

, Phantom Space   d   n

BYTE	208	209	210	211	212	213	214	215	216	217	218	219	220	221	222	223
HEX	20	13	4C	69	62	65	72	74	79	13	AC	20	61	6E	E4	20
DEC	32	19	76	105	98	101	114	116	121	19	172	32	97	110	228	32
ASC	^`	^S								^S	172	^`			228	^`
ALT	SPC	DC3								DC3	172	SPC			228	SPC
SYM			L	i	b	e	r	t	y				a	n		

Underline Toggle ← Underlined Text → Underline Toggle ,   d

BYTE	224	225	226	227	228	229	230	231	232	233	234	235	236	237	238	239
HEX	64	65	64	69	63	61	74	65	E4	20	74	EF	20	8D	0A	74
DEC	100	101	100	105	99	97	116	101	228	32	116	239	32	141	10	116
ASC									228	^`		239	^`	141	^J	
ALT									228	SPC		239	SPC	141	LF	
SYM	d	e	d	i	c	a	t	e			t					t

      d   o   "Soft" CR

BYTE	240	241	242	243	244	245	246	247	248	249	250	251	252	253	254	255
HEX	68	E5	20	70	72	6F	70	6F	73	69	74	69	6F	EE	20	74
DEC	104	229	32	112	114	111	112	111	115	105	116	105	111	238	32	116
ASC		229	^`											238	^`	
ALT		229	SPC											238	SPC	
SYM	h			p	r	o	p	o	s	i	t	i	o			t

e   n

BYTE	256	257	258	259	260	261	262	263	264	265	266	267	268	269	270	271
HEX	68	61	F4	20	61	6C	EC	20	6D	65	EE	20	61	72	E5	20
DEC	104	97	244	32	97	108	236	32	109	101	238	32	97	114	229	32
ASC			244	^`		236	^`			238	^`			229	^`	
ALT			244	SPC		236	SPC			238	SPC			229	SPC	
SYM	h	a			a	l			m	e			a	r		

    t   l   n   e

BYTE	272	273	274	275	276	277	278	279	280	281	282	283	284	285	286	287
HEX	63	72	65	61	74	65	E4	20	65	71	75	61	6C	2E	0D	0A
DEC	99	114	101	97	116	101	228	32	101	113	117	97	108	46	13	10
ASC							228	^`							^M	^J
ALT							228	SPC							CR	LF
SYM	c	r	e	a	t	e			e	q	u	a	l	.		

d   Newline

BYTE	288	289	290	291	292	293	294	295	296	297	298	299	300	301	302	303
HEX	0D	0A	4E	6F	F7	A0	20	77	E5	A0	20	61	72	E5	20	65
DEC	13	10	78	111	247	160	32	119	229	160	32	97	114	229	32	101
ASC	^M	^J			247	160	^`		229	160	^`			229	^`	
ALT	CR	LF			247	160	SPC		229	160	SPC			229	SPC	
SYM			N	o				w				a	r			e

Newline   w   Phantom Space   Phantom Space   e

BYTE	304	305	306	307	308	309	310	311	312	313	314	315	316	317	318	319
HEX	6E	67	61	67	65	E4	20	69	EE	20	E1	20	67	72	65	61
DEC	110	103	97	103	101	228	32	105	238	32	225	32	103	114	101	97
ASC						228	^`		238	^`	225	^`				
ALT						228	SPC		238	SPC	225	SPC				
SYM	n	g	a	g	e			i					g	r	e	a

d   n   a

BYTE	320	321	322	323	324	325	326	327	328	329	330	331	332	333	334	335
HEX	F4	20	63	69	76	69	EC	20	77	61	72	AC	A0	20	74	65
DEC	244	32	99	105	118	105	236	32	119	97	114	172	160	32	116	101
ASC	244	^`					236	^`				172	160	^`		
ALT	244	SPC					236	SPC				172	160	SPC		
SYM			c	i	v	i			w	a	r				t	e

t   l   ,   Phantom Space

BYTE	336	337	338	339	340	341	342	343	344	345	346	347	348	349	350	351
HEX	73	74	69	6E	E7	20	77	68	65	74	68	65	F2	A0	20	74
DEC	115	116	105	110	231	32	119	104	101	116	104	101	242	160	32	116
ASC					231	^`							242	160	^`	
ALT					231	SPC							242	160	SPC	
SYM	s	t	i	n			w	h	e	t	h	e				t

g   r   Phantom Space

BYTE	352	353	354	355	356	357	358	359	360	361	362	363	364	365	366	367
HEX	68	61	F4	20	8D	0A	6E	61	74	69	6F	EE	A0	20	6F	F2
DEC	104	97	244	32	141	10	110	97	116	105	111	238	160	32	111	242
ASC			244	^`	141	^J						238	160	^`		242
ALT			244	SPC	141	LF						238	160	SPC		242
SYM	h	a					n	a	t	i	o				o	

t   "Soft" CR   n   Phantom Space   r

WORDSTAR 259

BYTE	368	369	370	371	372	373	374	375	376	377	378	379	380	381	382	383
HEX	A0	20	61	6E	F9	A0	20	6E	61	74	69	6F	EE	20	73	EF
DEC	160	32	97	110	249	160	32	110	97	116	105	111	238	32	115	239
ASC	160	^`			249	160	^`						238	^`		239
ALT	160	SPC			249	160	SPC						238	SPC		239
SYM			a	n				n	a	t	i	o			s	

Phantom Space (370)   y (372)   Phantom Space (373)   n (380)   o (383)

BYTE	384	385	386	387	388	389	390	391	392	393	394	395	396	397	398	399
HEX	20	63	6F	6E	63	65	69	76	65	E4	20	61	6E	E4	20	73
DEC	32	99	111	110	99	101	105	118	101	228	32	97	110	228	32	115
ASC	^`									228	^`			228	^`	
ALT	SPC									228	SPC			228	SPC	
SYM		c	o	n	c	e	i	v	e			a	n			s

d (393)   d (397)

BYTE	400	401	402	403	404	405	406	407	408	409	410	411	412	413	414	415
HEX	EF	A0	20	64	65	64	69	63	61	74	65	E4	A0	20	63	61
DEC	239	160	32	100	101	100	105	99	97	116	101	228	160	32	99	97
ASC	239	160	^`									228	160	^`		
ALT	239	160	SPC									228	160	SPC		
SYM				d	e	d	i	c	a	t	e				c	a

o (400)   Phantom Space (401)   d (411)   Phantom Space (412)

BYTE	416	417	418	419	420	421	422	423	424	425	426	427	428	429	430	431
HEX	EE	A0	20	6C	6F	6E	E7	20	8D	0A	65	6E	64	75	72	65
DEC	238	160	32	108	111	110	231	32	141	10	101	110	100	117	114	101
ASC	238	160	^`				231	^`	141	^J						
ALT	238	160	SPC				231	SPC	141	LF						
SYM				l	o	n					e	n	d	u	r	e

n (416)   Phantom Space (417)   g (422)   "Soft" CR (424)

BYTE	432	433	434	435	436	437	438	439	440	441	442	443	444	445	446	447
HEX	AE	A0	20	20	57	E5	20	61	72	E5	20	6D	65	F4	20	6F
DEC	174	160	32	32	87	229	32	97	114	229	32	109	101	244	32	111
ASC	174	160	^`	^`		229	^`			229	^`			244	^`	
ALT	174	160	SPC	SPC		229	SPC			229	SPC			244	SPC	
SYM					W			a	r			m	e			o

. (432)   Phantom Space (433)   e (437)   e (441)   t (445)

BYTE	448	449	450	451	452	453	454	455	456	457	458	459	460	461	462	463
HEX	EE	20	E1	20	67	72	65	61	F4	20	62	61	74	74	6C	65
DEC	238	32	225	32	103	114	101	97	244	32	98	97	116	116	108	101
ASC	238	^`	225	^`					244	^`						
ALT	238	SPC	225	SPC					244	SPC						
SYM					g	r	e	a			b	a	t	t	l	e

n (448)   a (450)   t (456)

BYTE	464	465	466	467	468	469	470	471	472	473	474	475	476	477	478	479
HEX	66	69	65	6C	E4	20	6F	E6	20	74	68	61	F4	20	77	61
DEC	102	105	101	108	228	32	111	230	32	116	104	97	244	32	119	97
ASC					228	^`		230	^`				244	^`		
ALT					228	SPC		230	SPC				244	SPC		
SYM	f	i	e	l			o			t	h	a			w	a

                 d   f   t

BYTE	480	481	482	483	484	485	486	487	488	489	490	491	492	493	494	495
HEX	72	AE	20	20	57	E5	20	68	61	76	E5	20	8D	0A	63	6F
DEC	114	174	32	32	87	229	32	104	97	118	229	32	141	10	99	111
ASC		174	^`	^`		229	^`				229	^`	141	^J		
ALT		174	SPC	SPC		229	SPC				229	SPC	141	LF		
SYM	r				W			h	a	v					c	o

     .   e   e   "Soft" CR

BYTE	496	497	498	499	500	501	502	503	504	505	506	507	508	509	510	511
HEX	6D	E5	A0	20	74	EF	A0	20	64	65	64	69	63	61	74	E5
DEC	109	229	160	32	116	239	160	32	100	101	100	105	99	97	116	229
ASC		229	160	^`		239	160	^`								229
ALT		229	160	SPC		239	160	SPC								229
SYM	m				t				d	e	d	i	c	a	t	

         e   Phan-   o   Phan-   e
                tom   tom
               Space   Space

BYTE	512	513	514	515	516	517	518	519	520	521	522	523	524	525	526	527
HEX	20	E1	20	70	6F	72	74	69	6F	EE	20	6F	E6	20	74	68
DEC	32	225	32	112	111	114	116	105	111	238	32	111	230	32	116	104
ASC	^`	225	^`							238	^`		230	^`		
ALT	SPC	225	SPC							238	SPC		230	SPC		
SYM				p	o	r	t	i	o			o			t	h

         a   n   f

BYTE	528	529	530	531	532	533	534	535	536	537	538	539	540	541	542	543
HEX	61	F4	20	66	69	65	6C	64	AC	A0	20	61	F3	20	E1	A0
DEC	97	244	32	102	105	101	108	100	172	160	32	97	243	32	225	160
ASC		244	^`						172	160	^`		243	^`	225	160
ALT		244	SPC						172	160	SPC		243	SPC	225	160
SYM	a			f	i	e	l	d				a				

       t   ,   Phan-   s   a   Phan-
                                                 tom   tom
                                                 Space   Space

BYTE	544	545	546	547	548	549	550	551	552	553	554	555	556	557	558	559
HEX	20	66	69	6E	61	EC	A0	20	72	65	73	74	69	6E	E7	20
DEC	32	102	105	110	97	236	160	32	114	101	115	116	105	110	231	32
ASC	^`					236	160	^`							231	^`
ALT	SPC					236	160	SPC							231	SPC
SYM		f	i	n	a				r	e	s	t	i	n		

                      l   Phan-   g
                          tom
                       Space

WORDSTAR

BYTE	560	561	562	563	564	565	566	567	568	569	570	571	572	573	574	575
HEX	8D	0A	70	6C	61	63	E5	20	66	6F	F2	20	74	68	6F	73
DEC	141	10	112	108	97	99	229	32	102	111	242	32	116	104	111	115
ASC	141	^J					229	^`			242	^`				
ALT	141	LF					229	SPC			242	SPC				
SYM			p	l	a	c			f	o			t	h	o	s

"Soft" CR   e   r

BYTE	576	577	578	579	580	581	582	583	584	585	586	587	588	589	590	591
HEX	E5	20	77	68	EF	20	68	65	72	E5	20	67	61	76	E5	20
DEC	229	32	119	104	239	32	104	101	114	229	32	103	97	118	229	32
ASC	229	^`			239	^`				229	^`				229	^`
ALT	229	SPC			239	SPC				229	SPC				229	SPC
SYM			w	h			h	e	r			g	a	v		

e   o   e   e

BYTE	592	593	594	595	596	597	598	599	600	601	602	603	604	605	606	607
HEX	74	68	65	69	F2	20	6C	69	76	65	F3	20	74	68	61	F4
DEC	116	104	101	105	242	32	108	105	118	101	243	32	116	104	97	244
ASC					242	^`					243	^`				244
ALT					242	SPC					243	SPC				244
SYM	t	h	e	i			l	i	v	e			t	h	a	

r   s   t

BYTE	608	609	610	611	612	613	614	615	616	617	618	619	620	621	622	623
HEX	20	74	68	61	F4	20	6E	61	74	69	6F	EE	A0	20	6D	69
DEC	32	116	104	97	244	32	110	97	116	105	111	238	160	32	109	105
ASC	^`				244	^`						238	160	^`		
ALT	SPC				244	SPC						238	160	SPC		
SYM		t	h	a			n	a	t	i	o				m	i

t   n   Phantom Space

BYTE	624	625	626	627	628	629	630	631	632	633	634	635	636	637	638	639
HEX	67	68	F4	20	8D	0A	6C	69	76	65	AE	20	20	49	F4	20
DEC	103	104	244	32	141	10	108	105	118	101	174	32	32	73	244	32
ASC			244	^`	141	^J					174	^`	^`		244	^`
ALT			244	SPC	141	LF					174	SPC	SPC		244	SPC
SYM	g	h					l	i	v	e				I		

t   "Soft" CR   t

BYTE	640	641	642	643	644	645	646	647	648	649	650	651	652	653	654	655
HEX	69	F3	20	61	6C	74	6F	67	65	74	68	65	F2	20	66	69
DEC	105	243	32	97	108	116	111	103	101	116	104	101	242	32	102	105
ASC		243	^`										242	^`		
ALT		243	SPC										242	SPC		
SYM	i			a	l	t	o	g	e	t	h	e			f	i

s   r

BYTE	656	657	658	659	660	661	662	663	664	665	666	667	668	669	670	671
HEX	74	74	69	6E	E7	20	61	6E	E4	20	70	72	6F	70	65	F2
DEC	116	116	105	110	231	32	97	110	228	32	112	114	111	112	101	242
ASC					231	^`			228	^`						242
ALT					231	SPC			228	SPC						242
SYM	t	t	i	n			a	n			p	r	o	p	e	
					g				d							r

BYTE	672	673	674	675	676	677	678	679	680	681	682	683	684	685	686	687
HEX	20	74	68	61	F4	20	77	E5	20	73	68	6F	75	6C	E4	20
DEC	32	116	104	97	244	32	119	229	32	115	104	111	117	108	228	32
ASC	^`				244	^`		229	^`						228	^`
ALT	SPC				244	SPC		229	SPC						228	SPC
SYM		t	h	a			w			s	h	o	u	l		
					t			e							d	

BYTE	688	689	690	691	692	693	694	695	696	697	698	699	700	701	702	703
HEX	64	EF	20	73	6F	AE	20	1A	1A	1A	1A	1A	1A	1A	1A	1A
DEC	100	239	32	115	111	174	32	26	26	26	26	26	26	26	26	26
ASC		239	^`			174	^`	^Z	^Z	^Z	^Z	^Z	^Z	^Z	^Z	^Z
ALT		239	SPC			174	SPC	SUB	SUB	SUB	SUB	SUB	SUB	SUB	SUB	SUB
SYM	d			s	o											
		c				.		← Padded to End of File With Control-Z →

BYTE	704	705	706	707	708	709	710	711	712	713	714	715	716	717	718	719
HEX	1A	1A	1A	1A	1A	1A	1A	1A	1A	1A	1A	1A	1A	1A	1A	1A
DEC	26	26	26	26	26	26	26	26	26	26	26	26	26	26	26	26
ASC	^Z	^Z	^Z	^Z	^Z	^Z	^Z	^Z	^Z	^Z	^Z	^Z	^Z	^Z	^Z	^Z
ALT	SUB	SUB	SUB	SUB	SUB	SUB	SUB	SUB	SUB	SUB	SUB	SUB	SUB	SUB	SUB	SUB
SYM																

BYTE	720	721	722	723	724	725	726	727	728	729	730	731	732	733	734	735
HEX	1A	1A	1A	1A	1A	1A	1A	1A	1A	1A	1A	1A	1A	1A	1A	1A
DEC	26	26	26	26	26	26	26	26	26	26	26	26	26	26	26	26
ASC	^Z	^Z	^Z	^Z	^Z	^Z	^Z	^Z	^Z	^Z	^Z	^Z	^Z	^Z	^Z	^Z
ALT	SUB	SUB	SUB	SUB	SUB	SUB	SUB	SUB	SUB	SUB	SUB	SUB	SUB	SUB	SUB	SUB
SYM																

BYTE	736	737	738	739	740	741	742	743	744	745	746	747	748	749	750	751
HEX	1A	1A	1A	1A	1A	1A	1A	1A	1A	1A	1A	1A	1A	1A	1A	1A
DEC	26	26	26	26	26	26	26	26	26	26	26	26	26	26	26	26
ASC	^Z	^Z	^Z	^Z	^Z	^Z	^Z	^Z	^Z	^Z	^Z	^Z	^Z	^Z	^Z	^Z
ALT	SUB	SUB	SUB	SUB	SUB	SUB	SUB	SUB	SUB	SUB	SUB	SUB	SUB	SUB	SUB	SUB
SYM																

BYTE	752	753	754	755	756	757	758	759	760	761	762	763	764	765	766	767
HEX	1A	1A	1A	1A	1A	1A	1A	1A	1A	1A	1A	1A	1A	1A	1A	1A
DEC	26	26	26	26	26	26	26	26	26	26	26	26	26	26	26	26
ASC	^Z	^Z	^Z	^Z	^Z	^Z	^Z	^Z	^Z	^Z	^Z	^Z	^Z	^Z	^Z	^Z
ALT	SUB	SUB	SUB	SUB	SUB	SUB	SUB	SUB	SUB	SUB	SUB	SUB	SUB	SUB	SUB	SUB
SYM																

End of Gettysburg Address as a WordStar File

Gettysburg Address as a WordStar 2000 File

BYTE	0	1	2	3	4	5	6	7	8	9	10	11	12	13	14	15
HEX	7F	20	57	53	32	30	30	30	FF	31	2E	30	30	FF	FF	FF
DEC	127	32	87	83	50	48	48	48	255	49	46	48	48	255	255	255
ASC	^	^'							255					255	255	255
ALT	DEL	SPC							255					255	255	255
SYM			W	S	2	0	0	0		1	.	0	0			

Attn. Character | File I.D. | ←──── Version Number ────→ | Converted Spaces

BYTE	16	17	18	19	20	21	22	23	24	25	26	27	28	29	30	31
HEX	FF	20	31	4E	45	43	33	35	35	30	FF	FF	FF	FF	FF	FF
DEC	255	32	49	78	69	67	51	53	53	48	255	255	255	255	255	255
ASC	255	^'									255	255	255	255	255	255
ALT	255	SPC									255	255	255	255	255	255
SYM			1	N	E	C	3	5	5	0						

←─ Space ─→ | ←──────── Printer Identifier ────────→

BYTE	32	33	34	35	36	37	38	39	40	41	42	43	44	45	46	47
HEX	FF	20	20	20	20	20	31	37	20	7F	0A	7F	1C	20	30	20
DEC	255	32	32	32	32	32	49	55	32	127	10	127	28	32	48	32
ASC	255	^'	^'	^'	^'	^'				^	^J	^	^\	^'		^'
ALT	255	SPC	SPC	SPC	SPC	SPC			SPC	DEL	LF	DEL	FS	SPC		SPC
SYM							1	7							0	

←─ Space ─→ | ←── Formatted Line Count ──→ | File I.D. | Attn. Char. | Newline | Attn. Char. | Select Font | Previous Font | Space
  | ←──── Font ────→

BYTE	48	49	50	51	52	53	54	55	56	57	58	59	60	61	62	63
HEX	20	30	1C	7F	0A	7F	69	20	30	20	20	30	69	7F	7F	5E
DEC	32	48	28	127	10	127	105	32	48	32	32	48	105	127	127	94
ASC	^'		^\	^	^J	^		^'			^'			^	^	
ALT	SPC		FS	DEL	LF	DEL		SPC			SPC			DEL	DEL	
SYM		0					i		0			0	i			^

Subsequent Font | Select Font | Attn. Char. | Newline | Attn. Char. | Line Height | Previous Line Height | Space | Subsequent Line Height | Line Height | Attn. Char. | Attn. Char. | Header Offset
←── Font ──→ | ←──────── Line Height ────────→ | ←── Header Offset ──→

BYTE	64	65	66	67	68	69	70	71	72	73	74	75	76	77	78	79
HEX	20	20	36	5E	7F	7F	5F	20	20	36	5F	7F	7F	5B	01	41
DEC	32	32	54	94	127	127	95	32	32	54	95	127	127	91	1	65
ASC	^'	^'		^	^	^		^'	^'		^	^	^		^A	
ALT	SPC	SPC		DEL	DEL		SPC	SPC		DEL	DEL		SOH			
SYM			6	^			_			6	_			[		A

Header Offset in Lines from Top | Header Offset | Attn. Char. | Attn. Char. | Footer Offset | Footer Offset in Lines from Bottom | Footer Offset | Attn. Char. | Attn. Char. | Ruler | Old Left Margin | Old Right Margin
←──── Header Offset ────→ | ←──── Footer Offset ────→

WORDSTAR **265**

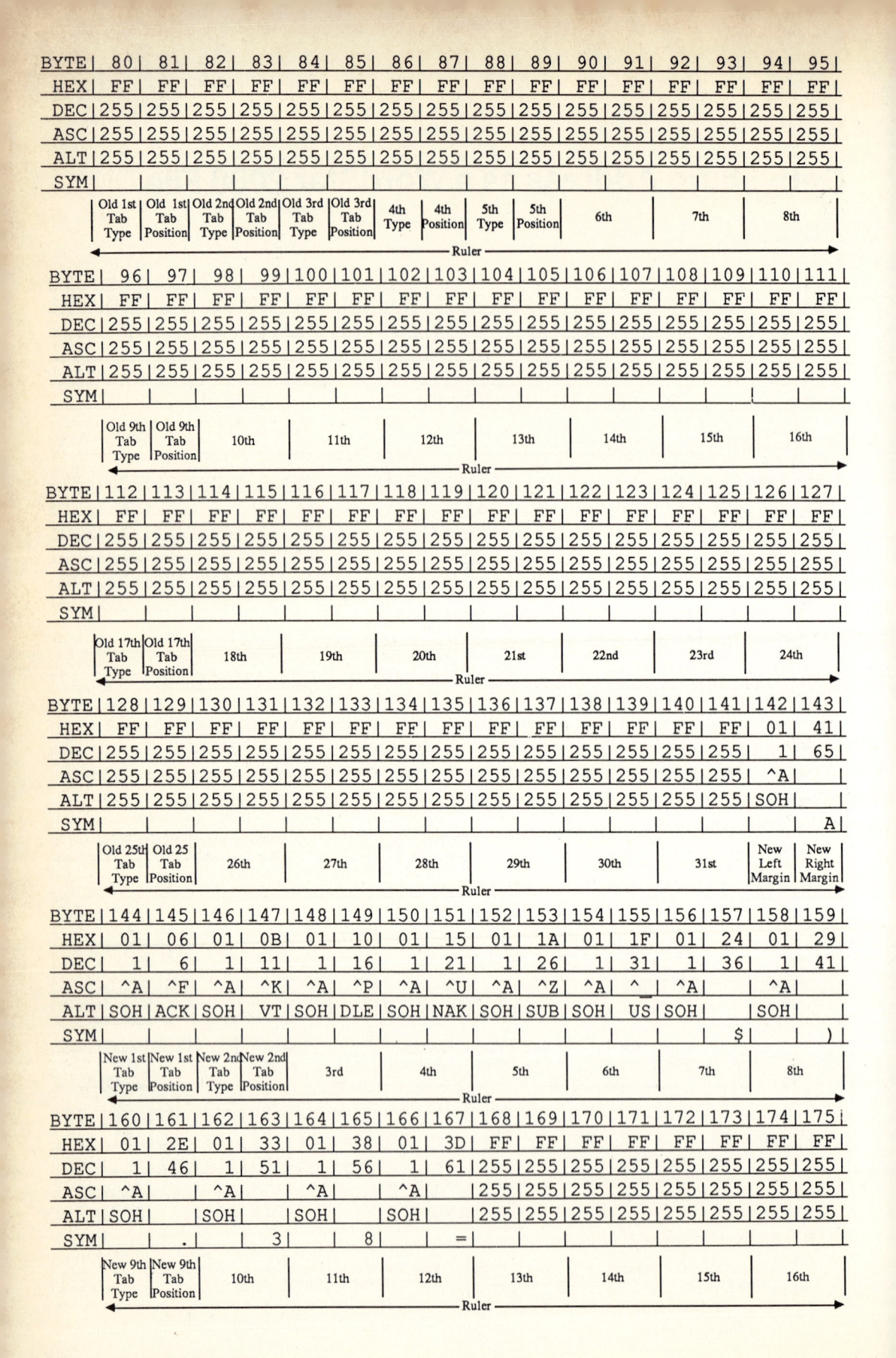

BYTE	80	81	82	83	84	85	86	87	88	89	90	91	92	93	94	95
HEX	FF	FF	FF	FF	FF	FF	FF	FF	FF	FF	FF	FF	FF	FF	FF	FF
DEC	255	255	255	255	255	255	255	255	255	255	255	255	255	255	255	255
ASC	255	255	255	255	255	255	255	255	255	255	255	255	255	255	255	255
ALT	255	255	255	255	255	255	255	255	255	255	255	255	255	255	255	255
SYM																
	Old 1st Tab Type	Old 1st Tab Position	Old 2nd Tab Type	Old 2nd Tab Position	Old 3rd Tab Type	Old 3rd Tab Position	4th Type	4th Position	5th Type	5th Position	6th		7th		8th	

← Ruler →

BYTE	96	97	98	99	100	101	102	103	104	105	106	107	108	109	110	111
HEX	FF	FF	FF	FF	FF	FF	FF	FF	FF	FF	FF	FF	FF	FF	FF	FF
DEC	255	255	255	255	255	255	255	255	255	255	255	255	255	255	255	255
ASC	255	255	255	255	255	255	255	255	255	255	255	255	255	255	255	255
ALT	255	255	255	255	255	255	255	255	255	255	255	255	255	255	255	255
SYM																
	Old 9th Tab Type	Old 9th Tab Position	10th		11th		12th		13th		14th		15th		16th	

← Ruler →

BYTE	112	113	114	115	116	117	118	119	120	121	122	123	124	125	126	127
HEX	FF	FF	FF	FF	FF	FF	FF	FF	FF	FF	FF	FF	FF	FF	FF	FF
DEC	255	255	255	255	255	255	255	255	255	255	255	255	255	255	255	255
ASC	255	255	255	255	255	255	255	255	255	255	255	255	255	255	255	255
ALT	255	255	255	255	255	255	255	255	255	255	255	255	255	255	255	255
SYM																
	Old 17th Tab Type	Old 17th Tab Position	18th		19th		20th		21st		22nd		23rd		24th	

← Ruler →

BYTE	128	129	130	131	132	133	134	135	136	137	138	139	140	141	142	143
HEX	FF	FF	FF	FF	FF	FF	FF	FF	FF	FF	FF	FF	FF	FF	01	41
DEC	255	255	255	255	255	255	255	255	255	255	255	255	255	255	1	65
ASC	255	255	255	255	255	255	255	255	255	255	255	255	255	255	^A	
ALT	255	255	255	255	255	255	255	255	255	255	255	255	255	255	SOH	
SYM																A
	Old 25th Tab Type	Old 25 Tab Position	26th		27th		28th		29th		30th		31st		New Left Margin	New Right Margin

← Ruler →

BYTE	144	145	146	147	148	149	150	151	152	153	154	155	156	157	158	159
HEX	01	06	01	0B	01	10	01	15	01	1A	01	1F	01	24	01	29
DEC	1	6	1	11	1	16	1	21	1	26	1	31	1	36	1	41
ASC	^A	^F	^A	^K	^A	^P	^A	^U	^A	^Z	^A	^_	^A		^A	
ALT	SOH	ACK	SOH	VT	SOH	DLE	SOH	NAK	SOH	SUB	SOH	US	SOH		SOH	
SYM														$		)
	New 1st Tab Type	New 1st Tab Position	New 2nd Tab Type	New 2nd Tab Position	3rd		4th		5th		6th		7th		8th	

← Ruler →

BYTE	160	161	162	163	164	165	166	167	168	169	170	171	172	173	174	175
HEX	01	2E	01	33	01	38	01	3D	FF	FF	FF	FF	FF	FF	FF	FF
DEC	1	46	1	51	1	56	1	61	255	255	255	255	255	255	255	255
ASC	^A		^A		^A		^A		255	255	255	255	255	255	255	255
ALT	SOH		SOH		SOH		SOH		255	255	255	255	255	255	255	255
SYM		.		3		8		=								
	New 9th Tab Type	New 9th Tab Position	10th		11th		12th		13th		14th		15th		16th	

← Ruler →

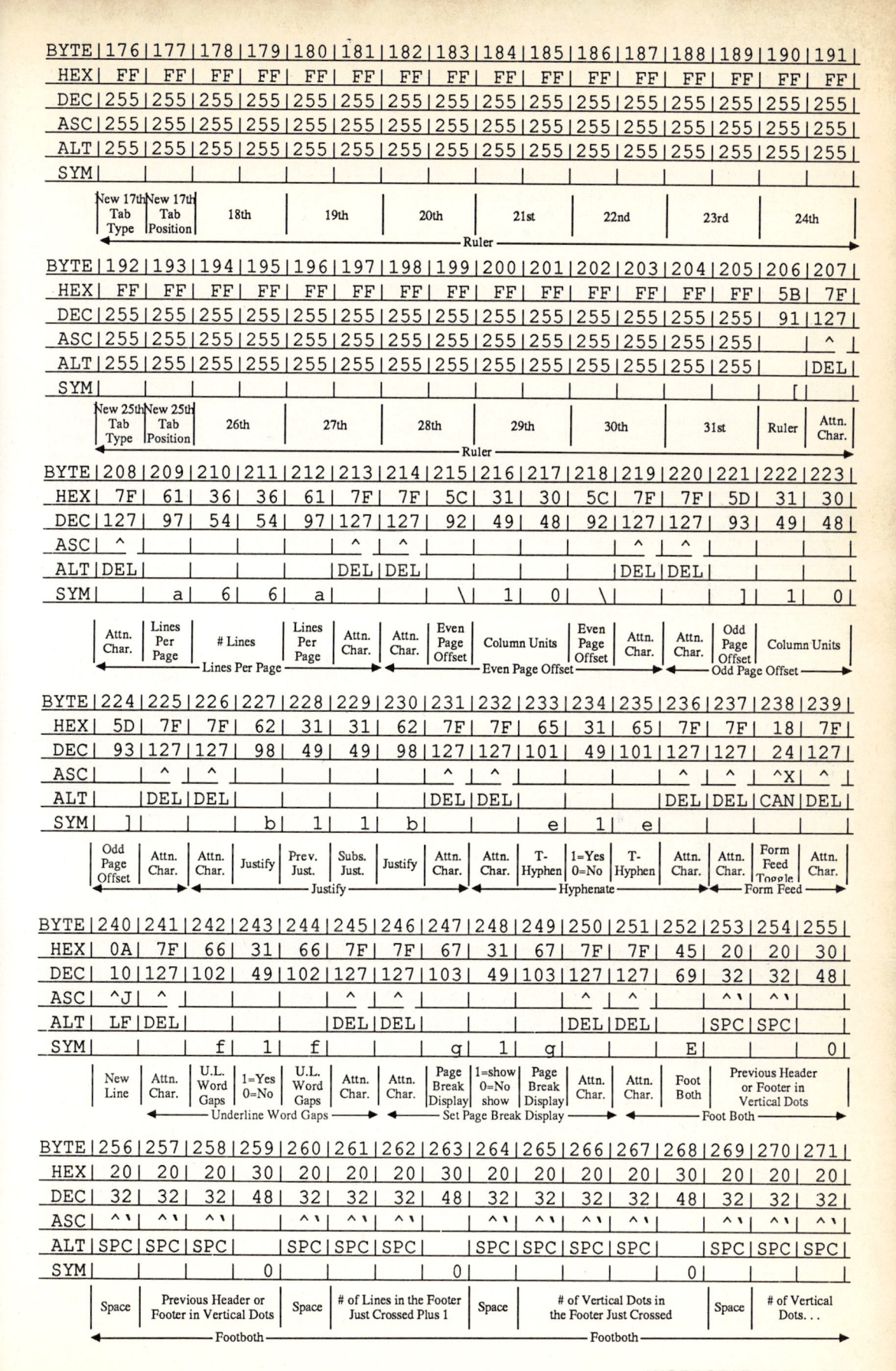

BYTE	176	177	178	179	180	181	182	183	184	185	186	187	188	189	190	191
HEX	FF	FF	FF	FF	FF	FF	FF	FF	FF	FF	FF	FF	FF	FF	FF	FF
DEC	255	255	255	255	255	255	255	255	255	255	255	255	255	255	255	255
ASC	255	255	255	255	255	255	255	255	255	255	255	255	255	255	255	255
ALT	255	255	255	255	255	255	255	255	255	255	255	255	255	255	255	255
SYM																
	New 17th Tab Type	New 17th Tab Position	18th	19th	20th	21st	22nd	23rd	24th
					Ruler				

BYTE	192	193	194	195	196	197	198	199	200	201	202	203	204	205	206	207
HEX	FF	FF	FF	FF	FF	FF	FF	FF	FF	FF	FF	FF	FF	FF	5B	7F
DEC	255	255	255	255	255	255	255	255	255	255	255	255	255	255	91	127
ASC	255	255	255	255	255	255	255	255	255	255	255	255	255	255		^
ALT	255	255	255	255	255	255	255	255	255	255	255	255	255	255		DEL
SYM															[	
	New 25th Tab Type	New 25th Tab Position	26th	27th	28th	29th	30th	31st	Ruler	Attn. Char.

BYTE	208	209	210	211	212	213	214	215	216	217	218	219	220	221	222	223
HEX	7F	61	36	36	61	7F	7F	5C	31	30	5C	7F	7F	5D	31	30
DEC	127	97	54	54	97	127	127	92	49	48	92	127	127	93	49	48
ASC	^					^	^					^	^			
ALT	DEL					DEL	DEL					DEL	DEL			
SYM		a	6	6	a			\	1	0	\			]	1	0
	Attn. Char.	Lines Per Page	# Lines	Lines Per Page	Attn. Char.	Attn. Char.	Even Page Offset	Column Units	Even Page Offset	Attn. Char.	Attn. Char.	Odd Page Offset	Column Units
		Lines Per Page				Even Page Offset			Odd Page Offset

BYTE	224	225	226	227	228	229	230	231	232	233	234	235	236	237	238	239
HEX	5D	7F	7F	62	31	31	62	7F	7F	65	31	65	7F	7F	18	7F
DEC	93	127	127	98	49	49	98	127	127	101	49	101	127	127	24	127
ASC		^	^					^	^				^	^	^X	^
ALT		DEL	DEL					DEL	DEL				DEL	DEL	CAN	DEL
SYM	]			b	1	1	b			e	1	e				
	Odd Page Offset	Attn. Char.	Attn. Char.	Justify	Prev. Just.	Subs. Just.	Justify	Attn. Char.	Attn. Char.	T-Hyphen	1=Yes 0=No	T-Hyphen	Attn. Char.	Attn. Char.	Form Feed Toggle	Attn. Char.
				Justify					Hyphenate				Form Feed

BYTE	240	241	242	243	244	245	246	247	248	249	250	251	252	253	254	255
HEX	0A	7F	66	31	66	7F	7F	67	31	67	7F	7F	45	20	20	30
DEC	10	127	102	49	102	127	127	103	49	103	127	127	69	32	32	48
ASC	^J	^				^	^				^	^		^\	^\	
ALT	LF	DEL				DEL	DEL				DEL	DEL		SPC	SPC	
SYM			f	1	f			g	1	g			E			0
	New Line	Attn. Char.	U.L. Word Gaps	1=Yes 0=No	U.L. Word Gaps	Attn. Char.	Attn. Char.	Page Break Display	1=show 0=No show	Page Break Display	Attn. Char.	Attn. Char.	Foot Both	Previous Header or Footer in Vertical Dots
			Underline Word Gaps			Set Page Break Display			Foot Both

BYTE	256	257	258	259	260	261	262	263	264	265	266	267	268	269	270	271
HEX	20	20	20	30	20	20	20	30	20	20	20	20	30	20	20	20
DEC	32	32	32	48	32	32	32	48	32	32	32	32	48	32	32	32
ASC	^\	^\	^\		^\	^\	^\		^\	^\	^\	^\		^\	^\	^\
ALT	SPC	SPC	SPC		SPC	SPC	SPC		SPC	SPC	SPC	SPC		SPC	SPC	SPC
SYM				0				0					0			
	Space	Previous Header or Footer in Vertical Dots	Space	# of Lines in the Footer Just Crossed Plus 1	Space	# of Vertical Dots in the Footer Just Crossed	Space	# of Vertical Dots...
		Footboth				Footboth

WORDSTAR 2000   267

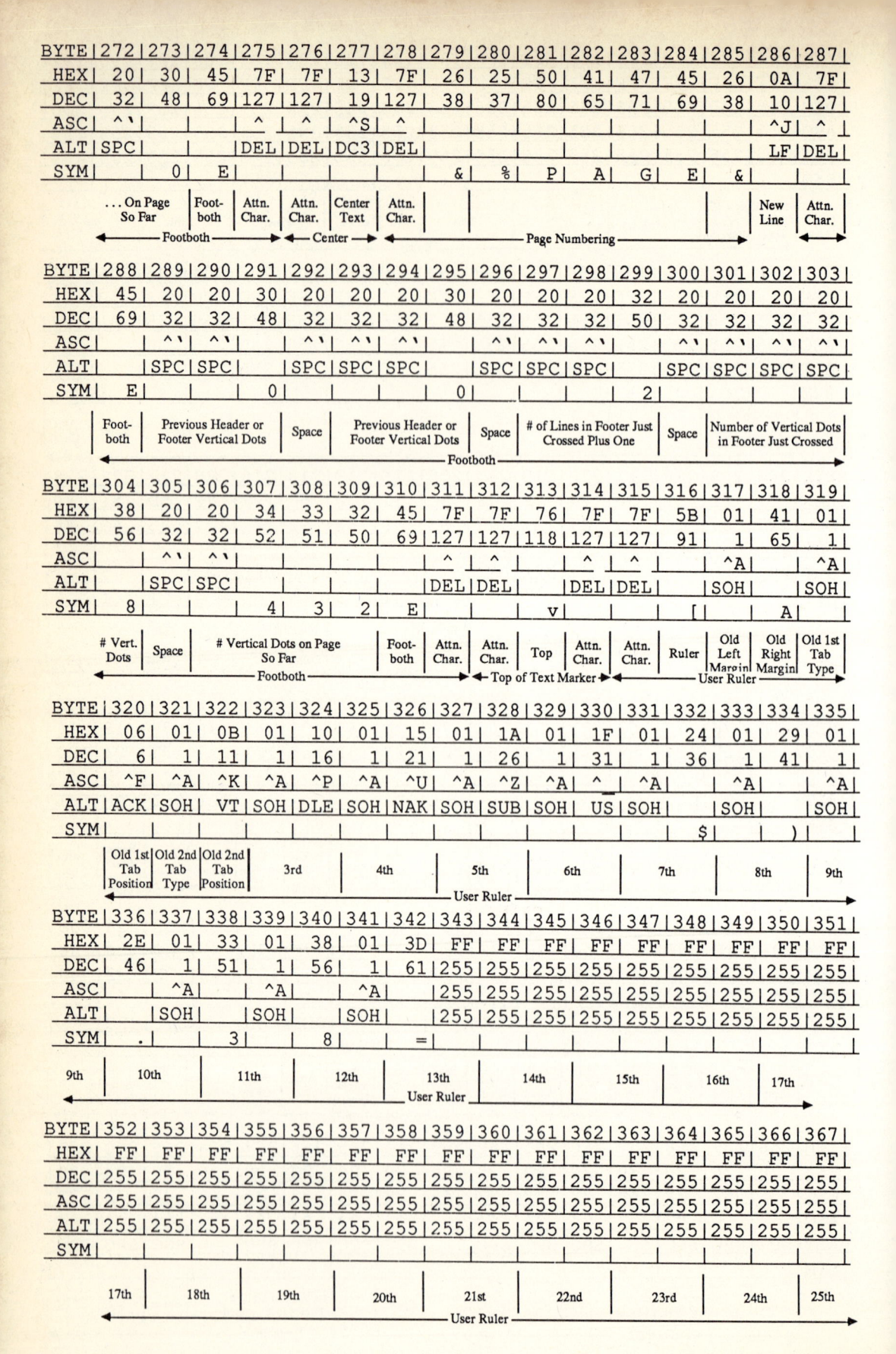

BYTE	272	273	274	275	276	277	278	279	280	281	282	283	284	285	286	287
HEX	20	30	45	7F	7F	13	7F	26	25	50	41	47	45	26	0A	7F
DEC	32	48	69	127	127	19	127	38	37	80	65	71	69	38	10	127
ASC	^`			^	^	^S	^								^J	^
ALT	SPC			DEL	DEL	DC3	DEL								LF	DEL
SYM		0	E					&	%	P	A	G	E	&		

...On Page So Far | Footboth | Attn. Char. | Attn. Char. | Center Text | Attn. Char. | | | | Page Numbering | | | | | New Line | Attn. Char.

←— Footboth —→ ←— Center —→ ←———— Page Numbering ————→

BYTE	288	289	290	291	292	293	294	295	296	297	298	299	300	301	302	303
HEX	45	20	20	30	20	20	20	30	20	20	20	32	20	20	20	20
DEC	69	32	32	48	32	32	32	48	32	32	32	50	32	32	32	32
ASC		^`	^`		^`	^`	^`		^`	^`	^`		^`	^`	^`	^`
ALT		SPC	SPC		SPC	SPC	SPC		SPC	SPC	SPC		SPC	SPC	SPC	SPC
SYM	E			0				0				2				

Footboth | Previous Header or Footer Vertical Dots | Space | Previous Header or Footer Vertical Dots | Space | # of Lines in Footer Just Crossed Plus One | Space | Number of Vertical Dots in Footer Just Crossed

←———————— Footboth ————————→

BYTE	304	305	306	307	308	309	310	311	312	313	314	315	316	317	318	319
HEX	38	20	20	34	33	32	45	7F	7F	76	7F	7F	5B	01	41	01
DEC	56	32	32	52	51	50	69	127	127	118	127	127	91	1	65	1
ASC		^`	^`					^	^		^	^	^A		^A	
ALT		SPC	SPC					DEL	DEL		DEL	DEL	SOH		SOH	
SYM	8			4	3	2	E			v			[		A	

Vert. Dots | Space | # Vertical Dots on Page So Far | Footboth | Attn. Char. | Attn. Char. | Top | Attn. Char. | Attn. Char. | Ruler | Old Left Margin | Old Right Margin | Old 1st Tab Type

←——— Footboth ———→ ←— Top of Text Marker —→ ←— User Ruler —→

BYTE	320	321	322	323	324	325	326	327	328	329	330	331	332	333	334	335
HEX	06	01	0B	01	10	01	15	01	1A	01	1F	01	24	01	29	01
DEC	6	1	11	1	16	1	21	1	26	1	31	1	36	1	41	1
ASC	^F	^A	^K	^A	^P	^A	^U	^A	^Z	^A	^_	^A		^A		^A
ALT	ACK	SOH	VT	SOH	DLE	SOH	NAK	SOH	SUB	SOH	US	SOH		SOH		SOH
SYM													$		)	

Old 1st Tab Position | Old 2nd Tab Type | Old 2nd Tab Position | 3rd | 4th | 5th | 6th | 7th | 8th | 9th

←———————————— User Ruler ————————————→

BYTE	336	337	338	339	340	341	342	343	344	345	346	347	348	349	350	351
HEX	2E	01	33	01	38	01	3D	FF	FF	FF	FF	FF	FF	FF	FF	FF
DEC	46	1	51	1	56	1	61	255	255	255	255	255	255	255	255	255
ASC		^A		^A		^A		255	255	255	255	255	255	255	255	255
ALT		SOH		SOH		SOH		255	255	255	255	255	255	255	255	255
SYM	.		3		8		=									

9th | 10th | 11th | 12th | 13th | 14th | 15th | 16th | 17th

←——————————— User Ruler ———————————→

BYTE	352	353	354	355	356	357	358	359	360	361	362	363	364	365	366	367
HEX	FF	FF	FF	FF	FF	FF	FF	FF	FF	FF	FF	FF	FF	FF	FF	FF
DEC	255	255	255	255	255	255	255	255	255	255	255	255	255	255	255	255
ASC	255	255	255	255	255	255	255	255	255	255	255	255	255	255	255	255
ALT	255	255	255	255	255	255	255	255	255	255	255	255	255	255	255	255
SYM																

17th | 18th | 19th | 20th | 21st | 22nd | 23rd | 24th | 25th

←————————————— User Ruler —————————————→

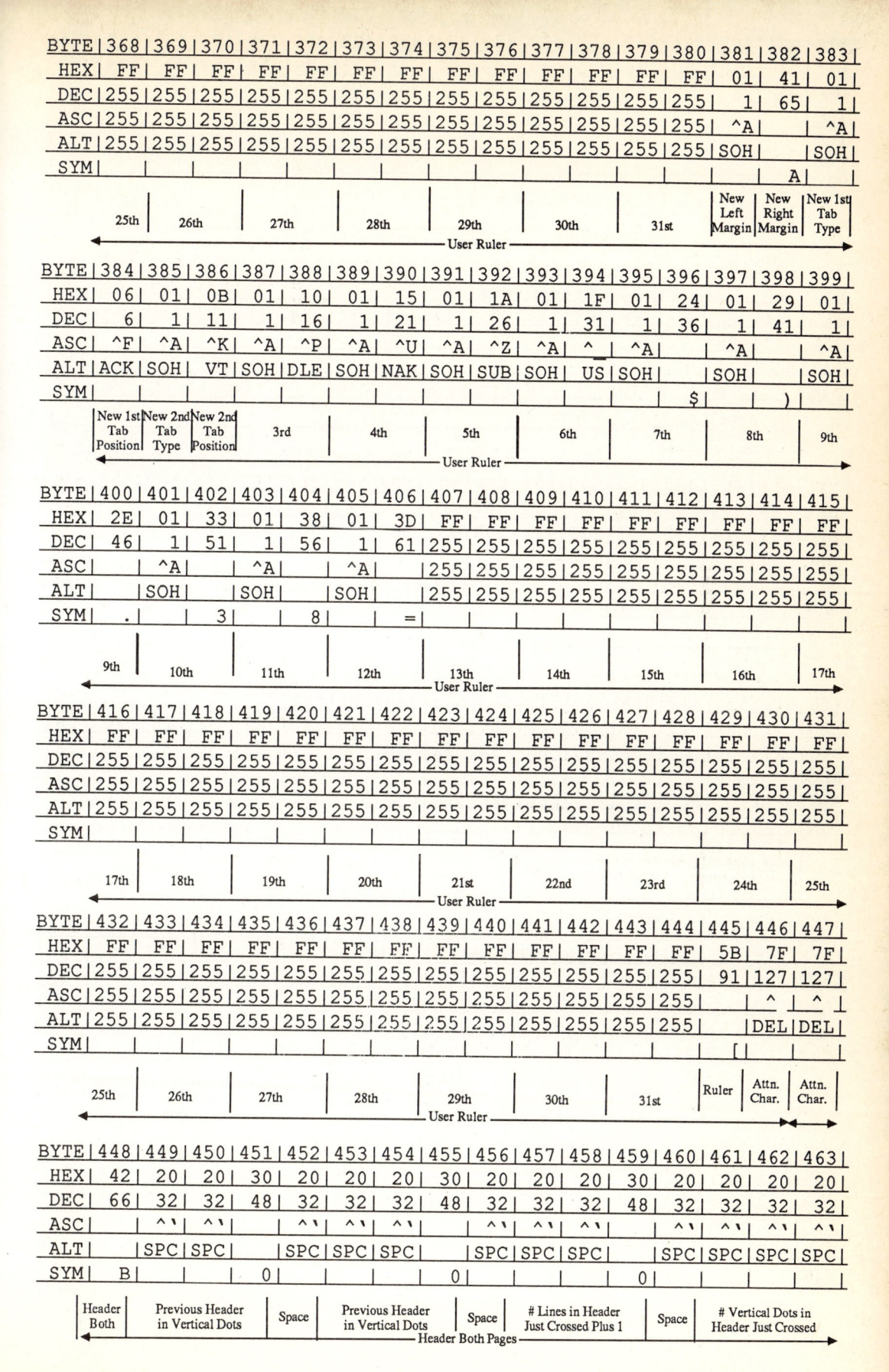

BYTE	368	369	370	371	372	373	374	375	376	377	378	379	380	381	382	383
HEX	FF	FF	FF	FF	FF	FF	FF	FF	FF	FF	FF	FF	FF	01	41	01
DEC	255	255	255	255	255	255	255	255	255	255	255	255	255	1	65	1
ASC	255	255	255	255	255	255	255	255	255	255	255	255	255	^A		^A
ALT	255	255	255	255	255	255	255	255	255	255	255	255	255	SOH		SOH
SYM															A	

25th — 26th — 27th — 28th — 29th — 30th — 31st | New Left Margin | New Right Margin | New 1st Tab Type
← User Ruler →

BYTE	384	385	386	387	388	389	390	391	392	393	394	395	396	397	398	399
HEX	06	01	0B	01	10	01	15	01	1A	01	1F	01	24	01	29	01
DEC	6	1	11	1	16	1	21	1	26	1	31	1	36	1	41	1
ASC	^F	^A	^K	^A	^P	^A	^U	^A	^Z	^A	^_	^A		^A		^A
ALT	ACK	SOH	VT	SOH	DLE	SOH	NAK	SOH	SUB	SOH	US	SOH		SOH		SOH
SYM													$		)	

New 1st Tab Position | New 2nd Tab Type | New 2nd Tab Position | 3rd — 4th — 5th — 6th — 7th — 8th — 9th
← User Ruler →

BYTE	400	401	402	403	404	405	406	407	408	409	410	411	412	413	414	415
HEX	2E	01	33	01	38	01	3D	FF	FF	FF	FF	FF	FF	FF	FF	FF
DEC	46	1	51	1	56	1	61	255	255	255	255	255	255	255	255	255
ASC		^A		^A		^A		255	255	255	255	255	255	255	255	255
ALT		SOH		SOH		SOH		255	255	255	255	255	255	255	255	255
SYM	.		3		8		=									

9th | 10th — 11th — 12th — 13th — 14th — 15th — 16th — 17th
← User Ruler →

BYTE	416	417	418	419	420	421	422	423	424	425	426	427	428	429	430	431
HEX	FF	FF	FF	FF	FF	FF	FF	FF	FF	FF	FF	FF	FF	FF	FF	FF
DEC	255	255	255	255	255	255	255	255	255	255	255	255	255	255	255	255
ASC	255	255	255	255	255	255	255	255	255	255	255	255	255	255	255	255
ALT	255	255	255	255	255	255	255	255	255	255	255	255	255	255	255	255
SYM																

17th — 18th — 19th — 20th — 21st — 22nd — 23rd — 24th — 25th
← User Ruler →

BYTE	432	433	434	435	436	437	438	439	440	441	442	443	444	445	446	447
HEX	FF	FF	FF	FF	FF	FF	FF	FF	FF	FF	FF	FF	FF	5B	7F	7F
DEC	255	255	255	255	255	255	255	255	255	255	255	255	255	91	127	127
ASC	255	255	255	255	255	255	255	255	255	255	255	255	255		^	^
ALT	255	255	255	255	255	255	255	255	255	255	255	255	255		DEL	DEL
SYM														[		

25th — 26th — 27th — 28th — 29th — 30th — 31st | Ruler | Attn. Char. | Attn. Char.
← User Ruler →

BYTE	448	449	450	451	452	453	454	455	456	457	458	459	460	461	462	463
HEX	42	20	20	30	20	20	20	30	20	20	20	30	20	20	20	20
DEC	66	32	32	48	32	32	32	48	32	32	32	48	32	32	32	32
ASC		^\	^\		^\	^\	^\		^\	^\	^\		^\	^\	^\	^\
ALT		SPC	SPC		SPC	SPC	SPC		SPC	SPC	SPC		SPC	SPC	SPC	SPC
SYM	B			0				0				0				

Header Both | Previous Header in Vertical Dots | Space | Previous Header in Vertical Dots | Space | # Lines in Header Just Crossed Plus 1 | Space | # Vertical Dots in Header Just Crossed
← Header Both Pages →

WORDSTAR 2000 269

BYTE	464	465	466	467	468	469	470	471	472	473	474	475	476	477	478	479
HEX	30	20	20	20	20	30	42	7F	7F	13	7F	7F	02	20	BB	03
DEC	48	32	32	32	32	48	66	127	127	19	127	127	2	32	187	3
ASC		^'	^'	^'	^'			^	^	^S	^	^	^B	^'	187	^C
ALT		SPC	SPC	SPC	SPC			DEL	DEL	DC3	DEL	DEL	STX	SPC	187	ETX
SYM	0					0	B									

| # Vertical Dots | Space | # of Vertical Dots on Page So Far / Header Both Pages | Header Both | Attn. Char. | Attn. Char. | Center Text / Center | Attn. Char. | Attn. Char. | Soft Space | Space | Two Characters / Soft Spaces |

BYTE	480	481	482	483	484	485	486	487	488	489	490	491	492	493	494	495
HEX	20	02	7F	4C	69	6E	63	6F	6C	6E	27	73	20	47	65	74
DEC	32	2	127	76	105	110	99	111	108	110	39	115	32	71	101	116
ASC	^'	^B	^										^'			
ALT	SPC	STX	DEL										SPC			
SYM				L	i	n	c	o	l	n	'	s		G	e	t

| Space | Soft Space | Attn. Char. / Soft Spaces | Text of Header |

BYTE	496	497	498	499	500	501	502	503	504	505	506	507	508	509	510	511
HEX	74	79	73	62	75	72	67	20	41	64	64	72	65	73	73	0A
DEC	116	121	115	98	117	114	103	32	65	100	100	114	101	115	115	10
ASC								^'								^J
ALT								SPC								LF
SYM	t	y	s	b	u	r	g		A	d	d	r	e	s	s	

| Text of Header | New Line |

BYTE	512	513	514	515	516	517	518	519	520	521	522	523	524	525	526	527
HEX	7F	42	20	20	30	20	20	20	30	20	20	20	32	20	20	20
DEC	127	66	32	32	48	32	32	32	48	32	32	32	50	32	32	32
ASC	^		^'	^'		^'	^'	^'		^'	^'	^'		^'	^'	^'
ALT	DEL		SPC	SPC		SPC	SPC	SPC		SPC	SPC	SPC		SPC	SPC	SPC
SYM		B			0				0				2			

| Attn. Char. | Header Both | Previous Header in Vertical Dots | Space | Previous Header in Vertical Dots | Space | # Lines in Header Just Crossed Plus One | Space | # Vertical Dots in Header Just Crossed |
| Concluding Header Information |

BYTE	528	529	530	531	532	533	534	535	536	537	538	539	540	541	542	543
HEX	20	38	20	20	34	31	36	42	7F	0A	7F	13	7F	7F	02	20
DEC	32	56	32	32	52	49	54	66	127	10	127	19	127	127	2	32
ASC	^'		^'	^'					^	^J	^	^S	^	^	^B	^'
ALT	SPC		SPC	SPC					DEL	LF	DEL	DC3	DEL	DEL	STX	SPC
SYM		8			4	1	6	B								

| # Vertical Dots Just Crossed | Space | # Vertical Dots on Page So Far / Concluding Header Information | Header Both | Attn. Char. | New Line | Attn. Char. | Center Text / Center Text | Attn. Char. | Attn. Char. | Soft Spaces / Soft Spaces | Space |

BYTE	544	545	546	547	548	549	550	551	552	553	554	555	556	557	558	559
HEX	03	05	20	02	7F	7F	05	7F	54	68	65	20	47	65	74	74
DEC	3	5	32	2	127	127	5	127	84	104	101	32	71	101	116	116
ASC	^C	^E	^'	^B	^	^	^E	^				^'				
ALT	ETX	ENQ	SPC	STX	DEL	DEL	ENQ	DEL				SPC				
SYM									T	h	e		G	e	t	t

| Two Characters | Space | Soft Spaces / Soft Spaces | Attn. Char. | Attn. Char. | Toggle Bold Face / Bold Face | Attn. Char. | Text in Bold Face |

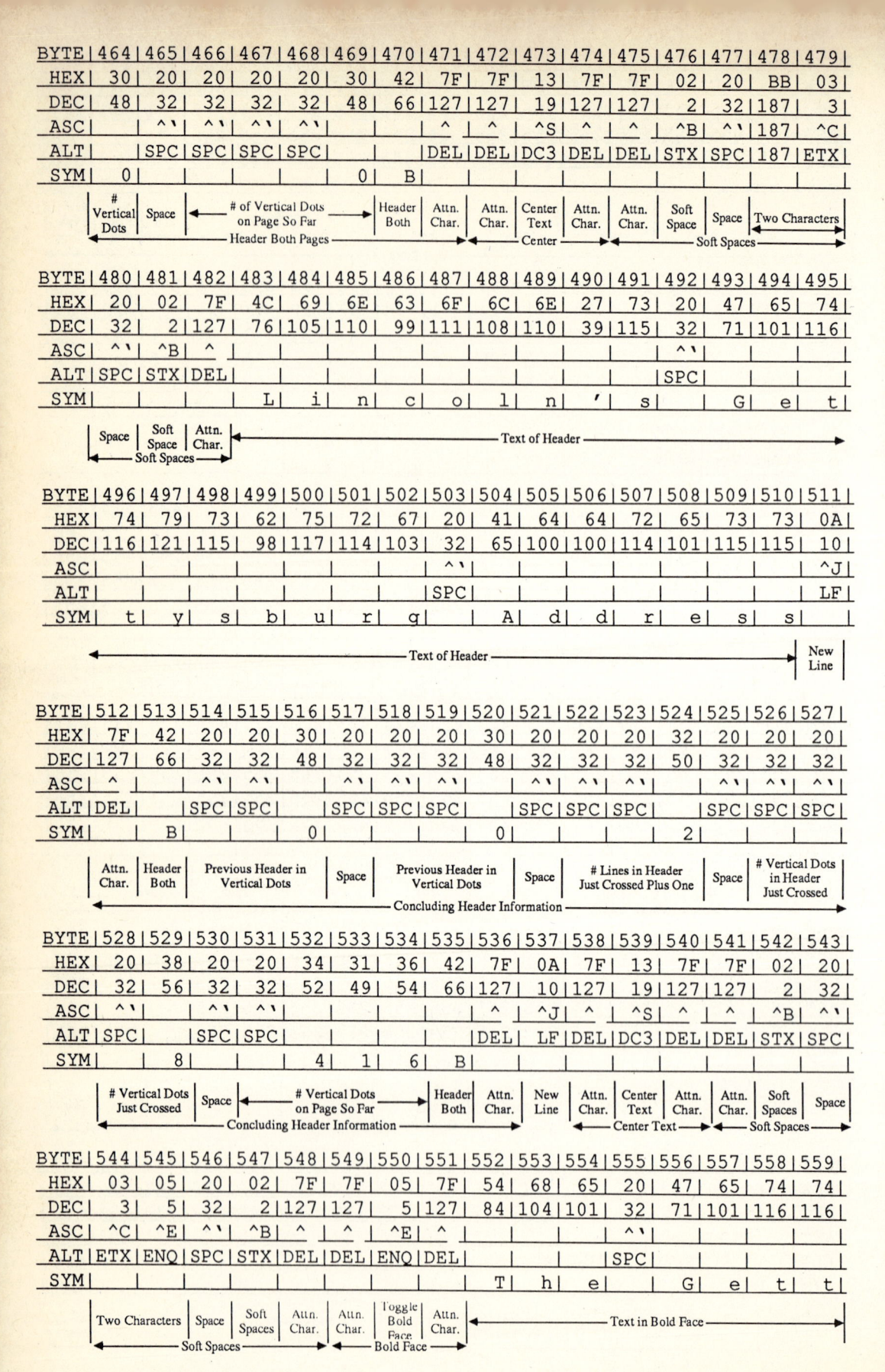

270 WORDSTAR 2000

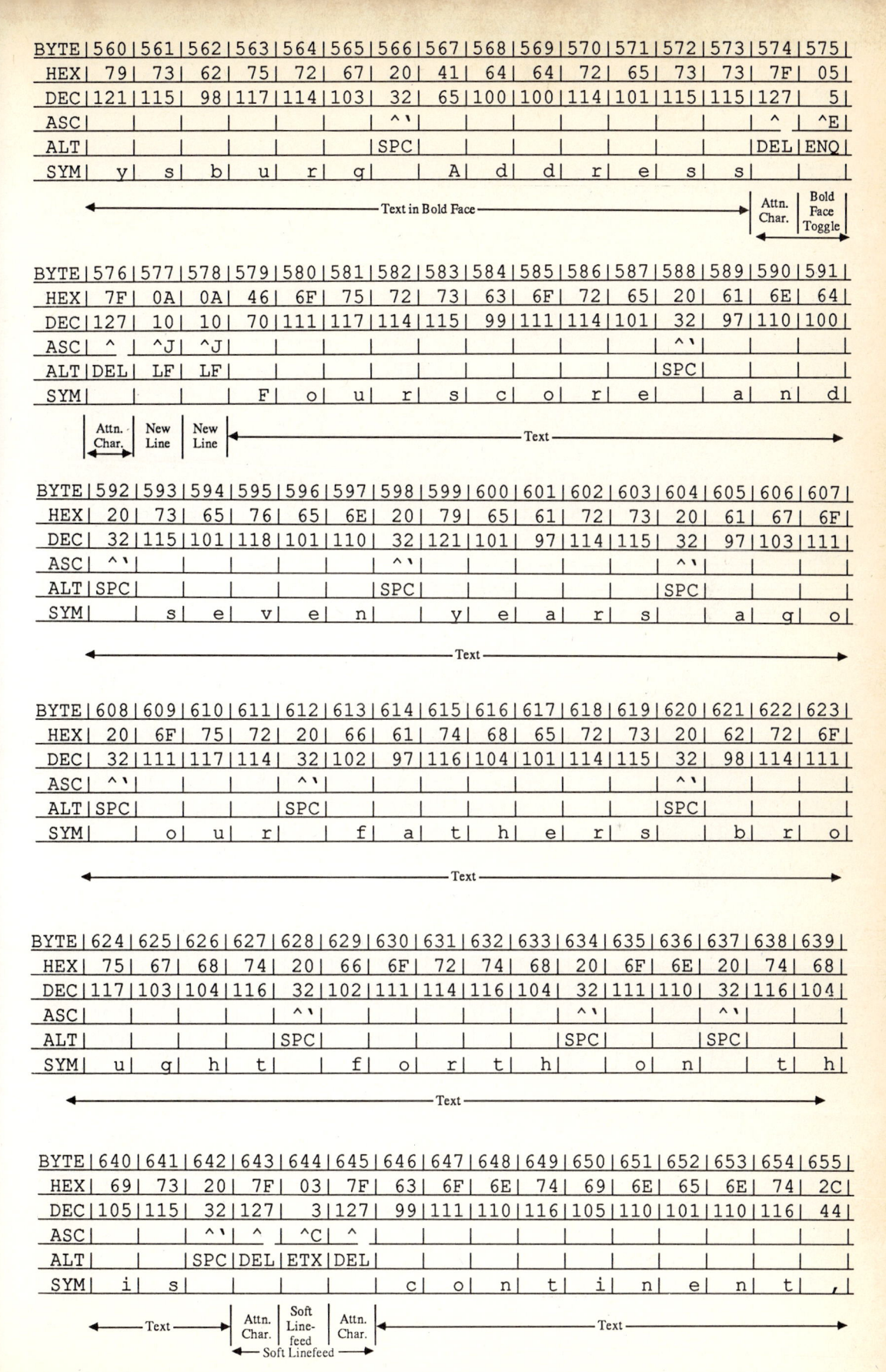

BYTE	560	561	562	563	564	565	566	567	568	569	570	571	572	573	574	575
HEX	79	73	62	75	72	67	20	41	64	64	72	65	73	73	7F	05
DEC	121	115	98	117	114	103	32	65	100	100	114	101	115	115	127	5
ASC							^`								^	^E
ALT							SPC								DEL	ENQ
SYM	y	s	b	u	r	g		A	d	d	r	e	s	s		

← Text in Bold Face → | Attn. Char. | Bold Face Toggle |

BYTE	576	577	578	579	580	581	582	583	584	585	586	587	588	589	590	591
HEX	7F	0A	0A	46	6F	75	72	73	63	6F	72	65	20	61	6E	64
DEC	127	10	10	70	111	117	114	115	99	111	114	101	32	97	110	100
ASC	^	^J	^J										^`			
ALT	DEL	LF	LF										SPC			
SYM				F	o	u	r	s	c	o	r	e		a	n	d

Attn. Char. | New Line | New Line | ← Text →

BYTE	592	593	594	595	596	597	598	599	600	601	602	603	604	605	606	607
HEX	20	73	65	76	65	6E	20	79	65	61	72	73	20	61	67	6F
DEC	32	115	101	118	101	110	32	121	101	97	114	115	32	97	103	111
ASC	^`						^`						^`			
ALT	SPC						SPC						SPC			
SYM		s	e	v	e	n		y	e	a	r	s		a	g	o

← Text →

BYTE	608	609	610	611	612	613	614	615	616	617	618	619	620	621	622	623
HEX	20	6F	75	72	20	66	61	74	68	65	72	73	20	62	72	6F
DEC	32	111	117	114	32	102	97	116	104	101	114	115	32	98	114	111
ASC	^`				^`								^`			
ALT	SPC				SPC								SPC			
SYM		o	u	r		f	a	t	h	e	r	s		b	r	o

← Text →

BYTE	624	625	626	627	628	629	630	631	632	633	634	635	636	637	638	639
HEX	75	67	68	74	20	66	6F	72	74	68	20	6F	6E	20	74	68
DEC	117	103	104	116	32	102	111	114	116	104	32	111	110	32	116	104
ASC					^`						^`			^`		
ALT					SPC						SPC			SPC		
SYM	u	g	h	t		f	o	r	t	h		o	n		t	h

← Text →

BYTE	640	641	642	643	644	645	646	647	648	649	650	651	652	653	654	655
HEX	69	73	20	7F	03	7F	63	6F	6E	74	69	6E	65	6E	74	2C
DEC	105	115	32	127	3	127	99	111	110	116	105	110	101	110	116	44
ASC			^`	^	^C	^										
ALT			SPC	DEL	ETX	DEL										
SYM	i	s					c	o	n	t	i	n	e	n	t	,

← Text → | Attn. Char. | Soft Line-feed | Attn. Char. | ← Text →
← Soft Linefeed →

WORDSTAR 2000 271

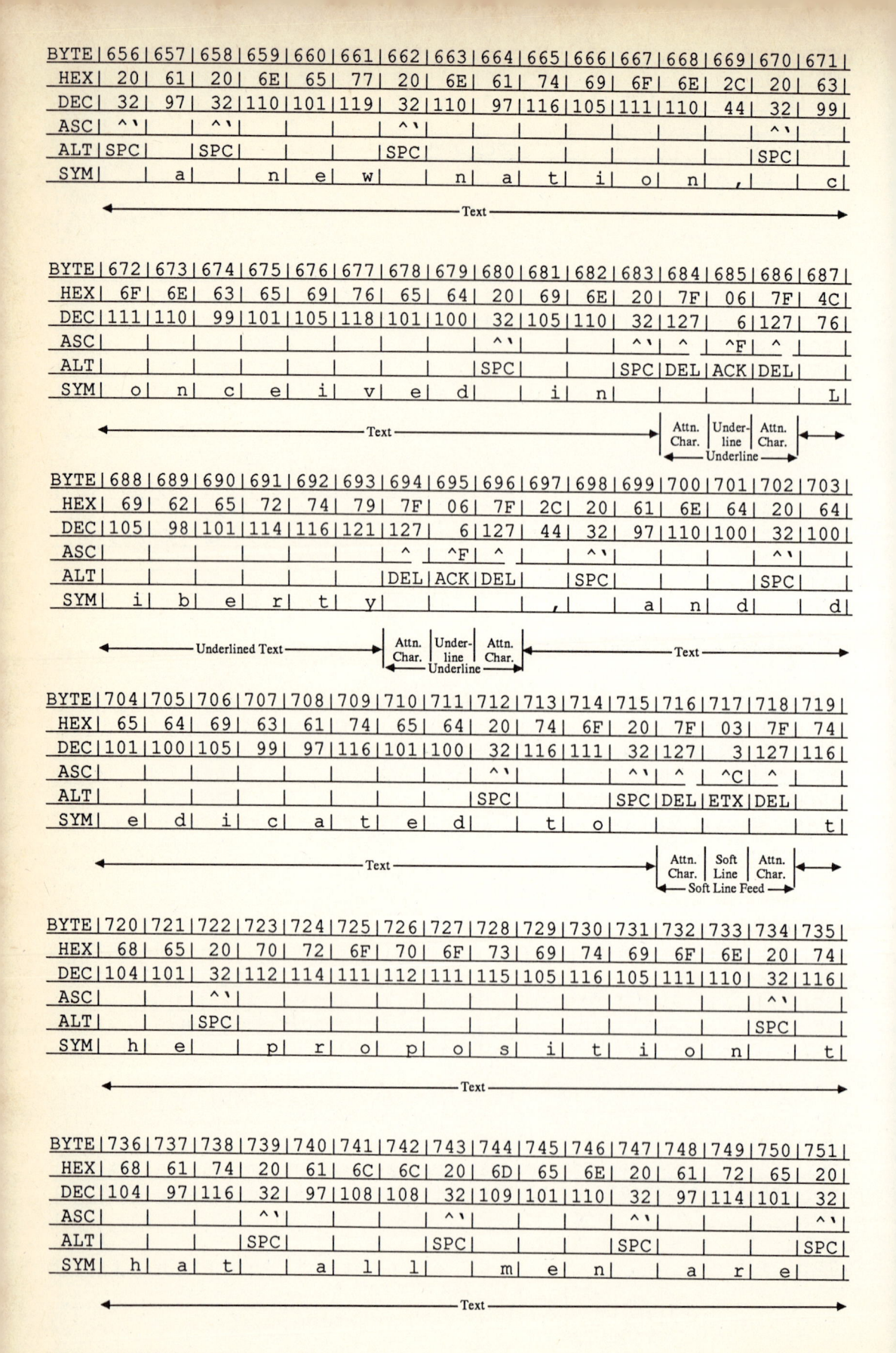

BYTE	656	657	658	659	660	661	662	663	664	665	666	667	668	669	670	671
HEX	20	61	20	6E	65	77	20	6E	61	74	69	6F	6E	2C	20	63
DEC	32	97	32	110	101	119	32	110	97	116	105	111	110	44	32	99
ASC	^`		^`			^`								^`		
ALT	SPC		SPC			SPC								SPC		
SYM		a		n	e	w		n	a	t	i	o	n	,		c

←———————————————— Text ————————————————→

BYTE	672	673	674	675	676	677	678	679	680	681	682	683	684	685	686	687
HEX	6F	6E	63	65	69	76	65	64	20	69	6E	20	7F	06	7F	4C
DEC	111	110	99	101	105	118	101	100	32	105	110	32	127	6	127	76
ASC									^`		^`		^	^F	^	
ALT									SPC		SPC	DEL	ACK	DEL		
SYM	o	n	c	e	i	v	e	d		i	n					L

←———————————— Text ————————————→ Attn. Char. | Under-line | Attn. Char. ←→
←— Underline —→

BYTE	688	689	690	691	692	693	694	695	696	697	698	699	700	701	702	703
HEX	69	62	65	72	74	79	7F	06	7F	2C	20	61	6E	64	20	64
DEC	105	98	101	114	116	121	127	6	127	44	32	97	110	100	32	100
ASC							^	^F	^		^`				^`	
ALT							DEL	ACK	DEL		SPC				SPC	
SYM	i	b	e	r	t	y				,		a	n	d		d

←— Underlined Text —→ Attn. Char. | Under-line | Attn. Char. ←——— Text ———→
←— Underline —→

BYTE	704	705	706	707	708	709	710	711	712	713	714	715	716	717	718	719
HEX	65	64	69	63	61	74	65	64	20	74	6F	20	7F	03	7F	74
DEC	101	100	105	99	97	116	101	100	32	116	111	32	127	3	127	116
ASC									^`		^`		^	^C	^	
ALT									SPC		SPC	DEL	ETX	DEL		
SYM	e	d	i	c	a	t	e	d		t	o					t

←———————————— Text ————————————→ Attn. Char. | Soft Line | Attn. Char. ←→
←— Soft Line Feed —→

BYTE	720	721	722	723	724	725	726	727	728	729	730	731	732	733	734	735
HEX	68	65	20	70	72	6F	70	6F	73	69	74	69	6F	6E	20	74
DEC	104	101	32	112	114	111	112	111	115	105	116	105	111	110	32	116
ASC			^`												^`	
ALT			SPC												SPC	
SYM	h	e		p	r	o	p	o	s	i	t	i	o	n		t

←———————————————— Text ————————————————→

BYTE	736	737	738	739	740	741	742	743	744	745	746	747	748	749	750	751
HEX	68	61	74	20	61	6C	6C	20	6D	65	6E	20	61	72	65	20
DEC	104	97	116	32	97	108	108	32	109	101	110	32	97	114	101	32
ASC				^`				^`				^`				^`
ALT				SPC				SPC				SPC				SPC
SYM	h	a	t		a	l	l		m	e	n		a	r	e	

←———————————————— Text ————————————————→

272 WORDSTAR 2000

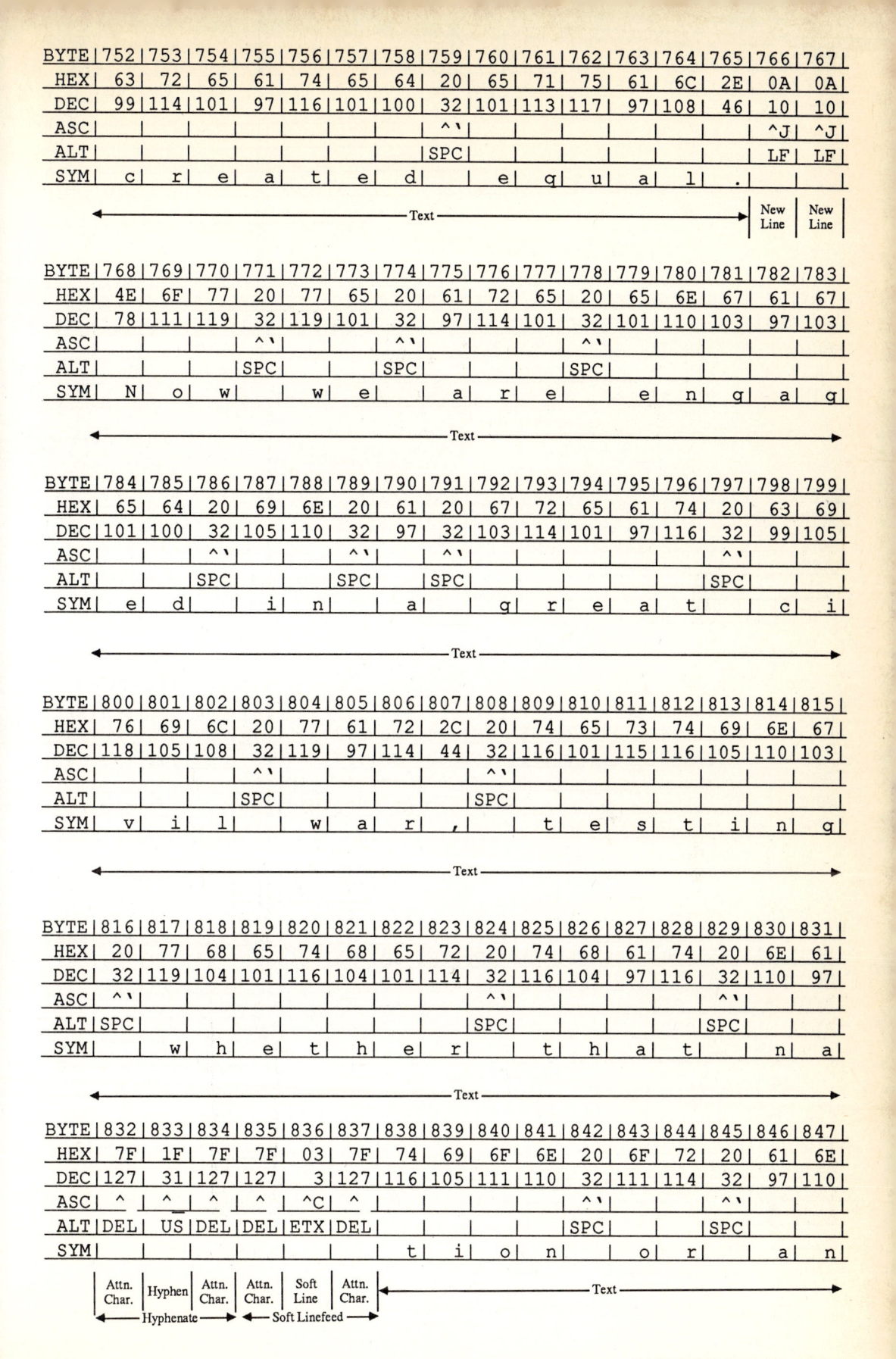

BYTE	752	753	754	755	756	757	758	759	760	761	762	763	764	765	766	767
HEX	63	72	65	61	74	65	64	20	65	71	75	61	6C	2E	0A	0A
DEC	99	114	101	97	116	101	100	32	101	113	117	97	108	46	10	10
ASC								^`							^J	^J
ALT								SPC							LF	LF
SYM	c	r	e	a	t	e	d		e	q	u	a	l	.	New Line	New Line

←———————————————— Text ————————————————→

BYTE	768	769	770	771	772	773	774	775	776	777	778	779	780	781	782	783
HEX	4E	6F	77	20	77	65	20	61	72	65	20	65	6E	67	61	67
DEC	78	111	119	32	119	101	32	97	114	101	32	101	110	103	97	103
ASC				^`			^`				^`					
ALT				SPC			SPC				SPC					
SYM	N	o	w		w	e		a	r	e		e	n	g	a	g

←———————————————— Text ————————————————→

BYTE	784	785	786	787	788	789	790	791	792	793	794	795	796	797	798	799
HEX	65	64	20	69	6E	20	61	20	67	72	65	61	74	20	63	69
DEC	101	100	32	105	110	32	97	32	103	114	101	97	116	32	99	105
ASC			^`			^`		^`						^`		
ALT			SPC			SPC		SPC						SPC		
SYM	e	d		i	n		a		g	r	e	a	t		c	i

←———————————————— Text ————————————————→

BYTE	800	801	802	803	804	805	806	807	808	809	810	811	812	813	814	815
HEX	76	69	6C	20	77	61	72	2C	20	74	65	73	74	69	6E	67
DEC	118	105	108	32	119	97	114	44	32	116	101	115	116	105	110	103
ASC				^`					^`							
ALT				SPC					SPC							
SYM	v	i	l		w	a	r	,		t	e	s	t	i	n	g

←———————————————— Text ————————————————→

BYTE	816	817	818	819	820	821	822	823	824	825	826	827	828	829	830	831
HEX	20	77	68	65	74	68	65	72	20	74	68	61	74	20	6E	61
DEC	32	119	104	101	116	104	101	114	32	116	104	97	116	32	110	97
ASC	^`								^`					^`		
ALT	SPC								SPC					SPC		
SYM		w	h	e	t	h	e	r		t	h	a	t		n	a

←———————————————— Text ————————————————→

BYTE	832	833	834	835	836	837	838	839	840	841	842	843	844	845	846	847
HEX	7F	1F	7F	7F	03	7F	74	69	6F	6E	20	6F	72	20	61	6E
DEC	127	31	127	127	3	127	116	105	111	110	32	111	114	32	97	110
ASC	^	^_	^	^	^C	^					^`			^`		
ALT	DEL	US	DEL	DEL	ETX	DEL					SPC			SPC		
SYM							t	i	o	n		o	r		a	n

Attn. Char. | Hyphen | Attn. Char. | Attn. Char. | Soft Line | Attn. Char. | ←———————— Text ————————→
←— Hyphenate —→ ←— Soft Linefeed —→

WORDSTAR 2000   **273**

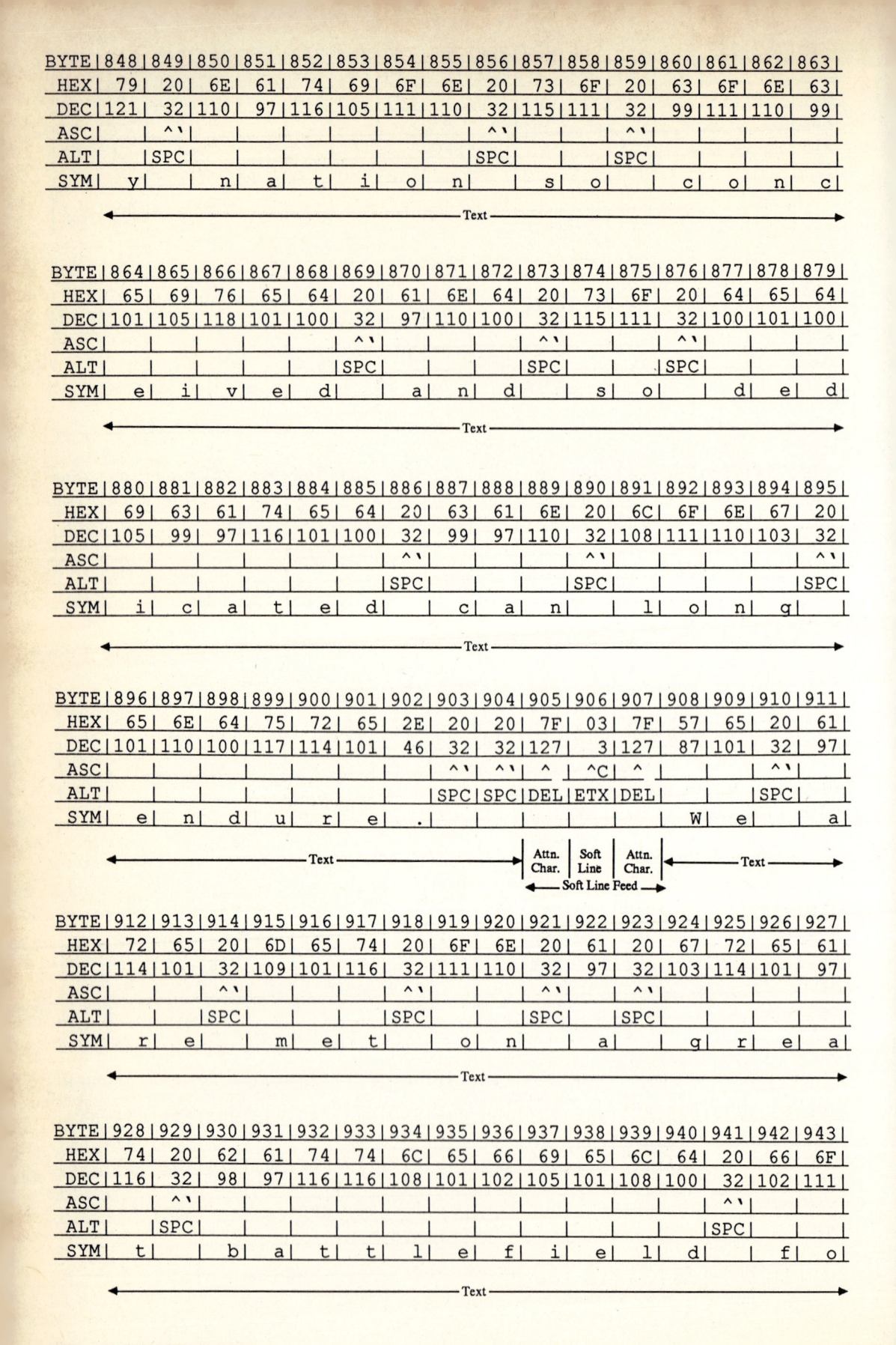

BYTE	848	849	850	851	852	853	854	855	856	857	858	859	860	861	862	863
HEX	79	20	6E	61	74	69	6F	6E	20	73	6F	20	63	6F	6E	63
DEC	121	32	110	97	116	105	111	110	32	115	111	32	99	111	110	99
ASC		^`					^`		^`							
ALT		SPC					SPC		SPC							
SYM	y		n	a	t	i	o	n		s	o		c	o	n	c

←———————————————— Text ————————————————→

BYTE	864	865	866	867	868	869	870	871	872	873	874	875	876	877	878	879
HEX	65	69	76	65	64	20	61	6E	64	20	73	6F	20	64	65	64
DEC	101	105	118	101	100	32	97	110	100	32	115	111	32	100	101	100
ASC					^`			^`		^`						
ALT					SPC			SPC		SPC						
SYM	e	i	v	e	d		a	n	d		s	o		d	e	d

←———————————————— Text ————————————————→

BYTE	880	881	882	883	884	885	886	887	888	889	890	891	892	893	894	895
HEX	69	63	61	74	65	64	20	63	61	6E	20	6C	6F	6E	67	20
DEC	105	99	97	116	101	100	32	99	97	110	32	108	111	110	103	32
ASC					^`				^`							^`
ALT					SPC				SPC							SPC
SYM	i	c	a	t	e	d		c	a	n		l	o	n	g	

←———————————————— Text ————————————————→

BYTE	896	897	898	899	900	901	902	903	904	905	906	907	908	909	910	911
HEX	65	6E	64	75	72	65	2E	20	20	7F	03	7F	57	65	20	61
DEC	101	110	100	117	114	101	46	32	32	127	3	127	87	101	32	97
ASC								^`	^`	^	^C	^			^`	
ALT								SPC	SPC	DEL	ETX	DEL			SPC	
SYM	e	n	d	u	r	e	.						W	e		a

←————— Text —————→ |Attn. Char.|Soft Line|Attn. Char.| ←————— Text —————→
←— Soft Line Feed —→

BYTE	912	913	914	915	916	917	918	919	920	921	922	923	924	925	926	927
HEX	72	65	20	6D	65	74	20	6F	6E	20	61	20	67	72	65	61
DEC	114	101	32	109	101	116	32	111	110	32	97	32	103	114	101	97
ASC			^`				^`			^`		^`				
ALT			SPC				SPC			SPC		SPC				
SYM	r	e		m	e	t		o	n		a		g	r	e	a

←———————————————— Text ————————————————→

BYTE	928	929	930	931	932	933	934	935	936	937	938	939	940	941	942	943
HEX	74	20	62	61	74	74	6C	65	66	69	65	6C	64	20	66	6F
DEC	116	32	98	97	116	116	108	101	102	105	101	108	100	32	102	111
ASC		^`												^`		
ALT		SPC												SPC		
SYM	t		b	a	t	t	l	e	f	i	e	l	d		f	o

←———————————————— Text ————————————————→

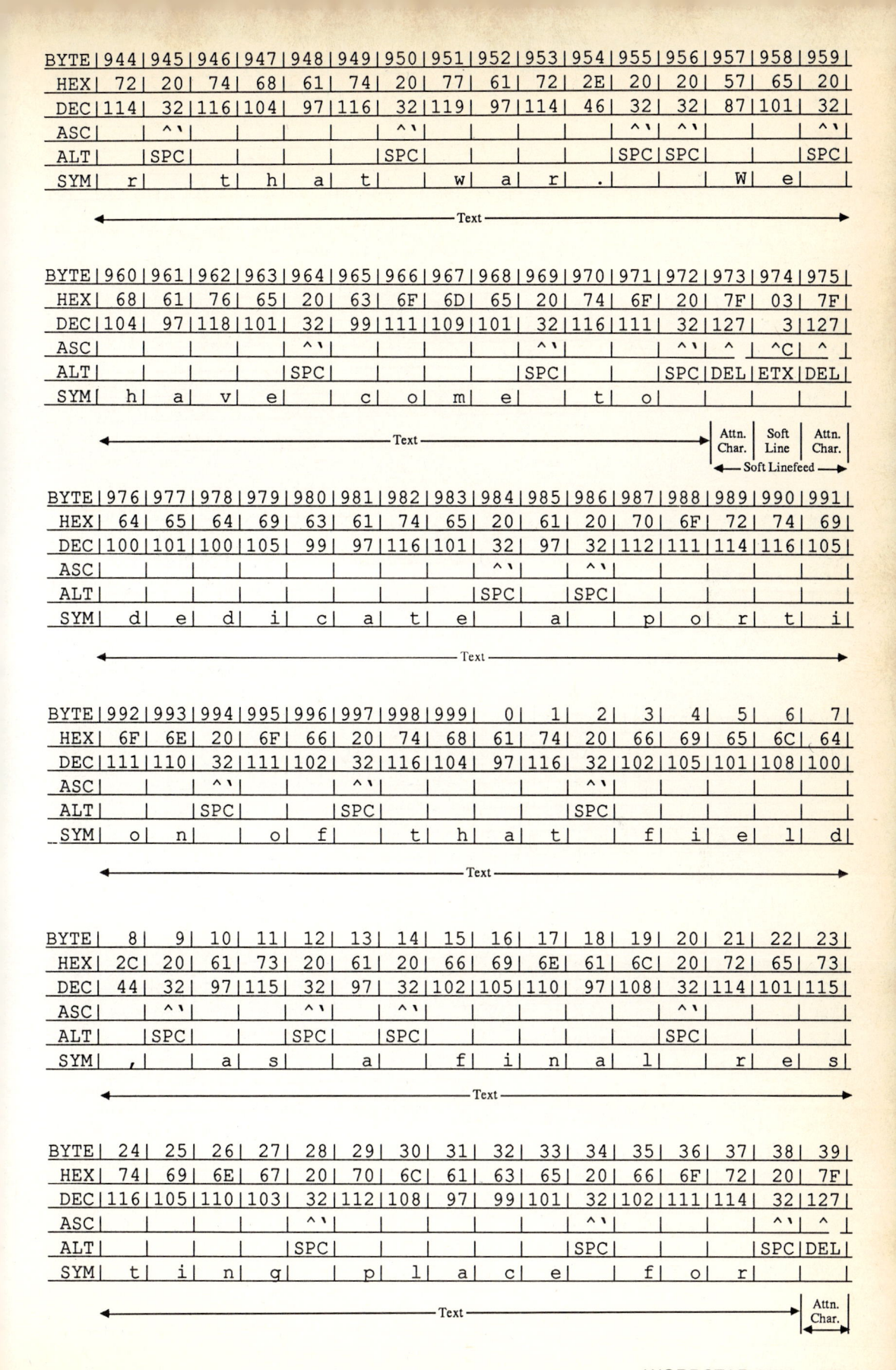

BYTE	944	945	946	947	948	949	950	951	952	953	954	955	956	957	958	959
HEX	72	20	74	68	61	74	20	77	61	72	2E	20	20	57	65	20
DEC	114	32	116	104	97	116	32	119	97	114	46	32	32	87	101	32
ASC		^'				^'						^'	^'			^'
ALT		SPC				SPC						SPC	SPC			SPC
SYM	r		t	h	a	t		w	a	r	.			W	e	

←———————————— Text ————————————→

BYTE	960	961	962	963	964	965	966	967	968	969	970	971	972	973	974	975
HEX	68	61	76	65	20	63	6F	6D	65	20	74	6F	20	7F	03	7F
DEC	104	97	118	101	32	99	111	109	101	32	116	111	32	127	3	127
ASC					^'					^'			^'	^	^C	^
ALT					SPC					SPC			SPC	DEL	ETX	DEL
SYM	h	a	v	e		c	o	m	e		t	o				

←———————— Text ————————→ Attn. Char. | Soft Line | Attn. Char.
←— Soft Linefeed —→

BYTE	976	977	978	979	980	981	982	983	984	985	986	987	988	989	990	991
HEX	64	65	64	69	63	61	74	65	20	61	20	70	6F	72	74	69
DEC	100	101	100	105	99	97	116	101	32	97	32	112	111	114	116	105
ASC							^'		^'							
ALT							SPC		SPC							
SYM	d	e	d	i	c	a	t	e		a		p	o	r	t	i

←———————————— Text ————————————→

BYTE	992	993	994	995	996	997	998	999	0	1	2	3	4	5	6	7
HEX	6F	6E	20	6F	66	20	74	68	61	74	20	66	69	65	6C	64
DEC	111	110	32	111	102	32	116	104	97	116	32	102	105	101	108	100
ASC			^'		^'						^'					
ALT			SPC		SPC						SPC					
SYM	o	n		o	f		t	h	a	t		f	i	e	l	d

←———————————— Text ————————————→

BYTE	8	9	10	11	12	13	14	15	16	17	18	19	20	21	22	23
HEX	2C	20	61	73	20	61	20	66	69	6E	61	6C	20	72	65	73
DEC	44	32	97	115	32	97	32	102	105	110	97	108	32	114	101	115
ASC		^'			^'		^'						^'			
ALT		SPC			SPC		SPC						SPC			
SYM	,		a	s		a		f	i	n	a	l		r	e	s

←———————————— Text ————————————→

BYTE	24	25	26	27	28	29	30	31	32	33	34	35	36	37	38	39
HEX	74	69	6E	67	20	70	6C	61	63	65	20	66	6F	72	20	7F
DEC	116	105	110	103	32	112	108	97	99	101	32	102	111	114	32	127
ASC				^'					^'						^'	^
ALT				SPC					SPC						SPC	DEL
SYM	t	i	n	g		p	l	a	c	e		f	o	r		

←———————————— Text ————————————→ Attn. Char.

WORDSTAR 2000

BYTE	40	41	42	43	44	45	46	47	48	49	50	51	52	53	54	55
HEX	03	7F	74	68	6F	73	65	20	77	68	6F	20	68	65	72	65
DEC	3	127	116	104	111	115	101	32	119	104	111	32	104	101	114	101
ASC	^C	^						^`				^`				
ALT	ETX	DEL						SPC				SPC				
SYM			t	h	o	s	e		w	h	o		h	e	r	e

Soft Line / Attn. Char. / ◀ Soft Linefeed ▶ ◀——————— Text ———————▶

BYTE	56	57	58	59	60	61	62	63	64	65	66	67	68	69	70	71
HEX	20	67	61	76	65	20	74	68	65	69	72	20	6C	69	76	65
DEC	32	103	97	118	101	32	116	104	101	105	114	32	108	105	118	101
ASC	^`					^`						^`				
ALT	SPC					SPC						SPC				
SYM		g	a	v	e		t	h	e	i	r		l	i	v	e

◀——————— Text ———————▶

BYTE	72	73	74	75	76	77	78	79	80	81	82	83	84	85	86	87
HEX	73	20	74	68	61	74	20	74	68	61	74	20	6E	61	74	69
DEC	115	32	116	104	97	116	32	116	104	97	116	32	110	97	116	105
ASC		^`					^`					^`				
ALT		SPC					SPC					SPC				
SYM	s		t	h	a	t		t	h	a	t		n	a	t	i

◀——————— Text ———————▶

BYTE	88	89	90	91	92	93	94	95	96	97	98	99	100	101	102	103
HEX	6F	6E	20	6D	69	67	68	74	20	6C	69	76	65	2E	20	20
DEC	111	110	32	109	105	103	104	116	32	108	105	118	101	46	32	32
ASC			^`						^`						^`	^`
ALT			SPC						SPC						SPC	SPC
SYM	o	n		m	i	g	h	t		l	i	v	e	.		

◀——————— Text ———————▶

BYTE	104	105	106	107	108	109	110	111	112	113	114	115	116	117	118	119
HEX	49	74	20	7F	03	7F	69	73	20	61	6C	74	6F	67	65	74
DEC	73	116	32	127	3	127	105	115	32	97	108	116	111	103	101	116
ASC			^`	^	^C	^			^`							
ALT			SPC	DEL	ETX	DEL			SPC							
SYM	I	t					i	s		a	l	t	o	g	e	t

◀— Text —▶ Attn. Char. / Soft Line / Attn. Char. ◀——— Text ———▶
◀ Soft Linefeed ▶

BYTE	120	121	122	123	124	125	126	127	128	129	130	131	132	133	134	135
HEX	68	65	72	20	66	69	74	74	69	6E	67	20	61	6E	64	20
DEC	104	101	114	32	102	105	116	116	105	110	103	32	97	110	100	32
ASC				^`								^`				^`
ALT				SPC								SPC				SPC
SYM	h	e	r		f	i	t	t	i	n	g		a	n	d	

◀——————— Text ———————▶

276 WORDSTAR 2000

BYTE	136	137	138	139	140	141	142	143	144	145	146	147	148	149	150	151
HEX	70	72	6F	70	65	72	20	74	68	61	74	20	77	65	20	73
DEC	112	114	111	112	101	114	32	116	104	97	116	32	119	101	32	115
ASC							^'				^'				^'	
ALT							SPC				SPC				SPC	
SYM	p	r	o	p	e	r		t	h	a	t		w	e		s

◄──────────────── Text ────────────────►

BYTE	152	153	154	155	156	157	158	159	160	161	162	163	164	165	0	0
HEX	68	6F	75	6C	64	20	64	6F	20	74	68	69	73	2E	XX	XX
DEC	104	111	117	108	100	32	100	111	32	116	104	105	115	46	0	0
ASC					^'		^'								XXX	XXX
ALT					SPC		SPC								XXX	XXX
SYM	h	o	u	l	d		d	o		t	h	i	s	.		

◄──────────────── Text ────────────────►

End of Gettysburg Address as a WordStar 2000 File

APPENDIX C

FilePrint Utility Source Code

This program will print out the contents of a PC-DOS text file in the same format that this Reference Guide uses in its Appendix. It is written in Turbo Pascal.

FilePrint asks for a file name, reads it, and prints the file. As written, it does no checking or error trapping. FilePrint is also limited in the size of the file it can print for two reasons: the byte numbers are integers, and there is about a 1:30 expansion ratio between the size of the file as it appears on disk, and the number of bytes FilePrint causes it to take up in memory. A 5000-byte file on disk can expand to over 150,000 characters in memory.

```
Program FilePrint (Input, Output);
{$U+}
{FilePrint Copyright 1985 by Jeff Walden.                            }
{All Rights Reserved, including those                                }
{ of international copyright.                                        }

Const
  Maxarraysize       =   47;
  NumberRecsPerLine  =   15; {48 bytes displayed per screen}
  CtrlCodes          =   33;
  EOM                =   '';

Type
  Flag         = Boolean;
  Character    = String[1];
  CellString   = String[3];
  RowName      = String[4];
  PathName     = String[64];
  BigString    = String[64];

  BytePTR      = ^DiskContents;
  DiskContents = Record
                   ByteNum : Integer;
                   Value   : Byte;
                   Prior   : BytePTR;
                   Next    : BytePTR;
                 End;

  DisplayRec   = Record
                   ByteNum         : Integer;
                   Value           : Byte;
                   TwoValHexChar   : CellString;
                   DecimalVal      : Integer;
                   ASCII_Contents  : CellString;
                   ALT_Display     : CellString;
                   Symbol          : CellString;
                 End;

  CTRLMnemonics = Record
                    Index : Integer;
                    Code  : CellString;
                  End;
Var {Global Variables}
  Display_Val_Array : Array [0..MaxArraySize] of DisplayRec;
  Control_Codes     : Array [0..CtrlCodes] of CTRLMnemonics;
  ActiveFile        : PathName;
  DiskFile          : File of Byte;
  Filehead          : BytePTR;
  Filetail          : BytePTR;
  Filepointer       : BytePTR;
  Newbyte           : BytePTR;
  Heaptop           : ^Integer;
  i                 : Integer;
```

(continued)

```
Procedure Read_Disk(Currentfile : Pathname);
  Var
    i, j, n      : Integer;
    x            : Integer;
    C            : Byte;
  Begin
    Mark(Heaptop);
    Filehead := NIL;
    i := 0;
    Assign(DiskFile, CurrentFile);
    Reset(DiskFile);
    While NOT EOF(DiskFile) Do
      Begin
        Gotoxy(1,1);
        Seek(DiskFile, i);
        Read(DiskFile, C);
        New(Newbyte);
        Newbyte^.Bytenum := i;
        Newbyte^.Value   := C;
        If Filehead = NIL Then
          Begin
            Filehead := Newbyte;
            Filehead^.Prior := NIL;
          End
        Else
          Begin
            Filetail^.Next := Newbyte;
            Newbyte^.Prior := Filetail;
          End;
        Filetail := Newbyte;
        Filetail^.Next := Nil;
        i := i + 1;
      End;       {While NOT EOF}
    Close(DiskFile);
    Write('File now closed - printing will begin.');
    Filepointer := Filehead;
  End;   {Read_Disk}

Procedure Load_File;
  Begin
    Release(Heaptop);
    Write('Enter Filename: ');
    Read(Activefile);
    Read_Disk(Activefile);
  End;

Procedure INIT;
  Var
    i : Integer;
  Begin
    ClrScr;
    Mark(Heaptop);
    For i := 0 to 32 Do
```

(continued)

```
      Begin
        With Control_Codes[i] Do
          Begin
            Index := i;
          End; {With Control_Codes[i] Do}
      End;'     {For i := 0 to 32 Do}


      Control_Codes[33].Index := 127;


      Control_Codes[0].Code    := 'NUL';
      Control_Codes[1].Code    := 'SOH';
      Control_Codes[2].Code    := 'STX';
      Control_Codes[3].Code    := 'ETX';
      Control_Codes[4].Code    := 'EOT';
      Control_Codes[5].Code    := 'ENQ';
      Control_Codes[6].Code    := 'ACK';
      Control_Codes[7].Code    := 'BEL';
      Control_Codes[8].Code    := ' BS';
      Control_Codes[9].Code    := ' HT';
      Control_Codes[10].Code   := ' LF';
      Control_Codes[11].Code   := ' VT';
      Control_Codes[12].Code   := ' FF';
      Control_Codes[13].Code   := ' CR';
      Control_Codes[14].Code   := ' SO';
      Control_Codes[15].Code   := ' SI';
      Control_Codes[16].Code   := 'DLE';
      Control_Codes[17].Code   := 'DC1';
      Control_Codes[18].Code   := 'DC2';
      Control_Codes[19].Code   := 'DC3';
      Control_Codes[20].Code   := 'DC4';
      Control_Codes[21].Code   := 'NAK';
      Control_Codes[22].Code   := 'SYN';
      Control_Codes[23].Code   := 'ETB';
      Control_Codes[24].Code   := 'CAN';
      Control_Codes[25].Code   := ' EM';
      Control_Codes[26].Code   := 'SUB';
      Control_Codes[27].Code   := 'ESC';
      Control_Codes[28].Code   := ' FS';
      Control_Codes[29].Code   := ' GS';
      Control_Codes[30].Code   := ' RS';
      Control_Codes[31].Code   := ' US';
      Control_Codes[32].Code   := 'SPC';
      Control_Codes[33].Code   := 'DEL';

   End;            {Procedure INIT}

Procedure Produce_Display_Val_Array;
   Var
      Lclpointer : BytePTR;
      i : Integer;
      ASCII_Contents : CellString;
      ALT_Display    : CellString;
```

(continued)

APPENDIX C   283

```pascal
Procedure HexIn_CharOut (HexIn : Byte;
                         Var Charout : CellString);
  Begin  {HexIn_CharOut}
    Case Hexin of
      0..9 : Str(HexIn:1,CharOut);
       10  : CharOut := 'A';
       11  : CharOut := 'B';
       12  : CharOut := 'C';
       13  : CharOut := 'D';
       14  : CharOut := 'E';
       15  : CharOut := 'F';
      Else   CharOut := 'X';
    End; {Case HexIn of}
  End;    {HexIn_CharOut}
Procedure Two_Char_Hex_Convert (Hex_Contents : Byte;
                         Var Hex_As_String : CellString);
  Var
    i, j     : Byte;
    TempStr : CellString;
  Begin  {Two_Char_Hex_Convert}
    Hex_As_String := '';
    i := Hex_Contents;
    j := Hex_Contents;
    i := i DIV 16;
    j := j MOD 16;
    HexIn_CharOut (i,Hex_As_String);
    HexIn_CharOut (j,TempStr);
    Hex_As_String := (Hex_As_String + TempStr);
  End;    {Two_Char_Hex_Convert}

Procedure Handle_Control_Codes (Hex_Contents    : Byte;
                         Var ASCII_Contents : CellString;
                         Var ALT_Display    : CellString);
  Const
    Offset = 64;
  Begin  {Handle_Control_Codes}
    ASCII_Contents := ('^' + (Chr(Hex_Contents + Offset)));
    Case Hex_Contents of
      0..32 : ALT_Display :=
                       Control_Codes[Hex_Contents].code;
        127 : ALT_Display := Control_Codes[33].code;
      Else    ALT_Display := '!!!!';
    End; {Case Hex_Contents of}
  End;    {Handle_Control_Codes}

Procedure Handle_Printing_Chars (Hex_Contents    : Byte;
                         Var ASCII_Contents : CellString;
                         Var ALT_Display    : CellString);
  Begin  {Handle_Printing_Chars}
    ASCII_Contents := ('  ' + (Chr(Hex_Contents)));
    ALT_Display := ASCII_Contents;
  End;    {Handle_Printing_Chars}
```

(continued)

```
Procedure Handle_HiBit_Chars (Hex_Contents      : Byte;
                          Var ASCII_Contents : CellString;
                          Var ALT_Display    : CellString);
  Begin   {Handle_HiBit_Chars}
    Str(Hex_Contents:3,ASCII_Contents);
    ALT_Display := ASCII_Contents;
  End;    {Handle_HiBit_Chars}
  Begin   {Produce_Display_Val_Array}
    LclPointer := Filepointer;
    ASCII_Contents := '';
    ALT_Display    := '';
      For i := 0 to MaxArraySize Do
         With Display_Val_Array[i] Do
            If Lclpointer <> NIL Then
               Begin
                 ByteNum       := Lclpointer^.ByteNum MOD 1000;
                 Value         := Lclpointer^.Value;
                 DecimalVal    := Value;
                 Two_Char_Hex_Convert (Value,TwoValHexChar);
                 Case Value of
                    0..32,127 : Begin
                                  Handle_Control_Codes (Value,
                                     ASCII_Contents, ALT_Display);
                                  Symbol := '';{ALT_Display;}
                                End;
                    33..126 : Begin
                                Handle_Printing_Chars (Value,
                                   ASCII_Contents, ALT_Display);
                                Symbol := Chr(Value);
                              End;
                    128..255 : Begin
                                 Handle_HiBit_Chars (Value,
                                    ASCII_Contents, ALT_Display);
                                 Symbol := Chr(Value);
                               End;
                      Else   Begin
                               ASCII_Contents := '!!!!';
                               ALT_Display    := '!!!!';
                               Symbol := '!';
                             End; {Else}
                 End; {Case}
                 Lclpointer := Lclpointer^.Next;
               End
            Else
               Begin
                 Bytenum := 0;
                 Value   := 0;
                 TwoValhexChar :='XX';
                 DecimalVal := 0;
                 ASCII_Contents := 'XXX';
                 ALT_Display := 'XXX';
                 Symbol := '';
               End;
  End;         {Produce_Display_Val_Array}                  (continued)
```

APPENDIX C

```
Procedure Printer_Dump;

   Const
     Pagewidth = 80;
     Printlen  = 55;
     VTABlen   =  3;
     FF = #12;
     CR = #13;
     LF = #10;

   Var
     PCount, i : Integer;
     CurrPTR : BytePTR;
     Rowcount: Integer;

   Procedure VerticalTab;
     Var
       i : Integer;
     Begin
       For i := 1 to VTABlen Do
          Writeln(LST);
     End;

   Procedure Underline;
     Const
       LLen = 70;
     Var
       i : Integer;
     Begin
       Write(LST,CR);
       For i := 0 to LLen Do
          Write(LST,'_');
     End;

   Procedure Dump_Array;
     Var
       i, k, j : Integer;
     Begin
       k := NumberRecsPerLine+1;
       For i := 0 to 2 Do
          Begin
            Write(LST,'BYTE|');
            For j := 0 to NumberRecsPerLine Do
               Write(LST,Display_Val_Array[(i*k)+j].ByteNum:3,'|');
            Underline;
            Writeln(LST);

            Write(LST,' HEX|');
            For j := 0 to NumberRecsPerLine Do
Write(LST,Display_Val_Array[(i*k)+j].TwoValHexChar:3,'|');
            Underline;
            Writeln(LST);
```

(continued)

```
              Write(LST,' DEC|');
              For j := 0 to NumberRecsPerLine Do
                Write(LST,Display_Val_Array[(i*k)+j].DecimalVal:3,'|');
              Underline;
              Writeln(LST);

              Write(LST,' ASC|');
              For j := 0 to NumberRecsPerLine Do
                Write(LST,Display_Val_Array[(i*k)+j].ASCII_Contents:3,'|');
              Underline;
              Writeln(LST);

              Write(LST,' ALT|');
              For j := 0 to NumberRecsPerLine Do
                Write(LST,Display_Val_Array[(i*k)+j].ALT_Display:3,'|');
              Underline;
              Writeln(LST);

              Write(LST,' SYM|');
              For j := 0 to NumberRecsPerLine Do
                If (Display_Val_Array[(i*k)+j].DecimalVal > 127) Then
                  Write(LST,'    |')
                Else
                  Write(LST,Display_Val_Array[(i*k)+j].Symbol:3,'|');
              Underline;
              Writeln(LST);

              VerticalTab;

            End;


     End;

Begin {Printer_Dump}
   CurrPTR := Filepointer;
   Filepointer := Filehead;
   Rowcount := 0;
   PCount := 1;
   While (Filepointer^.Next <> NIL) Do
     Begin
       Produce_Display_Val_Array;
       VerticalTab;
       Write(LST,Activefile,' Page#',PCount);
       VerticalTab;
       Dump_Array;
       PCount := PCount + 1;
       For i := 0 to MaxArraySize Do
         If (Filepointer^.Next <> NIL) Then
           Filepointer := Filepointer^.Next
         Else
           Filepointer := Filetail;
       Produce_Display_Val_Array;
       Dump_Array;
```

(continued)

```
        For i := 0 to MaxarraySize Do
           If (Filepointer^.Next <> NIL) Then
              Filepointer := Filepointer^.Next
           Else
              Filepointer := Filetail;
         Write(LST,FF);
      End;
   Filepointer := CurrPTR;
 End;   {Printer_Dump}



Begin
    INIT;
    Load_File;
    Produce_Display_VAl_Array;
    Printer_Dump;
    Release(heaptop);
    Writeln('Thank you for using FilePrint(tm).');
 End.
```